On the Governmen

MICHEL FOUCAULT

On the Government of the Living

LECTURES AT THE COLLÈGE DE FRANCE

1979-1980

Edited by Michel Senellart
General Editors: François Ewald and Alessandro Fontana

English Series Editor: Arnold I. Davidson

TRANSLATED BY GRAHAM BURCHELL

palgrave
macmillan

First published 2014 by
PALGRAVE MACMILLAN

Palgrave Macmillan in the UK is an imprint of Macmillan Publishers Limited,
registered in England, company number 785998, of Houndmills, Basingstoke,
Hampshire RG21 6XS.

Palgrave Macmillan in the US is a division of St Martin's Press LLC,
175 Fifth Avenue, New York, NY 10010.

Palgrave Macmillan is the global academic imprint of the above companies
and has companies and representatives throughout the world.

Palgrave® and Macmillan® are registered trademarks in the United States,
the United Kingdom, Europe and other countries

ISBN 978-1-349-54099-0   ISBN 978-1-137-49182-4 (eBook)
DOI 10.1057/9781137491824

This book is printed on paper suitable for recycling and made from fully
managed and sustained forest sources. Logging, pulping and manufacturing
processes are expected to conform to the environmental regulations of the
country of origin.

A catalogue record for this book is available from the British Library.

A catalog record for this book is available from the Library of Congress.

CONTENTS

1. Christian critique of the gnosis: dissociation of salvation and perfection, knowledge of God and knowledge of self; 2. The obligation to tell the truth about oneself in Western societies; 3. The form of power this presupposes.

FOREWORD

MICHEL FOUCAULT TAUGHT AT the Collège de France from January 1971 until his death in June 1984 (with the exception of 1977 when he took a sabbatical year). The title of his chair was "The History of Systems of Thought."

On the proposal of Jules Vuillemin, the chair was created on 30 November 1969 by the general assembly of the professors of the Collège de France and replaced that of "The History of Philosophical Thought" held by Jean Hyppolite until his death. The same assembly elected Michel Foucault to the new chair on 12 April 1970.[1] He was 43 years old.

Michel Foucault's inaugural lecture was delivered on 2 December 1970.[2] Teaching at the Collège de France is governed by particular rules. Professors must provide 26 hours of teaching a year (with the possibility of a maximum of half this total being given in the form of seminars[3]). Each year they must present their original research and this obliges them to change the content of their teaching for each course. Courses and seminars are completely open; no enrolment or qualification is required and the professors do not award any qualifications.[4] In the terminology of the Collège de France, the professors do not have student but only auditors.

Michel Foucault's courses were held every Wednesday from January to March. The huge audience made up of students, teachers, researchers and the curious, including many who came from outside France, required two amphitheaters of the Collège de France. Foucault often complained about the distance between himself and his "public" and of how few exchanges the course made possible.[5] He would have liked a seminar in which real collective work could take place and made a number of attempts to bring this about. In the final years he devoted a long period to answering his auditors' questions at the end of each course.

This is how Gérard Petitjean, a journalist from *Le Nouvel Observateur*, described the atmosphere at Foucault's lectures in 1975:

> When Foucault enters the amphitheater, brisk and dynamic like someone who plunges into the water, he steps over bodies to reach his chair, pushes away the cassette recorders so he can put down his papers, removes his jacket, lights a lamp and sets of at full speed. His voice is strong and effective, amplified by the loud-speakers that are the only concession to modernism in a hall that is barely lit by light spread from stucco bowls. The hall has three hundred places and there are five hundred people packed together, filling the smallest free space ... There is no oratorical effect. It is clear and terribly effective. There is absolutely no concession to improvisation. Foucault has twelve hours each year to explain in a public course the direction taken by his research in the year just ended. So everything is concentrated and he fills the margins like correspondents who have too much to say for the space available to them. At 19.15 Foucault stops. The students rush towards his desk; not to speak to him, but to stop their cassette recorders. There are no questions. In the pushing and shoving Foucault is alone. Foucault remarks: "It should be possible to discuss what I have put forward. Sometimes, when it has not been a good lecture, it would need very little, just one question, to put everything straight. However, this question never comes. The group effect in France makes any genuine discussion impossible. And as there is no feedback, the course is theatricalized. My relationship with the people there is like that of an actor or an acrobat. And when I have finished speaking, a sensation of total solitude ..."[6]

Foucault approached his teaching as a researcher: explorations for a future book as well as the opening up of fields of problematization were formulated as an invitation to possible future researchers. This is why the courses at the Collège de France do not duplicate the published books. They are not sketches for the books even though both books and courses share certain themes. They have their own status. They arise from a specific discursive regime within the set of Foucault's "philosophical activities." In particular they set out the program for a genealogy of knowledge/power relations, which are the terms in which he thinks of his work from the beginning of the 1970s, as opposed to the program of an archeology of discursive formations that previously orientated his work.[7]

The course also performed a role in contemporary reality. Those who followed his courses were not only held in thrall by the narrative that unfolded week by week and seduced by the rigorous exposition, they also found a perspective on contemporary reality. Michel Foucault's art consisted in using history to cut diagonally through contemporary reality. He could speak of Nietzsche or Aristotle, of expert psychiatric opinion or the Christian pastorate, but those who attended his lectures always took from what he said a perspective on the present and contemporary events. Foucault's specific strength in his courses was the subtle interplay between learned erudition, personal commitment, and work on the event.

♠

With their development and refinement in the 1970s, Foucault's desk was quickly invaded by cassette recorders. The courses—and some seminars—have thus been preserved.

This edition is based on the words delivered in public by Foucault. It gives a transcription of these words that is as literal as possible.[8] We would have liked to present it as such. However, the transition from an oral to a written presentation calls for editorial intervention: at the very least it requires the introduction of punctuation and division into paragraphs. Our principle has been always to remain as close as possible to the course actually delivered.

Summaries and repetitions have been removed whenever it seemed to be absolutely necessary. Interrupted sentences have been restored and faulty constructions corrected. Suspension points indicate that the recording is inaudible. When a sentence is obscure there is a conjectural integration or an addition between square brackets. An asterisk directing the reader to the bottom of the page indicates a significant divergence between the notes used by Foucault and the words actually uttered. Quotations have been checked and references to the texts used are indicated. The critical apparatus is limited to the elucidation of obscure points, the explanation of some allusions and the clarification of critical points. To make the lectures easier to read, each lecture is preceded by a brief summary that indicates its principle articulations.

The text of the course is followed by the summary published by the *Annuaire du Collège de France*. Foucault usually wrote these in June, some time after the end of the course. It was an opportunity for him to pick out retrospectively the intention and objectives of the course. It constitutes the best introduction to the course.

Each volume ends with a "context" for which the course editors are responsible. It seeks to provide the reader with elements of the biographical, ideological, and political context, situating the course within the published work and providing indications concerning its place within the corpus used in order to facilitate understanding and to avoid misinterpretations that might arise from a neglect of the circumstances in which each course was developed and delivered.

On the Government of the Living, the course delivered in 1980, is edited by Michel Senellart.

♠

A new aspect of Michel Foucault's "œuvre" is published with this edition of the Collège de France courses.

Strictly speaking it is not a matter of unpublished work, since this edition reproduces words uttered publicly by Foucault. The written material Foucault used to support his lectures could be highly developed, as this volume attests.

This edition of the Collège de France courses was authorized by Michel Foucault's heirs who wanted to be able to satisfy the strong demand for their publication, in France as elsewhere, and to do this under indisputably responsible conditions. The editors have tried to be equal to the degree of confidence placed in them.

FRANÇOIS EWALD AND ALESSANDRO FONTANA

---

1. Michel Foucault concluded a short document drawn up in support of his candidacy with these words: "We should undertake the history of systems of thought." "Titres et travaux," in *Dits et Écrits, 1954-1988*, four volumes, eds. Daniel Defert and François Ewald (Paris: Gallimard, 1994), vol. 1, p. 846; English translation by Robert Hurley, "Candidacy Presentation: Collège de France" in *The Essential Works of Michel Foucault, 1954-1984, vol. 1: Ethics: Subjectivity and Truth*, ed. Paul Rabinow (New York: The New Press, 1997) p. 9.
2. It was published by Gallimard in May 1971 with the title *L'Ordre du discours*, Paris, 1971. English translation by Ian McLeod, "The Order of Discourse," in Robert Young, ed., *Untying the Text* (London: Routledge and Kegan Paul, 1981).
3. This was Foucault's practice until the start of the 1980s.
4. Within the framework of the Collège de France.
5. In 1976, in the vain hope of reducing the size of the audience, Michel Foucault changed the time of his course from 17.45 to 9.00. See the beginning of the first lecture (7 January 1976) of *"Il faut défendre la société". Cours au Collège de France, 1976* (Paris: Gallimard/Seuil, 1997); English translation by David Macey, *"Society Must be Defended." Lectures at the Collège de France 1975-1976* (New York: Picador, 2003).
6. Gérard Petitjean, "Les Grands Prêtres de l'université française," *Le Nouvel Observateur*, 7 April 1975.
7. See especially, "Nietzsche, la généalogie, l'histoire," in *Dits et Écrits*, vol. 2, p. 137; English translation by Donald F. Brouchard and Sherry Simon, "Nietzsche, Genealogy, History" in *The Essential Works of Michel Foucault 1954-1984, vol. 2: Aesthetics, Method, and Epistemology*, ed., James Faubion (New York: The New Press, 1998), pp. 369-392.
8. We have made use of the recordings made by Gilbert Burlet and Jacques Lagrange in particular. These are deposited in the Collège de France and the Institut Mémoires de l'Édition Contemporaine.

Translator's Note

The French word *pénitence* may be translated in English as "penitence," where perhaps it is the sense of repentance, contrition, remorse, etcetera, that is accentuated, and "penance" in the narrower sense of the specific penalty or punishment (in the form of ascesis, discipline, mortification, etcetera) given for sins committed, and also in the more general sense of the whole sacrament of penance in the Catholic Church (comprising repentance, confession, the penalty or "satisfaction," and remission). In these lectures, the French *pénitence* translates the Latin *paenitentia*, which, in early Christian Latin, translates the Greek *metanoia* (conversion). The most common English word for *paenitentia/metanoia* in translations of the Bible (King James and Standard Revised versions) and of the early Church Fathers is "repentance." I have translated *pénitence* as either "repentance" or "penance" depending on the context. However, the reader should bear in mind that "repentance" perhaps falls short of the early Church sense of *paenitentia/metanoia*, and that in these lectures "penance" does not usually mean penalty or punishment, and, unless explicitly indicated, does not refer to the sacrament of penance.

The French *aveu* is usually translated into English as "confession," but can also be translated as avowal, admission, acknowledgement, etcetera. As Foucault notes in the lecture of 6 February 1980, when used with regard to Christianity, it is usually understood in the modern and religious, sacramental sense of confession (French: *confession*) as this has existed since the end of the Middle Ages. It is a central theme of these lectures that this form of confession is the result of "much more complex, numerous, and rich processes by which Christianity bound individuals to the obligation to manifest their ... individual truth" and that this sense of confession (*confession*) "seems to have covered over all other forms of confession (*aveu*)" (p. 103). Hence, *aveu*, in these lectures, covers a more extensive range of "reflexive truth acts" than just the modern or sacramental sense of *confession*. As with the French *aveu*, no single English word adequately captures the specific generality of this family of practices, and distinctions between these practices cannot be mapped directly onto the distinction in French between *aveu* and *confession*. I have translated *aveu* as confession throughout. In English, the word "confession" extends over the fields of both *aveu* and *confession* in French, but the limitations of the word, and of any other single term with regard to the variety of practices discussed by Foucault, should be kept in mind. It is perhaps worth noting that throughout his lectures at Dartmouth in 1980, "About the Beginning of the Hermeneutics of the Self,"* which were given in English, Foucault used the English "confession" where the French would have been *aveu*. Where it has seemed necessary or useful to mark the distinction between *aveu* and *confession*, the word being translated is indicated.

The following abbreviations are used in the endnotes.

ANF   *The Ante-Nicene Fathers. Translations of The Writings of the Fathers down to A.D. 325*

DÉ   *Dits et écrits*

EPA   *Les écrits des Pères apostoliques*

NPNF1   *A Select Library of Nicene and Post-Nicene Fathers of the Christian Church. First Series*

NPNF2   *A Select Library of Nicene and Post-Nicene Fathers of the Christian Church. Second Series*

PG   *Patrologia Graeca*

SC   *Sources Chrétiennes*

---

* "About the Beginning of the Hermeneutics of the Self: Two Lectures at Dartmouth" (1980), *Political Theory*, 21/2, May 1993.

one

9 JANUARY 1980

> *The hall of justice of Septimius Severus. Comparison with the story of Oedipus.* ∽ *Exercise of power and manifestation of the truth. Alethurgy as pure manifestation of truth. No hegemony without alethurgy.* ∽ *Constant presence of this relation between power and truth up to modern times. Two examples: royal courts,* raison d'État, *and the witch hunt (Bodin).* ∽ *The project of this year's course: to develop the notion of government of men by the truth. Shift with regard to the theme of power-knowledge: from the concept of power to that of government (lectures of the two previous years); from the concept of knowledge (*savoir*) to the problem of the truth.* ∽ *Five ways of conceiving of the relations between exercise of power and manifestation of the truth: the principles of Botero, Quesnay, Saint-Simon, Rosa Luxemburg, and Solzhenitsyn. The narrowness of their perspectives. The relation between government and truth, prior to the birth of a rational governmentality; it is formed at a deeper level than that of useful knowledge.*

THE HISTORIAN DIO CASSIUS recounts the following story[1] about the Roman Emperor Septimius Severus,[2] who, as you all know—well, at any rate, as I know since yesterday—ruled at the end of the second and beginning of the third century, between 193 and 211 I think. Septimius Severus had a palace built[3] in which there was, of course, a large ceremonial hall where he granted audience, delivered his judgments, and dispensed justice. On the ceiling of this hall, Septimius Severus had a representation of the star-studded sky painted, which did not represent just any sky, or any stars in no matter what position. What was exactly represented was the sky of his birth; the conjunction of the stars that presided over his birth and so over his destiny. His reasons for having this done are quite clear and explicit and fairly easy to reconstruct. For Septimius Severus the purpose was, of course, that of inscribing his particular and conjunctural judgments within the system of the world and of showing how the *logos* that presided over this order of the world, and over his birth, was the same *logos* that organized, founded, and justified his judgments. What he said in a particular circumstance in the world, in a particular *kairos*, as the Stoics would say, belonged precisely to the same order of things as that fixed once and for all on high. He also wanted to show how his reign was founded by the stars, that it was not an error that he, the roughneck from Leptis Magna, had seized power by force and violence, that it was not by chance or as the result of any human plot that he had seized power, but that he had been called to the position he occupied by the very necessity of the world. His reign, his seizure of power, which could not be founded by the law, was justified once and for all by the stars. Finally, third, it was a matter of showing his, the emperor's good fortune in advance, and how it was fated, inevitable, inaccessible, and the extent to which it was impossible for anyone, conspirator, rival, or enemy, to seize the throne that the stars had shown was due to him, and which henceforth nothing could overcome. His fortune was good, it was certain, the past indicated this, but for the future too things were definitively sealed. Thus, uncertain and particular actions, a past made of chance and luck, and a future which of course no one could know, but from which some might take advantage to threaten the emperor, were all turned into necessity and had to be seen as a truth on the ceiling of the hall in which he passed judgment. What manifested itself as power here, down below, I was going to say at ground level, could and had to be deciphered in truth in the night sky.

Severus was nevertheless a prudent man, since if he had his astral sky represented on the ceiling of the hall in which he passed judgment, there was however a small patch of this sky that he had not had represented, that he carefully hid, and that was represented only in another room, the emperor's own, to which only he and no doubt some of his household had access, and this small patch of astral sky, which no one had the right to see, which only the emperor knew, was, of course, what one calls the horoscope in the strict sense, that which enables one to see the hour, this being, of course, the hour of death. Of course, no one had access to the sky of death that fixed the end of the emperor's destiny, of his good fortune.

The star-studded sky of Septimius Severus, above his justice, is almost obviously the exact opposite of the story of Oedipus.[4] For after all, the destiny of Oedipus was not above his head in a star-studded sky represented on a ceiling, but attached to his feet, to his steps, to the ground and to the paths going from Thebes to Corinth and from Corinth to Thebes. His destiny was in his feet, under his feet; a destiny known to no one, neither him nor any of his subjects. A destiny that was going to lead him to his ruin, of course, and we should not forget that, at the start of Sophocles' play, when called upon by the population beset by the plague, we see Oedipus too deliver a solemn judgment. He too says what must be done, and he says: "the person whose defilement is responsible for the plague in the city of Thebes must be driven out."[5] He too, therefore, delivered a judgment, and one that is also inscribed in the inevitability of a destiny. But this inevitability of a destiny, which will take up again and give its meaning to the judgment pronounced by Oedipus, is precisely the trap into which he will fall. And whereas Septimius Severus dispensed his justice and delivered his judgments in such a way as to inscribe them in an absolutely visible order of the world that founded them in right, necessity, and truth, the unfortunate Oedipus delivered a fateful judgment that was inscribed in a destiny entirely shrouded in darkness and ignorance, and that as a result constituted his own trap.

And we might find another—somewhat contrived—analogy in the fact that while a fragment was missing from the sky on the ceiling of the hall where Septimius Severus held audience, there was a fragment of the mystery and destiny of Oedipus that was however not unknown. There was a shepherd who had seen what happened when Oedipus was born and who had seen how Laius was killed. It is this shepherd, hidden away in the countryside, who in the end will be sought out and who will give his testimony. And it is he who will say that Oedipus is the guilty one. So, deep in the countryside of Thebes there was a small piece of the destiny of Oedipus that was known and visible to at least one person.

There was something like the equivalent of the Emperor's private room, but it was the shepherd's hut. And in this shepherd's hut Oedipus's destiny came true or at any rate manifested itself. The emperor hid the sky of his death. The shepherd knew the secret of Oedipus's birth.

So you see then that the anti-Oedipus, of course, exists. Dio Cassius had already come across it.

You will say these are all somewhat cultural and artificial games, and that if Septimius Severus had represented over his head the star-studded sky that presided over his justice, destiny, and fortune, if he wanted men to read in truth what he did in terms of power in politics, these were only the games of an emperor whose good fortune had gone to his head. After all, it was quite natural for this African soldier who had risen to the summit of the Empire to seek to found in the heavens of a magical-religious necessity a sovereignty that the law, which was just as magical and religious moreover, could not recognize in him. And it was entirely natural for this man fascinated by Oriental cults to try to substitute the magical order of the stars for the reasonable order of the world, for that reasonable order of the world that his last but one predecessor, Marcus Aurelius, wanted to implement in a Stoic government of the Empire.[6] It was like the magical, oriental, religious echo of what the great Stoic Emperors of the second century wanted to do: govern the Empire only within a manifest order of the world and act in such a way that the government of the Empire be the manifestation in truth of the order of the world.

In fact, if it is true that the individual political situation of Septimius Severus, as well as the climate in which the notion of imperial government was reflected on in the second century, may justify Septimius Severus's concern to inscribe the exercise of his power in this manifestation of truth and thus justify his abuses of power in terms of the very order of the world, if this climate, this context, this particular conjuncture may justify it, I think it would nevertheless be very difficult to find an example of a power that is exercised without being accompanied, in one way or another, by a manifestation of truth. You will say that everyone knows this, that I am always saying it, regurgitating it, and repeating it. How, in fact, could one govern men without know-how, without knowledge, without being informed, without knowledge of the

order of things and the conduct of individuals? In short, how could one
govern without knowing what one governs, without knowing those one
govern, and without knowing the means of governing both these things
and these people? Nevertheless, and this is why I have dwelled somewhat on the example of Septimius Severus, I think the suspicion can
and should arise fairly quickly that it is not just and entirely a question
of this. In other words, it is not simply utilitarian, I was going to say
economic need that enables us to take stock of the phenomenon I have
tried to point out, namely the relation between exercise of power and
manifestation of the truth.

[First], it seems to me—and here again let's stick with the example of Septimius Severus—that this truth, the manifestation of which
accompanies the exercise of power, goes far beyond knowledge useful for
government. After all, what immediate, rational need could Septimius
Severus have for those stars that he had represented over his head and
the heads of those to whom he dispensed justice? We should not forget
that the reign of Septimius Severus was also the period of a number of
important jurists, like Ulpianus,[7] and that juridical knowledge, juridical reflection was far from being absent from Septimius Severus's own
politics.[8] And beyond the knowledge of jurists like Ulpianus, he needed
this supplementary, excessive, I was going to say non-economic manifestation of the truth. Second, what I think should be stressed is that
the very way in which this somewhat luxurious, supplementary, excessive, useless truth is manifested does not entirely belong to the order of
knowledge, of a formed, accumulated, centralized, and utilized* knowledge. In this example of the star-studded sky we see a kind of pure manifestation of truth: a pure manifestation of the order of the world in its
truth, a pure manifestation of the Emperor's destiny and of the necessity
that presides over it, a pure manifestation of the truth on which the
prince's judgments are ultimately founded. We are dealing with a pure,
fascinating manifestation whose principal intention is not so much to
demonstrate or prove something, or to refute something false, but simply to show, to disclose the truth. In other words, for Septimius Severus
it was not a question of procedures for establishing the truth of this or
that thesis, such as the legitimacy of his power or the justice of this or

---

* An inaudible word follows.

that judgment. It was not a question, therefore, of establishing the correctness of what is true as opposed to the false that is refuted and eliminated. Essentially it was a question of making truth itself appear against the background of the unknown, hidden, invisible, and unpredictable. So it was not so much a matter of organizing a knowledge, of the organization of a useful system of knowledge necessary and sufficient for the exercise of government. It was a matter of a ritual of manifestation of the truth maintaining a number of relations with the exercise of power that, even if calculation is not absent from them, certainly cannot be reduced to pure and simple utility, and what I would like to take up again a little is the nature of the relations between this ritual of manifestation of the truth and the exercise of power.

I say "ritual of manifestation of the truth" because what is involved here is not purely and simply what could be called a more or less rational activity of knowledge. It seems to me that the exercise of power, an example of which we can find in the history of Septimius Severus, is accompanied by a set of verbal or non-verbal procedures, which may thus take the form of recorded information, knowledge, information stored in tables, records, and notes, and which may also take the form of rituals, ceremonies, and various operations of magic, divination, the consultation of oracles, of gods. So what is involved is a set of verbal or non-verbal procedures by which one brings to light—and this may just as well be the sovereign's individual consciousness as the knowledge (*savoir*) of his counselors or as public manifestation—something that is asserted or rather laid down as true, whether in contrast, of course, with something false that has been eliminated, disputed, or refuted, or by dragging it out from the hidden, by dispelling what has been forgotten, by warding off the unforeseeable.

So I won't say simply that the exercise of power presupposes something like a useful and utilizable knowledge in those who [govern].* I shall say that the exercise of power is almost always accompanied by a manifestation of truth understood in this very broad sense. And, looking for a word that corresponds, not to the knowledge useful for those who govern, but to that manifestation of truth correlative to the exercise of power, I found one that is not well-established or recognized, since it

---

* M.F.: exercise it.

has hardly been used but once, and then in a different form, by a Greek grammarian of the third or fourth centuries—well, the experts will correct me—a grammarian called Heraclitus who employs the adjective *alēthourgēs* for someone who speaks the truth.[9] *Alēthourgēs* is the truthful. Consequently, forging the fictional word *alēthourgia*, alethurgy, from *alēthourgēs*, we could call "alethurgy" the manifestation of truth as the set of possible verbal or non-verbal procedures by which one brings to light what is laid down as true as opposed to false, hidden, inexpressible, unforeseeable, or forgotten, and say that there is no exercise of power without something like an alethurgy. Or again—since you know that I love Greek words and that in Greek the exercise of power is called "hegemony," although not in the sense we now give this word: hegemony is just the fact of being in the position of leading others, of conducting them, and of conducting, as it were, their conduct—I will say: it is likely that hegemony cannot be exercised without something like an alethurgy. This is to say, in a barbarous and rough way, that what we call knowledge (*connaissance*), that is to say the production of truth in the consciousness of individuals by logico-experimental procedures, is only one of the possible forms of alethurgy. Science, objective knowledge, is only one of the possible cases of all these forms by which truth may be manifested.

You will say that this is all academic debate and suchlike diversion, for, if we can say, speaking very generally, that for centuries there was no exercise of power, no hegemony, without something like rituals or forms of manifestation of the truth, that there was no hegemony without alethurgy, happily this has now all been brought down to much more effective and rational problems, techniques, and procedures than, for example, the representation of the star-studded sky over the Emperor's head, and that we now have an exercise of power that is rationalized as art of government, and that this art has given rise [to], or depends upon, a number of bodies of objective knowledge like the knowledge of political economy, of society, of demography, and of a whole series of processes.[10] I entirely agree. Well, I agree a bit, in part. And I am happy [to acknowledge] that the series of phenomena to which I have referred, through the story of Septimius Severus, is a sort of residual aura testifying to a certain archaism in the exercise of power, that all this has now almost disappeared and we have arrived at a rational art of government about which precisely I have spoken in the last two years' lectures. I would just like to note two things.

First of all, in this as in every other domain, what is marginal and what is residual still has its heuristic value when one examines it closely, and that in this order of things the too much or too little is very often a principle of intelligibility.

Second, no doubt too things have lasted for much longer than one thinks. And if Septimius Severus is fairly representative of, once again, a quite precise context at the end of the second and beginning of the third century, this history of the manifestation of truth, understood in the very broad sense of an alethurgy around the exercise of power, was not dispelled as if by magic, either under the influence of the mistrust that Christianity may have had for this kind of magical practice, or due to the effects of the progress of Western rationality from the fifteenth-sixteenth centuries. We could—I may return to this next week if I have time—refer to a very interesting article by Denise Grodzynski, published in a book edited by Jean-Pierre Vernant entitled *Divination et Rationalité*,[11] on the struggle conducted by the Roman Emperors of the third and fourth centuries against these magical practices and on the way in which there was to some extent an attempt to, as it were, purify the exercise of power of this ambience, [and which shows] clearly all the difficulties encountered and all the political stakes behind this.[12] But, much later, for example in the fifteenth and sixteenth centuries, at the beginning of the seventeenth century, we could also [speak about] the princely [and] royal courts of the end of the Middle Ages, of the Renaissance, and still of the seventeenth century, which, as we know, were very impor-tant political instruments. We know too what "cultural centers,"[13] as it is said, they were. And what does "cultural centers" [signify], what meaning did it have? Maybe we should say sites of manifestation of the truth rather than just centers of culture. It is quite clear that there were huge, immediately utilitarian reasons for the concern of Renaissance princes to bring together around them a number of activities, forms and bodies of knowledge, practices, and individuals who were what we would call cultural creators or vehicles. It is true that this involved cre-ating a core of competences around the prince precisely enabling him to assert his political power over the old, let's say feudal or in any case earlier structures.[14] It was also a matter of ensuring a centralization of knowledge at a time when a certain religious and ideological division was in danger of forming an excessively significant counterweight to the prince. In the period of the Reformation and Counter Reformation, it was a matter of being able to control to some extent the violence and intensity of these ideological and religious movements that were more or less imposed on the prince whether he liked it or not.

There is that. But I think the phenomenon of the court also represented something else and that in the court, and in the extraordinary concentration in the court of what we could call cultural activities, there was a sort of pure expenditure of truth or a pure manifestation of truth. Where there is power, where power is necessary, where one wishes to show effectively that this is where the power lies, there must be truth. And where there is no truth, where there is no manifestation of truth, it is because there is no power, or it is too weak, or incapable of being power. Power's strength is not independent of something like the manifestation of truth that goes far beyond what is merely useful or necessary to govern well. The strengthening of princely power that we see in the fifteenth, sixteenth, and seventeenth centuries called, of course, for the formation of a whole range of knowledge that could be said to be useful for the art of government, but also for a whole series of rituals, of manifestations of knowledge, from the development of humanist circles to the very strange and constant presence of sorcerers, astrologers, and seers in the entourage of the princes up until the beginning of the seventeenth century. The exercise of princely power, in the sixteenth century as in the time of Septimius Severus, could not dispense with a certain number of these rituals, and it would be interesting to study the character of the seer, sorcerer, and astrologer in the sixteenth and seventeenth centuries.

In a sense, *raison d'État*, some genetic moments of which I tried to reconstruct two years ago,[15] is actually a whole, let's say utilitarian and calculating reorganization of all the alethurgies peculiar to the exercise of power. It involved the development of a type of knowledge that would be, as it were, internal to and useful for the exercise of power. But the constitution of *raison d'État* was accompanied by a whole movement that was clearly its negative counterpart: the seers of the royal court must be driven out, the astrologer must be replaced by the kind of counselor who both possessed and invoked the truth, a real minister capable of providing the prince with useful knowledge. The constitution of *raison d'État* is the reorganization of all those manifestations of truth that were linked to the exercise of power and the organization of the courts.

As a result, we could—if anyone were interested—view the witch hunt at the end of the sixteenth century[16] as not having been purely and simply a phenomenon of the Church's and so, to an extent, State's reconquest of a whole stratum of population that, basically, had been only super- ficially converted to Christianity in the Middle Ages. Of course, this phenomenon is fundamental; I have absolutely no wish to deny it. The witch hunt was indeed a repercussion of the Reformation and Counter Reformation, that is to say, of an acceleration of Christianization, which had been rather slow and superficial in previous centuries. The witch hunt did indeed represent this. But there was also a witch hunt, a drive against seers and astrologers that took place in the higher strata and even in the royal entourage. And the exclusion of the seer from the courts is chronologically contemporary with the latter and with the most intense witch hunts in the lower strata. We should therefore see [here] an as it were forked phenomenon that looked in both directions; in the direc- tion of the prince's entourage and in the direction of the lower classes. That type of knowledge, that type of manifestation of truth, of produc- tion of truth, of alethurgy had to be eliminated both in the lower strata, for a number of reasons, and in the prince's entourage and court.

We can find here a character who is definitely important, and that is, of course, Bodin. Bodin, whom we know about on account of his *République*, who was one of the theorists of the new rationality that was to preside over the art of government,[17] also wrote a book on sorcery.[18] Now I know that there are people—their names and nationality are not important—who say: yes, of course, if Bodin does these two things, if he is both theorist of *raison d'État* and the great caster out of demon-mania, both demonologist and theorist of the State, this is quite simply because nascent capitalism needed labor and witches were also abortionists, it was a question of removing the checks to demography in order to be able to provide capital with the labor it needed in its factories of the nine- teenth century. You can see that the argument is not entirely convinc- ing (it is true that I caricature it). But for myself, it would seem more interesting to seek the two registers of Bodin's thought in the relation there must be between the constitution of a rationality specific to the art of government in the form, let us say, of a State reason in general and, on the other hand, the casting out of that alethurgy that, in the form of demon-mania, but also of divination, occupied a place in the knowledge of princes that *raison d'État* had to replace. This would certainly be a possible domain of study.[19]

So much for the introduction of some of the themes I would like to talk about this year. You can see that broadly it will involve elaborating somewhat the notion of the government of men by the truth. I have spoken a little about this notion in previous years.[20] What do I mean by "elaborate this notion"? It means, of course, something of a slight shift in relation to the now worn and hackneyed theme of knowledge-power. That theme, knowledge-power, was itself only a way of shifting things in relation to a type of analysis in the domain of the history of thought that was more or less organized by, or that revolved around the notion of dominant ideology. So there are two successive shifts if you like: one from the notion of dominant ideology to that of knowledge-power, and now, a second shift from the notion of knowledge-power to the notion of government by the truth.

There is, of course, a difference between these two shifts. If I tried to set the notion of knowledge-power against the notion of dominant ideology it is because I think three objections could be made to the latter. First, it postulated a badly constructed theory, or a theory not constructed at all, of representation. Second, this notion of dominant ideology was pegged, implicitly at least, and moreover without being able to rid itself of it in a clear way, to an opposition of true and false, reality and illusion, scientific and unscientific, rational and irrational. Finally, third, under the word "dominant," the notion of dominant ideology chose to overlook all the real mechanisms of subjection and as it were discarded the card, passing it on to another hand, saying: after all, it's for historians to find out how and why some dominate others in a society. In opposition to this I tried therefore to establish the notions of knowledge and power. The function of the notion of knowledge (*savoir*) was precisely to clear the field of the opposition between scientific and unscientific, the question of illusion and reality, and the question of true and false. Not so as to say that these oppositions did not have any sense or value—that was not what I wanted to say. I simply wanted to say that with knowledge (*savoir*) the problem was to be posed in terms of constitutive practices, of practices constitutive of domains of objects and concepts within which the oppositions of scientific and unscientific, true and false, reality and illusion could come into play. As for the notion of power, its main function was to replace the notion of system of dominant representations with the question or field of analysis of the procedures and techniques by which power relations are actually effectuated.

Now, the second shift in relation to this notion of knowledge-power involves getting rid of this in order to try to develop the notion of government by the truth; getting rid of the notion of knowledge-power as we got rid of the notion of dominant ideology. Well, when I say this I am being utterly hypocritical, since it is obvious that one does not get rid of what one has thought oneself in the same way as one rids oneself of what was thought by others. Consequently, I will certainly be more indulgent with the notion of knowledge-power than with that of dominant ideology, but it is for you to reproach me for this. So, in the inability to treat myself as I have treated others, I will say that passing from the notion of knowledge-power to that of government by the truth essentially involves giving a positive and differentiated content to these two terms of knowledge and power.

Over the last two years I have then tried to sketch out a bit this notion of government, which seemed to me to be much more operational than the notion of power, "government" being understood, of course, not in the narrow and current sense of the supreme instance of executive and administrative decisions in State systems, but in the broad sense, and old sense moreover, of mechanisms and procedures intended to conduct men, to direct their conduct, to conduct their conduct. And it is in the general framework of this notion of government that I tried to study two things, as examples: on the one hand, the birth of *raison d'État* in the seventeenth century,[21] understood not as theory or representation of the State, but as art of government, as rationality elaborating the very practice of government, and, on the other, contemporary American and German liberalism—this is what I did last year[22]—also being understood, not as economic theory or political doctrine, but as a certain way of governing, a certain rational art of government.

Starting this year, I would now like to develop the notion of knowledge in the direction of the problem of the truth. [...] [I would like] still, today, to remain somewhat at the level of generalities so as to try to situate the problem a bit better, given that the example of Septimius Severus and his star-studded sky is not completely adequate for grasping, for situating a bit more precisely the questions to be posed for an historical analysis. It is a commonplace to say that the art of government and, let's say, the game of truth are not independent of each other and that one cannot govern without in one way or another entering into the game of truth. These are all commonplaces, and to tell the truth, taking a completely provisional bearing, I think these common themes can be found in four or five main forms in modern political thought (I say "modern political thought" in the very broad sense of the term, that is to say, from the seventeenth century). Five ways of conceiving the possible relation between exercise of power and manifestation of the truth.

The first, oldest, very general, and very banal form, but which of course, for three centuries, had its innovatory force and produced the effects of a break, is quite simply that there cannot be any government without those who govern indexing their actions, choices, and decisions to a whole set of bodies of knowledge, of rationally founded principles, or exact knowledge, which do not arise simply from the prince's wisdom in general or from reason tout court, but from a rational structure specific to a domain of possible objects, which is that of the State. In other words, the idea of a State reason seems to me to have been in modern Europe the first way of reflecting on and trying to give a precise, assignable, manageable, and usable status to the relation between the exercise of power and the manifestation of the truth. In short, this would be the idea that the rationality of governmental action is *raison d'État*, and that the truth that has to be manifested is the truth of the State as object of governmental action. Let's call this Botero's principle, inasmuch as Botero was the first, or one of the first to give a systematic formulation of the principle of *raison d'État*.[23]

Second, a bit later, we come across another way of linking the art of government and the game of truth. At first sight it is a paradoxical, utopian mode of connection, and yet historically it was very important. It is the idea that, if in actual fact the government governs not through wisdom in general, but through the truth, that is to say through the exact knowledge of the processes that characterize the reality that is the State—that reality that constitutes population, the production of wealth, work, commerce—if it governs through the truth, then it will have to govern even less. The more it pegs its action to the truth, the less it will have to govern in the sense that the less it will have to take decisions that have to be imposed from above, in accordance with more or less uncertain calculations, on people who will accept them more or less well. If the truth can succeed in constituting the climate and light common to governors and governed, then you can see that a time must come, a kind of utopian point in history when the empire of the truth will be able to make its order reign without the decisions of an authority or the choices of an administration having to intervene otherwise than as the formulation, obvious to everyone, of what is to be done. The exercise of power will therefore only ever be indicator of the truth. And if this indication of the truth takes place in a sufficiently demonstrative manner, everyone will be in agreement with it and, when it comes to it, there will no longer be need for a government or government will be only the surface of reflection of the truth of the society and economy in a number of minds who will have to do no more than pass on this truth to those who are governed. Governors and governed will be as it were actors, co-actors, simultaneous actors of a drama that they perform in common and which is that of nature in its truth. Summarizing things considerably, this is Quesnay's idea,[24] the physiocratic idea: the idea that if men were to govern according to the rules of evidence, it would be things themselves, rather than men, that govern. Let us call this, if you like, Quesnay's principle, which, despite again its abstract and quasi-utopian character, was of great importance in the history of European political thought.

We can say that what took place later and what we see developing in the nineteenth century, in the domain of these reflections on the way to link truth and government, is basically only the development or dissociation of this physiocratic idea. In fact, in the nineteenth century you find the idea, which is also very banal but of great importance, that if the art of government is fundamentally linked to the discovery of a truth and to the objective knowledge of this truth, this implies the constitution of a specialized form knowledge, the formation of a category of individuals, also specialized in knowledge of this truth, and this specialization constitutes a domain that is not exactly specific to politics, but defines rather a set of things and relations that must, in any case, be imposed on politics. You can see that broadly speaking this is Saint-Simon's principle.[25]

Facing this and a bit later we find, so to speak, the opposite: if a number of individuals appear as specialists of the truth that is to be imposed on politics, this is basically because they have something to hide. That is to say, if it were to come about that all the individuals living in a society knew the truth and actually knew, in reality and in depth, what is happening, and what the apparent competence of others seeks only to hide, in other words, if everyone were to know everything about the society in which they live, the government would no longer be able govern and the revolution would take place immediately. Strip off the masks, discover things as they happen, become conscious of the nature of the society in which we live, of the economic processes of which we are the unconscious agents and victims, become aware of the mechanisms of exploitation and domination, and the government falls at once. There is an incompatibility, consequently, between the finally acquired evidence of what is really taking place, between the evidence acquired by all, and the exercise of government by a few. This is a principle, therefore, of universal awareness as principle of the overthrow of governments, regimes, and systems. This is what Rosa Luxembourg formulated in a famous phrase: "If everyone were to know, the capitalist regime would not last twenty four hours."[26]

To this we could add a much more recent way of understanding and defining the relations between the manifestation of truth and the exercise of power. This is the exact opposite of Rosa Luxemburg's approach. We could call this Solzhenitsyn's principle,[27] which amounts to saying: maybe if everyone knew, the capitalist regime would not last twenty-four hours, but, Solzhenitsyn says, if the socialist regimes stand firm it is precisely because everyone knows. It is not because the governed do not know what is happening, or it is not because some of them know but others do not, it is rather because they know and it is to the extent that they know, to the extent that everyone is actually aware of the evidence of what is happening, it is precisely to that extent that things do not change. This is, precisely, the principle of terror. Terror is not an art of government the aims, motives, and mechanisms of which are hidden. Terror is precisely governmentality in the naked, cynical, obscene state. In terror it is the truth and not the lie that immobilizes. It is the truth that freezes, it is the truth that, by its evidence, by that evidence manifest everywhere, renders itself intangible and inevitable.

So a balance sheet, if you like: *Raison d'État* or principle of rationality is Botero; economic rationality and principle of evidence is Quesnay; scientific specification of evidence and principle of competence is Saint-Simon; reversal of particular competence into universal awakening is the principle of general consciousness, Rosa Luxemburg; and finally, shared and fascinated awareness of the inevitable is the principle of terror or Solzhenitsyn's principle. Five ways of reflecting upon, analyzing, or at any rate localizing the relations between the exercise of power and the manifestation of the truth.

Obviously, I have not drawn up this table with any idea of it being exhaustive, or even to establish an off-hand view that would allow us to grasp what is essential to the whole and its coherence. I have done so only to give some reference points or rather to make a purely indicative list of some of the ways in which attempts have been made, in the modern period, to think the relations between art of government and knowledge of the truth, or again between exercise of power and manifestation of the truth. I have not listed them in this schematic fashion, one after the after and pinning them to a name, and so to a date, so as to say that each of them distinctively characterizes a very specific moment, that there was an age of rationality, an age of evidence, an age of competence. That was not my purpose. Nor have I wanted to show that they were linked in an inevitable transition from one to the other. And above all I did not want to say that the principle of terror, for example, was already inevitably contained, necessarily, in embryo, in nucleus, in the idea of a governmental rationality of the kind found in the seventeenth century in *raison d'État*. This is absolutely not what I wanted to say. Rather I have indicated some ways of thinking the relations between manifestation of truth and exercise of power solely in order to try to show you the narrowness of each of their points of view.

We could mark this narrowness by emphasizing the following. [On the one hand,] in all of these modern ways of reflecting upon government-truth relations, all of which are from the last three centuries, these relations are defined in terms of a certain reality, which would be the State or society. Society would be the object of knowledge, the site of spontaneous processes, the subject of revolts, the object-subject of fascination in terror. And, on the other hand, the other limitation of these analyses, is that they are produced according to a knowledge (*savoir*) that [would] always [have] the form of the more or less objective knowledge (*connaissance*) of the phenomena. Now I would like to attempt to go back beyond these different schemas. I would like to go back and show you how the relations between government and truth were not finally formed when society or the State appeared as possible and necessary objects for a rational governmentality. For the link between manifestation of truth and exercise of power to be made, we don't have to wait for the constitution of these new, modern relations between an art of government and, let's say, political, economic, and social rationality. The link between exercise of power and manifestation of truth is much older and exists at a much deeper level, and I would like to try to show you—by taking a very particular and precise example that does not fall within the domain of politics—how you cannot direct men without carrying out operations in the domain of truth, and operations that are always in excess of what is useful and necessary to govern in an effective way. The manifestation of truth is required by, or entailed by, or linked to the exercise of government and the exercise of power in a way that always goes beyond the aim of government and the effective means for achieving it.

It is often said that, in the final analysis, there is something like a kernel of violence behind all relations of power and that if one were to strip power of its showy garb one would find the naked game of life and death. Maybe. But can there be power without showy garb? In other words, can there really be a power that would do without the play of light and shadow, truth and error, true and false, hidden and manifest, visible and invisible? In other words, can there be an exercise of power without a ring of truth, without an alethurgic circle that turns around it and accompanies it? The star-studded sky over the head of Septimius Severus and the heads of those he judged, the star-studded sky as truth that was spread out implacably above the one who governs and those who are governed, that star-studded sky as manifestation of the truth, that star-studded sky, therefore, over all our heads, puts the political law in his hands.

That's it. Well, it is around these themes that I will try to proceed.

1. Dio Cassius, Greek historian (?155-?240 C.E.). Of the eighty books of his monumental *Roman History*, only books 37 to 59 have survived. The passage referred to by Foucault comes from Book 77, 11, as summarized by the Byzantine monk John Xiphilinus (end of the eleventh century). See *Dio's Roman History*, vol. IX, trans. E. Cary (Cambridge, Mass., and London: Harvard University Press/William Heinemann, The Loeb Classical Library, 1982 [1927]) pp. 261-263. "Severus, seeing that his sons were changing their mode of life and that the legions were becoming enervated by idleness, made a campaign against Britain, though he knew that he should not return. He knew this chiefly from the stars under which he had been born, for he had caused them to be painted on the ceilings of the rooms in the palace where he was wont to hold court, so that they were visible to all, with the exception of that portion of the sky which, as the astrologers express it, 'observed the hour' when he first saw the light; for this portion he had not depicted in the same way in both rooms. He knew his fate also by what he had heard from the seers; for a thunderbolt had struck a statue of his which stood near the gates through which he was intending to march out and looked toward the road leading to his destination, and it had erased three letters from his name. For this reason, as the seers made clear, he did not return, but died in the third year. He took along with him an immense amount of money." See the translation by E. Gros, Dion Cassius, *Histoire Romaine*, t. 10 (Paris: Firmin Didot, 1870) in which the reference is Book 76, 11: "Severus then turned his arms against Britain, because he saw his sons leading an intemperate life and the legions growing soft in idleness, and he did this, even though he knew that he would not come back. He knew this above all through knowledge of the stars under which he was born (he had them painted on the ceilings of the halls of his palace in which he dispensed justice; so that apart from the precise moment that related to the hour of his birth, to his horoscope, as one says, everyone could see them, because this moment did not appear the same on each side); he also knew through having heard it from the seers. In fact, on the base of a statue of himself, placed by the entrance through which his army had to leave, and looking over the road along which they passed, three letters from his name had been erased by the lightning that had struck it; and it is for this reason that, as the seers had declared, he did not return and died three years later. He took considerable sums with him on this expedition."

2. Lucius Septimius Severus (146-211 C.E.), Emperor of Rome 193-211. Born in Leptis Magna (Tripolitania—Modern Libya), he first exercised a variety of offices in Africa (senator, quaestor, proconsul), and then commanded the legions of Illyria which proclaimed him emperor after the violent death of Pertinax. Recognized by the Senate, he then defeated his two rivals, Pescennius Niger, recognized by the whole of Asia, and Albinus, elected by the legions of Britain.

3. This was no doubt the Septizonium (or Septizodium), a monument, which has now disappeared, built to the South East of the Palatine, the remains of which survived into the sixteenth century. It was demolished by Pope Sixtus V in 1588. The emperor fitted out a hall in which he was represented as the Sun surrounded by the seven planets.

4. Sophocle, *Œdipe-Roi* in *Œuvres*, vol. I, ed. and trans. P. Masqueray (Paris: Les Belles Lettres, 1922, 4th edition, 1946) [reference edition]; English translation by David Grene, Sophocles, *Oedipus the King*, in *Sophocles I, Three Tragedies*, ed. David Grene and Richard Lattimore (Chicago and London: The University of Chicago Press, 1991). See M. Foucault, *Leçons sur la volonté de savoir. Cours au Collège de France, 1970-1971* suivi de *Le Savoir d'Œdipe*, ed. D. Defert (Paris: Gallimard-Seuil, coll. "Hautes Études," 2011) p. 192 note 1; English translation by Graham Burchell, *Lectures on the Will to Know. Lectures at the Collège de France 1970-1971, and Oedipal Knowledge*, ed. Daniel Defert, English Series Editor, Arnold I. Davidson (Basingstoke and New York: Palgrave Macmillan, 2013), p. 200 note 1.

5. Ibid., 236-244, Fr., p. 149; Eng., p. 20. Foucault summarizes here the judgment pronounced by Oedipus before the Thebans.

6. Marcus Aurelius (121-180 C.E.), Roman Emperor from 161 to 180, author of the work known as the *Meditations*. He had two successors before Septimius Severus: his son Commodus (180-192), and then Pertinax (January-March 193), who were both murdered. On this figure of the philosopher-prince, see M. Foucault, *L'Herméneutique du sujet. Cours au Collège de France, 1981-1982*, ed. Frédéric Gros (Paris: Gallimard-Le Seuil, 2001), pp. 191-194; English translation by Graham Burchell, *The Hermeneutics of the Subject. Lectures at the Collège de France, 1981-1982*, English series editor, Arnold I. Davidson (Basingstoke and New York: Palgrave Macmillan, 2005), pp. 199-201.

On Septimius Severus' relation to Oriental cults, see J. Daniélous, *Origène* (Paris: La Table Ronde, "Le génie du christianisme," 1948), p. 35: "[The] invasion [of these cults, which began under the Antonines] reaches its peak with the expansion of the Syrian cults under the Severan dynasty. The head of the dynasty had, in fact, married the daughter of a great Syrian priest, Julia Domna. The latter introduced the Syrian cults to the court and, in particular, the cult of the sun."

7. Domitius Ulpianus (?170-228 C.E.), one of the major Roman jurisconsults, a member, with Papinian, of the Imperial Council, which, under Septimius Severus, became the principal organ of imperial administration. An important part of his work has been conserved thanks to the *Digest*, drafted in the sixth century on the order of Justinian, around a third of which is drawn from his writings.

8. He had himself had legal training.

9. See A. Bailly, *Dictionnaire grec-français* (1894), revised edition by L. Séchan and P. Chantraine (Paris: Hachette, 16th ed., 1950) p. 77: "ἀληθουργής [*alēthourgēs*]: who acts frankly, HERACL[IDE], All [= Homeric allegories], 67 (*alēthēs, ergon*)." Heraclitus, cited in the list of authors, p. xx, appears thus: "Grammarian, place and date unknown [E. Mehler ed., 1851]." For further clarifications, see Pseudo-Héraclite, *Allégories d'Homère*, text established and translated by F. Buffière (Paris: Les Belles Lettres, 1989 [1962]); Heraclitus, *Homeric Problems*, ed. and trans. Donald Andrew Russell and David Konstan (Society of Biblical Literature, 2005).

10. On these bodies of objective knowledge on which the art of government from the seventeenth-eighteenth centuries depends, see *Sécurité, territoire, population. Cours au Collège de France, 1977-78*, ed. Michel Senellart (Paris: Gallimard-Le Seuil, 2004); English translation by Graham Burchell, *Security, Territory, Population. Lectures at the Collège de France, 1977-78*, English series editor Arnold I. Davidson (Basingstoke and New York: Palgrave Macmillan, 2007), lectures of 1 February (the triangle of government-population-political economy), 29 March and 5 April 1978 (police, political economy), and *Naissance de la biopolitique. Cours au Collège de France, 1978-79*, ed. Michel Senellart (Paris: Gallimard-Le Seuil, 2004); English translation by Graham Burchell, *The Birth of Biopolitics. Lectures at the Collège de France, 1978-79*, English series editor, Arnold I. Davidson (Basingstoke and New York: Palgrave Macmillan, 2005), lectures of 10 January (the regime of truth characteristic of the age of politics), 17 and 24 January (the specific features of the liberal art of government).

11. Jean-Pierre Vernant, ed., *Divination et Rationalité* (Paris: Seuil, "Recherches anthropologiques," 1990 [1974]).

12. D. Grodzynski, "Par la bouche de l'empereur, Rome IVᵉ siècle," ibid., pp. 267-294.

13. See A.-M. Schmidt, "La cour de Henri II," in G. Gadoffre, ed., *Rencontres, 9: Foyers de notre culture*, (Lyon: éd. de l'Abeille, 1943) pp. 31-37; G. Gadoffre, "Foyers de culture," *Encyclopaedia Universalis* (online edition, 2008), which examines successively the university college, court society, the eighteenth century salon, and the romantic studio from the double point of view of the "mental universe" that takes shape in it and its relationship with the official institution, and especially the section: "Un foyer de culture greffé sur l'institution royale: la cour de Henri II."

14. On the political function of the court in the seventeenth century, which (with classical tragedy) constituted "a sort of lesson of public law"—"to organize a space for the daily and permanent display of royal power in all its splendor," see M. Foucault, *"Il faut défendre la société." Cours au Collège de France 1975-1976"* ed., M. Bertani and A. Fontana (Paris: Gallimard-Le Seuill, "Hautes Études," 1997), lecture of 25 February 1976, pp. 156-157; English translation by David Macey, *"Society Must Be Defended." Lectures at the Collège de France 1975-1976*, English series editor, Arnold I. Davidson (New York: Picador, 2003), pp. 175-176 [translation slightly modified; G.B.].

15. See M. Foucault, *Sécurité, territoire, population; Security, Territory, Population*, lectures of 8, 15, and 22 March 1978.

16. Foucault had already broached the question of witchcraft in his lectures of 1974-1975, *Les anormaux. Cours au Collège de France 1974-1975*, ed., M. Bertani and A. Salomoni (Paris: Gallimard-Le Seuil, 1999), lecture of 26 February 1975, pp. 190-191 and 203-201; English translation by Graham Burchell, *Abnormal. Lectures at the Collège de France 1974-1975*, English series editor Arnold I. Davidson (New York: Picador, 2003) pp. 204-206 and

pp. 208-216. At that time it was a question of distinguishing witchcraft from the phenomenon of possession: "… just as witchcraft was no doubt simultaneously the effect, point of reversal, and center of resistance to this wave of Christianization and its instruments—the Inquisition and its courts—so possession was similarly the effect and point of reversal of this other technique of Christianization, namely the confessional and spiritual direction" (pp. 213-214).

17. J. Bodin, *Les six livres de la République* (Paris: Jacques Du Puys, 1576; republication of 10th edition at Lyon: Jacques Cartier, 1593; Paris: Fayard, Corpus des Œuvres de Philosophie en Langue Française, 1986); English translation (abridged) by M.J. Tooley, as *Six Books of The Commonwealth* (Oxford: Basil Blackwell, 1955).

18. J. Bodin, *De la démonomanie des sourciers* (Paris: Jacques du Puy, 1580; 6th revised and expanded edition, 1587). The work went through 13 French editions up until 1616 and was published at least twenty five times in four languages. See P. Mesnard, "La démonomanie de Jean Bodin," in *L'Opera e il pensiero di G. Pico della Mirandola* (Florence: Istituto nazionale di studi sul Rinascimento, 1965), vol. II, pp. 333-356.

19. Several works on the *République/Démonomanie* connection have been published since this date. See, for example, M. Préaud, "La *Démonomanie*, fille de la *République*," in *Jean Bodin*, Actes du colloque interdisciplinaire d'Angers, 24-27 May 1984 (Angers: Presses Universitaires d'Angers, 1985), vol. 2, pp. 419-425, which recalls the presence of "sorcerers" among the Italian counselors of Catherine de' Medici, while stressing Bodin's own interest in astrology. In a different perspective, see R. Muchembled, *Le roi et la sorcière. L'Europe des bûchers (XVᵉ-XVIIIᵉ siècles)*, (Paris: Desclée, 1993) pp. 48-52 ("Jean Bodin, ou la *République* de Satan"); G. Heinsohn and O. Steiger, "Birth Control: The Political-Economic Rationale behind Jean Bodin's *Démonomanie*," in *History of Political Economy*, vol. 31, 3 (1999), pp. 423-448.

20. See M. Foucault, *Naissance de la biopolitique*, lecture of 10 January 1979, pp. 20-22; *The Birth of Biopolitics*, pp. 17-20.

21. See above, note 15.

22. See *Naissance de la biopolitique*; *The Birth of Biopolitics*, lectures of 31 January and 21 February, on German neo-liberalism or ordo-liberalism, and the lectures of 14 and 21 March on the American neo-liberalism of the Chicago School.

23. Giovanni Botero, author of *Della ragion di Stato libri dieci*, (Venise: Appresso i Gioliti, 1589 [4th, expanded edition, 1598]); French translation by G. Chappuys, *Raison et gouvernement d'Estat en dix livres* (Paris: Guillaume Chaudière, 1599); English translation by D.P. and J.P Waley, *The Reason of State and The Greatness of Cities* (New Haven: Yale University Press, 1956). See his definition of *raison d'État*, cited by Foucault in *Sécurité, territoire, population*, lecture of 8 March 1978, p. 243; *Security, territory, population*, p. 238: "The State is a firm domination over peoples; and Reason of State is the knowledge of the appropriate means for founding, preserving, and expanding such a domination."

24. On Quesnay and the physiocrats, see *Sécurité, territoire, population*, the lectures of 18 January 1978, p. 35, 1 February pp. 98-99, and 8 February p. 120, with regard to the notion of "economic government"; *Security, Territory, Population*, pp. 33-34 , p. 95, and p. 116.

25. Claude Henri de Roucroy, comte de Saint-Simon (1760-1825), author of *Du système industriel*, 1821, and of the *Catéchisme des industriels*, 1823-1824. In his works he defended a plan for the reorganization of society according to which "the government of men" must give way to "the administration of things": the movement of history and the progress of reason lead to the disappearance of politics to the advantage of a technocratic type of administration founded on the "capabilities" of experts and industrialists. "In the present state of enlightenment, the country no longer needs to be governed, but to be administered as cheaply as possible; now, it is only in industry that one can learn to administer cheaply"; *Du système industriel*, vol. I, 1821, cited in G. Gurvitch, *Claude-Henri de Saint-Simon. La physiologie social. Œuvres choisies* (Paris: PUF, "Bibliothèque de Sociologie Contemporaine," 1965), p. 126.

26. Rosa Luxemburg (1871-1919). This phrase could not be found in the four volumes of her *Œuvres* published by Maspero in 1969. Foucault's direct or indirect source may be C. Castoriadis, *L'institution imaginaire de la société* (Paris: Seuil, "Esprit," 1975), p. 150 note 41: "Rosa Luxemburg said: 'If all the population *knew*, the capitalist regime would not last twenty four hours.'" (I thank B. Harcourt for putting me on the track of this reference.)

27. Alexander Isaevich Solzhenitsyn (1918-2008), author, notably of *The Gulag Archipelago, 1918-1956*, published in 1973; French translation (Paris: Seuil, 1974-1976), three volumes; English translation by Thomas P. Whitney, (New York and London: Harper and Row/Collins, 1974). Foucault referred to Solzhenitsyn in *Sécurité, territoire, population*, lecture of 1 March 1978, p. 204; *Security, Territory, Population*, p. 201, with regard to his denunciation of terror as functional principle of socialist regimes, and in *Naissance de la biopolitique*, lecture of 14 February 1979, p. 136 (see p. 156 note 1); *The Birth of Biopolitics*, p. 130 (p. 151 note 1).

two

16 January 1980

The relations between government and truth (continued). ᔐ *An*
example of these relations: the tragedy of Oedipus the King.
Greek tragedy and alethurgy. Analysis of the play focused on the
theme of the kingship of Oedipus. ᔐ *Conditions of formulation of*
the orthon epos, *the just speech (*la parole juste*) to which one*
must submit. The law of successive halves: the divine and prophetic
half and the human half of the procedure of truth. The game of the
sumbolon. *Comparison of divine alethurgy and the alethurgy of*
slaves. Two historical forms of alethurgy: oracular and religious
alethurgy and judicial alethurgy founded upon testimony. Their
complementarity in the play.

LAST WEEK I BEGAN to outline the situation of the problem concerning the relations between exercise of power and manifestation of
truth. I tried to show you—well, at least to indicate the theme that
the exercise of power cannot take place and be carried out without
something like a manifestation of truth. I tried to emphasize [the fact
that] this manifestation of truth should not be understood merely as
the constitution, formation, and concentration of knowledge useful for
effective government, that it involved something else, that there was
something like a supplement with regard to that system of utility. What
also needs to be stressed (and maybe I did not do so enough last week)
is that when I speak of relations between manifestation of truth and
exercise of power, I do not mean that the exercise of power needs to
manifest itself in truth in the blaze of its presence and potency, and

that it needs, as it were, to publicly and manifestly ritualize its forms of exercise. What I would like to try to emphasize today is precisely that kind of supplement of manifestation of truth as much with regard to the constitution of knowledge useful for government as with regard to the necessary manifestation of power among us.

Clearly, the relations between manifestation of truth and exercise of power could be analyzed from a general ethnological point of view, which I, of course, would be incapable of undertaking. I would simply like here to take an example, a precise and definite case of the relationship between exercise of power and manifestation of truth, which will lead us—well, which I would like to lead us to this year's theme. I must apologize straightaway for this first example, which will serve as the starting point for the analyses that I would like to undertake this year, and for two reasons: not only is it a very hackneyed example, but it is one I have talked about a bit about at least, I don't know …, how long have I been here? It must be ten years, so I must have talked about it around nine years ago.[1] Well, I have made some soundings and it seems that few people remember it, which proves, thank heavens, that they do not stay here for nine years. Quite simply, it is, of course, the story of Oedipus the King.[2] The story of Oedipus the King clearly raises, in everyone's eyes, the problem of the relations between the exercise of power and the manifestation of the truth. And what I would like to propose to you today and next week is a sort of reading of Oedipus the King, not in terms of desire and the unconscious, but in terms of truth and power, an alethurgic reading if you like.

Of course, every Greek tragedy is an alethurgy, that is to say a ritual manifestation of truth; an alethurgy in the completely general sense of the term, since tragedy, of course, makes truth audible and visible through the myths and heroes, through the actors and their masks. In Greece, the stage, the theater is a site on which the truth is manifested, as the truth is manifested, albeit in a different way, at the seat of an oracle, or on the public square where one debates, on in the space where justice is dispensed. Tragedy tells the truth—at any rate, it is this problem of the truth-telling of tragedy that Plato will raise, and I will return to this problem later.[3] In this general sense, then, every tragedy is an alethurgy, but equally in a more precise, if you like, technical sense, tragedy is an alethurgy also in its internal organization inasmuch as it not only tells the truth, but it represents the truth-telling. In itself it is a way of revealing the truth, but it is also a way of representing the way in which, in the story it recounts, or in the myth to which it refers, the truth came to light. I refer here to Aristotle's well-known text in which he says that there are two essential elements in every tragedy.[4] First, peripeteia, or dramatic reversal, the movement internal to the tragedy through which the fortune of the characters is reversed, that the powerful become wretched and those who appear in the shape of anonymity are finally revealed to be the strong and powerful.[5] So, on one side reversal and, on the other, recognition, what Aristotle calls anagnōrisis, that is to say that not only is the fortune of the characters reversed in the course of the tragedy, but what was not known at the beginning is discovered at the end.[6] The character who was represented as ignorant to start with, finally comes to know at the end of the tragedy, or the one who was masked, concealed, whose identity is unknown, is finally revealed for what he is. So in tragedy there is a reversal and recognition and we can say that in most tragedies it is the reversal that brings about in some way the movement of recognition. It is because there is a reversal of the situation, because the fortune of the characters changes, that, in the final analysis, the truth appears, or the masks fall, or what was hidden is revealed. This is what happens, for example, in Electra,[7] [and] in Philoctetes.[8]

In Oedipus the King (and I refer here to an analysis by [Vernant[*]][9]), we can say that it is the opposite, and that the tragedy has the particular characteristic of it being the mechanism of recognition, the path and work of the truth itself that will lead to the reversal of fortune of the characters.[10] So, Oedipus the King, like every tragedy, turns out to be a drama of recognition, of the truth, an alethurgy, but a particularly intense and fundamental alethurgy, since it is the very mainspring of the tragedy. All this is well-known. What we are accustomed to emphasizing regarding anagnōrisis, recognition in Oedipus, is that this recognition—and it is precisely this that makes it the very motor of the tragedy—has what we may call a reflexive character: it is the same character who seeks to know, who carries out the work of the truth, and who discovers himself to be the very object of the search. Oedipus did not know at the start and will

---

* M.F.: Vidal-Naquet.

come to know at the end—but what does he know? He knows that he himself, the one who was ignorant, was the guilty one he was seeking. It is he who launched the arrow and it is he, finally, who finds himself to be the target. He is subjugated; unknowingly he submitted himself to his own decree. This is all in the text, it is all well-known.

But what I would like to stress is another aspect of the mechanics of recognition, not this cycle from subject to object but the problem of the technique, of the procedures and rituals by which recognition is actually carried out in this tragedy, the processes of manifestation of the truth. We know that Oedipus is the tragedy of ignorance, or the tragedy of the unconscious. In any case, it is certainly the drama of blindness. But I think we can see here also—I say "also" because there is no exclusive or imperialist character to the analysis I am proposing—a drama of multiple truths, of abundant truths, of truths in excess. Stress is always put on the problem of how and why Oedipus could not see everything that was before his eyes. Emphasis is always given to the problem of how and why Oedipus could not hear everything that was said to him, and the solution is sought precisely in what it was that was to be known, the content of which he could not fail to reject. No doubt. But I think we should also pose the problem: what then were the procedures, how were things said, what was the veridiction or what were the veridictions that followed their course through the tragedy of Oedipus and maybe account for the strange relations—in the character of Oedipus himself, in his discourse—between the exercise of his power and the manifestation of the truth or the relations that he himself maintains with the truth? It is not necessarily as desiring son or as murderer son, it is maybe also as king, as king called *turannos*[11] in a very precise sense, that Oedipus had that contorted relation to the truth we have heard about.

Oedipus the King. I would like to focus things a bit around this theme of the kingship of Oedipus. The first thing to appear in this play, which you are familiar with and I am not going to recount to you, is, as you know, the sequence by which the "progressive" discovery of the truth takes place,* the sequence that we could say is subject to a law of halves. Things are discovered or, at any rate, things are said and the truth is manifested, by successive halves. At the beginning, as you know, the

---

* M.F.: I put progressive in quotation marks.

plague having spread throughout Thebes, Creon has been sent to consult the oracle at Delphi. To the plague side, or the plague half if you like, the oracle at Delphi replies with the corresponding element that must get rid of the plague: this is quite simply the ritual of purification. Plague, purification. But purification of what? Of a defilement. What defilement? A murder. What murder? The murder of the old king Laius.[12] We have there the first half of the oracle or, anyway, the first half of what should be necessary and sufficient to bring an end to the plague in Thebes, that is to say, the precise designation of the act, the killing, the murder that caused the plague. We have the murder, the crime half, but as you know the oracle does not say the other, the murderer half. Who killed Laius? The oracle did not want to reply to that question and, as Oedipus says, one cannot force an oracle to reply when it does not want to.[13] So, the oracle has given half of the answer. The other half is missing. How are we to find out this other half and how are we to know who murdered Laius?

Here, two ways present themselves, which Oedipus and the coryphaeus debate. There is a first way proposed by Oedipus himself and this is the way of inquiry. Oedipus says: "it's quite simple: I am going to proclaim"—and he actually does proclaim—"that anyone who has any information concerning Laius's murderer must come forward to report it so that finally the truth will be discovered and the other half of the oracle, the hidden half of what the oracle said, will be revealed."[14] To this proposal, which is very significant and to which we will have to return, the chorus objects that it does not want this procedure, for it would be suspecting the people itself of having committed the crime.[15] There remains the second way—there are only two ways, the text says, and not a third—which is to consult the seer, the prophet, *theios mantis*, the divine seer:[16] Teiresias, who on one side is in fact closest to Apollo, the one who has received from Apollo himself the right to speak the truth, and of whom the text says, quite precisely, that he is king just like Apollo (the text juxtaposes the two characters—Phoebus[17] and Tieresias: *anakt' anakti*, king facing king).[18] So, king like Phoebus, like Apollo, seeing the same things, the text says, so having the same sight and knowledge.[19] He is, in a way, Apollo's brother. He is also his complement, since he is blind and, through the night of his eyes which do not see, he can know what the god Apollo knows, or rather, what is hidden by the light of the god who sees everything. He is in some way the double, the complement and other half of Phoebus, the double of the god himself and in fact it is as such that he contributes the missing half of Apollo's oracle. Apollo said: "it's a question of murder, and of the murder of Laius." Tieresias addressing Oedipus, adds: "you are the murderer."[20] And in this way he completes the other half. It should be said that he also adds a supplementary half, a half in excess. He says: "And furthermore, you have committed some other little trifles and one day you will discover the impurities that bind you to your family."[21] But this is, as it were, an extra half. When Tieresias says: "There you are, the one who killed is you," you can see that all there is to know is known. Between them, Apollo and Tieresias have said everything and nothing is missing. Nothing is missing from these two halves that complete each other, and yet it is not enough.

For whom is it not enough? Here, once again, the chorus and coryphaeus play a very important role in this mechanism of the alethurgy and discovery of the truth. First the coryphaeus and then the chorus say: "It is not enough." The coryphaeus says it first of all during the confrontation between Tieresias and Oedipus. Tieresias does not want to say what he knows. Pushed by Oedipus, he ends up saying it (we will see by what mechanisms) and that is when Oedipus says: "If you accuse me of being the murderer of Laius it is because you have evil thoughts about me, you are motivated by ill will, you have something against me and want to attack my power." What does the coryphaeus say at this point? He says: "The accusations of Tieresias are no more valid than the suspicions of Oedipus." That is to say, the coryphaeus refuses to choose between the seer and the king and sees the weakness of both. "Both of them," the coryphaeus says, "speak in anger,"[22] and so the words of both are to be questioned. Then, after the departure of Tieresias, the chorus speaks and repeats what the coryphaeus has said. It also refuses to take sides. And it says with regard to Tieresias, who has just left: "I cannot say he is right or wrong."[23] Why? In the first place, the chorus says: "because I am not one of those who see far ahead or look far behind, I see only what I have before my eyes. I see only my present."[24] Second, the chorus says, "the seer gives no proof"—and it uses the term *basano*[25]—"about either the past or the present." Third, the seer who has just spoken may well use the god's word as justification, but he is nevertheless still a man.[26] He is a man like others and to that extent he is subject to the same errors and the same requirements as any discourse of truth delivered by men. So he must provide his proofs. And finally, fourth, he says, it may well be that there are in fact men who know more than others. And maybe the seer is one these men who have received the power to know more than others. But it nevertheless remains that in the past Oedipus has given a number of proofs of his love for Thebes and of his ability to act for the good of the town, since he saved the town once before.[27] Oedipus has therefore given his proofs and these counterbalance the greater knowledge that the seer might receive from the god. There is a balance between the divine gift the prophet has received and the proofs actually given in the past by Oedipus, so that the chorus refuses to judge, because, it says, "before having seen"—he employs the verb *idoimi*—"with my eyes the seer's utterance justified, I would never approve the divine words."[28] Oedipus has in his favor some visible things, *phanera*.[29] It is these that prevent me, the chorus, from giving the necessary and sufficient credit to the divine words for me to accept what [the seer]* has said. Between divine words and visible things there is at present a debate that I cannot settle, and I cannot settle it because I do not see it. It is then the chorus's sight that has to decide between visible things and divine words. It is this instance that has to give proof, that has to decide between the two sides, and so long as it has not decided between them things will remain suspended. It is simply when "I will have seen" that there will be, the chorus says, "*orthon epos*, a just word."[30] The just word will be produced when the divine discourses, divine prophecies, and oracular utterances have fit together or found their complement or completion in the visible things and in what will have been seen. It is at that point, in that complementarity, that adjustment, that the *orthon epos*, the just word will be produced, the speech to which one must indeed submit, because it is the truth, and it is the law, the bond, and the obligation peculiar to the truth. So, the god-seer couple may well have told the whole story; it has not told the whole truth. The rest of the tragedy will unfold [in] the movement from the facts pronounced in the seer's and the god's discourse to the truth itself. So, with the seer and the god, we have the divine, prophetic, oracular, divinatory half of this procedure of truth.

---

* Inaudible word.

Obviously, the second half of the procedure of truth will be the human half. And this human half will itself be divided in two. One, the first half of the human half, will be devoted to the murder of Laius, and this alethurgy, this manifestation in truth of the murder, will in turn be divided in two, since, on the one hand, there will be Jocasta, who, having come to reassure Oedipus and going through her memories in an attempt to show that the seer could only tell lies, recounts what happened and says to Oedipus: "Reassure yourself, you could not have killed Laius because he was killed at the crossroads by robbers."[31] So, with memories, indirect memories of what she was told, of what she heard, Jocasta tells half of what happened, the half so to speak of the murder, or of the murder seen from the Theban side and from the side of the king's entourage. To which Oedipus, with his memories, only has to adjust his own recollections and say that, actually, he also killed someone at the place where three roads meet.[32] And he did not hear this; he did it himself and saw it with his own eyes. Jocasta heard half of it; Oedipus saw and did the other half. And once again we can say that at this point everything is known. The whole story, or, at any rate, the whole of the half that concerns the purification ordered by the oracle, has finally come to light. We now know what happened and who the murderer was. Everything is known, or rather everything would be known if there were not even so a little uncertainty, marked by the imprecision of hearsay knowledge, since Jocasta heard it said that Laius was killed by several bandits, whereas Oedipus knows full well that he was alone when he killed the old king.[33]

And it is this that will set off the second half of the human process of discovery of the truth. The person who would be and was, in reality, the only surviving witness of what happened will be sought out. But even before he arrives, a messenger from Corinth arrives on the scene, the messenger who informs Oedipus that Polybus is dead at Corinth, but who at the same time informs him that Polybus was not his real father, that he, Oedipus, is only a foundling, a child who had been confided to precisely this old messenger when he was a shepherd in Cithaeron.[34] Half, if you like, no longer of the story of the murder now, but of the birth, from the receiver's side if you like. We know that Oedipus was not the child of Polybus, we know that he was a foundling, and it is at this point that the slave arrives, the last slave, the one who witnessed the murder of Laius, but also the one to whom Oedipus had been confided when his parents wanted him killed. This slave arrives as a witness, as final witness, he who was hidden, who had hidden himself away in his hut for so many years so as not to tell the truth. He is brought onto the stage and it is he who is indeed forced to attest that Oedipus had been handed over to him to be exposed.[35] At this point, the Theban half, if you like, is fit together with the Corinthian half. The messenger from Corinth had said: "He was found." The slave from Thebes says: "I was the one who gave him and I was the one who received him from the hands of Jocasta." And we have there the last half that fits together and completes the whole. And these two ocular testimonies of the messenger from Corinth and the shepherd of Thebes, these two ocular halves fulfill the oracular pronouncement of the god and the seer.

With just two small hitches: there is still this problem of the "one and several." Was Laius killed by one person or several people? The question is unresolved. And it is never resolved in the text, so that, when it comes to it, we do not know and will never be able to know if it really was Oedipus who killed Laius. And, second, the Theban slave himself who received the abandoned child had heard it said that it was Jocasta's child and, after all, he is not certain of it. And here too, right to the end, nothing in the text will tell us if in fact Oedipus really was Jocasta's son. Only one person could tell, Jocasta, but she will kill herself and we will never know. So that even from the side of those visible things, those *phanera* that have to fulfill the oracular utterance in order to form in total a just, a right utterance, even at that level things will never be fully complete. As multiple as the fitting together of the pieces may be, there will always remain a certain hitch the function of which is, of course, to be determined.

Let us leave, for the moment anyway, these small lacunae. We see clearly therefore the mechanism of these halves that fit together: divine half, religious, prophetic, ritual alethurgy, with an oracular, divinatory half—the Phoebus half, the Tieresias half; and then a human half, the individual alethurgy of memory and inquiry, with a murder half, one part of which is held by Jocasta and another by Oedipus; and then a birth half, the birth of Oedipus, one part of which comes from Corinth, brought by the messenger, and the other half in Thebes, buried, hidden in a slave's hut. We have then six holders of the truth who group together two by two to create a play of halves which complete each other, match up, and fit into each other. In a way it is the game of six halves. And it needed no less than these six halves to constitute the *orthon epos*, the right speech (*parole droite*) that will be the culminating point of the alethurgy.[36]

We have then statically a game of six halves. We should note one or two things straightaway. First, the totalization of these fragments takes place in a quite distinctive and easily recognizable form. You see that there is not exactly an arithmetic addition, that is to say it is not a matter of six characters coming one after the other, each knowing a small fragment of truth, and who, by adding each of these fragments to the five others, end up forming the whole truth. In fact, it is a question of alignments of complementary fragments that take place two by two with, if you like, the totality of the truth at each level. The totality of the truth was basically said by the gods. The totality of the truth is, if not completely said, at least grasped fully by Oedipus and Jocasta when they recall their memories. And finally, the totality of the truth is said once again, a third time, by the servants and slaves. In short, in each of the three groups you have two different persons each of whom holds one of the fragments of the truth. First of all, at the level of the gods, there is succession. The oracle speaks first of all, and then the seer. Then there is Oedipus and Jocasta who confront each other in the interplay of discussion. And then there are the two slaves who encounter each other, as it were, by chance and fortune, the one being summoned at the moment when the other, for completely different reasons, has come from Corinth. At each level a there is a bond, a very strong bond between these characters. On the one hand, there is the bond between the god and his seer, since the seer receives his power to speak the truth from the god himself. He is invested with this power by the god. Second, of course, there are the bonds we know about between Oedipus and Jocasta, and there are those that we do not yet know, bonds that are again very strong, no longer divine but juridical: they are husband and wife. And finally, there is a bond of friendship, *philia*, between the two shepherds. They recall, in fact, and this is what authenticates their testimony, that they were both shepherds in Cithaeron, that they met every winter and that they had formed bonds of friendship. Each is therefore bound by a kind of pact: friendship pact down below, juridical pact at mid-level, and finally religious pact or bond at the upper level. The game of these two halves that fit together between two characters who form between them bonds of this kind is what is called in Greek the *sumbolon*: that figure, that material object, that shard of pottery which is broken in two and possessed by the two persons who have formed a certain pact. And when it is necessary to authenticate the pact or when one comes to claim from the other what is due to him or when they want to reactivate their pact, the fit of the two halves authenticates what has happened and validates their bond.[37] It is the authentication of a private alliance between families, it is the recognition of one individual by another, it is the mark validating a message, it is all this, it is this form that is in play in Oedipus, and moreover Oedipus says so in the text itself: "I will not be able to follow the criminal's tracks for long if I do not have in my hands some symbol, *sumbolon*"[38]—in the sense of: if I do not have in my hands some piece, a part of a piece rather that can be fit together with the corresponding, complementary part of the same piece and that will authenticate what I know. The truth will be obtained therefore, and will only be obtained through this game of the *sumbolon*, of a half or rather of a part that will fit together with another, held by someone bound to the first by a religious, juridical, or friendship bond.

You have seen, and I am not going to dwell on this, that this circulation of the *sumbolon*, which is basically the guiding thread that can be followed throughout the whole play, takes place on a descending scale that is quite evident since we start at the level of the god and his seer. Then, at mid-level we have royalty, Jocasta and Oedipus, who almost discover the murder, and then, right down below we have the two servants, shepherds and slaves, one the Corinthian servant of Polybus, the other the Theban servant of Jocasta and Laius, and it is these who finally carry out the fitting together of the two halves of the *sumbolon*, who rejoin what belongs to Corinth and what belongs to Thebes, who rejoin murder and birth, who get the son of Laius and the supposed son of Polybus to coincide. In this way, rediscovering across the years their friendship of the time when they were shepherds together in Cithaeron, through their memories they pass from hand to hand the child Oedipus, of whom each keeps half, as it were, in hand, so that Oedipus finds that he is himself this *sumbolon*, this shard broken in two, with a Theban half and a Corinthian half. At the end of the play, he who was fragmented finds his unity again, or again ends up double. Oedipus is these two halves and at the same time a double being,[39] and the monstrosity of Oedipus consists precisely in being perpetually double, since he is both son and husband of his mother, father and brother of his children. And you know that whenever he speaks he thinks he is saying one thing and in fact another signification slips in, such that each of his utterances is double. Oedipus is by definition the double character, he is that *sumbolon* whose two halves, in being superimposed, both discover his unity and reveal his monstrous duality.

But this is another question, [which] concerns precisely the nature of Oedipus's power. I would like to leave to one side today the problem of Oedipus's knowledge and the relation between his power and what he knows, in order to concern myself with the two other levels, the higher and the lower, the side of the gods and that of the slaves. [In what concerns the level of Jocasta and Oedipus][*] from a certain point of view, and putting the question in terms of conscious and unconscious, we may, of course, wonder to what extent Oedipus and Jocasta did not know. [It is] moreover quite striking that in the commentators or annotators of the text of *Oedipus the King*, we always [find] little notes: is it really likely, for example, that Jocasta never recounted to Oedipus how Laius died? But [the question of] verisimilitude seems to[†] me, [on the one hand,] not to be effective for the actual analysis of the text and, [on the other,] to pose the problem in terms of the conscious and unconscious, whereas I would like to pose it in terms of knowledge (*savoir*), in terms of ritual and the manifestation of knowledge, in other words in terms of alethurgy. If we pose the problem in these terms, we can say that in actual fact Oedipus and Jocasta finally speak the truth without knowing it and that they are not the true vectors of alethurgy, only its intermediaries. On the other hand, the alethurgy strictly speaking, that is to say, the ritual and complete formulation of the truth, is effectively accomplished twice: once at the level of the gods, that is to say at the level of Phoebus and Tieresias, and then at the level of the slaves and servants. It is given twice, but obviously not in the same way. And I

---

[*] Foucault begins here a sentence left unfinished: "Once again, what is striking in these two levels is that ... —and it is much more striking, moreover, than for the level of Oedipus and Jocasta, because Oedipus and Jocasta."

[†] M.F.: this is a problem of verisimilitude which seems to me.

think that the comparison between the two alethurgies, that of the gods and that of the slaves, may perhaps enable us then to locate the specificity of Oedipus's knowledge.

So, let's compare divine alethurgy and the alethurgy of slaves. First, the gods, like the slaves, are instances of truth, holders of truth, subjects of truth, if you like, who are questioned. They do not speak unless questioned, but obviously the question and the way of questioning are not the same. One consults the god and awaits his answer. Once [the answer] is given, it is given and there is nothing more one can do. One cannot question him further. However enigmatic his answer may be, however incomplete in the view of those who hear it, even if it turns out in the end to be absolutely complete, there is nothing one can do about it, one just has to make do and deal with it. There is no question of constraining the god. The question and answer game with the god is played once and for all and when it is over one must make do with the result.

Tieresias, like the god, is also someone one consults and to whom one puts questions. But already the system of constraints by which one draws out answers by questioning him is a bit different. Tieresias has to be pressed to come. He does not come of his own accord and he says and continues to repeat: "I should not have had to come, I didn't want to come, I didn't want to answer."[40] Tieresias is appealed to and ends up answering. Why? For two reasons. First, he answers because he is appealed to as the person responsible for taking care of a number of things regarding the city, and quite precisely for telling the truth for the good of the city.[41] If the seer refuses to speak, if he keeps quiet when the city is threatened, when it is already in the midst of misfortune, then he is not performing his role, he is not exercising his function. As protector of the city, as the one whose task is to give advice so that the city is in fact well governed and safely led to port without shipwreck, the seer must not shirk his duty, he must speak. And then he spoke for a second reason. When he finally says: "the murderer is you," Oedipus gets angry and tells him: "You present yourself in fact as a seer whereas you are nothing else but my enemy, and I can do a number of things against you and as king I am as powerful as you." To which Tieresias replies: "If you are powerful facing me, I too am powerful facing you and am no less than you, like you I am a king."[42] So that Tieriesias, who at the beginning was presented as a king like Phoebus, appears on another side, this is his other face, as no less a king than Oedipus himself. And it is in this challenge, in this joust between these two royal characters that Tieresias will finally speak the truth and the whole truth. It is you, says Tieresias; no it is you, Oedipus will say. And who is responsible for what happens and the evil, Tieresias or Oedipus? The joust leaves the problem in suspense. So Tieresias is someone one questions, but he is not questioned in the way that Phoebus is questioned. One questions Tieresias as power to power, king to king, in a joust of equality between the sovereign and himself.

The third extraction of truth will be carried out with the slaves and servants. They too will be questioned. But, of course, the question put to the slaves will not have the same form and will not follow the same procedures as the consultation of the god or the questions put to Tieresias, the prophet. One of the two servants is questioned as a messenger who brings news and from whom information is requested. But what is particularly interesting is the interrogation of the last shepherd, the one who holds all of the truth, since he had received Oedipus, had not carried out the order to kill him, had given him to the Corinthian and, finally, had witnessed the murder of Laius. So, the one who knows everything, who is basically the symmetrical counterpart of the god, the one who maybe knows even more than Tieresias, who knows no less than Phoebus, is questioned. And in a way this interrogation[43] is the asymmetrical counterpart of the oracular consultation that we did not witness but whose result is reported by Creon at the beginning of the play.[44] In what does the interrogation consist? It is very simple. You will recognize it quickly. First, he is asked: "Are you who you claim to be?" He is asked to authenticate his identity and the Corinthian is asked: "The slave you have brought here, is this Theban slave really the one you have told us about and who gave Oedipus to you?" "Yes," the Corinthian replies, "he is the one standing before you." And the Theban authenticates his identity by saying: "Yes, I am a slave born in the king's palace." Having established this, he will be questioned according to a technique of interrogation. He is asked: "Do you remember what took place? Who gave you the child that you then handed over to the Corinthian? What was the intention of the person who gave you the child?" And finally, to be sure of extracting from him the whole truth, he is threatened with torture. "If you don't want to talk willingly," Oedipus says, "you will be forced to talk." And then, faced with a new refusal, Oedipus adds: "Well, if you refuse to speak you will die."[45] Such is the consultation of the slave, if I can put it that way, which corresponds to the questioning of the god at the start of the play. So that is the technique of interrogation.

Second, there is not only a difference in the procedure for extracting the truth but [also], of course, in the very modality of the gods' as opposed to the slaves' knowledge. The gods' knowledge, nevertheless, just as that of the slaves, is a certain way of combining looking and discourse, or seeing and saying. But the seeing and saying are obviously not combined by the gods, by the god and his seer, in the same as the way they are by slaves. The god in fact sees everything. Why? Because he is himself the light that lights up everything and renders them visible. The god's gaze is so to speak connatural with the things that are there to be seen; the light in the god's eyes is the same as that which lights up the world. The world is visible only because in the god's gaze there is a light that makes things visible, to the god himself and to all men. There is connaturalness, consequently, of the light that inhabits the god's gaze and the visibility of things. We could say the same about speech. If the god's word is always truthful it is for the good reason that it is both a power that states and a power that pronounces. It tells of things and makes them happen. It says what will happen and binds men, things, and the future in such a way that it cannot not happen. Under these conditions, how could the god not speak the truth? His knowledge, the god's knowledge, as light and discourse, as seeing and saying, is infallible since it is indissociable from what makes things visible and what makes them happen. The same force enables the god to see and at the same time makes them visible. The same force enables the god to say what will happen and constrains them to happen. It is in this sense that Tieresias, who inherits the god's power, can say: "The force of truth lives in me."[46] The force of truth from divination is not what enables someone to see in advance what is going to happen, it is the connaturalness of the power of telling it and the power of making it happen. Force of the light-gaze and of the statement-bond.

With the servants, of course, seeing and saying are combined in a completely different way and are of a completely different nature. What is seeing for the servants, from the slaves' point of view? Obviously it is not seeing things that one makes visible oneself. It is rather witnessing, as powerless men, a spectacle imposed from outside, by the will of men, by the decisions of kings, and by what happens to them. Slaves are present only as spectators. Everything unfolds before them, around them, without any connaturalness with the law, without any commonality with those who command. They obey—with one or two little hitches that we will come back to—but they are present only as powerless spectators. Consequently, in what is the truth of their gaze rooted? In the fact that, precisely, they were present, they were present themselves, seeing with their own eyes and acting with their own hands. In the scenes between the Corinthian slave and the Theban slave, all the testimonies are quite distinctive at the level of the vocabulary. Addressing himself to Oedipus, for example, the Corinthian says: "I was the one that found you in a valley of Cithaeron. I was there because I was watching over my flock. I was the one that untied your pierced feet. It was to me that another shepherd gave you."[47] It is therefore simply and fundamentally the law of presence that authenticates what the Corinthian may say. And when pressed and asked: "But where did this child that someone gave you come from?" the law of presence obliges the Corinthian to say that he does not know. "I do not know. But the person who put you, Oedipus, in my hands is the one who could tell you."[48] And it is at that point that the shepherd from Cithaeron comes in, the one who gave Oedipus to the Corinthian. Well, the Theban shepherd will reply in the same way. He is asked: "Was it not you that handed the child to the Corinthian?" And the answer is: "I was the one that handed him over."[49] A bit further on he says: "It was to me that Jocasta gave him,"[50] and again: "I refused to kill him because I took pity on him and I gave him to another."[51] So, the whole relationship of seeing and telling the truth is not structured here around the power to make things appear in a visibility that is the visibility of their very nature and that authorizes the god's gaze to foresee them since he makes them visible. It is structured around the presence of characters, the identity of the witness, and the fact that it is he himself, *autos*, who sees and speaks. He in his identity authenticates the god's word. In the case of the god and the seer, it was the force of the truth that lived in them. They had no need to be present. Phoebus was far away from what happened. He is far away when he is consulted. It is from afar that he launches his decrees on men. Tieresias is distant in the sense that he is blind, and Oedipus will criticize him somewhat for this. But in the case of the servants, the force of the truth does not dwell in them. They found themselves, as if by chance, on the scene of the truth. They are in the truth and not inhabited by it. It was they who inhabited the truth, or who, at least, frequented a reality, facts, actions, and characters on which they can deliver, in the name of their identity, in the name of the fact that they are themselves and are still the same, under these conditions, a true discourse.[52]

The third difference between the alethurgy of the gods and the alethurgy of the slaves—this is almost obvious and follows from the first two—concerns time. The truth-telling of the oracle and the seer is situated, of course, on the axis of the present and the future and always takes the form of the injunction. The seer and the god never look to the past. To Oedipus, who is looking for the truth, neither the god nor the seer respond: "Well, this is what happened." They always say something that is situated on the present-future axis and in the form of the injunction. First, they say, for example, what remedy must be employed: the defilements must be driven out, the pollution must not be left to grow until it becomes incurable, or they indicate the order to which it is necessary to submit: "I command you to obey the law that you yourself proclaimed and from this day to speak to no one," Tieresias tells Oedipus.[53] Or again the seer and the god uncover the invisible that no one yet sees, but the present invisible. Neither the seer nor the god say to Oedipus: "You are the one who killed." They say: "You are the one who is now the criminal," or: "unawares you are presently living in a loathsome relationship." And finally, of course, they tell of the event that will take place: "From two directions, the fearsome double-footed curse shall drive you out."[54] Opposite this, the truth-telling of the slaves is situated entirely on the axis of the past. If they tell the truth, it is because they remember. And they can tell the truth only in the form of memory. They say nothing, of course, about the future. And what would the present be if not the law imposed on them, or the order or threat hanging over them, and which comes from the kings and those who give them orders? The slaves can look only to the past. The Theban slave tries to take refuge behind forgetfulness so as not to speak the truth and, facing him, the Corinthian messenger keeps saying to him: "But let's see, revive your memories. I am

sure he remembers. You recall handing me the child?"[55] Whereas the
oracle binds the men to whom he speaks because he tells them: That
which must come about is the same as that which the god brings about,
human truth telling can do nothing but submit to another law, not the
law that makes things happen, but the law of memory and recollection,
the weight of what has happened and that cannot not have happened
because it happened. And furthermore, the words employed to designate this divine alethurgy and the word employed to designate this
human alethurgy, actually the alethurgy of the slave, is characteristic.
The ritual word for designating the alethurgy of oracular discourse is
phēmi,[56] that is to say, not just: I say, but: I proclaim, I assert, I decree, at
the same time, I state and I pronounce. I say that it will be so and I say
that it is taking place. While on the other side, the word is *omologeō*,[57]
I acknowledge, I admit, yes, this is indeed what happened and I cannot
avoid the law of what happened. One proclaims and decrees; the other
avows and testifies.

So you can see that it is easy to locate the two modes of manifestation of the truth, the two profoundly different alethurgies that are easy
to recognize and name. That of the gods is completely recognizable for
the good reason that it says clearly what it is. It is the religious and
ritual alethurgy of oracular consultation. The other is clearly not much
more difficult to recognize, although it is not named in the text because
it belongs to historical realities that are relatively new in the period
in which Sophocles was writing. These are quite simply the rules of
judicial procedure, those new rules of judicial procedure established by
constitutions and laws in a number of Greek cities at the end of the
sixth and especially at the beginning of the fifth century, and particularly in Athens.[58] Judicial alethurgy, which involves an inquiry to which
all those who know come to tell on pain of punishment, the summoning
of witnesses, the interrogation and confrontation of witnesses, and, in a
very precise fashion, the possibility and right to torture a slave so that
he tells the truth. In the Athenian city, the slave was someone whose
death could be put in the balance with regard to the truth. He could be
threatened with death so that he tell the truth, and he was the only one
from whom one could extract the truth under the threat of death. What
Sophocles puts face-to-face are quite simply the two great procedures in
classical Greece that defined the way of giving rise to the manifestation

of truth according to rules that can authenticate and guarantee this manifestation.

That it was a matter of two historically ascribable forms of alethurgy is easily confirmed by a small episode at the start of the play, at any rate in the first half, that is to say, the episode between Creon and Oedipus, in which Creon, after he has reported the god's disquieting but still equivocal oracle, and having brought Tieresias, finds himself accused by Oedipus of having hatched a plot against him. "If you have reported such a bad oracle and especially if you have brought Tieresias who accuses me, it is because you want to take power in my place."[59] We will come back to this problem of Oedipus's power. But for the moment, how is the conflict between Creon and Oedipus in this scene settled? As you know, Jocasta intervenes. She comes out from the palace and says: "Stop your argument." At this point Creon offers to swear that he did not invent the god's message and that he did not plot with Tieresias to say threatening words concerning Oedipus. And, in actual fact, he makes a solemn oath saying: "It is not me."[60] Now this was a judicial procedure older than inquiry and questioning. It was the procedure by which the aristocracy settled its own conflicts. One of the parties swore and, as a result, voluntarily exposed himself to the gods' vengeance if he was not telling the truth and, at that point, the one before whom one swore an oath was obliged to suspend his accusation and not pursue it. The task of taking vengeance on the accused if he was lying when rejecting the accusation on oath is handed over to the god.[61] It is a perfectly definable and recognized judicial procedure that precisely the procedures of inquiry, the procedures of questioning, etcetera, were tending to suppress.

This episode between Creon and Oedipus and the way in which their conflict is pacified, provisionally, plays what could be called a completive and structural role in the gradation from the gods to the slaves. The oracle is the veridiction of the gods; the oath is the veridiction of kings and chiefs; testimony is the veridiction of the others or of those who serve. But I think—and I will stop here—that the true and great tension between the veridiction of the gods and the veridiction of slaves, between oracular alethurgy and the alethurgy of testimony, arises from the fact that both alethurgies say exactly the same thing. The slaves say neither more nor less than the gods, or rather they say it clearly and, as a result, they say it better. But above all, how could the alethurgy of the gods have taken place, and right through to the end, and how could it have constituted an *orthon epos*, a complete and inevitable manifestation of the truth, without the alethurgy of the slaves? And in fact this is played out at two levels and in the following way. First: what was required for the god's prophetic utterance to be brought to term and for its prediction at the birth of Oedipus—that he will kill his father and have sex with his mother—to be or become true? A number of things were needed, and what do we find at the center of them? Well, the lie of the slaves, for if the slave to whom Jocasta gave the infant Oedipus had in fact done what he was told to do, he would have killed Oedipus. But he did not kill him; he disobeyed. He handed him over to another slave and did not say so. The other slave had taken him back to Corinth, given him to Polybus, and said nothing throughout Oedipus's childhood. And when Oedipus left Corinth so as not to kill his father and mother, the slave still said nothing. Disobedience, lie, silence. It is thanks to this that the god's prophetic utterance could in fact be realized. The god's word could be verified because there was an interplay of truth and lie in human discourse, or in the discourse of slaves. And, in a way, taking not the play but the myth to which it refers, the truth of the prediction by Phoebus could only pass through the lie, silence, and disobedience of men. It is because there was this game of truth that the god was finally right. But what happens in the play itself? What happens is that, as we have seen, throughout the play, the word of the gods is not believed. The prophetic utterance, the oracular utterance remains enigmatic and no one succeeds in interpreting it and, if things had remained there, nothing would be known. Oedipus would remain king and no one would have known that he had killed his father and slept with his mother. The same is true of the seer's word. He had told the things nevertheless, but the chorus did not want to hear and, not hearing it, the truth could not come to light. Consequently it needed this specific alethurgy of the slaves, it needed this procedure of questioning, it needed the law of memory to be imposed on the slaves and to force them to say what they had seen, it needed their presence, it needed them to have been there themselves and to be the same as they are now, present on the scene once again, for the play itself finally to unfold as an alethurgy, and for what was said in a sort of enigmatic and suspended truth at the beginning of the play to become the inevitable truth to which Oedipus is forced to submit and the spectators themselves have to recognize. So without this truth-telling of the slaves, the truth-telling of the gods would not have had any purchase and the play could not have taken place. On the one hand, it needed therefore the falsehood of the slaves for the telling of the gods to become true and it needed the truth-telling of the slaves for the uncertain truth-telling of the gods to become an inevitable certainty for men.

So there is the linkage of the two alethurgic mechanisms that frame Sophocles' play. Obviously, at the center of the play there is still the problem of Oedipus. What was his ignorance? What was his relation to these truth-tellings that surrounded him, threatened him, and finally forced him to submit to his destiny? I will speak about this next week.

1. Elected to the Collège de France in April 1970 as holder of the chair of *History of Systems of Thought*, Foucault began his teaching on 2 December the same year (see *L'ordre du discours*, Paris: Gallimard, 1971; English translation by Ian McLeod, "The Order of Discourse" in Robert Young, ed., *Untying the Text* (London: Routledge and Kegan Paul, 1981): so, nine years and a few weeks before this lecture.

2. Foucault dealt with *Oedipus the King* for the first time in the last lecture of the 1970-1971 course, "The Will to Know" (see *Leçons sur la volonté de savoir*, pp. 177-185; *Lectures on the Will to Know*, pp. 183-199). He subsequently returned to the text several times: see "Le savoir d'Œdipe"; "Oedipal Knowledge," lecture given at the University of Buffalo in March 1972 (published as an appendix in *Leçons sur la volonté de savoir*, pp. 225-251; *Lectures on the Will to Know*, pp. 229-261; see D. Defert, "Situation du cours"; "Course Context," ibid., Fr., p. 277; Eng., pp. 279-280); "La vérité et les formes juridiques" (1974), *Dits et Écrits*, II, no. 139, pp. 538-646; "Quarto," I, pp. 1406-1490; English translation by Robert Hurley, "Truth and Juridical Forms" in *Essential Works of Foucault 1954-1984. Vol. 3. Power*, ed. James D. Faubian (New York: New Press, 2000) (second lecture) in which he sets out to show "how the tragedy of Oedipus, the one we can read in Sophocles ... is representative and in a sense the founding instance of a definite type of relation between power and knowledge (*savoir*), between political power and knowledge (*connaissance*), from which our civilization is not yet emancipated" (p. 17); *Mal faire, dire vrai* (Louvain and Chicago: Presses Universitaires de Louvain and University of Chicago Press, 2012), lecture of 28 April 1981, pp. 47-87. See also *Le gouvernement de soi et des autres. Cours au Collège de France 1982-1983*, ed. Frédéric Gros (Paris: Gallimard-Le Seuil, 2008), pp. 78-80 (see note 11 by F. Gros, p. 89); English translation by Graham Burchell, *The Government of Self and Others. Lectures at the Collège de France, 1982-1983*, English series editor Arnold I. Davidson (Basingstoke and New York: Palgrave Macmillan, 2010) pp. 83-85 and p. 94 note 11.

3. See Plato, *The Republic*, trans. Desmond Lee (London and Harmondsworth: Penguin Books, 2nd revised edition, 1987) Book IX, 602c-605d, on criticism of the effects of dramatic poetry (comedy and tragedy); see Book X, 600e, p. 429: "We may assume, then, that all the poets from Homer downwards have no grasp of truth but merely produce a superficial likeness of any subject they treat, including human excellence." Foucault does not return to this topic in the rest of the course.

4. We cite the text used by Foucault (see "Le savoir d'Œdipe," p. 251, note 1 by D. Defert; "Oedipal Knowledge," p. 258 note 1): Aristote, *Poétique*, 11, 9, in J. Voilquin and J. Capelle, *Art rhétorique et Art poétique* (Paris, Garnier, "Classiques Garnier," 1944) p. 455: "two parts constitute the story: reversal (*péripétie*) and recognition." A third element is *pathos*, the moving event or the violent effect (11, 9-10, p. 455); English translation by I. Bywater, *Poetics*, in *The Complete Works of Aristotle*, Volume Two, ed. Jonathan Barnes (Princeton: Princeton University Press, Bollingen Series LXXI, 2, 1984), p. 2324: "reversal of fortune," "reversal and discovery"; "A third part is suffering...an action of a destructive or painful nature"; see J.-P. Vernant, "Ambiguïté et renversement. Sur la structure énigmatique d'"Œdipe Roi"" in J. Pouillon and P. Maranda, eds., *Échanges et Communications. Mélanges offerts à Claude Lévi-Strauss à l'occasion de son soixantième anniversaire* (Paris-The Hague: Mouton, 1970) vol. II, pp. 1253-1273, reprinted in J.-P. Vernant and P. Vidal-Naquet, *Mythe et tragédie en Grèce ancienne* (Paris: La Découverte, 1972) vol. 2, pp. 99-131 (106) and in ibid., *Œdipe et ses Mythes* (Paris: Ed. Complexe, 1986) pp. 25-53 (p. 28); English translation by Janet Lloyd as "Ambiguity and Reversal: On the Enigmatic Structure of *Oedipus Rex*," in Jean-Pierre Vernant and Pierre Vidal-Naquet, *Myth and Tragedy in Ancient Greece*, trans. Janet Lloyd (New York: Zone Books, 1988).

5. Aristote, *Poétique*, 11, 2, p. 453: "Reversal is a change of the action in an opposite direction to that which had been indicated"; Aristotle, *Poetics*, p. 2324: "A reversal of fortune is the change of the kind described from one state of things within the play to its opposite." He cites notably the example of Oedipus; Fr., pp. 453-455: "Thus, in *Oedipus* the messenger who arrives thinks he is going to please Oedipus and free him from his disquiet on the subject of his mother, but by making him know he produces the opposite effect"; Eng., p. 2324: "... for instance in *Oedipus*: here the opposite state of things is produced by the Messenger, who, coming to gladden Oedipus and to remove his fears as to his mother, reveals the secret of his birth."

6. Ibid., 11, 4, Fr., p. 455: "Recognition, as the name indicates, makes ignorance pass to knowledge, changing friendship into hatred or inversely in the characters destined to happiness or misfortune"; Eng., p. 2324: "A discovery is, as the very word implies, a change from ignorance

to knowledge, and thus to either love or hate, in the personages marked for either good or evil fortune." He again cites the example of Oedipus: ibid., 11, 5-6, Fr.: "The most beautiful recognition is that which arises in the course of a reversal of fortune, as happens in Oedipus"; Eng.: "The finest form of discovery is one attended by reversal, like that which goes with the discovery in *Oedipus*."

7. *Electra*, tragedy by Sophocles written before the tragedy with the same name by Euripides. Aristotle does not give this as an example.

8. *Philoctetes*, tragedy by Sophocles (409 B.C.E). Again, Aristotle does not give this as an example.

9. See J.-P. Vernant, "Ambiguity and Reversal."

10. See ibid., p. 117: "Aristotle ... points out that in *Oedipus Rex* the recognition is finest because it coincides with the peripeteia. Oedipus' recognition in effect has bearing upon none other than himself. And the hero's final self-identification constitutes a complete reversal of the action ...." See above, note 6.

11. See the title of the tragedy: OIDIPOUS TURANNOS.

12. Sophocle, *Œdipe-Roi*, ed. and trans. P. Masqueray (Paris: Les Belles Lettres, "Collection des universités de France," t. 1, 4th edition, 1946, reference edition) 87-107, pp. 75-76; English translation by David Grene, Sophocles, *Oedipus the King*, in *Sophocles I, Three Tragedies*, ed. David Grene and Richard Lattimore (Chicago and London: University of Chicago Press, 1991) pp. 13-15.

13. Ibid., 280-281, Fr., p. 151: "no one has the power to force the gods to act against their will"; Eng., p. 21: "... but to put compulsion on the Gods/against their will—no man can do that."

14. Ibid., 224-232, Fr., p. 149; Eng., pp. 19-20. Here, as in the rest of his commentary, Foucault paraphrases or freely translates the text.

15. Ibid., 276-279, Fr., p. 151; Eng., p. 21. It is the coryphaeus who is speaking.

16. Ibid., 298, Fr., p. 151: "the seer, inspired by the god"; Eng., p. 22: "the godly prophet."

17. Sometimes Foucault says "*Phoibos*" and sometimes, as in Masqueray's translation, "*Phœbos*." Not being able to choose between these two versions on the basis of the manuscript, we have stayed with the version, following the Greek, adopted in "Le savoir d'Œdipe"; "Oedipal Knowledge" [that is, here, Phoebus: G.B.].

18. Ibid., 284, Fr., p. 151; Eng., p. 21. Literally: Tieresias, king (*Anakt' anakti ...*) who sees the same things as king Phoebus (... *Phoibō*).

19. Ibid., 284-285, see the previous note.

20. Ibid., 353, Fr., p. 154: "you are the criminal"; Eng., p. 25: "you are the land's pollution." Tieresias repeats his assertion at 362; see below, note 56.

21. Ibid., 366-367, Fr., p. 154; Eng., p. 26: "I say that with those you love best/you live in foulest shame unconsciously/and do not see where you are in calamity."

22. Ibid., 404-405, Fr., p. 156; Eng., p. 28: "both have spoken ... in anger."

23. Ibid., 485, Fr., p. 158; Eng., p. 31: "I do not approve what was said/nor can I deny it."

24. Ibid., 486-488, Fr., p. 158; Eng., p. 31.

25. Ibid.,491, Fr., p. 158.; Eng., p. 31. The word appears again at 510 when the chorus contrasts the proof Oedipus gave of his wisdom and his love for Thebes, when faced by the winged Virgin, with the lack of proof on the part of Tieresias.

26. Ibid., 500, Fr., p. 159; Eng., p. 31.

27. Ibid., 507-511, Fr., p. 159; Eng., p. 32. See above, note 25, with regard to *basanō*.

28. Ibid., 504-505, Fr., p. 159.: "... I would not approve those who accuse Oedipus"; Eng., p. 32: "I would never agree/with those that find fault with the king."

29. Ibid., 506-507, Fr., p. 159: "For it was visible to all (*phanera gar*) that in the past he defeated the winged virgin"; Eng., p. 32: "For once/in visible form the Sphinx/came on him and all of us/saw his wisdom ...."

30. 504, Fr., p. 159; Eng., p. 32: "the word/proved right beyond doubt."

31. Ibid., 715-716, Fr., p. 166-167: *ōsper g'ē phatis xenoi pote gēstai phoneuous en trimais amaksitois*; "everyone says so, some foreign robbers killed him, long ago, where three roads meet"; Eng., p. 41: "the king, was killed by foreign highway robbers/at a place where three roads meet—so goes the story."

32. Ibid., 726-755, Fr., p. 167-168; Eng., pp. 42-43.

33. Ibid., 842-847, Fr., p. 171; Eng., p. 47.

34. Ibid., 942 et seq., 1025 et seq.

35. Ibid., 1110 *et seq*. On the shepherd's double testimony (on the birth of Oedipus and on the murder of Laius), see 754-756, 834-847, 1051-1053.

36. See already, "La vérité et les formes juridiques," p. 557/p. 1425; "Truth and Juridical Forms," p. 19, on this "pure form," the rule of halves," to which the "mechanism of the truth" conforms in *Oedipus the King*.

37. See "La vérité et les formes juridiques," p. 560/p. 1428; "Truth and Juridical Forms," p. 22, where Foucault defines the *sumbolon* in the following way: "It is an instrument of power and its exercise whereby a person who holds some secret or power breaks some ceramic object in half, keeping one part and entrusting the other to an individual who is to carry the message or certify its authenticity. By fitting these two parts together it is possible to verify the authenticity of the message, that is, the continuity of the power exercised."

38. *Œdipe-Roi*, 220-221, p. 149: "*Ou gar an makran ikneuon autos, mē ouk ekōn ti sumbolon*"; "alone I would not be able to follow the criminal's track if you were not to give me some clue"; *Oedipus the King*, p. 19: "For I would not/be far upon the track if I alone/were tracing it without a clue."

39. On the essentially double character of Oedipus, see J.-P. Vernant, "Ambiguity and Reversal," pp. 119-121, who relates it to the "logical schema of reversal, corresponding with the ambiguous type of thought that is characteristic of tragedy" (p. 121).

40. See *Œdipe-Roi*, 318, p. 152; *Oedipus the King*, p. 23; 343-344: Fr., p. 153; Eng., pp. 24-25; 432: Fr., p. 156; Eng., p. 29.

41. Ibid., 303-304, Fr., p. 152; Eng., pp. 22-23.

42. Ibid., 408-410, Fr., p. 156; Eng., p. 28.

43. Ibid., 1118 et seq.

44. Ibid., 95-98, 100-101, 103-104, and 106-107, Fr., pp. 144-145; Eng., pp. 14-15.

45. Ibid., 1152, Fr. p. 183; Eng., p. 61.

46. Ibid., 356, Fr., 154; Eng., p. 25: "the truth is what I cherish/and that's my strength."

47. Ibid., 1026-1034, Fr., p. 178; Eng., pp. 54-55.

48. Ibid., 1038, Fr., p. 178; Eng., p. 55.

49. Ibid., 1157, Fr., p. 183; Eng., p. 61.

50. Ibid., 1171-1174, Fr., pp. 183-184; Eng., pp. 62-63.

51. Ibid., 1178-1181, Fr., p. 184; Eng., p. 63.

52. See "La vérité et les formes juridiques," (second lecture), p. 561/p. 1429; "Truth and Juridical Forms," p. 23: "the entire *Oedipus* play is a way of shifting the enunciation of the truth from a prophetic and prescriptive type of discourse to a retrospective one that is no longer characterized by prophecy but, rather, by testimony." [Translation slightly modified; G.B.]

53. *Œdipe-Roi*, 350-352, p. 154; *Oedipus the King*, p. 25.

54. Ibid., 417-418, Fr., p. 156; Eng., p. 28: "A deadly footed, double striking curse,/... shall drive you forth/out of this land ...."

55. Ibid., 1132-1143, Fr., p. 182; Eng., p. 60.

56. Ibid., 362, Fr., p. 154: Tieresias: "*Phonea se phēmi tandros ou xēteis kurein*"; "I assert that you are the murderer of the man whose killer you seek"; Eng., p. 26: "I say you are the murderer of the king/whose murderer you seek." See also 366, Fr., p. 154: "I claim (*phēmi*) that unawares you are living in the most shameful relations ..."; Eng., p. 26: "I say that with those you love best/ you live in foulest shame unconsciously."

57. *Omologein*: admit, avow, confess, acknowledge. On the derivative *exomologein* in Christian vocabulary, see below, the ninth lecture. According to B.W. Beatson, *Index graecitatis Sophocleae* (Cambridge and London: Simpkin & Marshall, 1830), not paginated, the only occurrence of the word in Sophocles is in *Philoctetes*, 980, trans. David Greene in David Grene and Richmond Lattimore, eds., *Sophocles II* (Chicago and London: University of Chicago Press, 1969) p. 234: Odysseus to Philoctetes: "Yes, I, I and no other [robbed you of your arms]. I admit that [*omologō*]."

58. On the contrast between the two alethurgies, see the *Leçons sur la volonté de savoir*, lecture of 17 March 1971, pp. 178-179; *Lectures on the Will to Know*, pp. 184-186. See also "La vérité et les formes juridiques," (third lecture), p. 570/p. 1438; "Truth and Juridical Forms," p. 33: "*Oedipus the King* is a kind of compendium of the history of Greek law"; and Fr., p. 571/p. 1439; Eng., pp. 33-34, regarding the birth of the inquiry, that form of judicial discovery of the truth which Foucault sees as one of the great conquests of Athenian democracy.

59. *Œdipe-Roi*, 532-542, p. 160; *Oedipus the King*, p. 33.
60. Ibid., 644-645, Fr., p. 164; Eng., p. 38.
61. See *Leçons sur la volonté de savoir*, lecture of 27 January 1971, pp. 73-74; *Lectures on The Will to Know*, pp. 74-76, regarding the dispute between Menelaos and Antilochos (Homer, *The Iliad*, XXIII, 566-592) over this "test of the truth" by which the one who swears enters a universe dominated by the power of the gods: "With his imprecation, the person who swears leaves it to the power of the gods. That is what will decide" (p. 76). Foucault returns at length to this example in *Mal faire, dire vrai*, lecture of 22 April 1981, pp. 15-25. See also "La vérité et les formes juridiques" (second lecture), pp. 555-556/pp. 1423-1424; "Truth and Juridical Forms," pp. 17-19, where, on the basis of the same example, he relates the "old and very archaic practice of the test of the truth" to Sophocles' tragedy: "Creon replies to Oedipus according to the old formula of the dispute between warriors."

three

23 JANUARY 1980

Oedipus the King *(continued)*. ◡ *The object of this year's lectures: the element of the "I" in procedures of veridiction. As a result of what processes has telling the truth in the first person been able to establish itself as manifestation of truth? Relations between the art of governing men and self-alethurgy.* ◡ *The question of Oedipal knowledge. In what does his* tekhnē *consist? Contrast with the ways of being of Creon and Teiresias. Specifically Oedipal activity:* euriskein *(finding, discovering). The search for clues (*tekmēria*). Characteristics of* tekmērion. *Oedipus, operator of the truth he seeks. Discovery as art of government.* ◡ *The power of Oedipus. Central place of this theme in the play. Oedipus, incarnation of the classic figure of the tyrant; victim of his tyrannical usage of the procedure of truth that he himself puts to work. Difference from the* gnōmē *(opinion, advice) by which he resolved the riddle of the Sphinx and saved the town.*

I WOULD LIKE TO finish with Oedipus [today]. I am not very sure that the ultra-aggressively and bluntly positivist interpretation I am giving you is entirely true. I see at least a sign of it in the fact that I have just left my copy of *Oedipus* at home and [so] there are things that I will not be able to tell you. Too bad. Punished!

Last week I tried to show you how in Sophocles' play we see the coherent and systematic development on both sides of Oedipus, framing and of course trapping him, of two modes of truth, of veridiction, of telling the truth, of what I shall call two types of alethurgy that match each other, finally fit together, and close up around Oedipus. These two forms of alethurgy, and precisely on condition that they fit into each other and join together, form together the good, the right account, the "*orthon epos*" that is finally bearer of the truth, of the truth itself and the whole truth. One of these alethurgies, these forms of veridiction, the veridiction that nothing escapes, that dominates time and pronounces eternal decrees from afar, is of course the oracular and religious veridiction. And then, on the other side, there is another truth-telling that appears and develops at the end of the play, closing it, the truth-telling that is extracted gradually, bit by bit, element by element. This is a truth-telling that complies with the form, the law, and the constraints of memory, and it pronounces only on what [the subject]* has seen with his own eyes. Religious and interpretative alethurgy, therefore, on the one hand, which is authorized by the force of a name: "It is because I am the servant of Loxias," says Teiresias, "that I can say what I say"[1]—referring therefore to Phoebus. And, on the other hand, a judicial alethurgy, which is authorized only by the fact of being able to say "I," "myself," "I was there myself," "I myself saw," "I gave with my own hands," "I received with my own hands," "*ego*." I think we have an important element here, or anyway (and if I stressed this last week, it is for a reason of method or, let's say, of progression) this is what I would like to study a little this year, that is to say, if you like, the element of the first person, of the "I," of the "*autos*," of the "myself" in what could be called alethurgy or veridiction or the rites and procedures of veridiction.

In a completely schematic, arbitrary way, which would horrify any historian who is at all serious, let us all the same say this. If you take the ritual, canonical forms of veridiction in archaic Greek texts, whether in Homer, or Hesiod, or the poets of the sixth century, then the presentation of truth-telling as the enunciation, formulation, or manifestation of the truth is authorized by a power that is always prior to or anyway external to the person who is speaking. In Homer, when the king or a chief gets up to give his advice and to present his opinion as the right and true opinion, to justify and authenticate his truth-telling he seizes hold of a staff of command that is at the same time both the sign of his power and the seal of the truth of what he is going to say. The poet

_____
* M.F.: he.

never begins without invoking a divinity, that of Memory, who deposits in him precisely a certain speech, a certain word, a certain utterance of which he is to be only the bearer. But if this utterance holds the truth, it is precisely to the extent that it has been authenticated and stamped by Memory, by Memory as a goddess.[2] We could also say that in the same way dreams speak the truth—a whole study could be made of the dream as alethurgy, in what and why [it] speaks the truth[3]—precisely because I am not the master of the dream and something else happens to me in the dream, someone else emerges, someone who speaks, who gives signs, and this is where the astonishing, almost constant and universal element of the dream that speaks the truth is formed in Western, as well as other civilizations. And if it speaks the truth, it is precisely because it is not me who speaks in my dream. So, if you like, you have this strong tendency, this inclination in a whole series of civilizations, and in any case in archaic Greek civilization, to reveal and authenticate truth-telling by the fact that the one who speaks is not the one who holds the truth, and the truth that passes into his telling comes to him from elsewhere.

The problem is how and for what reasons truth-telling came to authenticate its truth, be asserted as manifestation of truth, precisely to the extent that the person speaking can say: It is me that holds the truth, and it is me that holds the truth because I saw it and because having seen it, I say it. This identification of truth-telling and having-seen-the-truth, this identification between the person speaking and the source, origin, and root of the truth, is undoubtedly a multiple and complex process that was crucial for the history of the truth in our societies.

This constitution of an alethurgy that revolves round the *autos*, the myself, the himself, the I, can be seen through a number of processes [and] phenomena. For example, in the history of judicial institutions, the appearance of the witness as someone who was present and who, having been present, can say "that was the truth," is one of the phenomena through which we see the emergence of that interlocking of the first person with alethurgy. [Identical] phenomena can also be found in the development of the practice of the journey and the travel story. It is already quite clear in Herodotus[4] how a number of things are asserted as true because there were witnesses and because there was a witness who had witnessed what someone had seen and, from witness to witness, the

chain of witnesses ends by constituting the truth, always on condition
that this alethurgy, this manifestation of the truth, refers to an *autos*, to
someone who can say "myself." All this is, of course, a lengthy history
that does not exactly end up with, but arrives at a decisive point when
Descartes can say "myself" with regard to some evident truths of math-
ematics itself. So it is this whole history of the relations between *autos*
and alethurgy, between the myself and truth-telling that interests me in
the history of the truth in the West.

What I would like to study a little this year is, of course, only a fragment of all this. But let's return to Oedipus for the moment. Between
the alethurgy of the seer and the alethurgy of the witness, Oedipus is, of
course, the one who does not know. He is ignorant of what happened.
He is imprudent, since not only does he not know, but he does not
know that he would do better not to know. Ignorant Oedipus, imprudent Oedipus is also, perhaps, unconscious Oedipus, since how could
he not know, at bottom, what he thinks he does not know? Fine, this
is familiar, known. However, at the level of a naive reading, it remains
that throughout the text Oedipus is the bearer of quite explicit signs
of knowledge. Of course, all these references in the text to Oedipus's
knowledge have to be read at two levels, each of these utterances has a
double meaning, since in the mind of the listener who hears them, all
these signs of knowledge refer to the fact that we know all that Oedipus
does not know, and when he says: "I know," we know that basically he
did not know. And so, all these expressions that emphatically mark his
knowledge refer in fact to his ignorance. But I think the signs of Oedipal
knowledge do not get all their meaning from the sole fact that they refer,
by a sort of play on words, to his real ignorance. I think that the signs
of Oedipal knowledge form a perfectly coherent set and that Oedipus's
knowledge is a specific knowledge that has a distinctive form and that is
perfectly describable in comparison with the other types of knowledge,
whether of the seer [or] the witness.

What is this Oedipal knowledge?[5] I would like to begin by referring
to a very brief passage that seems to me to be significant for characterizing the knowledge peculiar to Oedipus. At the moment of his argument
with Teiresias, at the point when Teiresias tells him: "You are the guilty
one, you want to drag the truth from me. Fine, here it is, don't look for
it elsewhere: the person who killed Laius is you. You killed Laius and I

could tell of many other things you have done," Oedipus interrupts him and throws at him a strange invocation, since he does not say: "this is not true, I am innocent, I could not have done it," but says: "*O ploute kai turanni, kai tekhnē tekhnēs*"; "Oh wealth, Oh—*turanni*—Oh power, *tekhnē tekhnēs*, supreme art, art of arts," so then: "Oh wealth, Oh power, Oh art of all the arts, what jealousy you arouse!"[6] And after that, he reproaches Teiresias with having said what he said, for having made his accusations, only out of jealousy for that *O ploute kai turanni, kai tekhnē tekhnēs*. Three terms, in the middle of which there is the term *turanni*, to which we will come back, "power," and this term "power" appears flanked by its two adjacent goddesses, if you like, wealth on the one hand, and then *tekhnē tekhnēs*, the supreme art. So Oedipus says: "In this whole story that concerns me, and in which I stand accused, it is not my innocence, it is not a murder I have committed that is at issue, it is not that, it is wealth, power, and *tekhnē tekhnēs*." What does Oedipus mean when he thus puts at the center of what is at stake between him and Teiresias, consequently at the very center of the play, this power that has a wealth aspect and an aspect, a side of *tekhnē tekhnēs*, supreme art?

This expression, supreme art, art of arts, is noteworthy for a number of reasons. First, I do not think you will ever find power characterized as a *tekhnē*, as a technique, an art, in the archaic texts, or anyway not before the end of the sixth century. Second, on the other hand, obviously one of the absolutely fundamental themes of all political discussion, of philosophical debate in the fifth and fourth centuries is the extent to which the exercise of political power calls for, entails something like a *tekhnē*, a knowledge (*savoir*), a technical knowledge, a know-how that would justify apprenticeship, the development of laws, formulae, and ways of doing things. So here, with this expression, we are at the very heart of a political-philosophical debate, or of a debate about the theory and practice of politics in the fifth century, and so in the period of Sophocles. Finally, this expression captures my attention for a very particular reason, which is that, as you know, the expression *tekhnē tekhnēs* remains a typical, almost ritual expression by which the art of government is constantly characterized up until the seventeenth century. *Tekhnē tekhnēs*, supreme art, will designate political art in general, and it will designate especially the art of governing men in general, be this in the collective form of a political government, or in the individual form of spiritual direction. And there is, of course, the famous text by Gregory Nazienzen, to which we will return at much greater length this year, which, eight centuries after Sophocles, defines spiritual direction as *tekhnē tekhnēs*,[7] characterizing spiritual direction in a way that remains absolutely constant up until the eighteenth century.[8] *Tekhnē tekhnēs* is then the art of directing souls.[9]

If I lay some stress on this expression, it is precisely because what I would like to do this year is study the relation between this *tekhnē tekhnēs* as supreme art, that is to say, art of governing men, and alethurgy. To what extent does the art of governing men entail something like a manifestation of truth? Not so much how, in what way, are the relations between the art of governing men and alethurgy generally formed, but how, in what way, are the relations formed [between] the art of governing men and what I will call self-alethurgy, that is to say those forms of manifestation of truth that revolve around the first person, around the "I" and the "myself"? I would like to touch on these themes of *tekhnē tekhnēs* and self-alethurgy.

Let us know return to this *tekhnē* of Oedipus to find out in what it consists. Oedipus's *tekhnē* contrasts with two other ways of doing things or ways of being. Obviously it is in clear contrast with Creon's way of doing things or way of being. Actually, there is a rather interesting passage in the play when Creon defends himself against Oedipus and [the latter] says: "If you have reported such an unfavorable oracle, and if you then sought out the seer, it is because you are envious of my position and want to take the throne." Defending himself, Creon replies—and his plea, moreover, is entirely in the same vein as at least one genre of sophistic discourse, that is to say, defense at the level of plausibility: "What you say is not true, because it is implausible.[10] And there are a number of reasons why it is implausible that I should envy you." [It is] these reasons that I would like to look at.

I cannot be jealous of you, Creon says, because basically I have a good life. What is my life? Well, he says, it is the life of a king without having to be one or without having to do a king's job. We could say, if you like, that this is a Louis-Philippe type of assertion, of the kind: I reign, but I do not govern. In fact, if we look at his words, he says exactly that. "As the son of Laius, the brother of Jocasta, and as your brother-in-law, what do I have? On the one hand, I have *archē*, that is to say, I am in the first rank, I am among the foremost and, on the other hand, I have *dunasteia*, power."[11] Power is a rather enigmatic word that is employed by Plato, for example, to designate aristocratic regimes and is precisely opposed to *turannis*.[12] *Turannis* is the power of just one. *Dunasteia*, on the other hand, is a kind of power possessed in common and shared by a number of people. How do they share it? Creon's text indicates something of this inasmuch as he says: In what does my life consist as one of the foremost, having *dunasteia*, power? Quite simply in this: That you are the king, you are obliged to give me presents, and whenever I ask for something, you give it to me. On the other hand, the common people, knowing that I have *dunasteia*, power, appeal to me. In this way I find myself in a both privileged and intermediary position between government and those who are governed. Presents and a whole circuit of exchanges, promises, commitments, and favors converge on me. I am as it were surrounded by both, by the person who commands and those who are commanded, and in this function as intermediary I enjoy all the advantages without having any of the cares. In other words, Creon is the man of the bond—of the bond that binds him to his brother-in-law and the aristocracy, on the one hand, and to the common people on the other. He is the man of the bond, but not the man of action strictly speaking. Moreover, we have confirmation that he is the man of the bond in an episode I referred to last week, when precisely at the end of this argument he will propose, by swearing on oath, to assure Oedipus that he has nothing against him and has not falsified the message. He is the man of the bond; he is the man of the oath. This is what enables him to live like a king without being one, without having to govern. Everything comes to him through this series of exchanges and commitments. He does not need a *tekhnē* to live in this way. All he needs is simply to respect the laws, rules, habits, commitments, and all the bonds that unite him with both the king and the people. What is respect for the bonds? Ultimately it means being moderate, temperate, thoughtful, and wise. And he formulates his own knowledge using the word "*sōphronein*": to be moderate, that is what I know.[13]

Opposite this there is Teiresias. Whereas Creon has no *tekhnē*, Teiresias has a *tekhnē* that enables him to interpret oracles. What is this *tekhnē*? The application of the term *tekhnē* to the mantic, to divination is absolutely traditional. It is employed a number of times in *Oedipus* with regard to divination. [No doubt] not always, but a considerable number of times, it is employed in an ironic or negative way. For example, Oedipus himself employs the word *tekhnē* to designate what Teiresias does and the way in which he interprets the god's signs or words. But how does he speak of it? At the time of the events we are now trying to sort out, [he says]—that is, what took place at the time of the death of Laius—and when no one was able to say exactly what took place: "Was the seer then exercising his *tekhnē*?"[14] The answer can only be: "Yes, he was"—which is immediately followed up with: "if so, then how come he did not know the truth?"[15] Here the word *tekhnē* has an ironic sense, just as in the other retort when he says: "You, with all your *tekhnē*, were not able to solve the riddle that I solved, that is to say the riddle of the Sphinx."[16] So here, *tekhnē* is employed in an ironic sense, powerless *tekhnē*. And the word *tekhnē* reappears on another occasion, in the important dialogue between Jocasta and Oedipus, but this time in a completely negative sense. This is when Jocasta, in a much more radical manner than Oedipus himself, says to Oedipus: "But don't worry about what the seer may say. You know that no mortal has ever possessed the *mantikē tekhnē*, no mortal has ever possessed the art of divination."[17] That is to say, the art of divination does not exist, at least among mortals. So, the existence of a mantic *tekhnē* is radically challenged.

In fact, what characterizes Teiresias's practice, which Oedipus and Jocasta seem to deny can be called *tekhnē*, are two things we referred to last week. On the one hand, if Teiresias speaks the truth, this is not exactly a *tekhnē* for the excellent reason that Teiresias has a natural bond with the truth. He is born with the truth, the truth is born in him, the truth grows like a plant within his body, or as another body in his body. Hence all these expressions, for example: the truth that *empephuken*, that comes naturally with him.[18] The truth is born in him. Teiresias says: "I nourish the truth in me,"[19] and Oedipus says: "You know the truth, *suneidōs*,[20] you know it immediately." So, there is no technique, since there is this connaturalness—or at any rate, this claim to connaturalness—of Teiresias and the truth. And on the other hand, by what processes is Teiresias able to formulate the truth and discover it in himself? Well, by an activity for which he employs a quite precise and particular word, which is *phronein*.[21] *Phronein*, that is to say, thinking, reflecting, withdrawing into oneself, penetrating the depths of one's thought. And such indeed is Teiresias's activity that, in his dispute with Oedipus, at the point when he is going to leave the stage, turning towards Oedipus and the chorus, Teiresias tells them: "But you know well, you do not think, *ou phroneit*, you do not reflect."[22]

So, you have Creon, who is a man of *sophronein*, of moderation, the one who knows his bonds and how to respect them, and then there is the *phronein* of Teiresias, which is a way of sinking into himself, into his thoughts, in order to find the truth with which he is connatural.

What is the *tekhnē* of Oedipus in relation to this? If there is absolutely no question of speaking of Creon's *tekhnē*, and if the *tekhnē* of Teiresias is no doubt not a *tekhnē*, Oedipus, on the other hand, does claim to be a man of *tekhnē*. And the most frequently recurring word in the text for characterizing his *tekhnē* is *euriskein*, that is to say, "to find," "to discover." There is a whole series of texts: "The town appeals to you that you may find some help," *eurein*, at 42. At 68: "I will tell the anxious people the solution I have found," *ēuriskon*. Later, Oedipus will reproach the Thebans for not having undertaken to "discover, *euriskein*, the murderer" when Laius was murdered. And this is what Oedipus will do. He will try to discover him. He will try to discover him himself. You find this at 120,[23] 258,[24] and 304.[25] When he is arguing with Creon, he says: "Ah, at last, I have discovered the plot hatched against me" (546). Elsewhere Teiresias also says it, at a given moment, when he is about to leave the stage, he says: "all these things, are you not clever at finding them? It's for you to find them yourself."[26]

So, we have: Creon, who maintains his moderation; Teiresias, who is deep in his thoughts, *phronein*; Oedipus, who sets off to discover the truth, *euriskein*, who discovers. You will say that there is at least one thing he discovered, the first that I have spoken about and which is the solution to the riddle of the Sphinx. Now, and this is a bit of a riddle about the riddle, Oedipus never says anywhere in the text that he discovered the solution to the riddle of the Sphinx. He does not use the word *euriskein* with regard to the riddle of the Sphinx; he says that he mastered it, *gnōmē*.[27] *Gnōmē* is completely different from the series of words deriving from *euriskein*, "to find." It is a rather pallid, bland, neutral word that means viewpoint, opinion, way of thinking, way of judging. So it was not with this specifically Oedipal activity to which he binds his destiny, it was not with this activity that consists in setting off in search to discover the truth that he solved the riddle of the Sphinx. He solved it by a completely different type of activity, to which we will have to return at the end, which is *gnōmē*, opinion. I mastered the Sphinx and the riddle of the Sphinx, I thus cured the city of all its ills, I set it back on its feet, I set it right when it was cast down by misfortune thanks to *gnōmē*, thanks to my viewpoint, my opinion, and not by the search for the truth.

Let us now return to the *euriskein* of Oedipus, leaving to one side this problem of *gnōmē*, which was employed just to solve the riddle. In what does the *euriskein* of Oedipus consist, this activity of searching to which he will bind his fate and which will underpin the whole play? To find, to discover, is, of course, the act by which someone who does not know becomes someone who knows. Oedipus is always saying: I was not there at the time of the deeds; I know nothing about what happened; you were there, you should know something; I cannot know. As a result, the problem for Oedipus is how he can transform himself from someone who did not know into someone who knows. This transformation of the one who did not know into the one who knows is, as you know, the Sophists' problem, Socrates' problem, and will still be Plato's problem. It is the whole problem of education, rhetoric, and the art of persuading. It is, ultimately, the whole problem of democracy. In order to govern the city, does one need to transform those who do not know into those who know? Is it necessary to transform all those who do not know into people who know? Or in order to govern the city is there a certain knowledge that some need to possess, but not others? Does one discover this knowledge and can one form it in someone who does not yet know but will end up knowing? All these problems of the technique of transformation of non-knowledge into knowledge are, I think, at the heart of philosophical-political, pedagogical, and rhetorical debate, of the debate on language and the utilization of language in fifth century Athens.

So, Oedipus has to be transformed from a man who does not know into a man who knows. How will this transformation take place? And here the vocabulary is quite clear, quite clear-cut and insistent. Oedipus can become the one who knows, starting from his non-knowledge, thanks to marks, signs, clues, and markers to be found on the way, on the trail, which will enable him to steer the ship and finally enable him, on the basis of these events, to infer the truth and what happened. The word for this interpretation of signs that will finally lead him to the truth is not [the one] that designates the seer's interpretation, for example. It is the word *tekmairetai*.[28] And these elements, signs, and marks are designated at several points by the word *tekmērion*,[29] that is to say, mark, clue. It is a word that is both precise and complex.

First, you find it in an [author]* like Alcmaeon, for example, who says the following, which is very significant and which it seems to me the Oedipus story, well the tragedy by Sophocles, echoes: "the gods have certainty, whereas we men have *tekmērion*, we have the clue, the sign."[30] It is a word, therefore, that marks quite well a type of knowledge that is absolutely different from the knowledge one may get from communicating with the gods or by listening to what they say. It is also a word that has a scientific usage, since in the fifth century you find *tekmērion* employed simply to designate any type of demonstration. A mathematical demonstration may be called *tekmērion*. Later, in Aristotle, you find a contrast between the *tekmērion* that gives the truth in an indubitable way, the absolutely certain sign, and the *eikos* or the *sēmeion*, which is the probable, the likely sign.[31] Here, In Sophocles' play, the word *tekmērion* is obviously employed in a much less rigorous way than in Aristotle; it is assimilated to or employed at the same level as *sēmeion*.[32] In fact, there is a clearly medical coloring of the vocabulary here. Moreover, the whole of *Oedipus* is permeated by the medical metaphor, since the evil that has befallen Thebes is, of course, the plague and what is at issue is curing the town of the plague. So it is indeed a medical practice that Oedipus puts to work: confronted with the town's sickness, uncovering the signs, elements, indications, and symptoms by which the cause itself of sickness can be tracked down. You see here an intertwining of medicine and law that is already essential and fundamental in fifth century Greece, but that will be fundamental and essential for the whole of Western civilization. Ultimately it could be said that Oedipus is a medical and legal matter. At any rate, if we consider it at the level of the procedures of truth put to work in the play, it is one of the first articulations of a judicial with a medical form of alethurgy.

In what does the *tekmērion*, the *tekmēria* that Oedipus is putting together in order to arrive at the truth and to transform himself from a

---

* M.F.: poet.

man who does not know into one who does, consist? It consists of elements that can function in four different directions. It goes, of course, from the present to the past, that is to say: we are presently in a disastrous situation, we must find the cause of these events; this cause is in events now past and forgotten; we must therefore go back from the present to the past. The *tekmērion* also goes from past to present, and this is clear in Jocasta's argument when, discussing with Oedipus, she tells him: But after all, you know that already a number of oracles have been pronounced without being followed by any effect; consequently, oracles do not always speak the truth, and since the old ones did not speak the truth, you can conclude that the oracles given to you now are no more true. Be reasonable, come to a conclusion from the past to the present, Jocasta says, employing the term *tekmērion*.[33] The third direction goes from presence to absence. The *tekmērion* is what Oedipus has in his hands, something that he sees, that he knows, something he has been told, and he must trace the people who said this, or who know why it was said. Going back to the past from presence to absence. And the *tekmērion* is also the element that also allows one to pass from absence to presence, since this way of proceeding involves passing from those who have heard talk about the story, from those who have heard it said that there were people who knew, of going from these, who consequently were absent from the scene, to those who really witnessed the murder and saw it with their own eyes. So it is necessary to go from absence to presence. Roughly, if you like, this whole game of *tekmērion* is a game that complies with the law of presence and the law of the gaze. It is necessary to arrive finally at presence itself and at the gaze itself, the gaze of people who were themselves present.

This is what will transform Oedipus from the one who does not know into the one who knows. Now—and this is another aspect of Oedipal *euriskein*—he wants to make this discovery himself. He wants to make it himself in that he does not trust anyone else; he wants to resolve the question himself. Throughout the text Oedipus is constantly saying: "I came myself to inform myself, I myself want to know what this plague ravaging Thebes is, I myself want to listen to the citizens' prayer, I myself want to know who the person is who heard talk of a witness, I myself want to see the witness." That is to say, Oedipus himself must be the operator of this truth. And it is Oedipus himself who must

produce this alethurgy in the form of discovery, and who must produce
it entirely and up to the famous final scene, well one of the last scenes,
when we see him in the presence of those who saw the scene themselves.
At this point, Oedipus is the master of the truth. From start to finish
he has been the operator who, advancing from *tekmērion* to *tekmērion*, has
arrived in the physical presence on stage of those who were, of the one
who was physically present at the crime. It turns out that this *autos* will
turn around and the "himself," who was the operator of the truth, will
be the object of the discovery. But this is another question. Once again, I
am placing myself at the level of the procedures of truth, just at the level
of the alethurgies.

Now, what did Oedipus aim to discover by this *euriskein*? Whereas
Teiresias's knowledge bore on the gods' decrees, Oedipal research does
not bear on these decrees but rather on what actually happened, which
may or may not conform to the gods' decrees. That is to say, for Oedipus
the activity of *euriskein*, of discovery, is basically a double-sided activity. On the one hand, the discovery must bring to light the event itself,
the fortune or misfortune of men, the encounters. What took place
when Laius arrived at the fork where three roads meet? What happened there? How did the encounter with his murderer come about?
So, the discovery bears on the event, on the encounters, the intersec-
tion of things, series, actions, and men. And the aim of this discovery,
on the other hand, is to escape the gods' decrees by discovering these
events, or to limit their effects, or anyway to weigh up what is or is not
in conformity with these decrees. The *euriskein* thus discovers the way
of not submitting entirely and definitively to the gods' decrees. It is a
way of steering a course between these decrees and avoiding them if
possible. It is an art of making out the reefs, of discovering where they
are hidden, of avoiding running into them. It is a way guiding the ship
through the reefs to port. This is why Oedipus, who claims to be the
man of discovery, of *euriskein*, is always saying: "me, after all, I have to
govern the ship," *kubernan*.[34] The art of discovery is then an art of the
rudder. And here we are thus at the heart, well at the point of another
problem, which is: what is the relation between this activity of discovery that Oedipus makes his own, his own art, that he claims for himself
and for himself alone, and the practice of government, the art of pilot-
ing the ship between the reefs?

So, some words now on power... Throughout the play, Oedipus basically hears only the problem of power. Everyone around him speaks
of the plague, of the dangers the town faces, of the misfortune of men.
He is told of the need to find the guilty person. He is told: But you
are the guilty one. He is told: But there must be people who know.
Oedipus really does want to set off in search of the truth, but primarily
because it is a question of his power and inasmuch as it is a question
of his power. For him, the game is not the game of the truth. It is the
game of power. And he plays the game of the truth only to the extent
that for him power is put in question. This is very clear throughout the
text and especially in the first part when the problem is posed. When
told about the plague and that the inhabitants of Thebes are appealing
to him, he says immediately: "In fact, I really must concern myself with
this plague in Thebes, because the misfortune destroying the town also
affects me."[35] When people speak to him about the murder, when he is
told: The oracle has said that the reason for the plague at Thebes is the
fact that the king, Laius, was killed, Oedipus says straightaway: Well
then, we must find the guilty person. Why must he be found? To save
Thebes? Absolutely not. "The guilty person must be traced for it could
well be that he will attack me too."[36] And Oedipus confirms that it is
his power that is in question, saying: "If we discover the guilty person
and it proves that the guilty person has dwelled in my home or has some
relation to me, I will banish myself," that is to say I agree to losing my
power if there is anything between me and the assassin.[37] And when
he is arguing with the prophet Teiresias, and Teiresias accuses him, he
does not defend himself by saying: Your accusations are false, because I
was not there at the time of the murder, because I am an unfortunate
stranger who arrived by chance and have nothing to do with all this. Not
at all. At this point he absolutely does not speak in terms of truth. He
says: "What you say is not true, because what you really have in mind is
to threaten my power, and I shall defend this power against you."[38] It is
the same with Creon. He does not say to Creon: Teiresias lied. He says:
"You have plotted with him against me in order to take my power."[39]
And finally, when with Jocasta, at the final moment of the discovery, the
messenger has just told Oedipus, in front of Jocasta: But you are not the
son of Polybus, Oedipus notes the panic of Jocasta, who is beginning
to understand and see the truth. But what does Oedipus hear at the

moment the truth is being discovered? He says: "Jocasta is ashamed of me and judges me unworthy of power, for I am only a foundling. I may not have parents, it is true, but I am at least the son of *tukhē*, the son of fate. And this fully authorizes me to take and exercise power. I am not an unworthy son. The obscurity of my parents is compensated for by the fact that fate has picked me out to become king."[40] In any case, for Oedipus it is a question of power until practically the end, and that is what preoccupies him throughout the play. This is so true, moreover, that at the end when the disaster is accomplished, he says: "Now I can only obey."[41] [And] Creon tells him: "Do not seek always to command and be the master, *kai gar akratēsas*,"[42] an expression that plays on the words and means at the same time: you rose to the summit *and* now you have become completely without power, *a-kratēs*.[43] And the last retort of the Chorus, the last phrase is: "No doubt you solved the riddle and you were *kratistos*, and now here you are completely ruined."[44] This expression echoes the invocation that was pointed out right at the start of the play, when Oedipus is greeted in the form of *kratunōn Oidipous*, Oedipus the powerful.[45] So what is at issue is power in a sense, at least from the point of view of Oedipus. This is the first thing I wanted to note.

The second is this. At the center of the play, exactly halfway through, at the end of the first half when, as you know, Phoebus has been consulted, Teiresias has been consulted, and Jocasta has unintentionally revealed to Oedipus that he was probably the murderer of Laius, after this first half of gods and kings, and before the other half of testimonies and slaves, and in which the truth will be accomplished, between these two halves there is a song of the chorus.[46] A song of the chorus that, strangely, appears unrelated to what has just taken place. Suddenly, first of all, they sing of praise of the law. The chorus comes in at the point where we are waiting for the messengers who will tell the truth and perhaps exonerate Oedipus or maybe prove his guilt. Suddenly, at this moment, the chorus praises the law that it says is born of Olympus, is the child of Zeus and not of mortals, the child of a single father, that is never exposed to forgetfulness, and that finally is inhabited by a god who never grows old. Tyrants, the chorus says, are against the law. Tyrants are immoderation, they are fortune with its highs and lows that raise men to the summit and then plunge them down, breaking their feet. Then, joining to this condemnation of tyrants the curse and sacrilege of those who everywhere walk with pride, who seek only their own advantage, who violate the inviolable, the chorus says, may Zeus see these, for respect of the gods is disappearing and even the oracles are no longer believed.

This is both a very surprising and very clear text. It is very clear because, of course, it is about Oedipus. It is about nothing else but Oedipus. The word *turannos*, which is employed in the passage,[47] refers to the title itself of the play, and there is a series of very clear allusions: the man with the broken feet[48] is, of course, Oedipus, or again, what is meant by "the laws have only a single father,"[49] if not a reference to the fact that Oedipus had at least one father too many, since he had assassinated him and that what's more had two of them. Having only one father is to be unlike Oedipus. So it is a perfectly clear text, since it is addressed to Oedipus, but by that very fact it is completely surprising, since, throughout the first part, the chorus manifested only attachment, affection, and faithfulness towards Oedipus. In its previous intervention, it had said to Oedipus after his dispute with Creon: "In any case, I do not know where the truth lies, I do not know which of you is right, I cannot therefore give an opinion, but I know one thing, which is that given the services you have rendered me, first of all I cannot believe that you are the guilty one, and in any case I will never abandon you."[50] So beyond the truth of the accusations, the chorus affirmed a fundamental attachment to Oedipus. And now, without anything truly new having been introduced, save that the truth is on the move and rushing towards the stage, but it has not yet arrived, the chorus has already dropped Oedipus and given a negative picture of Oedipal power.

What then is this power of Oedipus that is actually at the heart of the play, since Oedipus hears only this and the chorus, situated in the middle of the play, indicates that this is what it is about? The title, the words of the chorus, and several expressions we come across in the text indicate that this power is tyrannical power. Tyrannical power: not understanding this word in its pejorative sense, of course. What this refers to is a perfectly precise historical figure, a frequent, current, almost universal institution in the Greek world at the turn of the sixth and fifth centuries and which we should not forget that although to a great extent it had disappeared or entered into strong decline during the fifth century, although at the time of Sophocles the immediately political problem of tyranny was no longer posed—at least, not consist-ently—in the sixth and fifth centuries tyranny was and remained the point of departure, the matrix, as it were, of political thought in Greece, and there were several reasons for this. First of all, because democra-cies, where they existed, were effectively established through tyranny. It was through tyranny that democracy was established in Athens, for example; the tyrants were, so to speak, the willing or unwilling authors of democracy.[51] And in any case it was always in relation to this tyranny that the theory of political power was developed in Greece for at least a century. Tyranny was always a constant and ambiguous model for politi-cal thought in Greece. And after all, it could be said that tyranny was for Greek political thought what the revolution has been for modern European political thought, that in relation to which, ultimately, one must always situate oneself and that has to be thought of as passage, transition, foundation, or upheaval.

Now this figure of the tyrant, this political figure therefore, which is not immediately negative, which is positive and negative, this problem-atic figure of the tyrant comprises a number of features that can be found very clearly in Oedipus as in the political thought contemporary with or later than Sophocles. I leave aside the specifically mythical features, which the practice of tyranny in the sixth and fifth centuries always marked, for example: the tyrants in Greece always referred themselves to a heroic model that authenticated, as it were, the seizure of power. During—how to put it?—stagings, concerted ceremonies of power, the tyrant appeared as the one who, born in a town, was either driven from it, or disappeared, or went into voluntary exile, and who then returns to his town and through some exploit becomes qualified to take power and is reinserted in the town through a new system of bonds and, pos-sibly, marriage. The Oedipal story could be described as a typical story of tyranny. Let's say, in any case, that the historical tyrants always made sure of re-inscribing their seizure of power within a mythical landscape of this kind. To that extent Oedipus is indeed the typical tyrant.

But let's leave this, which is something of the general framework of the drama. In the play itself, Oedipus appears with these tyrannical features—tyrannical, again, in the sense of a very precise political figure. First, Oedipus is someone who has experienced a changeable destiny, that is to say he was not born with power, or he was not born at the heart of power. Unlike Creon, he was not always on the side of *archē*, in the front rank. Highs and lows have continually alternated in his life. "The years which have grown with me," he says, "have made me great and small in turns."[52] Second, Oedipus saved the city, and a typical feature of tyrannical existence that justifies the tyrant and gives him the absolute right to exercise power, even though he was not born amongst the great or did not remain among them, is that at a given moment, during a battle, or some confrontation, when it was a matter of a decision or when there was civil war in the city, he provided a service to the city, he accomplished an exploit. Thus Oedipus can say that he was like a rampart, a tower against the city's enemies.[53] He enabled the city to breathe and sleep. He set the city right, raised it up, *orthōsai polin*.[54] Now this expression of setting the city right, putting it straight, making it *orthē*, is the same expression that Solon, the law-giver (*nomothetēs*) and sort of tyrant, uses to describe his own action in imposing laws on Athens or giving it laws.[55] Third, this salvation of the city by the tyrant establishes, constitutes, founds a relationship of gratitude, debt, affection, and love between the tyrant and the town, which is very different from obligatory veneration for the statutory chief. The test that Oedipus overcame in triumphing over the Sphinx was, as the text itself says, "a proof" of Oedipus's benevolence towards the city.[56] As a result, the city naturally has a corresponding benevolence towards Oedipus. This is why, referring to this salvation previously assured by Oedipus, the chorus can say: "Know that I would be insane if I were to abandon you, who, when my country was suffering, put it on the right path."[57] So, there is a bond between Oedipus and the city itself, that is to say, with the *plēthos*, the people. Hence there is a new feature, that of solitude. Inasmuch as he is the one who, alone, saved the city and to whom the entire city is individually bound, the tyrant, and so Oedipus, is a solitary chief. "He shot his arrow beyond the others," the text says, "he was swept up by happiness, he mastered it, he alone solved the riddle."[58] And since he was alone in solving the riddle, alone in saving the city, since he is the one to whom alone the city will be grateful, since the bond is established between him alone and the entire city, a consequence and further feature of tyrannical power is that he takes the town to be his. And he takes it to be his own property so much that Creon objects, saying to him: "I too am a chief; I am part of the city. Thebes does not belong to you alone."[59]

From the point of view of Oedipus, the fact that he assured the city's salvation means that a sort of property deed was established. The town has now become his and so the orders he gives and the decisions he takes will have their sole foundation in him, in his will, and not at all in terms of an order of law and *nomos*. His conduct will not be regulated by this universal law. He says so moreover: "If I saved the town, what do I care about the rest?"[60] And when he is told: But the order you gave to Creon—at the time of the dispute—is unjust, Oedipus [replies]: "That doesn't matter; he will have to obey even so."[61] And so, the action and power of Oedipus is not organized by reference to the universality of that *nomos*, that law that has only one father, that is born on Olympus, the law in which a god lives who does not age.[62] It is not that immobile and immortal law. It is simply his will, and his will defined according to what? Precisely, his care in leading the town like a ship through the reefs,[63] avoiding encounters, rocks, tempests, and every harmful event. That is to say, his power is organized by the need to govern, by *tuchē*, by the series of events by which men are linked, bound together in a completely different way than by the law that lays down their conduct according to the gods' eternal will.[64] And you see the *euriskein* of Oedipus and his power exactly correspond to each other. If he is obliged to govern by discovering, it is because discovering enables him to locate the reefs, rocks, and encounters, to locate through the gods' decrees the *tuchē*, and the government, the exercise of power that corresponds to this is precisely tyrannical in this respect—and this is what fundamentally characterizes tyrannical power: it is not organized by reference to the principle of the *nomos*; as best it can with the means and knowledge peculiar to the tyrant, it merely tries to follow *tuchē*, destiny, and not the *nomos*.

Now, by exercising his power in this way and bringing the activity of discovery into play in order to arrive at a *tuchē*, a destiny that involves him killing his father and having children by his mother, Oedipus condemns himself where he sought to discover another guilty person, and, above all, he shows that this *tuchē* is nothing other than the very thing the gods foresaw in advance and from which they forged the destiny that was to close tightly round men. Consequently, Oedipus's discovery is at the same time his condemnation. All this is well known. But does this mean that the drama refers to an invalidation of this form of alethurgy (the discovery of the truth itself through clues that lead to those who were in actual fact its witnesses and actors)? I do not think so, since it is precisely through this game of discovery that Thebes is ultimately saved and the anger of the gods against the people of Thebes is removed through the emergence of the real truth. This truth had to be discovered for Thebes to be saved, and since neither divination nor any other means had enabled this truth to be brought to light, an alethurgy of this kind really was necessary. On the other hand, what is condemned in the drama is that someone should claim to be master of this kind of alethurgy and wants to use this way of discovery for his own advantage, so as to get away with it, to reveal a play of chance encounters and coincidences that will enable him to escape the destiny that the gods have fixed for him. So it is that master of truth who is condemned.

So we can say that inasmuch as the tragedy of Oedipus is in itself an alethurgy, well inasmuch as it involves revealing a truth, the truth that emerges is this: the way in which Oedipus arrived at the truth is no doubt the only one that could give a real, effective content to those prophecies of the gods that in the first half remained uncertain and were not embodied in a manifest truth. The process is good, the procedure is good, but the context of tyrannical power within which Oedipus wanted to get it to work, in other words, the reference of this procedure of truth to the single master who tries to use it in order to govern by himself, to guide the ship of the town and his own ship through the reefs of destiny, it is this usage which condemns—condemns what? Well, the very person who [resorted to it]. So that the procedure really is in fact an effective procedure of manifestation of the truth and purification of the city. But on the other hand, the use to which Oedipus puts it, the tyrannical use, indexed to *tuchē* and so opposed to the gods' decrees, is what is thereby condemned. And in actual fact, what happens at the end of the drama is that the procedure of discovery set in motion by Oedipus himself enables the witnesses, the slaves, the least peasants hidden away in their huts to say: Yes, I was there, *autos*, I gave with my own hands, I received with my own hands, I saw with my own eyes—which precisely gives a content of truth to the prophecy of Teiresias and the gods' decrees. The two alethurgies will actually join up, the second having been called for by Oedipus, but fitting this second to the first makes Oedipus *the* surplus character, the one who has to be suppressed for Thebes really to be saved. Oedipus is a supernumerary of knowledge and not an unconscious. He was surplus in this procedure of truth that must now be displayed as manifestation of the truth in the people, in the *plēthos*, within the citizens, in the minds of slaves. That is where the truth must be found, the truth that saves the city from all its dangers by confirming precisely what the gods said.

There remains a little problem I raised earlier that must now be resolved. So Oedipus set in motion this procedure of truth that turned round against him and condemned him because of his tyrannical use of it. But you will say that Oedipus made use of his knowledge, of his skill, of his *tekhnē tekhnēs* at least once in a positive way: this was when, arriving on the road leading to Thebes, he encountered the Sphinx, solved the riddle, and saved Thebes. But precisely what was it that Oedipus used to solve the problem posed by the Sphinx? The *tekhnē tekhnēs*? Is it the game of *tekmēri[a]* going back from a clue to someone's presence to the truth? Absolutely not. I told you that, precisely, the term *euriskein* is never employed to designate the way in which Oedipus solved the problem. He solved it by *gnōmē*, by that simple opinion, that way of thinking, that viewpoint, that judgment.[65] Now *gnōmē* is a technical term that is part of the political-judicial vocabulary of fifth century Greece.[66] *Gnōmē* is the view that the citizen gives and is called upon to give after the explanations provided by the rhetors, the politicians, those who know, or following a trial in which the different elements of the case have been set out, in which the clues, the *tekmēria*, have been developed; at that point, the citizen as juror or the magistrate is called upon to give his view, *gnōmē*, and it is this view that seals the destiny of the accused and thus fulfills the gods' [decrees]. Oedipus is someone who, at a given moment, actually saved the town, not by using the knowledge of discovery, the *tekhnē tekhnēs*, [but] by his *gnōmē*, his judgment, by that judicial activity, and it is when he wanted to use the methods of discovery of the truth within the exercise of a tyrannical power linked to the game of fortune and misfortune, that the game of the truth led him precisely to misfortune.

That's it for Oedipus. So, next week I will try to pass on more directly to the subject of this year's course, that is to say the problem [of the relation between] *autos* and alethurgy. What is this game of the myself or oneself within procedures of truth?

1. *Œdipe-Roi*, 410, p. 156; *Oedipus the King*, p. 28.
2. See, M. Detienne, *Les Maîtres de vérité dans la Grèce archaïque*, (Paris: Maspero, 1973 [1967]), ch. 2; English translation by Janet Lloyd as *The Masters of Truth in Archaic Greece* (New York: Zone Books, 1996), ch. 2, "The Memory of the Poet." See in particular pp. 42-43, where the author refers to J.-P. Vernant, "Aspects mythiques de la mémoire," *Journal de psychologie*, 1959, pp. 1-29; reprinted in J.-P. Vernant, *Mythe et pensée chez les Grecs* (Paris: Maspéro, 1971), vol. 2, pp. 80-107; English translation as "Mythical Aspects of Memory" in *Myth and Thought Among the Greeks* (London: Routledge and Kegan Paul, 1983), pp. 75-105.
3. See M. Foucault, *Le souci de soi* (Paris: Gallimard, 1984), pp. 17-18; English translation by R. Hurley, *The Care of the Self* (New York: Random House, 1985, and Harmondsworth: Viking, 1986), pp. 5-6, regarding *The Interpretation of Dreams* of Artemidorus (second century C.E.), a representative work of ancient dream criticism (*onirocritique*).
4. Hérodote, Ἱστορίαι/*Histoires*, trans., P. Legrand (Paris: Les Belles Lettres, 1946); English translation by A.D. Godley, *Herodotus*, vols. I-IV (Cambridge, Mass., and London: Harvard University Press/William Heinemann, Loeb Classical Library, 1936). See F. Hartog, *Le miroir d'Hérodote* (Paris: Gallimard, 1980, new revised and expanded edition 2001 "Folio"), Part II, ch. 2: "L'œil et l'oreille." See in particular pp. 396-407, on the "Herodotean autopsy," "the eye as mark of enunciation, of an 'I have seen' as intervention of the narrator in his account in order to prove" (p. 396); "… the traveller's eye marks out the space and cuts out more or less known zones (from what I have seen with my own eyes, what others have seen, up to what no one has seen)" (p. 398); on the function of enunciation in the first person (p. 433 et seq.).
5. On this question, see "La vérité et les formes juridiques" (second lecture), pp. 566-567/ pp. 1434-1435, "Truth and Juridical Forms," pp. 28-30.
6. Ibid., 380, Fr., p. 155: "Oh wealth, power, superiority of art"; Eng., p. 27: "Wealth, sovereignty, and skill outmatching skill."
7. Grégoire de Nazianze, *Discours théologique* (362), II, French translation by J. Bernardi (Paris: Cerf, Sources Chrétiennes/SC, No. 247, 1978), pp. 110-111; English translation by Charles Gordon Browne, Gregory Nazienzen, *Orations* in Philip Schaff and Henry Wace, eds., *A Select Library of Nicene and Post-Nicene Fathers of the Christian Church. Second Series [NPNF2]*, vol. VII (Grand Rapids, Michigan: W.B. Eerdmans, 1893), p. 208. See I. Hausherr, *Spiritual Direction in the Early Christian East*, trans. Anthony P. Gythiel (Kalamazoo: Cistercian Publications, Cistercian Studies Series, No. 116, 1990), p. 52.
8. See *Sécurité, territoire, population*, lecture of 15 February 1978, p. 154; *Security, Territory, Population*, pp. 150-151. Foucault does not return to this text in the rest of the course. For a more developed commentary, see *Mal faire, dire vrai*, lecture of 13 May 1981, pp. 174-175.
9. See H. Brémond, Introduction to J. Brémond, *Les Pères du désert* (Paris: Librairie Victor Lecoffre, "Les moralistes chrétiens," ed., J. Galabada, 2nd edition, 1927), p. xiv: "… the desert Fathers, if they did not create from start to finish—and who knows?—at least organized, constructed, as if nothing had been done before them, and in such a way that posterity will have almost nothing to add to the edifice, that magnificent thing, 'the celestial art of bewitching the evils of others,' as Cassian said [*Conferences*, 18, 17 [There is no chapter 17 to conference 18; G.B.]], in a word the direction of souls" (cited by I. Hausherr, *Spiritual Direction*, p. 2).
10. *Œdipe-Roi*, 583-615, pp. 162-163; *Oedipus the King*, pp. 36-37.
11. 593, Fr., p. 162; Eng., p. 36.
12. Foucault returns to this notion in 1983 in his lectures, *Le gouvernement de soi et des autres. Cours au Collège de France 1982-1983*, éd. Frédédric Gros (Paris: Gallimard-Le Seuil, 2008), lecture of 2 February, First hour, p. 144, and lecture of 9 February, Second hour, p. 200 (concerning Plato, *Republic*, 473d); English translation by Graham Burchell, *The Government of Self and Others. Lectures at the Collège de France 1982-1983*, English series editor, Arnold I. Davidson (Basingstoke and New York: Palgrave Macmillan, 2010), p. 158 and p. 217.
13. *Œdipe-Roi*, 589, p. 162; *Oedipus the King*, p. 36: "self-control."
14. Ibid., 562, Fr., p. 161; Eng., p. 34: "profession."
15. Ibid., 568, Fr.: "How is it then that this clever man did not say what he says today?"; Eng.: "Why did our wise old friend not say this then?"
16. Ibid., 390-398, Fr., p. 155; Eng., p. 27.
17. Ibid., 709, Fr., p. 166: "… learn that no mortal being understands anything of the divinatory art"; Eng., p. 41: "learn that human beings have no part in the craft of prophecy."

18. Ibid., 299, Fr., p. 151: "who alone among men possesses the truth within him" (literally: "the only man in whom the truth grows naturally"); Eng., p. 22: "in whom alone of mankind truth is native."

19. Ibid., 356, Fr., p. 154; Eng., p. 25.

20. Ibid., 330, Fr., p. 153; Eng., p. 24; see too 704, Fr., p. 166; Eng., p. 41 (Jocasta, with regard to Creon).

21. Ibid., 462, Fr., p. 157: Teiresias to Oedipus: "if you convict me of lying, say then that divination gives me no knowledge (*phronein*)"; Eng., p. 30: "if you find me mistaken, say I have no skill in prophecy."

22. Ibid., 328, Fr. p. 153: "all of you are foolish (*ou phroneit*)"; Eng., p. 24: "All of you here know nothing." This passage is right at the start of the exchange between Oedipus and Teiresias, when the latter, in order not to have to say what he knows, makes as if to leave. Compare with 436, Fr., p. 157, where Teiresias is defined as "reasonable, *emphrōn*" (… *emphrones*); Eng., p. 29: "Wise."

23. Ibid., 120, Fr., p. 145: "A single detail could do much to discover (*exeuroi*)"; Eng., p. 16: "If we could even find a slim beginning in which to hope, we might discover much."

24. Ibid., 258, Fr., p. 150: "On the contrary, you must investigate (*exereunan*)"; Eng., p. 20: "Search it out."

25. Ibid., 304, Fr., p. 152: "to defend [the city], to save it…, we find (*exeuriskomen*) only you [Teiresias]"; Eng., p. 22: "My lord, in you alone we find a champion."

26. 440, Fr., p. 157; Eng., p. 29: "But it's in riddle answering that you are strongest."

27. Foucault returns to this notion at the end of the lecture.

28. See below, note 33 (Jocasta, with regard to Oedipus).

29. The word *tekmērion*, employed several times in *Electra* (774, 904, 1109), does not appear in *Oedipus the King*. Apart from *tekmairetai* (see previous note), the only occurrence of one of its derivatives is *dustekmarton* (adjective formed from *tekmairō*) at 109: "Where will we discover this difficult trail" (literally: "this trace difficult to discover," *tode ichnos dustekmarton*) of an old crime?" Oedipus asks; Eng., p. 15: "Where would a trace of this old crime be found?" See C. Ginzburg, "Aristote et l'histoire, encore une fois" in *Rapports de force. Histoire, rhétorique, preuve* (Paris: Gallimard-Le Seuil, "Hautes Études," 2003), p. 50, which refers (p. 55 note 31) to B. Williams, *Shame and Necessity* (Berkeley: University of California Press, 1993), pp. 58-59.

30. Alcmaeon of Croton, a "follower of Pythagoras," according to Diogenes Laertius, at the beginning of the fifth century; he was thought to have been the first to practice the dissection of animals. Only some fragments of his work survive, including that recorded by Diogenes Laertius, to which Foucault refers. English translation by R.D. Hicks, Diogenes Laertius, *Lives of Eminent Philosophers* (Cambridge, Mass., and London: Harvard University Press and William Heinemann, Loeb Classical Library, 1925), Vol. II, Book VIII, ch. 5, pp. 396-397: "Of things invisible, as of mortal things, only the gods have certain knowledge; but to us, as men, only inference from evidence is possible (*ōs d' antropois tekmairestai*)."

31. Aristotle, *Prior Analytics*, Book II, 27, 70^{b}1, trans., A.J. Jenkinson, in *The Complete Works of Aristotle*, The Revised Oxford Translation, ed., Jonathan Barnes (Princeton, Princeton University Press/Bollingen Series LXXI 2, 1984), Vol. One, p. 113; *Rhetoric*, I, 2, 1357^{b}1-24, trans., W. Rhys Roberts, *The Complete Works of Aristotle*, Vol. Two, pp. 2157-2158. On this distinction, see R. Barthes, *L'aventure sémiologique* (Paris: Seuil, "Points," 1985), pp. 134-135: *tekmērion*, certain indication; *eikos*, likely; *sēmeion*, sign. See also C. Ginzburg, "Aristote et l'histoire, encore une fois," pp. 47-50, on Aristotle's relation to Thucydides in the use of *tekmērion*.

32. See *Œdipe-Roi*, 710, p. 166: (Jocasta): "In a few words I will give you proof (*sēmeia*) [that no mortal understands anything of the divinatory art]"; *Oedipus the King*, p. 695: "Of that I'll show you a short proof [that human beings have no part in the craft of prophecy]"; 1059, Fr., p. 179: (Oedipus) "It is not admissible that with such indications (*indices, sēmeia*) I do not discover my birth"; Eng., p. 57: "With such clues I could not fail to bring my birth to light." On the absence of a distinction between the two words, *tekmērion* and *sēmeion* before Aristotle, see C. Ginzburg, "Aristote et l'histoire, encore une fois," p. 49, and M.F. Burnyeat, "The Origins of Non-Deductive Inference," in J. Barnes et al., eds., *Science and Speculation: studies in Hellenistic theory and practice* (Cambridge: Cambridge University Press, 1982), p. 196, note 10.

33. *Œdipe-Roi*, 851-858, pp. 171-172; *Oedipus the King*, p. 47. It is later, at 916, Fr., p. 174, that Jocasta, addressing the city leaders, tells them: "Oedipus does not interpret (*tekmairetai*) the

new oracles by the old, like a man of sense"; Eng., p. 49: "For Oedipus ... not conjecturing, like a man of sense, what will be from what was ...."

34. This expression does not appear in the text. However, see ibid., 923, Fr., p. 174: (Jocasta); Eng., p. 49: "he's pilot of our ship." See below, note 63.

35. Ibid., 60-61, Fr., p. 143; Eng., p. 13.

36. Ibid., 137-141, Fr., p. 146: "It is not for distant friends, it is for myself that I will remove this pollution. Whoever killed this king might well want to take vengeance on myself with the same hand: so in coming to his aid I serve my own cause"; Eng., pp. 16-17: "For when I drive pollution from the land I will not serve a distant friends' advantage, but act in my own interest. Whoever he was that killed the king may readily wish to dispatch me with his murderous hand; so helping the dead king I help myself."

37. Ibid., 249-251, Fr., p. 150; Eng., p. 20.

38. Ibid., 380-403, Fr., p. 155; Eng., pp. 27-28.

39. Ibid., 532-538 and 642-643, Fr., p. 160 and p. 164; Eng., p. 33 and p. 38.

40. Ibid., 1076-1085, Fr., p. 180; Eng., p. 58.

41. Ibid., 1516, Fr., p. 196; Eng., p. 75.

42. Ibid., 1522-1523, Fr., ibid.: "Cease wanting always to be the master (kratein), for what your earlier victories (kai gar akratēsas) have brought you have not always followed you in life." This retort follows the following exchange: "Oedipus: Take me away then from here.—Creon: Come then and leave your children.—Oedipus: Do not take them from me, I beg you"; Eng., pp. 75-76: "Oedipus: Now lead me away from here.—Creon: Let go the children, then, and come."—"Oedipus: Do not take them from me.—Creon: Do not seek to be master in everything, for the things you mastered did not follow you throughout your life."

43. See Le savoir d'Œdipe, p. 235; Oedipal Knowledge, p. 240: "And this same word is immediately repeated twice: first by Creon in the following line in a play on words (akratēsas [1523] in which are heard both the summits (akras) to which he has risen and the power of which he has been stripped, a-kratein); and then by the Chorus two lines further on ...."

44. Œdipe-Roi, 1524-1527, pp. 196-197: "... see this Oedipus, who figured out the famous riddles. The powerful man (kratistos ēn anēr), what citizen did not look on him without envy for his prosperity? And now into what a terrible flood of misfortune he has rushed headlong!"; Oedipus the King, p. 76: "... behold this Oedipus,—him who knew the famous riddles and was a man most masterful; not a citizen who did not look with envy on his lot—see him now and see the breakers of misfortune swallow him!"

45. Ibid., 14, Fr., p. 141; Eng., p. 11.

46. Ibid., 863-910, Fr., pp. 172-173; Eng., pp. 47-49.

47. Ibid., 873, Fr., p. 172: "Pride engenders the tyrant (Ubris phuteuei turannon)"; Eng., p. 48: "Insolence breeds the tyrant."

48. Ibid., 878, Fr., ibid.; Eng., ibid.

49. Ibid., 867-868, Fr., ibid.; Eng., ibid.

50. Ibid., 689-696, Fr., pp. 40-41; Eng., pp. 40-41.

51. The democracy established in Athens at the end of the sixth century followed the tyranny of Peisistratus and his sons, overthrown by the intervention of Sparta. After the Peloponnesian War (431-404), Sparta imposed on Athens the oligarchic Council of Thirty, also called the "Thirty tyrants." Democracy was reestablished in 403.

52. Œdipe-Roi, 1083, p. 180; Oedipus the King, p, 58: "the months, my brothers, marked me, now as small, and now again as mighty."

53. Ibid., 1200-1201, Fr. p. 185; Eng., p. 64.

54. Ibid., 39 and 51, Fr., p. 142 and p. 143; Eng., p. 12.

55. Solon (638 c. to 558 c. B.C.E.), Athenian legislator. Foucault had already made this comparison in "Le savoir d'Œdipe," p. 236; "Oedipal Knowledge," pp. 241-242. With regard to the description of Solon as "law-giver (nomothetēs) and sort of tyrant," see Leçons sur la Volonté de savoir, lecture of 17 February 1971, p. 123; Lectures on the Will to Know, p. 129, where Foucault, tracing the political transformations of the seventh and sixth centuries, writes: "... often too tyranny, having come to its end, led to the organization of a written law and sometimes served as intermediary [to democracy] (Solon, Peisistratus, Cleisthenes)." See too ibid., lecture of 3 March 1971, Fr. pp. 150-154; Eng., pp. 157-163, on "the eunomia of Solon."

56. Œdipe-Roi, 510, p. 159: "It is on good proof that he made himself loved by the city"; Oedipus the king, p. 32: "and all of us saw his wisdom and in that test he saved the city. So he will not be condemned by my mind."

57. Ibid., 690-695, Fr., p. 166; Eng., p. 40.
58. Ibid., 1196-1200, Fr., pp. 184-185; Eng., p. 64.
59. Ibid., 630, Fr., p. 163; Eng., p. 38.
60. Ibid., 443, Fr., p. 157; Eng., p. 29.
61. Ibid., 628, Fr., p. 163; Eng., p. 37.
62. See ibid., 865-871, Fr., p. 172; Eng., p. 48.
63. On this classical metaphor of government, see 56 (the city compared to a ship) and 922-923, Fr., p. 174: (Jocasta) "we are all afraid, like sailors who see the pilot of the ship panic-stricken"; Eng., p. 49: "… we are all afraid; he's the pilot of our ship and he is frightened." See above, note 34.
64. On the relation of Oedipus to *tuchē*, see 1080, Fr., p. 180: "I consider myself the son of beneficent Fortune"; Eng., p. 58: "I account myself a child of Fortune, beneficent Fortune." In *Le savoir d'Œdipe*, p. 243; *Oedipal Knowledge*, p. 248-249, Foucault notes that "it is no doubt Jocasta who expresses best the tyrant's relation [to] his knowledge and destiny, when she says that what controls (*kratei*) man are the things of fate (*ta tēs tukhēs*); and that what is best, strongest (*kratiston*), is to live as one has the power to do (*opōs dunaito tis*). Interplay between the force of *Tukhē* and the power of man: such is the lot of the one who considers the signs of divination and the terror they convey to be nothing (977-983)."
65. See above, note 27.
66. See *Le savoir d'Œdipe*, p. 252, note 20 by D. Defert; *Oedipal Knowledge*, p. 259, note 42: "Herodotus (I, 207-208) employs *gnōmē* to refer to counsel given in political deliberations."

four

30 JANUARY 1980

> Oedipus the King *(end): why Oedipus is not punished.* ∽
> *Reminder of the general problem studied this year: the genesis
> of the relations between government of men, manifestation of the
> truth, and salvation. Rejection of analysis in terms of ideology.
> Theoretical work as movement of continuous displacement. New
> explanation of the approach adopted: posing the question of the
> relationship the subject maintains with the truth on the basis of his
> relationship to power. At the basis of this approach, an attitude
> of systematic suspicion with regard to power: the non-necessity of
> all power whatever it may be. Difference from anarchism. An
> anarcheology of knowledge. Return to the analyses of (a) mad-
> ness, (b) crime and punishment.* ∽ *The double sense of the word
> "subject" in a power relationship and in manifestation of truth.
> The notion of truth act and the different modes of insertion of the
> subject (operator, witness, object) in the procedure of alethurgy.* ∽
> *Field of research: early Christianity. Perspective of this course: to
> study it not from the point of view of its dogmatic system, but from
> the point of view of truth acts. Tension in Christianity between
> two regimes of truth: that of faith and that of confession (*aveu*).
> Between Oedipus and Christianity, examination of alethurgy of
> the fault in Philo of Alexandria.*

[...] TWO OR THREE ELEMENTARY and simple lessons. First lesson: for some, and in particular for kings, it is no doubt preferable not
to know who they are, where they come from, what they have done

with their own hands, and what they have seen with their own eyes; preferable maybe for kings, but the fact remains that power, power in general, could not be exercised if truth were not manifested. Oedipus would certainly have been happier if he had continued not knowing until the end of his life, but as you know, there could be no peace for Thebes so long as the truth had not come out. So, manifestation of the truth, manifestation of alethurgy is necessary for the exercise of power.

Second lesson: in these procedures that enable the truth to come out, of course, the oracles say a lot and the seers know a lot about it. Both are capable of telling the truth, but, as you have seen, to a certain extent this truth remains insufficient. The gods and those who speak for them are quite capable of binding the destiny of men, and yet they are power-less to carry out completely the alethurgy that is required for order to reign in cities and power to be exercised properly. To a certain extent they remain powerless. To a certain extent what they say is not listened to and remains without effect, without credibility. And Sophocles' play shows that the manifestation of the truth will be [complete],* the circle of alethurgy will be closed only when it has passed through individuals who can say "I," when it has passed through the eyes, hands, memory, testimony, and affirmation of men who say: I was there, I saw, I did, I gave with my own hand, I received into my own hands. So, without what could be called this point of subjectivation in the general procedure and overall cycle of alethurgy, the manifestation of the truth would remain incomplete.

The third lesson, which is also very simple and elementary, is that, as a result, the manifestation of the truth, the alethurgic procedure, does much more than make known what was unknown, than reveal what was hidden. Because for all that, in the conclusion of Oedipus and maybe, we could say, in the interstice between *Oedipus the King* and *Oedipus at Colonus*, there is something a little paradoxical.[1] This is that when all is said and done there is a remainder in this story of Oedipus: the remain-der is Oedipus, or rather it is his punishment, that is to say, that he is not punished. We should not forget that at the beginning of the play when Creon returns with the oracle from Delphi, he says clearly that the oracle demands that the person who is the source of the defilement that

---

* Inaudible word.

brought plague to Thebes be punished. And two types of punishment
are indicated quite explicitly in the oracle: he must either be driven out
or be killed. "The guilty," says the oracle, "must be banished or pay for
murder with their murder."[2] Now, as you are well aware, Oedipus is
not put to death and he is not even exiled. He demands it, but he suffers neither of the two punishments. He is blinded, of course, and you
will say that he blinded himself in self-punishment, but this is not the
case, for after blinding himself he does not say that he did so to punish
himself, but because, for him, the light, his sight, and the spectacle of
his crime were incompatible.[3] And he considers himself so little punished that precisely after this he raises the question of punishment and
says to Creon: "Exile me, I know the god ordered that I be killed, but
I would like to be exiled or to withdraw on Cithaeron."[4] But Oedipus
remains at Thebes. At the end of the play we see the palace doors shut
behind him, and there he will remain, in the palace, in the very place of
his defilement, at the heart of Thebes, at the center of this town whose
destruction his crime had caused—or failed to cause—and yet Thebes
is freed and the plague has disappeared. That is to say, it is not, as the
oracle demanded, the exile, suppression, elimination, or murder of the
guilty person that was needed to liberate Thebes. The necessary and sufficient condition for the liberation of Thebes was that the truth come
out. The history of the liberation of Thebes is simply an effect of light,
and nothing more. Things come to light and the plague disappears and
order is reestablished. The alethurgy in itself—quite apart from the pure
and simple effects of knowledge that would have made it possible to
determine who was guilty and then, as a result, punish him—goes well
beyond the pure and simple effects of useful knowledge. We do not just
need the truth in order to discover a guilty person whom we will then
be able to punish. It suffices that the truth be shown, that it be shown
in its ritual, in its appropriate procedures, its regulated alethurgy, for
the problem of punishment no longer to be posed and for Thebes to be
liberated.

*   *   *

These then are the three themes that I wanted to emphasize: [first],
the relationship between manifestation of truth and exercise of power;
second, the importance and necessity for this exercise of power of a

truth that manifests itself, at least in certain of its points, but absolutely indispensably in the form of subjectivity; finally, third, the effect of the manifestation of this truth in the form of subjectivity, the effect of this manifestation beyond, let's say, immediately utilitarian relations of knowledge. Alethurgy, the manifestation of the truth, is much more than making known.

In the following lectures I would like to take up these three themes again a bit more tightly and a bit better than by this pure and simple identification. Once again, the question I would like to raise is this: how is it that, in our type of society, power cannot be exercised without truth having to manifest itself, and manifest itself in the form of subjectivity, and without, on the other hand, an expectation of effects of this manifestation of the truth in the form of subjectivity that go beyond the realm of knowledge, effects that belong to the realm of the salvation and deliverance of each and all? Generally speaking, the themes I would like to take up this year [are] these: how have the relations between the government of men, the manifestation of the truth in the form of subjectivity, and the salvation of each and all been established in our civilization?

I am well aware that this problem or these themes are familiar and hackneyed. After all, there are quite respectable analyses in terms of ideology that have a ready-made answer for these problems and explain that if, in fact, the exercise of power, the manifestation of the truth in the form of subjectivity, and salvation for all and each are linked, it is quite simply through the effects peculiar to what one calls an "ideology." Roughly speaking, this amounts to saying: inasmuch as men worry more about salvation in the other world than about what happens down here, inasmuch as they want to be saved, they remain quiet and peaceful and it is easier to govern them. The government of men by that truth they effectuate in themselves and that is good (*salutaire*) for them, in the strong sense, would reside precisely in those effects peculiar to what we call "ideology." Now I have to say that the idea that the more men are concerned for their salvation in the hereafter the easier it is to govern them down here on earth does not seem to me to be in proper accord with a number of little things we are familiar with in the ancient or recent history of relations between revolution and religion. So maybe the problem is not so simple and maybe we should not conduct the analysis from the angle of analyses in terms of ideology.

I come back once again to what I am constantly returning to, that is to say, the rejection of analysis in terms of ideology, the rejection of the analysis of men's thought, behavior, and knowledge in terms of ideology. I have insisted on this rejection of ideological analysis many times. I have returned to it, I think, in practically all of the annual courses I have given (it must be for at least nine or ten years now),[5] and even so I would like to return to it again, for a very simple reason. This is that each time I return to it I think, well anyway I would like, I hope to have carried out a very slight displacement. And this leads me to something like a sort of secret, which is that for me theoretical work—and I am not in any way saying this out of pride or vanity, but rather with a profound sense of my inability—does not consist in in establishing and fixing the set of positions on which I would stand and the supposedly coherent link between which would form a system. My problem, or the only theoretical work that I feel is possible for me, is leaving the trace, in the most intelligible outline possible, of the movements by which I am no longer at the place where I was earlier. Hence, if you like, this constant need, or necessity, or desire to plot, so to speak, the points of passage at which each displacement risks resulting in the modification, if not of the whole curve, then at least of the way in which it can be read and grasped in terms of its possible intelligibility. This plotting, consequently, should never be read as the plan of a permanent structure. It should not be subject to the same requirements as those imposed on a plan. Once again, it is a matter of a line of displacement, that is to say not of a line of a theoretical structure, but of the displacement by which my theoretical positions continually change. After all, there are quite a few negative theologies; let's say that I am a negative theorist.

So, a new course, a new line. And once more we return to the same themes, hoping for displacement and the new form of intelligibility. So, what does this rejection of analysis in terms of ideology mean?[*] There is what I think is a traditional, old, and furthermore perfectly respectable way of posing the philosophical-political question (inasmuch as there may be a philosophy that is not philosophical-political) that consists in this: when the subject voluntarily submits to the bond of the truth,

---

* M.F. adds: This year we could say the following.

in a relationship of knowledge (*connaissance*), that is to say, when, after providing himself with its foundations, instruments, and justification, the subject claims to deliver a discourse of truth, what can he say about, or for, or against the power to which he is involuntarily subject? In other words, what can the voluntary bond with the truth say about the involuntary bond that ties us and subjects us to power? I think this is the traditional way of posing the philosophical-political question. But I think we can also try to take the same problem the other way round. Not by positing first of all the right of access to the truth, not by establishing first of all this voluntary and as it were contractual bond with the truth, but by posing first of all the question of power in the following way: what does the systematic, voluntary, theoretical and practical questioning of power have to say about the subject of knowledge and about the bond with the truth by which, involuntarily, this subject is held? In other words, it is no longer a matter of saying: given the bond tying me voluntarily to the truth, what can I say about power? But, given my desire, decision, and effort to break the bond that binds me to power, what then is the situation with regard to the subject of knowledge and the truth? It is not the critique of representations in terms of truth or error, truth or falsity, ideology or science, rationality or irrationality that should serve as indicator for defining the legitimacy or denouncing the illegitimacy of power. It is the movement of freeing oneself from power that should serve as revealer in the transformations of the subject and the relation the subject maintains with the truth.

You can see that this form of analysis—like any other analysis of this type, moreover, and like the opposite analysis—rests more on a standpoint than a thesis. But this is not exactly the standpoint of, say, the *epochē*, of skepticism, of the suspension of all certainties or of all thetic positions of the truth. It is an attitude that consists, first, in thinking that no power goes without saying, that no power, of whatever kind, is obvious or inevitable, and that consequently no power warrants being taken for granted. Power has no intrinsic legitimacy. On the basis of this position, the approach consists in wondering, that being the case, what of the subject and relations of knowledge do we dispense with when we consider no power to be founded either by right or necessity, that all power only ever rests on the contingency and fragility of a history, that the social contract is a bluff and civil society a children's story, [and]

that there is no universal, immediate, and obvious right that can everywhere and always support any kind of relation of power. Let us say that
if the great philosophical approach consists in establishing a methodical
doubt that suspends every certainty, the small lateral approach on the
opposite track that I am proposing consists in trying to bring into play
in a systematic way, not the suspension of every certainty, but the non-
necessity of all power of whatever kind.

You will tell me: there you are, this is anarchy; it's anarchism. To
which I shall reply: I don't quite see why the words "anarchy" or "anarchism" are so pejorative that the mere fact of employing them counts
as a triumphant critical discourse. And second, I think there is even so
a certain difference. If we define, very roughly—and I would be quite
prepared moreover to discuss or come back to these definition, which
I know are very approximate—in any case, if we define anarchy by two
things—first, the thesis that power is essentially bad, and second, the
project of a society in which every relation of power is to be abolished,
nullified—you can see that what I am proposing and talking about is
clearly different. First, it is not a question of having in view, at the
end of a project, a society without power relations. It is rather a matter of putting non-power or the non-acceptability of power, not at the
end of the enterprise, but rather at the beginning of the work, in the
form of a questioning of all the ways in which power is in actual fact
accepted. Second, it is not a question of saying all power is bad, but
of starting from the point that no power whatsoever is acceptable by
right and absolutely and definitively inevitable. You can see therefore
that there is certainly some kind of relation between what is roughly
called anarchy or anarchism and the methods I employ, but that the
differences are equally clear. In other words, the position I adopt does
not absolutely exclude anarchy—and after all, once again, why would
anarchy be so condemnable? Maybe it is automatically condemned only
by those who assume that there must always, inevitably, essentially be
something like acceptable power. So the position I am proposing does
not exclude anarchy, but you can see that in no way does it entail it, that
it does not cover the same field, and is not identified with it. It is a matter of a theoretical-practical standpoint concerning the non-necessity of
all power, and so as to distinguish this theoretical-practical position on
the non-necessity of power as a principle of intelligibility of knowledge

itself, instead of employing the word "anarchy" or "anarchism," which would not be appropriate, I shall make a play on words, since this is currently not very fashionable,* let's again go a little against the trend and engage in word games (which are, moreover—well, I recognize that mine are very bad). So I will say that what I am proposing is rather a sort of anarcheology.

(Incidentally, having said this, if you like to read some of the interesting philosophy books currently being published—there are not that many—, rather than those making more noise, I recommend Feyerabend's book on science, which has just come out in Seuil.[6] No one is talking about it, but here is something interesting on the problem of anarchy and knowledge).

This is something of the meaning I give to an approach I have tried to [follow].† And to go back over things just a little—well, I am not going to endlessly recommence the same cycle—if you like, let us take the problem of the history and analysis of madness. What was at stake from the purely methodological point of view was the following. Whereas an analysis in terms of ideology would have consisted in asking: given the reality of madness—universalist position—and given human nature, the essence of man, of non-alienated man, man's fundamental freedom—humanist position—on the basis of these universalist and humanist positions, what are the grounds and conditions governing the system of representation that has led to a practice of confinement with its well-known alienating effects and need for reform. This would have constituted a, let's say, ideological type of study. The anarcheological type of study, on the other hand, consisted in taking the practice of confinement in its historical singularity, that is to say in its contingency, in the sense of its fragility, its essential non-necessity, which obviously does not mean (quite the opposite!) that there was no reason for it and is to be accepted as a brute fact. That the practice of confinement is intelligible implies that we can understand the at once perfectly intelligible but fragile fabric within which this practice came about. In other words, it was not a matter of starting from a universal that says: this is madness. It did not involve starting from a humanist position saying: this

---

* M.F. adds: they create a lot of problems.
† M.F.: carry out.

is human nature, the human essence, human freedom. Madness had to be taken as an *x* and the practice alone grasped, as if one did not know, and proceeding without knowing, what madness is. And from there it was a matter of seeing what type of relations of knowledge (*connaissance*) were founded by this practice itself, with their structuring and determining effects in the field of knowledge (*savoir*), of theory, medicine, and psychiatry, but also with their effects in the experience of the subject regarding the division of reason and unreason, whether or not the subject is thought to be ill. In other words, to the series: universal category—humanist position—ideological analysis and reform program, is opposed a series: refusal of universals[7] (I do not say nominalism for a host of reasons, the main one being that nominalism is a very specific and technical conception, practice, and philosophical method) so, refusal of universals—anti-humanist position—technological analysis of mechanisms of power and, instead of reform program: further extend points of non-acceptance.

In the same way, the problem with regard to crime and its punishment was not: given delinquency in our society, and given human nature, the human essence, is prison the best means to use and how can it be improved? The problem was: behind the self-evidence of an imprisonment that claims to be a both natural and rational physical sanction of crime, what was the singular, fragile, and contingent system of relations of power that served to support it and get it seen as acceptable, notwithstanding its inadequacy for its objectives, the inadequacy of its point of departure and of its point of arrival? So, rather than set up delinquency itself or man himself as measure of the prison and its possible reform, the question was how this practice of imprisonment, this practice of punishment in our societies, on the one hand modified the real practice of illegalities, but also constituted this doublet of legal subject and criminal man, subject of right and *homo criminalis*, in which our penal practice lost its way and still endlessly loses its way.

[After this] turn of the spiral on what has been done, let's now return to the question I would like to talk about this year: the government of men through the manifestation of truth in the form of subjectivity. Why, in what form, in a society like ours, is there such a deep bond between the exercise of power and the obligation for individuals to become themselves essential actors in the procedures of manifestation of the truth, in the procedures of alethurgy needed by power? What is the relationship between the fact of being subject in a relation of power and a subject through which, for which, and regarding which the truth is manifested? What is this double sense of the word "subject," subject in a relation of power, subject in a manifestation of truth?

To designate this insertion of the subject, of the subject as such, in the procedures of manifestation of the truth, in alethurgy, from now on I will use a word, an expression that the theologians of the Middle Ages frequently used with regard to the sacrament of penance. They distinguished three elements in the sacrament of penance: the part coming under contrition, *actus contritionis*; the part coming under satisfactions, that is to say the acts by which, as we say now, one does penance—this was the *actus satisfactionis*; and then, in the middle, there was that which concerned the formulation by the subject himself of the faults to which he attested having committed, and which the theologians called the *actus veritatis*, the act of truth.[8] Well, I will call truth act (*acte de vérité*) the part that falls to a subject in the procedures of alethurgy, the part that may be defined (1) by the subject's role as operator of the alethurgy, (2) by the subject's role as spectator of it, and (3) by the subject's role as the object itself of the alethurgy. In other words, in the procedure of manifestation of the truth the subject may be the active agent thanks to which the truth comes to light. Let's say, more or less, that in Greek sacrifice the priest who ritually performs a number of acts—cuts up the animal properly and shows what it is in the butchered animal that manifests the truth, or at any rate gives an answer to the question put and therefore responds to men's disquiet, uncertainty, or ignorance—is, inasmuch as he reveals the truth, its operator. He is nothing more than its operator, since he is not in question in the manifestation of truth, and although it is true that he is a spectator, the main spectators are those around him. Anyway, here, in the act by which, in the sacrificial ritual itself, he reveals that which provides an answer to ignorance, which makes known, the person carrying out the sacrifice is an operator of truth. Second, one may be inserted in the procedure of alethurgy as witness, that is to say, at certain points alethurgy may need individuals who say: yes, I saw, I was there, I remember, it is certain because it took place before my own eyes. This role of the individual as witness in the procedure of alethurgy is the second way of accomplishing the truth act. Finally, third, one may be inserted in the procedure of alethurgy and one may accomplish a truth act within this cycle when the truth one discovers through this procedure concerns oneself. We have there what we may call a reflexive truth act, and it is quite evident that the purest and also historically most important form of this reflexive form of the truth act is what we call confession (*l'aveu*), when someone can say: this is what I did, this is what took place in the depths of my conscience, these are the intentions I had, here is what, in the secret of my life or the secret of my heart, constituted my fault or my merit. At that point we have a truth act in which the subject is at once the actor of the alethurgy, since it is he who by his discourse reveals and brings into the light something that was in shadow and darkness. Second, he is its witness, since he can say: I know that it took place in my conscience and I saw it with the inner gaze that I focus on myself. And finally, third, he is its object, since it is a matter of him in his testimony and in the manifestation of truth he carries out. The term truth act may focus in fact on these three roles of actor, witness, or reflexive object, but more specifically, since what I would like to talk about is confession, when I say "truth act," I will not specify "reflexive truth act," and unless otherwise qualified the term will designate the reflexive truth act.

We have now more or less tightened up the problem: why and how does the exercise of power in our society, the exercise of power as government of men, demand not only acts of obedience and submission, but truth acts in which individuals who are subjects in the power relationship are also subjects as actors, spectator witnesses, or objects in manifestation of truth procedures? Why in this great system of relations of power has a regime of truth developed indexed to subjectivity? Why does power require (and for thousands of years in our societies, has required) individuals to say not only, "here I am, me who obeys," but in addition, "this is what I am, me who obeys, this is who I am, this is what I have seen, this is what I have done"?

Such then is the problem. It goes without saying—I think the way in which I have specified the subject indicates this sufficiently—that I will try to tighten up a bit this historical problem of the formation of a relation between the government of men and truth acts, well, reflexive truth acts, by approaching it from the angle of Christianity and early Christianity.

Generally, when the question of the government of men and regime of truth is raised with regard to Christianity, we think of the system of Christian dogma, that is to say, of the fact that, compared with the ancient Greek, Hellenistic, and Roman world, Christianity actually introduced a regime of truth that is at once very singular, very new, and also quite paradoxical. It is, of course, a regime of truth constituted by a body of doctrine that, [on the one hand,] depends upon a permanent reference to a text and, on the other hand, refers to an institution that is also permanent, and that changes and maintains something as enigmatic as tradition. So, a body of doctrine, but also truth acts required of the faithful, non-reflexive truth acts, but truth acts in the form of beliefs, acts of faith, professions of faith. When we speak of government of men and regime of truth in Christianity we are generally thinking of this side of things; the system of dogma and faith, dogma and belief. If we foreground this side of things it is for the reasons I was just talking about, namely preference for analysis in [terms]* of ideology, since it is precisely not in terms of truth acts (that is to say, the perspective of acts of faith) that the problem is analyzed, but in terms of the ideological nature of the content of the dogma and beliefs.†

Now, given the perspective I am adopting, in the first place you will understand that I will not privilege the content of beliefs in the regime of truth, but rather the truth act itself, and [second], it is not so much truth acts in the form of acts of faith that I would like to study as other acts that define, I think, or that punctuate, that articulate another regime of truth present in Christianity that is less defined by the act of faith or profession of faith in a dogmatic content revealed in a text and carried on in an institutionalized tradition. I would like to talk about another regime of truth: this is a regime defined by the obligation for individuals to have a continuous relationship to themselves of knowledge, their obligation to discover, deep within themselves, secrets that elude them, their obligation, finally, to manifest these secret and individual truths by acts that have specific, liberating effects that go well beyond the effects of knowledge. In other words, there is a whole regime of truth in Christianity that is not so much organized around the truth act as

---

* M.F.: form.
† M.F. adds: which will...[one or two inaudible words].

act of faith, but around the truth act as act of confession. The regimes of faith and confession in Christianity are very different, since what is involved in the case of faith is adherence to an inviolable and revealed truth in which the role of the individual, and therefore of the truth act, the point of subjectivation is essentially in accepting this content and in agreeing to demonstrate that one accepts it—this is the meaning of the profession of faith, of the act of profession of faith—whereas in the other case, in confession, it is not at all a matter of adhering to a content of truth, but of exploring individual secrets, and of exploring them end-lessly. We can say, more or less, from the point of view that interests us here at any rate, that Christianity has been constantly traversed by this extraordinary tension between the two regimes of truth, the regime of faith and the regime of confession.

That there has been profound tension does not mean that there have been two heterogeneous and unrelated regimes. After all, we should not forget that the notion of confession (*confession*), the meaning of the word "confession" in the Latin Church, is precisely at the fork, as it were, of these two regimes, since in the Latin of the Church Fathers, practically up to the seventh and eighth century, the confessor, the word "*confessor*" refers to someone who is prepared to make the profession of faith right to the end, that is to say to the point of risking death.[9] And gradually, connected up to this meaning of "confessor" is the other meaning of the word "confession," in the sense of confession of self (*aveu*). Confession (*confession*) becomes confession of self (*aveu*), and the *confessor* is the one who organizes, regulates, and ritualizes this confession of self and draws from it the effects that much later, from the twelfth century, will become sacramental effects. So, Christianity really is, at bottom, essentially, the religion of confession, to the extent that confession (*confession*) is the hinge of the regime of faith and the regime of confession of self, and, seen from this perspective, Christianity is underpinned by two regimes of truth.

Second, there is further proof that the two regimes of truth, that of faith and that of confession of self (*aveu*), are not two heterogeneous and incompatible elements, but deeply and fundamentally related, in the fact that, in practice, every development of one of the two regimes has been accompanied by the development or reorganization of the other. After all, if the practice of confession, in the sense of confession of self (*aveu*), of penitential confession, was so strongly developed from the end of the second to the fifth century, it was precisely to the extent that there was the problem of heresy, that is to say, of the definition of what the dogmatic content of the act of faith must be, and it is indeed in this settling of accounts with heresy (this too being a notion that was utterly foreign to the Greco-Roman world), therefore in the definition of the dogmatic content of the faith, that the practices of confession of self are developed. [...] When the practice of penitential confession, of penitential confession of self, is codified in an extremely juridical manner, and for several centuries, it was precisely at a time when Christianity was once again confronted with heresy—the Cathar heresy—and it was in the struggle against this heresy that the practice of confession also developed. So, you see, there is a constant correlation between the two meanings of the word "confession (*confession*)" and the reorganizations that both of them are induced to develop.

Finally, we can say that the major fault line in Christianity in the Renaissance, that is to say the division between Catholicism and Protestantism was still around this fundamental problem. What, ultimately, was Protestantism, if not a certain way of taking up the act of faith as adherence to a dogmatic content in the form of a subjectivity that enables the individual to discover this same content in himself, deep within himself, according to the law and testimony of his conscience. In other words, it is as operator of truth, as actor, witness, and object of the truth act that the individual discovers deep within himself what is to be the law and rule of his belief and act of faith. In Protestantism* we have a certain way of linking the regime of avowal and the regime of truth that precisely enables Protestantism to reduce the institutional and sacramental practice of penitential avowal, even to the extent of nullifying it, since precisely avowal and faith come together again in [a type]† of truth act in which adherence to the dogmatic content has the same form as the relation of self to self in subjectivity exploring itself.‡

---

* M.F. adds: a new way of linking to each other, completely differently from the old way, the relation (well, the Protestants are not so different from the old, but it doesn't matter ...).
† M.F.: a form.
‡ M.F. adds: So, two regimes of truth and, and—why am I telling you this? [a period of hesitation]. I no longer know. It doesn't matter, yes, well, it was to tell you that it is about avowal that I would like to talk to you, of that aspect of Christianity through which, alongside and intertwining with the regime of truth typical of the dogma and faith, there is this other regime of truth that defines and imposes a certain type of relation of self to self.

Of course, when I say that with Christianity an extremely complex, rich, dense, and new regime of truth appears in the Hellenistic and Roman world I am saying something that is both banal and not entirely true. Just as a bridge, an indication almost without explanation, inasmuch as things are clear, I would like to quote you a passage from Philo of Alexandria that seems to me quite a good reference point between Oedipus, about whom I spoke last week, and the Christian practices I will talk about in the weeks to come. So, Philo of Alexandria lived at the time of the beginnings of Christianity and was not a Christian himself but [at the confluence]* of Hebraic and Greek culture. In *De somniis*, the treatise on dreams, in the first book, chapter 15,[10] Philo stops for a moment on a passage from the Bible, which he found in Numbers, 25, 1-4, in which we see the Hebrew people giving themselves over to idolatrous practices and worshipping the god Baal. So the Hebrews, led by their concupiscence,† start to worship the god Baal, offering him sacrifices and eating the sacrificial meat, which is, of course, the absolute sin against God and his commandments. Seeing this, the Eternal, of course, gets angry, flares up against Israel and turns to Moses. What does he say to Moses? He says: "Assemble all the chiefs of the people, hang the guilty before the Eternal facing the sun, that the Eternal's anger turn away from Israel."[11] Being utterly incompetent, I am not able to tell you what commentary, analysis, or explanation could be [given] of this text within Hebraic culture. Let's say anyway that the wholly naive and superficial reading that we may make is nonetheless relatively clear: it is the entire people of Israel who, moved by concupiscence, sacrifice to Baal and offer him animals and eat them; the entire people is guilty. In his anger, God tells Moses to take the chiefs, to punish those of them who are guilty, and as a result God's anger will be softened and he won't have to punish the people. In other words: the sin of all and God's anger against all the people; separation of the chiefs from the people; holding the chiefs (or some of them) to be guilty, they are to be hung facing the sun and in this way the anger of the Eternal will turn away from Israel. Now Philo's text is utterly strange because it comments on the text saying: We have here the idea that conscience has to accept that,

---

* M.F.: on the borders [but he hesitates on the end of the word].
† M.F. adds: I no longer remember exactly, well good, led by...

whatever happens, it will never escape God's gaze. Even if we think the sin is hidden, even if we commit it in the most secret part of ourselves, we must realize that God sees all and that we will never escape his gaze. On the other hand, if conscience, says Philo—still commenting on the text and saying that what he is saying is the very meaning of the text— instead of hiding in the deepest recesses of itself, agrees to open itself and, he says in very beautiful expression, "unravel the folds in which it hid its actions," if it accepts then to lay the sin it has committed before it and "place it under the eyes of the universal inspector, as in the light of the sun," if then conscience "declares that it repents of its past errors of judgment, the fruit of thoughtlessness; if it recognizes that nothing is invisible to God, that he knows and sees all, not only accomplished actions but the numberless crowd of projected actions," then and by the sole fact of having unfolded the folds within which it hid itself, by the sole fact of having displayed its sins, by the sole fact of having brought them into the full light, so it will be purified: "It will be purified and amended, and it will have appeased the impending and well-grounded wrath of the dispenser of justice. But for this the soul must open itself to repentance, *metanoia*, younger brother of perfect innocence."[12]

You can see that this commentary is really both very interesting and paradoxical, and interesting because paradoxical, due to all its distortions of the Biblical text, which, once again, said: the people have sinned, God is angry, he orders the chiefs to be punished, and this pacifies his anger. And this is so clear in the text that in the following paragraph, in order to redouble as it were this mechanism, we see a Hebrew, I know longer know who, accompanied by an idolatrous woman, worshipper of Baal, and another Hebrew, faithful to the law of Moses, kills both of them, the man and the woman, as a result of which God's anger is pacified.[13] So it really is this mechanism between the sin of all and the responsibility of some, between punishment of an individual sin and forgiveness granted to all, that underlies the Biblical text. Philo says something else entirely. He says: The Biblical text shows that if you do not hide your sins, if you acknowledge them, set them out before your eyes, bring them out into the open, you will be forgiven. What is Philo's basis for saying this? It is a single word of the text, the small phrase in which the Eternal, addressing Moses, tells him to: "Assemble all the chiefs of the people, hang the guilty before the Eternal facing the sun." He hangs his whole commentary on: "facing the sun."[14] In fact, the passage I am quoting is from *De somniis*, chapter 15, where precisely he is attempting to discover the different allegorical meanings of the sun in the Bible. And it is on this basis that he completely re-jigs the Bible story. He completely omits the real punishment of the chiefs, one of whom is well and truly hung and another is killed by a spear. He completely omits the punishment and proceeds as if solely coming into the sunlight sufficed for the sin, first, to escape judgment, second, escape punishment, and third, be entirely and completely purified. Solely coming into the sunlight turns God's anger away. In other words, according to Philo, commenting on this text on the basis of the single element of this phrase, it is the force of illumination in itself, the effect of light, that is to say, the alethurgy of the sin itself, the alethurgy carried out by the sinner, actor of the sin, actor of the alethurgy, witness of the sin, witness of the alethurgy and taking himself as the object itself of this manifestation, that constitutes the mechanism by which the Eternal's forgiveness is granted.

Of course, there is no direct or indirect relation between this text and that of Oedipus I talked about last week. But you see that we find again this theme, much older than Christianity, which already traversed all Greek culture, which we can locate in Oedipus, which appears clearly in Philo and which then, through extremely complex elaborations, will be taken up again in Christianity, this same theme of the relationship between the sun and justice. And in relation to the Biblical text that showed that the non-punishment of the people was linked to the punishment of the chiefs, we can say that Philo Oedipalizes by making a collective alethurgy in which each can say, "this is what I myself have done, this is what I myself am, this is what I myself have seen," at once the principle of forgiveness, the purifying mechanism, and the basis for a return to the law and, as a consequence, the reestablishment of the just power of Moses and God.

Again, I have quoted this text to tell you that this theme of alethurgy or, if you like, of reflexive truth acts, the alethurgies by which individuals are called upon to manifest what they are themselves, at the heart of themselves, this alethurgy was, throughout ancient culture and continuously at least since the Greek fifth century, thought to be absolutely indispensable for the realization of power in its just and legitimate essence: no just and legitimate power if individuals do not tell the truth about themselves and in return it is enough, or at any rate it is necessary that individuals tell the truth about themselves for power actually to be reestablished according to laws that are those of the sun, of the sun that organizes the world and the sun that lights up the depths of conscience.

There you are. So then, next week we will move on to Christianity itself.

1. Sophocle, *Œdipe à Colone*, trans. P. Masqueray (Paris: Les Belles Lettres) vol. 2, 437-441, pp. 171-172, where, regretting having punished himself too much for his faults, Oedipus deplores having been forced into exile long after he blinded himself: "With time, when my pain had lost all its bitterness, when I had begun to understand that my rage, in its transport, had punished me too cruelly for my earlier faults, it was then that the city drove me from its territory, after so many years"; English translation by David Grene, *Oedipus at Colonus* in *Sophocles I*, ed. David Grene and Richmond Lattimore (Chicago and London: University of Chicago Press, 1991) p. 99: "But when time had gone by, and all the agony had mellowed, when I felt my agony had outrun itself in punishing my former sins—it was then and then the city drove me out—after all that time!"
2. *Œdipe roi*, 100-101, p. 144; *Oedipus the King*, p. 15.
3. Ibid., 1329-1338; Fr., pp. 189-190; Eng., p. 69.
4. Ibid., 1451-1453; Fr., p. 194; Eng., p. 73.
5. The critique of the analysis of power in terms of ideology was developed for the first time in the 1973 course, *La société punitive*, lecture of 28 March. Foucault subsequently returned to this subject only in the three following courses: "*Il faut défendre la société*," lecture of 14 January 1976, p. 30; "*Society Must Be Defended*," pp. 33-34; *Sécurité, territoire, population*, lecture of 18 January 1978, pp. 49-50; *Security, Territory, Population*, pp. 48-49; *Naissance de la biopolitique*, lectures of 10 January 1979, p. 21, and 17 January, p. 37; *The Birth of Biopolitics*, p. 19 and p. 35. For a clarification on this question, in addition to the recapitulation set out by Foucault in the first lecture of this course, see the "Entretien avec Michel Foucault," conducted by A. Fontana and P. Pasquino which first appeared in *Microfisica del potere* (Turin: Einaudi, 1977), then *DÉ, III*, p. 148/"Quarto," II, pp. 148; English translation as "Truth and Power" in *Essential Works of Foucault 1954-1984. Volume Three. Power*, pp. 119-120. See also P. Veyne, "L'idéologie selon Marx et selon Nietzsche," *Diogène*, 99 (July-September 1977) pp. 93-115.
6. P. Feyerabend, *Against Method. Revised Edition* (London: Verso, 1988). The author (1924-1994) supported an epistemological anarchism ("Science is an essentially anarchic enterprise," p. 9) according to which, every methodology having its limits, "there is only *one* principle that can be defended under *all* circumstances and in *all* stages of human development. It is the principle: *anything goes*" (p. 19). In an interview with G. Pessis-Pasternak, "Paul Feyerabend, anarchiste de la connaissance," *Le Monde Dimanche*, 28 February 1982, p. XI, he declared however: "I do not think I am an anarchist, although I have written an anarchistic book. Equally, although I have defended anarchistic epistemology, it is not obvious for all that that I like it. It seemed to me indispensable to defend it, since so many scientists, defenders of reason, are found on the other side. I wanted to prove that their arguments were not so irreducible as they claimed. What is the best way of demonstrating this? By defending an opposite point of view. But I never revealed my own opinion."
7. On this theoretical position, see *La volonté de savoir* (Paris: Gallimard, "Bibliothèque des Histoires," 1976) p. 123; English translation by Robert Hurley, *The History of Sexuality. Volume One: An Introduction* (New York and London: Random House/Allen Lane, 1978/1979), p. 93, regarding power: "One needs to be nominalistic, no doubt"; *Naissance de la biopolitique*, lecture of 10 January 1979, p. 5, and Course summary, p. 323; *The Birth of Biopolitics*, p. 3 and pp. 317-318. On "the need to test a nominalist method in history," Foucault refers to Paul Veyne: see by the latter, *Comment on écrit l'histoire* (Paris: Le Seuil, 1971, republished in "Points Histoire"), pp. 89-93, and "Foucault révolutionne l'histoire" (in ibid., pp. 207-211); English translation by Catherine Porter, "Foucault Revolutionizes History" in Arnold I. Davidson, ed., *Foucault and His Interlocutors* (Chicago and London: University of Chicago Press, 1997), pp. 150-154, and the article "Foucault" in D. Huisman, ed., *Dictionnaire des philosophes* (Paris: PUF, 1984) p. 943 (reprinted in *DÉ, IV*, p. 634/ "Quarto," II, p. 1453; English translation by Robert Hurley, "Foucault" in Michel Foucault, *Essential Works of Foucault 1954-1984. Volume Two: Aesthetics, Method, and Epistemology*, ed., James D. Faubion (New York: The New Press, 1998), p. 461: "a systematic skepticism toward all anthropological universals."
8. An expression employed by Tommaso de Vio (Thomas Cajetan) 1469-1534. In the *Dits et Écrits* the editor of the Course summary refers to *De Confessione quaestiones*, in *Quaestiones quodlibetales*, Paris, Regnault, 1530 (*DÉ, IV*, no. p. 125/"Quarto," II, p. 944; English translation by Robert Hurley, "On the Government of the Living" in *The Essential Works of Foucault 1954-1984. Volume One: Ethics, Subjectivity and Truth*, ed., Paul Rabinow (New York: New Press: 1997) p. 81 and p. 85). Foucault had read Cajetan very closely, as is shown by a bundle of 62 pages of notes in

his dossiers drawn principally from the *Peccatorum summula* (Douai, 1613). One of the pages contains the following notes, taken from the *De confessione* in *Opuscula Omnia*: "Is it necessary to confess completely hidden mortal sins? 1. Some say that it is not necessary, that human jurisdiction cannot deal with sins reserved for the divine jurisdiction. 2. Cajetan establishes the opposite. [a]. Divine wisdom does not exempt any sin from the '*materia judicii pœniten-tialis*,' it includes the sins whose first seat is the heart. [b]. Confession (*confession*), '*quae est actus veritatis*,' is an act of penance: the accused accuses himself of everything without excep-tion. [c]. The Lateran Council said that every individual, of both sexes, must confess '*peccata omnia*.'" The *Opuscula Omnia* having gone through many editions, we refer to the Lyon edition, apud haeredes Iacobi Iuntae, 1562, p. 72b (*De confessione quaestiones*, Quaestio II: "*An peccata mortalia totaliter occulta (ut sunt peccata in solo corde) sint necessario confitenda*"). The indissoluble unity of the acts of the penitent, contrition, confession, satisfaction (which are like its "mat-ter," distinct from its "form," contained in the words of absolution), emphasized by Cajetan several times, is clearly reaffirmed by the Council of Trent. See *Le saint concile de Trente œcumé-nique et général*, trans. abbé Chanut, 3rd ed. (Paris: S. Mabre-Cramoisy, 1686), 14th session (25 November 1551), ch. 3: "Of the parts and effects of the Sacrament of Penance": "The Acts of the Penitent himself, which are Contrition, Confession, and Satisfaction, are like the matter of this Sacrament; & these same Acts, as divine institution are required in the Penitent for the integrity of the Sacrament, and for the full and perfect remission of sins, are called also in this sense the parts of Penance." This division of the parts of penance is attested, from the twelfth century, in the *Sentences* of Pierre Lombard, IV, XVI, 1 (see PL 192, col. 877). It is taken up by Alexandre de Halès, *Glossa in quatuor libros Sententiarum*, IV, d. 16, t. 4, Quaracchi, 1957, p. 252 (cited by P. Adnès, "Pénitence," *Dictionnaire de spiritualité ascétique et mystique/DS*, 1984, col. 971) and vigorously reaffirmed by Thomas Aquinas, *Summa Theologica*, Part Three, Quaestio 90, 1-4.

9. On the semantic evolution of the word *confessio* in ecclesiastical Latin, see J. Ratzinger, "Originalität und Überlieferung in Augustins Begriff der '*Confessio*,'" *Revue des Études Augustiniennes*, 3 (1957), pp. 376-392. See especially pp. 380-381, on the first meaning of pro-fession of faith of martyrs before the tribunal (references to Tertullian, Cyprian, and Optato de Mileve), and p. 381 on *confessio*-exomologesis (reference to Tertullian, *De paenitentia*, 9, 2). See too A. Solignac, introduction to Saint Augustine, *Confessions* (Paris: Desclée de Brower, "Bibliothèque Augustinienne," 1962), Vol. XIII, p. 9, note 1, which refers to the previous article.

10. Philon d'Alexandrie, *De Somniis*, introd. and trans., P. Savinel (Paris: Cerf, "Œuvres de Philon d'Alexandrie," no. 19, 1962). The division into chapters does not correspond to the Savinel edition whose translation Foucault quotes. English translation by C.D. Yonge, *Philo of Alexandria* (Philo Judaeus), *On The Doctrine that Dreams Are Sent from God*, in *The Works of Philo Judaeus, The Contemporary of Josephus*, Vol. II (London: Henry G. Bohn, 1854).

11. Ibid., I, 89, p. 61: "Seize for me, God says, all the chiefs of the people and make an example of them for the people in the face of the sun: then the Lord's anger will turn away from Israel"; Eng., ibid., Book I, XV, p. 310: "Take all the chiefs of the people, and make an example of them unto the Lord in the face of the sun, and the anger of the Lord shall be turned from Israel." See *Numbers* 25, 4, trans. Robert Alter in, *The Five Books of Moses* (New York and London: W.W. Norton and Company, 2004), p. 818: "Take the chiefs of the people and impale them to the Lord before the sun, that the LORD's flaring wrath turn away from Israel."

12. Ibid., I, 91, Fr., p. 61: "If intelligence, having imagined that it could do wrong unbeknownst to God, saying to itself that it is impossible for Him to see everything, commits a sin in the most secret part of ourselves; if after this, either by itself or under the direction of someone, has the idea that it is impossible for something to escape God's gaze; if it opens itself and unravels the folds in which it hid all its actions so as to lay them out before it and place them under the eyes of the universal inspector as in the light of the sun; if it declares that it repents of its past errors of judgment, the fruit of thoughtlessness; if therefore it recognizes that nothing is invisible to God, that He knows and sees all, not only accomplished actions but the number-less crowd of projected actions, then, it is purified, amended, and as proof of belief it will have appeased the impending and well-grounded wrath of the dispenser of justice. But for this the soul must open itself to repentance, *metanoia*, younger brother of perfect innocence"; Eng., ibid., I, XV, p. 311: "Because, even if the mind, fancying that though it does wrong it can escape the notice of the Deity as not being able to see everything, should sin secretly and in dark places,

and should after that, either by reason of its own notions or through the suggestions of some one else, conceive that it is impossible that anything should be otherwise than clear to God, and should disclose itself and all its actions, and should bring them forward, as it were, out of the light of the sun, and display them to the governor of the universe, saying that it repents of the perverse conduct which it formerly exhibited when under the influence of foolish opinion for that nothing is indistinct before God, but all things are known and clear to him, not merely such as have been done, but even such are merely hoped or designed, by reason of the boundless character of his wisdom, it then is purified and benefited, and it propitiates the chastiser who was ready to punish it, namely, conscience, who was previously filled with just anger towards it, and who now admits repentance as the younger brother of perfect innocence and freedom from sin." Foucault returns at greater length to this notion of *metanoia* in the lecture of 13 February, below p. 000.

13. Numbers, 25, 6-8 (the Israelite who brings the idolatrous woman does not have a name).
14. *De somniis*, I, 89, p. 61; *On Dreams*, I, XV, p.310: "in the face of the sun."

five

6 FEBRUARY 1980

Studying Christianity from the point of view of regimes of truth. ↶ *What is a regime of truth? Reply to some objections. Consequences for the anarcheology of knowledge. Work to be put in the perspective of a history of the will to know.* ↶ *The act of confession* (aveu) *in Christianity. Confession* (confession), *in the modern sense, the result of a complex regime of truth at work since the second century C.E. The three practices around which the connection between manifestation of truth and remission of sins was organized:* (I) *baptism,* (II) *ecclesial or canonic penance,* (III) *examination of conscience.* ↶ (I) *Baptism in the first and second centuries; starting from Tertullian: from the idea of the two ways to that of original stain. The three matrices of moral thought in the West: the models of two ways, the fall, and the stain.*

SO, IN THE FOLLOWING lectures we will be studying Christianity—well, obviously, some very partial aspects of Christianity: considering these aspects not from the point of view of ideology, as I explained to you last week, but from the point of view of what I propose to call regimes of truth. By regime of truth I mean that which constrains individuals to a certain number of truth acts, in the sense I defined last week. A regime of truth is then that which constrains individuals to these truth acts, that which defines, determines the form of these acts and establishes their conditions of effectuation and specific effects. Roughly speaking, a regime of truth is that which determines the obligations of individuals with regard to procedures of manifestation of truth. What does the addition of this notion of obligation mean in relation to the notion of manifestation of truth? How does the truth oblige, in addition to the fact that it is manifested? Is it legitimate to suppose that the truth obliges on the other or on this side of these rules of manifestation? In other words, is it really legitimate to speak of regime of truth? What is the legitimacy, the foundation, the justification of a notion like that of regime of truth? I would like to talk a bit about this today, to start with at least.

Regime of truth. We speak of a political regime, in a way that may not be very clear or well-defined but is nevertheless relatively satisfactory, to designate in short the set of processes and institutions that more or less forcefully bind or oblige individuals to comply with decisions that emanate from a collective authority within the framework of territorial units in which this authority exercises a right of sovereignty. We may speak also of a penal regime, for example, here again to designate the set of processes and institutions by which individuals are bound, determined, or forced to submit to laws of general bearing. So, if that is the case, why not speak of regime of truth to designate the set of processes and institutions by which, under certain conditions and with certain effects, individuals are bound and obliged to make well-defined truth acts? Why not, after all, speak of truth obligations in the same way as there are political constraints or legal obligations? Are not obligations to do this or that and obligations to tell the truth, up to a point, of the same type or, at any rate, can we not transfer the notion of political regime and juridical regime to the problem of truth? It would involve truth obligations that impose acts of belief, professions of faith, or confessions with a purifying function.

There seems to be an immediate objection to the idea that there is a regime of truth and that regimes of truth can be described in their specificity. It will be said: you speak of regime of truth and when we ask for examples of this you take the example of Christianity and speak of acts of belief, profession of faith, confessions, and confession. That is to say, all the obligations you talk about, all these truth obligations you refer to, basically concern only non-truths, or else they are indifferent to the fact of whether or not it is a matter of truth, of true or false. In fact, what does this bond of obligation, which would bind individuals to the truth or oblige them to posit something as true, signify if not precisely that it is not truth or that [it] makes no difference whether it is true or false? To put it more clearly, I shall say the following: for there to be a truth obligation, or again for something like an obligation to be added to the intrinsic rules of manifestation of the truth, it must either involve precisely something that cannot be manifested or demonstrated by itself as true and that needs as it were this supplement of force, this *enforcement*, this supplement of vigor and obligation, of constraint, which means that one really will be obliged to posit it as true, although one knows that it may be false, or one is not sure that it is true, or it is not possible to demonstrate that it is true or false. After all, it does need something like an obligation to believe in the resurrection of the flesh, or the trinity, or things like that. In other words, in this type of act we are not dealing with a genuine truth obligation, but rather with what could be called the coercion of the non-true or the coercion and constraint of the unverifiable. Or again we could speak of regime of truth, of truth obligation, for procedures like, for example, teaching or information, which are exactly the same whether truths, lies, or errors are involved. Teaching is exactly the same, and the obligations it comprises are exactly the same, whether it is stupidities or truths being taught. So, in these cases we may well speak of obligation, but precisely to the extent that the truth as such is not involved.

On the other hand, when it is a question of truth, the notion of regime of truth becomes in a way superfluous, and the truth, at bottom, no doubt has no need of a regime, of a regime of obligation. There is no need to invoke a specific system of obligations whose role would be to impress the truth, to give it a force of constraint, to subject individuals to it, if it really is true. There is no need of a specific constraint for one to become the subject of truth, the operator in a manifestation of truth. The truth is sufficient unto itself for making its own law. And why? Quite simply because the coercive force of the truth resides within truth itself. In the search for and manifestation of the truth, what constrains me, what determines my role, what calls on me to do this or that, what obliges me in the procedure of the manifestation of the truth is the structure of truth itself. It is truth itself, and that's all. It is indeed self-evident, and the fundamental and founding characteristic of the self-evident in procedures of manifestation of the truth is the exact coincidence of the manifestation of truth and my obligation to recognize and posit it as true. By virtue of this, self-evidence is the best proof and demonstration that there is no need for a regime of truth to be added, as it were, to truth itself. Truth itself determines its regime, makes the law, and obliges me. It is true, and I submit to it. I submit to it, since it is true, and I submit inasmuch as it is true.

So it seems possible to keep, to uphold the notion of regime of truth only when something other than the truth is involved, or when it is a matter of things that are basically indifferent to truth or falsity, but when it is a question of truth itself there is no need for a regime of truth.

However, this objection to the idea of a regime of truth, and against the project of analyzing regimes of truth in general, does not seem entirely satisfactory to me. In actual fact, it seems to me that when we say that it is truth and truth alone that obliges in the truth we are in danger of failing to grasp what I think is an important distinction. We should not confuse two things. On the one hand there is the principle that truth is *index sui*,[1] that is to say, removing its specifically Spinozist signification, the principle that only the truth can legitimately show the true, that at any rate only the game of truth and falsity can demonstrate what is true. But for all that truth is *index sui*, this does not mean that the truth is *rex sui*, that the truth is *lex sui*, that the truth is *judex sui*. That is to say, the truth is not creator and holder of the rights it exercises over men, of the obligations the latter have towards it, and of the effects they expect from these obligations when and insofar as they are fulfilled. In other words, it is not the truth that so to speak administers its own empire, that judges and sanctions those who obey or disobey it. It is not true that the truth constrains only by truth. To put things very simply, in an almost or completely infantile way, I shall say the following: in the most rigorously constructed arguments imaginable, even in the event of something being recognized as self-evident, there is always, and it is always necessary to assume, a certain assertion that does not belong to the logical realm of observation or deduction, in other words, an assertion that does not belong exactly to the realm of the true or false, that is rather a sort of commitment, a sort of profession. In all reasoning there is always this assertion that consists in saying: if it is true, then I will submit; it is true, *therefore*[*] I

---

* Underlined in the manuscript.

submit; it is true, therefore I am bound. But this "therefore" of the "it is true, therefore I submit; it is true, therefore I am bound," is not a logical "therefore," it cannot rest on any self-evidence, nor is it univocal moreover. If in a certain number of cases, in a certain number of games of truth, like precisely the logic of the sciences, this "therefore" goes so much without saying that it is as if it is transparent and we do not notice its presence, it nevertheless remains the case that standing back a bit, and when we take science as precisely an historical phenomenon, the "it is true, therefore I submit" becomes much more enigmatic, much more obscure. This "therefore" that links the "it is true" and the "I submit," or which gives the truth the right to say: you are forced to accept me because I am the truth—in this "therefore," this "you are forced," "you are obliged," "you have to submit," in this "you have to" of the truth, there is something that does not arise from the truth itself in its structure and content. The "you have to" internal to the truth, immanent to the manifestation of the truth, is a problem that science in itself cannot justify and account for. I think this "you have to" is a fundamental historical-cultural problem.

As an example, which is also very elementary, I will say this: imagine two logicians who are arguing and whose reasoning together leads to a proposition that both acknowledge as being a true proposition, although it was denied by one of them at the start of the discussion. At the end of this argument, the one who had denied the proposition at the start and who, at the end, recognizes it, will say explicitly or implicitly: it is true, therefore I submit. What happens when he says "it is true, therefore I submit"? If he says "it is true," it is not insofar as he is a logician, well, I mean it is not because he is a logician that the proposition is true. If the proposition is true, it is because of the logic or that, anyway, the logic chosen was such and such, with its symbols, rules of construction, axioms, and grammar. Therefore, for the proposition to be true, it is necessary and sufficient that there was logic, that there were rules of this logic, rules of construction, rules of syntax, and that this logic works. It is therefore the logic, defined in its specific structure, that assures the fact that the proposition is true. But when he says "it is true, therefore I submit," he does not utter this "therefore" because it is part of the logic. It is not part of the logic, for it is not the truth of the proposition that, in fact, actually constrains him, it is not because it is logical, it is because

he is a logician, or rather it is insofar as he *is doing** logic, for it is not his
status or qualification as logician that means that he submits (he might
well not be a professional logician and he would submit the same), but
because he is doing logic, that is to say, because he constitutes himself, or
has been invited to constitute himself as operator in a certain number of
practices or as a partner in a certain type of game. And it happens that
this game of logic is such that truth will be considered to have in itself,
and without further consideration, a constraining value. Logic is a game
in which the whole effect of truth will be to constrain any person playing the game and following the regulated procedure to acknowledge it as
true. We can say that with logic we have a regime of truth in which the
fact that it is a regime disappears, or at any rate does not appear, because
it is a regime of truth in which the demonstration as self-indexation of
truth is accepted as having an absolute power of constraint. In logic,
regime of truth and self-indexation of truth are identified, so that the
regime of truth does not appear as such.

To take another extremely hackneyed example, when Descartes says
"I think, therefore I am,"[2] between the "I think" and the "I am," you
have a "therefore" that is theoretically unanswerable—well, that we may
suppose is theoretically unanswerable, and allow that it is—a "therefore" theoretically unassailable, but behind [which] is hidden another
"therefore," which is this: it is true, therefore I submit. The explicit
"therefore" of Descartes is that of truth that has no other origin than
itself and its intrinsic force, but under this explicit "therefore" is another
implicit "therefore." This is of a regime of truth that is not reduced to
the intrinsic character of truth. It is the acceptance of a certain regime
of truth. And for this regime of truth to be accepted the subject who
reasons must be qualified in a certain way. This subject may well be subject to every possible error, every possible illusion of the senses, he may
even be subject to an evil genius who deceives him.[3] However, there is
a condition for the machine to function and the "therefore" of "I think,
therefore I am" to have probative value. There has to be a subject who
can say: when it is true, and evidently true, I will submit. There has to
be a subject who can say: it is evident, therefore I submit. That is to say,
there must be a subject who is not mad.[4] The exclusion of madness is

---

* M.F. stresses this word, underlined in the manuscript.

therefore the fundamental act in the organization of the regime of truth that will have the particular property of being such that, when it is evident, one will submit, that will have the particular property that it will be truth in itself that will constrain the subject to submit. There is no king in geometry, that is to say no supplement of power is useful or necessary for doing geometry. But if a royal voice in geometry is not necessary, there cannot be any voice of madness in philosophy or any other rational system. There must not be any madman, that is to say, there cannot be any people who do not accept the regime of truth.

And, speaking generally, what is science, Science* in the singular? Is there a sense in putting this word "science" in the singular? Leaving aside, if you will, the problem of the rule of the game, of the grammar of science, of its structure—is there one or several? This is a problem—but if we pose the question in terms of regime of truth, I think we can say that actually it is legitimate to speak of Science (*la* science).† Science would be a family of games of truth all of which submit to the same regime, although they are not subject to the same grammar, and this very specific, very particular regime of truth is a regime in which the power of the truth is organized in a way such that constraint is assured by truth itself. It is a regime in which the truth constrains and binds because and insofar as it is true. And on that basis, I think it must be understood that science is only one of the possible regimes of truth and that there are many others. There are many other ways of binding the individual to the manifestation of truth, and of binding him to the manifestation of truth by other acts, with other forms of bond, according to other obligations and with other effects than those defined in science, for example, by the self-indexation of truth. There are numerous regimes some of which, for example, have a history and domain close to scientific regimes strictly speaking, for example alchemy in relation to chemistry. Whatever objects they may have in common, I do not think the difference is simply the degree of rationality, but in the fact that they are subject to two different regimes of truth, that is to say the acts of truth and the bonds of the subject with the manifestation of the truth are not at all the same in the case of alchemy as in that of chemistry.[5]

---

* "*la* science": again, M.F.'s emphasis.
† Again, underlined in the manuscript.

So you have regimes of truth that are historically and geographically close to science. You have other regimes of truth that are quite coherent and complex and very distant from scientific regimes of self-indexation of truth, and it is precisely this side of regimes of truth that I would like to study a little this year, taking as an example that coherent and complex set of practices comprising self-examination, the exploration of the secrets of conscience, the confession (*aveu*) of these secrets, and the remission of sins.

Generally, and to finish with this rather over-long introduction, I shall say that the problem for the archeology or (an)archeology* of knowledge will not be an overall study of the relations of political power and knowledge (*savoir*) or scientific knowledge (*connaissances*). The problem will be regimes of truth, that is to say, the types of relations that link together manifestations of truth with their procedures and the subjects who are their operators, witnesses, or possibly objects. You can see that his means not making any binary division on one side of which would be science, in which the triumphant autonomy of truth and its intrinsic powers would reign, and on the other side all the ideologies in which the false, or the non-true, would have to arm itself or be armed by a supplementary and external power in order to take on, improperly, the force, value, and effect of truth. Such an archeological perspective therefore absolutely excludes the division between the scientific and the ideological. [It] implies rather that we take the multiplicity of regimes of truth into consideration [and] the fact that every regime of truth, whether scientific or not, entails specific, more or less constraining ways of linking the manifestation of truth and the subject who carries it out. And finally, third, this perspective entails that the specificity of science is not defined by opposition to all the rest or to all ideology, but simply as one among many other possible and existing regimes of truth. This also entails a different approach from that of the history of the sciences, inasmuch as the role of the latter is basically to show how in this particular regime comprising science or the sciences, but which is unquestioned as regime of truth, truth gradually constrains men, humbles their presumptions, extinguishes their dreams, suppresses their desires, and tears out their images by the roots. In contrast, the archeological history

---

* Manuscript orthography.

I am putting forward, will involve going a bit in the other direction and therefore will not consist in allowing that truth, by right and without question, has a power of obligation and constraint over us, but in shifting the accent from the "it is true" to the force we accord truth. This type of history will not therefore be devoted to the way in which truth succeeds in tearing itself from the false and breaking all the ties in which it is held, but will be devoted, in short, to the force of truth and to the ties by which men have gradually bound themselves in and through the manifestation of truth. Basically, what I would like to do and know that I will not be able to do is write a history of the force of truth, a history of the power of the truth, a history, therefore, to take the same idea from a different angle, of the will to know.[6]

Force of truth, will to know, power of the truth, in short, a history of this in the West, of which, of course, at the very most I will be able to give only some fragments which I would like to focus around this more precise question: how in the West have men been bound and how have they been led to bind themselves to very specific manifestations of truth in which, precisely, it is they themselves who must be manifested in truth? How has Western man bound himself to the obligation to manifest in truth what he himself is? How has he bound himself, as it were, at two levels and in two ways, on the one hand, to the obligation of truth, and second, to the status of object within this manifestation of truth? How have men bound themselves to the obligation to bind themselves as object of knowledge (*savoir*). It is this sort of *double bind*, modifying of course the meaning of the term, that basically I have constantly wanted to analyze, [by showing]* how this regime of truth, by which men find themselves bound to manifest themselves as object of truth, is linked to political, juridical, etc., regimes. In other words, the idea is that from politics to epistemology, the relation should not be established in terms of ideology, or in terms of utility. It should not be established through notions like law, prohibition, and repression, but in terms of regime, of regimes of truth connected to juridico-political regimes. There is a regime of madness that is at once regime of truth, juridical regime, and political regime. There is a regime of disease. There is a regime of delinquency. There is a regime of sexuality. And it is in this

---

* M.F.: and to show also.

ambiguity or in this articulation that the word regime tries to mark out that I would like to grasp the connection between what is traditionally called the political and the epistemological. The regime of knowledge (*savoir*) is the point where a political regime of obligations and constraints and this particular regime of obligations and constraints that is the regime of truth are articulated.

[So], we shall try to tackle the question of Christianity seen from the point of view of regimes of truth, regimes of truth* that for the most part it did not invent but that it at least established, extended, institutionalized, and generalized. Clearly, straightaway I put regimes of truth in the plural—and here I return to what I referred to last week—inasmuch as Christianity defined at least two great poles of regimes of truth, two great types of acts that I tried to point out to you are not independent of each other, but are nonetheless very different types with very different morphologies. On the one hand there is what could be called the regime of truth that revolves around acts of faith, that is to say, acts of truth that constitute acceptance-commitment, adherence-fidelity with regard to certain contents that have to be considered true, acceptance-commitment that does not consist merely in affirming the truth of these things in and for itself, but must also give some external guarantees, proofs, authentications in accordance with a number of rules of conduct or ritual obligations. So that merely situates the domain of acts of faith, those with which I will not be concerned. And then, on the other hand, there is another pole in Christianity, another regime of truth, or anyway another frontier of the general regime of truth. This is the frontier that concerns what we may call acts of confession (*aveu*).

When we speak of the act of confession (*aveu*), with regard to Christianity, we think of course of the famous confession (*confession*), in the modern sense of the word "confession," the sense it has taken, roughly, from the end of the Middle Ages, that is to say, the verbalization of sins committed, a verbalization that has to take place in an institutional relationship with a partner, the confessor, who is qualified to hear it, to fix a penalty, [and] to grant remission. In fact, the verbal organization of the confession (*confession*), of the act of confession (*aveu*) in the form we are

---

* M.F. adds: I will just indicate it, at least in dotted lines, in the course of some presentations [*exposés*].

familiar with since the end of the Middle Ages, is only the result, and the as it were most visible and superficial result, of much more complex, numerous, and rich processes by which Christianity bound individuals to the obligation to manifest their truth, their individual truth. More precisely, behind this confession (*confession*), such as we have known it since the end of the Middle Ages, and which seems to have covered over all other forms of confession (*aveu*), we must uncover again a whole regime of truth in which Christianity, from the origin, or at any rate from the second century, imposed on individuals the obligation to manifest in truth what they are, not simply in the form of a consciousness of self that would make it possible to assure, according to the formula of ancient and pagan philosophy, the control of oneself and one's passions, but in the form of a manifestation in depth of the most imperceptible movements of the "mysteries of the heart,"[*7] and no longer simply in the form of a simple examination of oneself by oneself, but in the form of a complex relationship with another, or with others, or with the whole church community, all with a view to extinguishing a certain debt arising from evil and in this way redeeming the chastisements earned by this evil and promised as punishment. In other words, since the origin Christianity established a certain relation between the obligation of the individual manifestation of truth and the debt of evil. How were the obligation to individually manifest one's truth and the extinction of the debt of evil articulated in Christianity? This is what I would now like to talk about.

This connection between the manifestation of individual truth and the remission of sins was organized in three ways, at three levels, around three important practices, two of which are canonical and ritual, and the third of which is a somewhat different type. The first two are, of course, baptism and ecclesial or canonic penance. The third, which I believe will actually have much more importance than the other two, notwithstanding its not exactly ritual or canonic character, is spiritual direction (*direction de conscience*). I would like now to study a little these three things, these three forms of bond between individual manifestation of truth and remission of sins.

So first, baptism. Let's take things, if you will, at the level of their simplest ritualization as presented in the texts. After the New Testament, the

---

* In quotation marks in the manuscript.

first text to give us some indications about baptism in early Christianity is the *Didache*,[8] a text from the beginning of the second century which formulates little more than a few ritual rules regarding baptism. What do we find in the *Didache*? Well, we do not find any direct link between the remission of sins or purification, on the one hand, and truth acts. The *Didache* refers [to such acts] only with regard to the prior teaching that the person who is not yet called a catechumen, let's say that the postulant must follow. Before baptism, the postulant must be taught "all the preceding,"[9] and all the preceding is what is found in the first chapters, namely, [on the one hand,] the distinction between the two ways, the way of life and that of death,[10] and, on the other hand, the precepts that characterize the way of life, that is to say, a number of major prohibitions, those of homicide, adultery, and theft, a number of moral prescriptions of daily life, and finally, of course, the fundamental obligations with regard to God.[11] This then is what the postulant must learn for baptism; this is the relation that must be established between him and the truth. He is the disciple, someone taught, and he is taught a truth. And it is simply when he has learned this truth that he has access to baptism, which has the function of purification, a purification that is not assured by the teaching itself, by the work of the truth, but by two other things. First, by fasting, which always had the function of purification in the ancient tradition, to which the postulant of course must submit, but to which those who participate in the baptism in one way or another must also submit, that is to say, the baptizer and a number of other persons who are present as witnesses, guarantors, participants, co-actors in the procedure of baptism itself.[12] It is fasting that ensures purification, and it is water, the water of baptism,[13] that, according to its traditional symbolism,[14] is supposed to wash away the stains and sins of which the [postulant]* may have been guilty in his former life. So, there is a certain obligation of truth, but which is nothing more than the prior teaching, and then, on the other hand, there are the rituals of purification. There is no direct connection between them, at least in this text of the *Didache* from the beginning of the second century.

Second, from the middle of the second century, that is to say in the literature of those called the Apologists,[15] there is a quite precise

---

* M.F.: baptizer.

elaboration of these relations between truth act and purification. In a text like Justin's *First Apology*, which dates from around 150,[16] baptism is defined not only in terms of its ritual, but more and especially in its meaning. We learn here that baptism must and can only be given to "those who believe that the things we have taught and said are true."[17] This takes up exactly what we found already in the *Didache*: no baptism without prior teaching. An obligation, therefore, to acquire this truth, a bit more however than in the *Didache*. The *Didache* speaks only of teaching. Here, you see that the teaching must be, as it were, sanctioned in the subject by a specific act that is not just that of apprenticeship, but is the act of faith. The subject must not only have learned some things, he must believe they are true. As for the baptism itself, Justin's *Apology*—and I think we find this again in the texts of the same period and immediately after—gives it three meanings, well, three quite specific effects.

First, baptism is something that marks and seals the belonging of the baptized, not just to the ecclesial community, but also to God, and to God more fundamentally than to the ecclesial community. Baptism is a seal, according to the Greek word, *sphragis*.[18] It is a seal, a mark. Second, baptism assures a second birth, *anagenēsis, palliggenesia*, rebirth or new birth,[19] that is to say, for man there are two possible generations, well one necessary and the other possible. One is necessary for man in the sense that he is not master of it: it is a generation that happens to him, says Justin, *anagkē*, by necessity, and in *agnoia*, in ignorance. He is born without knowing, by necessity.[20] How is he born? He is born of a moist seed thanks to the *mixis* of our parents, thanks to the sexual relationship of our parents.[21] This is man's first generation, that to which every living person is subject, blindly and by necessity. The life that flows from this birth is evidently a life of bad inclinations and habits.[22] In relation to this life formed in ignorance, the outcome of necessity, born from humidity, and devoted to bad inclinations and bad habits, baptism will be a second birth, a rebirth thanks to which we cease being "children of *anagkē* and *agnoia*" and become "children of *proairesis* and *epistēmē*." We are children of choice and knowledge,[23] two notions—*proairesis* and *epistēmē*—which are of course terms of Stoic origin that characterize the conditions of the virtuous act.[24] By this second birth we are, as it were, put in the position that was previously defined for the Stoic sage or anyway for virtuous acts according to Stoic philosophy, that is to say, determined by the conscious and voluntary choice of individuals once they have acquired full, or at any rate sufficient knowledge of the order of the world in general. It is therefore a se[cond birth characterized by the fact]* that it puts us on the good way, at the start of a new life that will not be impure, will not be devoted to bad inclinations. But this second life is also characterized by the fact that there is choice and knowledge (*savoir*), that is to say a certain type of knowledge (*connaissance*). This is the second characteristic of baptism as defined by Justin. Finally, still in this passage in which Justin defines baptism, we see a third meaning, a third effect of baptism. This is that baptism, thus placed in the realm of choice and knowledge, puts the baptized in the light. That is to say, baptism is illumination (*phōtismos*).[25] Baptism, then, is seal, rebirth, and illumination, "illumination" being understood in the sense that [the word] had at the time, that is to say, at the same time, an immediate and total relationship of knowledge with God, the subject's assimilation with and resemblance to God, and finally recognition of oneself through this light that enlightens us about God, or rather that comes from God and, illuminating God, enlightens us at the same time. The baptized is someone who is illuminated in his thought, and those who have been purified by baptism, those rather who have been renewed in baptism after the long cycle of education that has taught them the truth, and after the act of faith by which they have affirmed the truth of what they have learned, are illuminated in their thought.

So, in baptism we have a cycle that starts with teaching, is continued with the act of faith, is carried on by free choice and knowledge, and ends with illumination. You see then that baptism, in its entirety, is a certain cycle of truth, that through this ritual act by which the salvation of individuals must be assured there is, on the one hand, purification and remission of previous sins, but also something else, a whole way of truth the stages of which are absolutely specific and different from each other: teaching, faith, choice, knowledge, illumination. We find evidence for baptism having this function of procedure of truth, of the insertion of individuals in the way of the truth and in the illumination of the truth, not only in Justin, but in contemporary and also later texts. For

---

* Conjecture: cassette being turned over.

example, a bit later Clement of Alexandria will say that baptism is the *to tes alētheias sphragis*, the seal of truth.[26]

Let's leave things like that for the moment. I merely wanted to give you a sort of somewhat rapid sketch of what may have been said by the main patristic texts concerning baptism, and now we come to what I believe constitutes the great mutation of the conception of baptism and of the relations between purification and truth. It is, of course, in Tertullian that we find this.

Tertullian,[27] at the turn of the second and third century, contributed a considerable elaboration of the three themes that we can pick out in Justin, that is to say, the themes of the seal, rebirth, and illumination. I think the elaboration of these three themes takes place in Tertullian for a whole host of reasons to which we will have to come back later, but let's say that it takes place essentially—simply from the point of view of the theory of baptism—around the conception of original sin, since you know it was Tertullian who had this marvelous idea of inventing the original sin, which did not exist before him.[28] Tertullian is the one who replaced the idea, which was clear in the *Didache* but is also found in the Pseudo-Barnabas,[29] of the two ways (the way one follows when one does not belong to God and the way one follows once one is devoted to him), with the idea that no man is born without crime, *nullus homo sine crimine*.[30] The birthright of every person is to be a sinner. Man is not someone who has to choose between two ways, the bad way if he does not know God and does not belong to him, and the good if he knows God and belongs to him. Man is in any case someone who is born a sinner. Man is not simply someone who strays onto the path of death before finding the right way of life. He is someone who has sinned from birth.

Original stain. I think there have only ever been three great matrices of moral thought in the West (I don't know about other civilizations, so I won't talk about them): you have had the matrix of the two ways, the matrix of the fall, and the matrix of the stain. That is to say, we think morality only either in the form of a choice between two ways, the good and the bad, or as the necessary course when, starting from an earlier, original, and fundamental fallen state, the individual's task, and the task of humanity, is to get back from that state to the original, lost and forgotten state. And finally you have morality in the form of the problematic of the stain: there has been a fault, an evil, pollution, a stain, and the problem of morality, of moral comportment, of moral conduct is how one can erase this stain. The two ways, the fall, and the stain seem to me to be the three models of morality and the three sole major possibilities in which morality has been able to define itself and develop as an art of the conduct of individuals: either set them on the good way, or tell them how to get back from the fall to the original state, or tell them how to erase the blot and the stain. I think the strength of Christianity, and one of the reasons why it has been what it has and had the ascendancy we are familiar with, is that it succeeded, and in particular thanks to works like those of Tertullian, in combining the three models, the old model of the two ways, found in the *Didache*, the model of the fall, found, of course, in the Bible, and the model of the stain, which was, I believe, elaborated in a very particular way by Tertullian. And Christianity, as morality, has functioned through the system of supports that have existed between the three fundamental models of the two ways, the fall, and the stain. I think that the other major ethical systems that the West has managed to produce would fall under a same analysis—well, I mean that we could find the same three models at work. After all, with Marxism it's the same thing. You have the model of the fall, alienation and dis-alienation. You have the model of the two ways: Mao Zedong. And you have, of course, the problem of the stain of those who are originally soiled and must be purified: Stalinism. Marx, Mao, Stalin; the three models of the two ways, the fall, and the stain.

So let's return to Tertullian and let's say that it was he who very specifically elaborated the problem, the form of the stain and the inheritance of the stain, with obviously a series of fundamental consequences with regard to baptism and the specific effects one should expect from it.[*] I have talked a little about Tertullian now, and [I will continue] next week.

---

[*] M.F. hesitates whether to continue and decides, in the end, that "we can stop there."

1. See Spinoza, Letter LXXVI to Burgh, in *The Correspondence of Spinoza*, ed., and trans., A. Wolf (London: Frank Cass & Co., 1966), p. 352: "the truth reveals itself and the false." (*est enim verum index sui, et falsi*). See also *The Ethics*, trans. Samuel Shirley (Indianapolis/Cambridge: Hackett Publishing Company, 1982), Part II, Scholium to Proposition 43, p. 92: "just as light makes manifest both itself and darkness, so truth is the standard both of itself and falsity" (*sicut lux seipsam, et tenebras manifestat, sic veritas norma sui, et falsi*).

2. Descartes, *Discours de la méthode* (1637), Part 4, in *Œuvres philosophiques*, ed. F. Alquié (Paris: Garnier, 1963) vol. I, p. 604 (AT, VI, 33); English translation by Robert Stoothoff, *Discourse on the Method*, in *The Philosophical Writings of Descartes*, Vol. I, p. 127: "*I am thinking, therefore I exist*"; See too *Les Principes de la Philosophie*, Part One, "Des principes de la connaissance humaine," I, 7, ibid., (1973) Vol. III, p. 95 (AT, IX, II, 28); English translation by John Cottingham, *Principles of Philosophy*, in ibid., p. 195.

3. *Méditations métaphysiques*, I, ibid. (1967), vol. II, p. 412: "some evil genius" (Latin text, p. 181: *genium aliquem malignum*") (AT, IX, 18); English translation by John Cottingham, *Meditations on First Philosophy*, in *The Philosophical Writings of Descartes*, Vol. II (Cambridge: Cambridge University Press, 1984), p. 15: "some malicious demon"; See too, II, Fr., pp. 417-418: "I suppose that that there is someone extremely powerful and, if I may say so, malicious and cunning, who employs all his forces and industry to deceive me"; Eng., p. 18: "I am supposing that there is some supremely powerful and, if it is permissible to say so, malicious deceiver, who is deliberately trying to trick me in every way he can."

4. See the reading of this passage already put forward in *Folie et Déraison. Histoire de la folie à l'âge classique* (Paris: Plon, 1961, republished Paris: Gallimard, "Bibliothèque des Histoires," 1972), pp. 55-58 and p.199; English translation by Jonathan Murphy and Jean Khalfa, *History of Madness* (London and New York: Routledge, 2006), pp. 44-46 and p. 181, and in "Mon corps, ce papier, ce feu" in ibid., Appendix II, pp. 583-603; *DÉ*, II, 102, pp. 245-268/ "Quarto," I, pp. 1113-1136; English translation, "My body, this paper, this fire," in *History of Madness*, pp. 550-574, in reply to Derrida's essay in *L'Écriture et la Différence* (Paris: Seuil, coll. "Tel Quel," 1967), pp. 51-97; English translation by Alan Bass, *Writing and Difference* (Chicago: University of Chicago Press, 1980) pp. 31-63. For the first version of this text see also, "Réponse à Derrida" published in the Japanese review *Paideia*, no. 11, 1972; *DÉ*, II, 104, pp. 281-295; "Quarto," I, pp. 1149-1163; English translation "Reply to Derrida," in *History of Madness*, pp. 575-590. On the difference of perspective, however, between his 1961 analysis and his reply to Derrida, see Foucault's letter to J.-M. Beryssade of November 1972, in *[Cahier de] L'Herne*, 95: *Michel Foucault*, 2011, pp. 92-94.

5. See "La vérité et les formes juridiques," pp. 586-587; "Truth and Juridical Forms," pp. 50-51 where Foucault relates alchemical knowledge to the model of the test and explains its disappearance by the emergence of a new knowledge that "took the inquiry matrix as its model."

6. On the project of a history of the will to know, see the inaugural lecture at the Collège de France of December 1970, *L'ordre du discours* (Paris: Gallimard, 1971), pp. 16-23; English translation by Ian McLeod, "The Order of Discourse," in Robert Young, ed., *Untying the Text* (London: Routledge and Kegan Paul, 1981), pp. 52-56, and the course of 1970-1971, *Leçons sur la volonté de savoir*, p. 217; "Course Summary" in *Lectures on the Will to Know*, p. 224: "The course this year begins a series of analyses which seek to put together, fragment by fragment, a "morphology of the will to know." Sometimes this theme of the will to know will be taken up in specific historical research; sometimes it will be treated for itself and in its theoretical implications."

7. On this expression, see for example, Basile de Césarée [Saint Basil of Caesaraea], *Regulae fusius tractatae*, PG, 31, 889-1052, Interrogatio XXI: "*Quod omnia etiam cordis arcana [to krupta tēs kardias] sint praeposito detegenda*" (*Les grandes règles*, Quaestio 26: "That one must reveal all to the superior, including the secrets of the heart ..."; see *Règles monastiques de saint Basile*, Éd. De l'abbaye de Maredsous, 1969); Cassien, *Institutions cénobitiques*, 12, 6, trans., J.-C. Guy (Paris: Cerf, SC No. 109, 1965) p. 459; English translation by Boniface Ramsey, John Cassian, *The Institutes*, Twelfth Book, VI, 2 (New York/Mahwah, N.J.: The Newman Press, "Ancient Christian Writers" No. 58, 2000), p. 257: "the secrets of his conscience"; Cassien, *Conférences*, 19, 12, trans. Dom E. Pichery (Paris: Cerf, SC No. 54, 1955-1959; 2nd ed., t. I, No. 42, 1966; t. II, no. 54, 1967; t. III, No. 64, 1971), see t. III, p. 50: "... the solitary himself can recognize by certain signs whether the root of this or that vice exists in the depth of his soul. On condition however that he does not seek to show his purity, but applies himself to offering it inviolate to

the sight of he from whom the most intimate secrets of the heart (*cordis arcana*) cannot be hid"; English translation by Boniface Ramsey, John Cassian, *The Conferences* (New York: Newman Press, "Ancient Christian Writers" No. 57, 1997), Nineteenth Conference, Chapter XII, p. 678: "Thus even the solitary, who strives not to show his purity to human beings but to manifest it inviolate before him from whom no secrets of the heart can be hidden, perceives from telltale indications whether the roots of each vice are implanted in him."

8. *La doctrine des douze apôtres (Didachè)*, [*Didakhē kuriou dia tōn dōdeka apostolōn tois ephnesin*] introd., trans., and notes by W. Rordorf and A. Tuilier (Paris: Cerf, SC, no.248bis, 1978, 2nd and expanded ed., 1998) [hereafter: *Didachè*]. Foucault does not use this edition in the rest of the course, but that translated by Hemmer in *Les Pères apostoliques*, I–II, trans. H. Hemmer and G. Ogier (Paris: A. Picard et Fils, 1907 [hereafter: Hemmer]) and, for the Greek text and translation, that of R.-F. Refoulé in *Les écrits des Pères apostoliques* (Paris: Cerf, 1962 [hereafter: *EPA*]). [There are a number of English translations of the *Didache*, many of them available online. I have consulted various translations to give an English version that seems to me to be closest to the French translations given by Foucault. A readily available version can be found in *Early Christian Writings. The Apostolic Fathers*, trans. Maxwell Staniforth (Harmondsworth: Penguin Books, 1968) and English page references will be to this, *Didache*; G.B.] This catechistic, liturgical, and disciplinary manual is a compilation of various documents brought together in the Christian communities, the text of which, discovered in 1875 and first published in 1883, goes back to the Church of the first and second centuries.

9. *Didachè*, 7, I, p. 171; *EPA*, p. 44; *Didache*, p. 230: "all the preliminaries"; see A. Benoit, *Le baptême chrétien au second siècle* (Paris: PUF, 1953), p. 5.

10. *Didachè*, 1, I, p. 142; *EPA*, p. 37: "There are two ways, one of life, the other of death; but the difference between these two ways is great"; *Didache*, p. 227: "There are two Ways: a Way of Life and a Way of Death, and the difference between these two Ways is great." This theme of Jewish origin (Hemmer, p. 2, refers to Jeremiah 21, 8 and Deuteronomy 30, 15-19), "was part of the catechetic material of the synagogue for the instruction of proselytes" (A. Benoit, *Le baptême chrétien*, p. 22). On the Jewish origin of the first six chapters, see the "Introduction" in Hemmer, p. xxxi.

11. *Didachè*., 1-5, pp. 142-169; *EPA*, pp. 37-44; *Didache*, pp. 227-230.

12. *Didachè*, 7, 4, p. 173; *EPA*, p. 45; *Didache*, p. 231.

13. *Didachè*, 7, 1, p. 171; *EPA*, p. 44; *Didache*, p. 230.

14. This symbolism, no trace of which is found in the New Testament, derives from the interpretation of Christ's baptism by John the Baptist as an "exorcism of the waters [having] purified the River Jordan, and with it, all the waters" (A. Benoit, *Le baptême chrétien*, p. 68).

15. The traditional naming of the Apologetic Fathers or Apologetes designates "a group of Christian writers of the second half of the second century who tried to defend Christianity from attacks on it made by pagans, and who attempted to make it understood by educated men of their time" (A. Benoit, *Le baptême chrétien*, p. 138). Justin is the only one of them, however, to speak of baptism.

16. Justin, *Apologia*, I, 61, PG, 6, col. 419-422; trans. L. Pautigny, *Première apologie de saint Justin* (Paris: A. Picard et Fils, "Textes et documents pour l'étude historique du christianisme," 1904). A new French translation by C. Munier appeared recently: *Apologie pour les chrétiens* (SC, no. 507, 2006); English translation by Alexander Roberts and James Donaldson as, Justin Martyr, *The First Apology of Justin Martyr*, ch. LXI, in A. Cleveland Coxe, ed., *The Ante-Nicene Fathers. Translations of The Writings of the Fathers down to A.D. 325* [hereafter, *ANF*], Vol. I: *The Apostolic Fathers with Justin Martyr and Iranaeus*, (Grand Rapids, Michigan: W. B. Eerdmans, 1994). The reference to this text, later than the writings of the apostolic Fathers referred to later in the course, is justified here, immediately after the *Didache*, by the fact that we find here "the first description of the sacrament [of baptism] that is the least bit complete in Christian literature" (A. Benoit, *Le baptême chrétien*, p. 143).

17. Ibid., col. 420 B; Fr., 61, 2, p. 127; Eng., ch. LXI, p. 183: "As many as are persuaded and believe that what we teach and say is true." Foucault here offers his own translation of the text.

18. On the definition of baptism as seal (*sphragis*), see G. Bareille, "Baptême (d'après les Pères grecs et latins)," *Dictionnaire de théologie catholique*/DTC, II, 1905, col. 179-180, which refers to various uses of the metaphor (baptism as seal of Christ, which represents God's alliance with the regenerated soul, seal of faith, seal of the regeneration that incorporates us into Christ's

flock). See too F.J. Dölger, *Sphragis. Eine altchristliche Taufbezeichnung in ihren Beziehung zur profan und religiösen Kultur des Altertums*, (Paderborn, F. Schöningh, "Studien zur Geschichte und kultur des Altertums," Band 5, Heft. 3/4, 1911) (a good summary of his analyses is found in A. Benoit, *Le baptême chrétien*, pp. 98-103), and A.-G. Hamman, "La signification de σφραγίς [*sphragis*] dans le Pasteur d'Hermas," *Studia Patristica*, 4, 1961, pp. 286-290. The word is not found in the passage Foucault comments on. According to Benoit, *Le baptême chrétien*, p. 97, it is "in the second epistle of Clement [that] the equivalence baptism = *sphragis*" appears for the first time in an "indubitable" way: see VII, 6, VIII, 6, and VI, 9. The word, as designation of baptism, is found in Tertullian, *De paenitenia*, 6, Clement of Alexandria, *Quis dives salvetur*, 42, 1, and Hermas, *Similitude*, XVI, 2-7, XVII, 4. Comparing the baptismal doctrines of Hermas and Justin, Benoit emphasizes notably the following difference: "Justin does not speak of '*sphragis*' ... but he uses the term '*phôtismos*' to designate baptism, a term which is not found in Hermas" (*Le baptême chrétien*, p. 184). On this latter notion, see the passage from Justin, below (pp. 105-106). The triple characterization of baptism as regeneration (*paliggenesia*), seal (*sphragis*), and illumination (*phôtismos*) is set out by F.J. Dölger, *Der Exorzismus im altchristlichen Taufritual. Eine religionsgeschichtliche Studie* (Paderborn: F. Schöningh, "Studien zur Geschichte und kultur des Altertums," Band III, heft. 2/3, 1909), pp. 3-4 (on Foucault's use of this article, see P. Chevallier, "Foucault et les sources patristiques," *Cahier de L'Herne: Michel Foucault*, 2011, p. 139).

19. Justin, *Apologie*, PG, col. 420C; *Première Apologie*, 61, 3, p. 129: "… they are led by us to the place where there is water, and there, in the same manner in which we were regenerated (*anegennatêuen*), they in turn are themselves regenerated (*anagennantai*)" (literally: "they are regenerated by the same sort of regeneration (*anagennêseos*) as we have been regenerated"; *The First Apology*, ch. LXI, ANF, Vol. I, p. 183: "Then they are brought by us where there is water, and are regenerated in the same manner in which we were ourselves regenerated." See also Fr., 66, I, p. 141: "… no one can take part [in the Eucharist] if he…has not been bathed for the remission of sins and regeneration (*anagennêsin*)"; Eng., ch. LXVI, p. 185: "no one is allowed to partake [of the Eucharist] but the man who…has been washed with the washing that is for the remission of sins, and unto regeneration." The second word, *palliggenesia*, however, is not in the text. As P. Chevalier, "Foucault et les sources patristiques," p. 138, clarifies, it "appears in Justin only in a fragment available at the end of the edition of his works by the Abbot Migne, in his great patrology of the nineteenth century." See F.J. Dölger, *Der Exorzismus*, p. 3, which refers to the expression of the *Épitre à Tite*, 3, 5: "*loutran paliggenesias*." The word is also employed, in relation with the "second baptism" of post-baptismal penance, by Clement of Alexandria in *Quis dives salvetur*, 42, PG 9, col. 650 D, and by Origen, with regard to regeneration by water (see J. Daniélou, *Origène*, p. 72).

20. Ibid., col. 421 A; Fr., 61, 10, p. 129: "In our first generation we are born ignorant and according to the law of necessity (*agnoountes kat anagkēn*)"; Eng., LXI, p. 183: "at our birth we were born without our own knowledge or choice … the children of necessity and of ignorance."

21. Ibid.; Fr., ibid.: "… of a moist seed, in the mutual union of our parents"; Eng., ibid.: "by our parents coming together."

22. Ibid.: Fr., ibid.: "… and we come into the world with bad habits and perverse inclinations"; Eng., ibid.: "(we) were brought up in bad habits and wicked training."

23. Ibid.: Fr., 61, 10, pp. 130-131: "So that we do not remain children of necessity and ignorance, but of choice and science (*alla proaireseôs kai epistēmēs*)"; Eng., ibid.: "in order that we may not remain the children of necessity and of ignorance, but may become the children of choice and knowledge."

24. On this concept, introduced by Aristotle into philosophical language (see *Nicomachean Ethics*, trans. W. D. Ross and revised by J.O. Urmson, in *The Complete Works of Aristotle*, ed. Jonathan Barnes, I, 1, 1094 a, p. 1729, and III, 2, 1111 b-1112 a, pp. 1755-1756 (Tricot: "deliberate, preferential choice") and to which Epictetus accords a central place in his thought (see his *Discourses*, Book I, 17, 21-27; Book II, 10, 1-3, *et passim*). "For Epictetus, the disposition which renders nature capable of the moral act is *proairesis*, which helps us limit our desires and actions to things that are in our power; it is what controls opinions (*dogmata*) and decides on our representations (*phantasiai*)" (C. Munier, Introduction to Tertullien, *La pénitence*, p. 37, which refers to M. Spanneut, *Permanence du stoïcisme*, Gembloux, 1973, pp. 74-78). See also the old but still remarkable work (referred to by Foucault in *Le souci de soi*, p. 270; *The Care of the Self*, p. 236)

of A. Bonhöffer, *Epiktet und die Stoa* (Stuttgart: F. Frommann, 1968), pp. 259-261 [the title given in *Le soucie de soi/Care of the Self* is in fact *Epiktet und das Neue Testament*, 1911; G.B.] and A.-J. Voelke, *L'idée de volonté dans le stoïcisme* (Paris: PUF, 1973), pp. 142-160 (*"proairesis"* as choice, moral person, and divine element according to Epictetus).

25. Justin, *Apologia*, col. 421 B; *Première Apologie*, 61, 12, p. 131: "This ablution is called illumination (*phōtismos*) because the mind of those who receive this doctrine is illuminated (*photisomenōn*)"; *The First Apology*, LXI, p. 183: "And this washing is called illumination, because they who learn these things are illuminated in their understandings." On the meaning of this word, see A. Benoit, *Le baptême chrétien*, pp. 165-168.

26. The expression may not in fact come from Clement of Alexandria. It is found in the *Extraits de Théodote*, published under his name, translated by F. Sagnard (Paris: Cerf, SC no. 23, 1948, 2nd ed., 1970), § 86, p. 211: "Even animals without reason show, by the seal they bear, to whom each belongs ... Just the same, the faithful soul which has received the seal of the Truth (*to tes alētheias sphragisua*) 'carries the mark of Christ' (*Galatians*, 6, 17)." Theodotus belonged to the Gnostic group of the Valentinians, to the criticism of which Tertullian, after Iranaeus (*Adversus Haeresis/Against Heresies*) devoted a special treatise: *Contre les Valentiniens*, trans., commentary and index by J.-C. Fredouille (Paris: Cerf, SC nos. 280-281, 1980); English translation by Alexander Roberts, *Against the Valentinians*, in A. Cleveland Cox, ed., *ANF, Vol. III: Latin Christianity: Its Founder, Tertullian*, Parts I-III (Grand Rapids, Michigan: W.B. Eerdmans, 1994). But as Benoit points out, *Le baptême chrétien*, p. 74, "in the *Extraits de Théodote*, it is difficult to determine what comes from Clement of Alexandria, who collected them, and what from the thought of Theodotus," adding that, according to the editor of the text, "this passage seems to come from Clement." Sagnard, in a note of p. 210 of the *Extraits*, describes the extract 86 as a "very fine passage, worthy of Clement of Alexandria"; see appendix F of his edition, pp. 229-239, "Le baptême au deuxième siècle et son interprétation valentinienne" (on the image of the "seal": pp. 235-239).

27. Born at Carthage, in a pagan family, Tertullian (?160-?220) converted around 195 ("one is not born, one becomes Christian," he writes in his *Apologetic*), after having started a career as a jurist. Around 205 he joined the Montanists (see below, lecture of 5 March, p. 220, note 29). For the abundance of his writings, the vigor of his style, and the originality of his thought, he is considered to be the first Latin theologian. Foucault's first reference to this author (he does not cite him in the 1978 lectures on the Christian pastorate) is in the interview "Le jeu de Michel Foucault" (1977) in *DÉ*, III, no. 206, p. 313; "Quarto" II, p. 313; English translation by Colin Gordon, "The Confession of the Flesh," in Michel Foucault, *Power/Knowledge. Selected Interviews and Other Writings 1972-1977*, ed. Colin Gordon (Brighton: The Harvester Press, 1980), p. 211, with regard to the problematic of the flesh: "The basic originator of it all was Tertullian ... Tertullian combined within a coherent theoretical discourse two fundamental elements: the essentials of the imperatives of Christianity—the '*didache*'—and the principles by way of which it was possible to escape from the dualism of the Gnostics."

28. On the doctrine of original sin according to Tertullian, see A. Gaudel, "Péché originel," DTC, XII, 1933, col. 363-365. "Taken together, his assertions sketch out a theology of original sin which Saint Augustine will later develop" (col. 365); F. Refoulé, Introduction to *Traité du baptême* (Paris: Cerf, SC, no. 35, 2002 [see below p. 000, note 5]), p. 13: "Tertullian is the first to teach the doctrine of original sin, although he did not see all its consequences. "*Nulla anima sine crimine, quia nulla sine boni semine*" [*De Anima*, 41, 3], he will say in one of those oratorical formulae which characterize his style." See too the commentary of C. Munier on *De paenitentia*, which, p. 15, note 12, refers to A. d'Alès, *La théologie de Tertullian* (Paris: G. Beauchesne, 1905), pp. 120-127, pp. 264-268, and p. 197 (with regard to II, 3, p. 147): "In An. [*De Anima*], 39-40, he clearly distinguishes the sin caused by the demon in the life of each individual, and the state of corruption, which comes from original sin: *pristini corruptio*, and which is washed away by baptism. Adam's sin does not only constitute a chronological priority and pernicious example; all his descent is infected in its deepest roots; through heredity it carries and transmits (*tradux*) a propensity to evil; it is, in the strong sense, a sinful race, from generation to generation (*semen delicti*)."

29. *Epître de Barnabé*, Introduction, translation, and notes P. Prigent and R.A. Kraft (Paris: Cerf, SC, no. 172, 1971) (on the designation of the author as Pseudo-Barnabas, see the Introduction, p. 27); English translation by Alexander Roberts and James Donaldson, revised by A. Cleveland

Coxe, *The Epistle of Barnabas* in *ANF, Vol. I*. The doctrine of the Two Ways (the Way of Light
and the Way of Darkness), the source of which would be a manual of morality of Jewish origin,
is set out in the concluding chapters XVIII-XX, pp. 147-149. On the relations between *The
Epistle of Barnabus* and the *Didache* regarding the teaching of the Two Ways, see the introduction to the *Épître de Barnabé*, and to the *Didaché*, pp. 12-20, and the latter, pp. 22-34. See also
A. Benoit, *Le baptême chrétien*, p. 3. However, Foucault does not use the "Sources chrétiennes"
edition. See below, lecture of 27 February, p. 172 and note 14.

30. See above, note 28.

six

13 FEBRUARY 1980

Tertullian (continued): the relation between purification of the soul and access to the truth in the preparation for and act of baptism. Reminder of the general framework of this analysis: the relations between truth act and ascesis. Novelty of Tertullian's doctrine. ∽ The problem of the preparation for baptism. Tertullian's argument against the Gnostics and the attitude of some postulants towards baptism. His doctrine of original sin: not only perversion of nature, but introduction of the other (Satan) in us. The time of baptism, a time of struggle and combat against the adversary. Fear, essential modality of the subject's relationship to himself; importance of this theme in the history of Christianity and of subjectivity. ∽ Practical consequence: the "discipline of repentance (pénitence)." New sense of the word in Tertullian. Diffraction of metanoia. Repentance extended to the whole of life. Repentance as manifestation of the truth of the sinner to God's gaze. Dissociation of the pole of faith and the pole of confession.

TODAY, I WOULD LIKE to explain a little how Tertullian defines the relation between purification of the soul and access to the truth in the preparation for and act of baptism. For those who may be surprised that one should be interested in this and occupied with it at a level of detail that is of relatively little importance for our everyday concerns, I would like to say that the aim of these sketches around these problems is to trace a dotted line, to draw an outline—once again, I am returning to what I was saying at the beginning—for a history of truth. A history of truth, not from the point of view of relations or structures of objectivity, or of intentionality, but from the point of view of acts of subjectivity, or of the subject's relationship to himself, understood not only as a relationship of self-knowledge, but as a relationship of exercise of self on self, elaboration of self by self, transformation of self by self, that is to say, the relations between the truth and what we call spirituality, or again: truth act and ascesis, truth act and experience in the full and strong sense of the term, that is to say, experience as that which qualifies the subject, enlightens it about itself and about the world and, at the same time, transforms it.

So, let's take up the problem of the relations between purification and access to the truth in Tertullian. With regard to baptism, I think that the relation Tertullian establishes between purification and access to the truth is very different from that established by those we may call his predecessors, that is to say, the apostolic Fathers or the apologists of the second century. At the turn of the second and third century, Tertullian, I think, introduced a number of changes into this system of relations between purification and truth. We can summarize these changes in a couple of words, in order to skim over a little in advance what I am going to say, so that things may be quite clear. It seems to me that with Tertullian or, anyway, through Tertullian's texts, we can see a phenomenon that will have echoes and back-up in other authors in his period. In any case, we can find the following changes in him and no doubt others. On the one hand, the soul, in baptism—preparation for baptism, act of baptism—does not appear simply in a process that gradually qualifies it as subject of knowledge (*savoir ou connaissance*). In preparation for baptism and in the ritual of baptism, the soul is placed in a process that constitutes it, certainly still as subject of knowledge (*savoir ou connaissance*), but equally and in a certain way as object of knowledge (*connaissance*). And second, it seems to me that the relationship between purification and access to the truth in Tertullian and in some of his contemporaries does not take simply, or exclusively, or even in a dominant way the form of teaching, but it takes the form, the structure of what could be called the test, and this is what I would like to try to clarify a little now.

So, the relation between truth and purification as the constitution of a relationship in which the soul is the object of knowledge (*connaissance*) and, second, constitution, structuring of a relationship not so much of teaching, but of test.

Let's take first of all the problem of the preparation for baptism.* What takes place in this preparatory phase, which should lead to baptism itself, and in what does it consist? You recall—we were saying this last week—the texts of the apostolic Fathers and the apologists define the period of preparation for baptism as primarily a period of teaching. What does this mean? It means that the aim is to turn the postulant into a subject of knowledge (*connaissance*). He must be transformed into a subject of knowledge, that is to say: first, he is taught some truths, which are the truths of the doctrine and the rules of the Christian life, and in this way he is lead, from teaching to teaching, to a belief that he must manifest and affirm in a particular truth act, the profession of faith, one of the fundamental aspects of baptism. This baptism, through the rite in which it consists, calls on the Holy Spirit, which, descending into the soul, brings a light, an illumination that gives the soul, in short, an access to the truth that is not just a content of knowledge, a series of dogmas to be believed or of objects to be known, but, for the one who knows, is at the same time his own life that has now become eternal just as the truth he knows is eternal. Baptism produces a life of light, a life without shadow, without taint, without death, and thus you can see that, from teaching to participation in eternal life, the preparation for baptism is basically a long path of initiation in which the postulant at baptism is gradually qualified as a subject of knowledge at increasingly higher levels, to the point at which he becomes, as it were, the truth itself. He has become the truth. So, an enormous structure of teaching is developed in this way throughout this preparation for baptism.

In comparison with this absolute privilege of teaching—I will come back to this shortly, but we find this privilege of teaching in the pure state, in the most striking form, if you like, in Clement of Alexandria, with the great arrangement of all his thought around themes and in the form of teaching, with the *Protreptic*,[1] the *Pedagogue*,[2] and then the *Stromata*,[3] which represents the didascalic level or higher teaching for

---

* M.F. adds: that is to say the period of initiation, during which the postulant, the one who in the second century was not yet called, but at the period of Tertullian was already beginning to be called catechumen ... [sentence unfinished].

those precisely who attain the life of purity and perfection—in contrast with this structure of teaching, which seems to have dominated the second century and which is still dominant at the end of the second century in some authors like Clement of Alexandria, I think there is a considerable shift of emphasis with Tertullian. It is a shift of emphasis that we can symbolize, or pinpoint, through a passage, a phrase found in the *De paenitentia*, in chapter six, in which Tertullian, speaking of baptism, says: "We are not bathed in the baptismal water in order to be purified, but we are bathed in the baptismal water because we are purified."[4] It is clear that, with regard to the whole theoretical and practical balance of what we have seen concerning the meaning and effects of baptism, we have here a considerable change that can be broken down in the following way. What does it mean if we now say that we are bathed in the baptismal water because we have been purified? First, of course, a perceptible, manifest chronological shift that means that purification will pass—or seems anyway to have to pass—from the act of baptism itself to procedures that precede it and to the whole time of preparation prior to baptism. So, there is a chronological shift. Second, another shift—again, I am situating myself at the level of appearances: all of this has to be analyzed, but it seems that the burden of purification is shifted also, since the earlier texts made the baptismal rite the factor of purification and, consequently, made God the one who assures purification in the rite. Now, however, it is we ourselves who must arrive before God, at the baptism, already purified, as if it is we ourselves who have to purify ourselves. So, there is not only a chronological shift, but a move from God to man as the operator of purification. Finally, third, it seems that, with this idea, preparation for baptism [must] not be simply the initiation into a truth and the constitution of the postulant as a subject of knowledge, but that much more, or anyway as well as the game of truth in this initiation, there [must] be a game of the pure and impure, a game of morality. And there is therefore a shift, let's say, from truth to morality, or an inversion of the order between truth and purification in Tertullian's thought, since, in the previous system, it was in fact the initiation into the truth, the progressive constitution of the subject of knowledge, that assured purification. But now we require purification to take place even before the moment that is to produce illumination in the baptism. As a result, the relation between truth and purification is inverted. It is purification, it seems to me, that must lead to the truth.

These inversions are what appear through this passage and obviously we must examine it more closely in order to know what it actually says when it says that we must arrive at baptism already purified and that it is because we are purified that we are bathed in the baptismal water.

So, first remark. Obviously, there is no question of Tertullian denying the intrinsic effectiveness of the rite, or the reality of the act that takes place in it, or the principle that it is indeed the baptismal water that, in actual fact, purifies us, that is to say, renders us substantially, ontologically pure. The treatise Tertullian devotes to baptism itself, De baptismo, which dates from exactly the turn of the second and third century,[5] is precisely directed against a number of movements which were all of a more or less dualist or Gnostic inspiration and which rejected the effectiveness of the baptismal rite. These different movements rejected the rite and effectiveness of baptism for a number of reasons.

To indicate just two of them I shall say the following: first—and we will come back to this later because it is very important—for the Gnostics,[6] or generally for all the movements inspired by Gnosticism, the soul does not need to be purified in itself, it does not need, as it were, to see its own substance or its own nature relieved, released from the stain of sin, because for the Gnostics the soul (at any rate, the soul of the person who is to be elected), is not in itself stained, it is imprisoned within a world of matter and evil. For this reason there would be no sense in wanting to purify it; it has to be freed. It has to return to its homeland, find its memory, return to where it came from, it has to find again its kinship with God, but it does not have to purify itself. It is right therefore to reject the rite of baptism. The other reason is that for the Gnostic, or someone inspired by Gnosticism, there is something scandalous in the rite of baptism in itself, since baptism, by using something like water, that is to say a material substance, claims to purify something purely spiritual, of the same nature as God, with something that is matter, which is precisely evil and impurity. How could the impure purify the pure? Absurdity! This was in fact the position of a certain group inspired by Gnosticism that existed (were rampant, as Christian historians say) at Carthage at the time of Tertullian—these were the Nicolaitans,[7] and in particular a woman,[8] leader of the sect, who said: How can a drop of water wash away death?[9]

To this criticism of the baptismal rite and of its effectiveness, Tertullian replies—and here we see quite well that, for him, the baptismal rite well and truly has a purifying effect—first of all, with a reminder of the spiritual values of water found in Scripture. Throughout its texts, Scripture constantly emphasizes the spiritual effectiveness of water, or at any rate the spiritual value of water, which is not matter that participates in evil because it is matter, but matter that always has a certain privilege at the very heart of matter. First, on what did the spirit of God rest before the creation of the world? Over what did the spirit of God sit enthroned? Over what did it hover? Well, over the water.[10] The water is God's seat and, consequently, the mark of his sovereignty. Second, when God created man, he fashioned him. He fashioned him with his hands, taking earth, taking clay, but, Tertullian says, how could he have fashioned the human being, the body of man in its complexity and perfection, if he had only clay, only earth, and not water? Water made it possible to fashion man, to make a man from matter,[11] a man who is precisely in the image and likeness of God, as the text says.[12] So, the likeness and image of God, the effect of God's fashioning of man, is in fact linked to the existence of water. It is through water that something like a likeness of God to man could come about. Third, it was the water of the Flood that happily purified the surface of the Earth of all sinners.[13] It was the water of the Red Sea that separated the Jewish people from its pursuing enemies and so freed it.[14] Water was spiritual food in the desert when Moses made it spring from the rock.[15] Water, finally, is the source of healing in the pool of Bethsaida.[16*] So, throne of divine sovereignty, element of God's image, purification of the Flood, freedom with the Red Sea, spiritual food, healing: you can see that, according to Tertullian, throughout Scripture water has constantly been the very form through which God enters into a relationship with the world, with matter, with his creature.

So, baptism, in its materiality, as rite, is inscribed in this long series of relations between God and man. God and his creature, God and the

---

* The manuscript adds: To this spiritual value, [obscurely][a] recognized by the pagans, Christ's baptism adds the action of the Holy Spirit.

[a] Conjecture.

world. It is one of God's forms of action on his creatures. Baptism has
the naturalness guaranteed by Scripture, well by antiquity at any rate.
Hence the principle concerning baptism formulated by *De baptismo*:
"happy sacrament of Christian water that, washing away the stains of
our dark past, delivers us to the freedom of our eternal life."[17] So, notwithstanding the phrase I quoted earlier, Tertullian does maintain the
principle of the baptismal rite and its purifying effectiveness. Only,
where things begin to change is when Tertullian wonders about certain
attitudes displayed by some postulants as a result of their belief in the
effectiveness of baptism. These attitudes are blameworthy for a number
of reasons, some moral and others theological.

Some people, in fact, as a result of the way in which they interpret
the effectiveness of the baptismal rite, say to themselves: since baptism
must purify them of all the sins they have committed anyway, why go
to repent of all the sins they have actually committed, why be distressed
by them, feel remorse for them, why even rid themselves of them, since
when they come to baptism, the effectiveness of the rite will assure them
total, entire, and definitive purification? Hence those postulants who
prepare themselves for baptism in only a superficial, light, and futile
way, and who thus commit a sin of pride and presumption in asking
God to forgive them for what they themselves have not even repented or
corrected. These people rush into baptism, get themselves baptized as
quickly as possible, before sufficient preparation.[18]

And then there is the opposite attitude that consists in saying to oneself: since baptism will free me from every sin and purify me anyway, but
that once purified of these sins I must not fall again and after baptism
all the sins I committed previously will be definitively prohibited,[19] why
not delay baptism as long as possible, steep myself in sin, and then get
myself baptized later.[20] This attitude* was an absolutely fundamental
point of debate for centuries and centuries in the Church with regard
to baptism, but especially later with regard to penance—we will see it
again—that is to say: delaying as much as possible the point at which
one will, so to speak, take the plunge and belong to a world of purity
from which one will not be able to fall without being definitively condemned. It is in fact the whole status of the pure, the elect, the perfect

---

* M.F. adds: which was very important.

that is thus in question in this debate, and basically, for Christianity to gain acceptance for an early baptism, on the one hand, and an equally early and renewed penance, [on the other], ultimately it had to abandon the idea of perfection, of purity, which was absolutely fundamental in all the religions of salvation of Antiquity. Someone pure has to be not completely pure. Someone purified has to remain a little impure, for if he has in actual fact acquired the status of total purity, if he is in actual fact one of the perfect, really elect, and if he is conscious of himself as one of the elect, then he will have a different status within the world, within matter, within creation, in the midst of other men, and he will no longer be able to do what he wants to do. This dimorphism of the pure and the impure, of the perfect and those who are not perfect, of the chosen and those not chosen, will be one of the most fundamental and problematic points of dogma, organization, and the pastorate through-out Christianity.

Anyway, these were the two attitudes Tertullian was dealing with and are what force him, on his own admission, to rethink a little what preparation for baptism must be.[21] What, he asks, is behind these two attitudes of either hastening to be baptized without going through a sufficient preparation, or delaying baptism as long as possible in order to be able to sin as much as possible with peace of mind? Obviously, there is a series of grave errors, some concerning God and others the nature of sin. With regard to the nature of God, the error appears straightaway, and it is an error that is also an offense. Both these attitudes assume, in effect, that by purifying anyway, automatically, and in an absolutely effective way, the rite is something that obligates God. That is to say, that the baptismal rite actually requires God to purify me, and because God is constrained in this way I can either not prepare sufficiently for baptism, or alternatively I can delay it for as long as possible. In other words, behind these two attitudes there is the idea that the rite is imposed on God as it is on men, or rather that it is imposed on God in a much more imperative, constraining, and oppressive way than it is on men themselves, since men choose the moment of baptism, they do not prepare themselves for it. But when someone submits to the rite, God is obliged to forgive. In this way, Tertullian says in *De paenitentia*, these two attitudes transform God's generosity into slavery.[22] One enslaves God, and one enslaves him to man's will. First error, first offense.

But I will pay a bit more attention to the other error, or errors, because they concern our subject more directly. They concern sin, the nature of sin, and what we are, we others, insofar as we are sinners. In fact—and here I think we touch on an important point—Tertullian, you know, was the one who invented original sin, or at any rate, elaborated it. He elaborated it on the basis of, or rather against two ideas which were, as it were, familiar both to the ancient world and to the Christianity of the first two centuries. These two conceptions are the idea of sin as a blot, a stain, on the one hand, and the idea of sin as a fall on the other. Not, to be sure, that Tertullian abandoned either of these ideas, but he considerably elaborated and shifted them. First, for Tertullian, the original sin is not simply a stain, a blot, a sort of shadow that has slipped in between the soul and the light, thus establishing a darkness between them that has to be dispelled by illumination or purification. Original sin is more than that. What marks man's soul from birth is of course that it is expressed, that it manifests itself as blot, stain, shadow, forgetfulness, ignorance, but it is fundamentally a perversion of nature and a perversion of our nature.

Of course, for Tertullian, all this is inscribed in a whole conception, I was going to say, of the heredity of sin—well, he works out a theory of the transmission of the original sin by the seed,[23] starting from the idea, which was very widespread in Antiquity and first formulated by Democritus, that the individual's seed—the seed in the strict sense of the term, the sperm—is no more than a sort of decoction, or foam rather, which emanates from the whole body[24] and is expressed in the ejaculation of the sperm, so that in the sperm man is entirely split. There is again the idea of masculine ejaculation as symmetrical to feminine childbirth. Another being comes from feminine childbirth, but we should not forget that there was also a sort of splitting of the being, and of the whole being, in masculine ejaculation. This is an old idea which Tertullian takes up and combines with the idea, more his own, that there are two seeds,[25] that of the soul and that of the body, two very different seeds, the former being a material seed, and the latter being equally a seed that he calls corporeal, but the body of the soul not being the same as the body of the body, okay fine ... These two seeds are profoundly and intimately combined with each other, and anything that happens to stain one of the seeds, anything that happens to taint one of the seeds, is equally transferred to the other, so that they are interdependent in their taint, stain, or imperfection. From the original sin, which was indeed at first a stain, the successive seeds disseminated through the whole of humankind have [therefore] given to each being born from the relay of this seed a profoundly perverted nature. It is not just the stain that has been communicated, it is nature itself that has been corrupted, to the point that Tertullian tells us that basically we have "another nature."[26]

To that extent, you see that purification cannot be merely an effect of the light that replaces darkness and forgetfulness with the illumination of knowledge. It requires a sort of thoroughgoing renewal of our nature. Then the problem arises of whether evil is another substance and a radically other nature. Tertullian is forced to keep to a median line between a dualist conception of an absolutely evil matter opposed to an absolutely good nature and a Platonic type of conception of fault as stain, taint, and forgetfulness, and he refers to what I think is the very important metaphor of the growth of living beings. Basically, if we take an animal, it is of course the same from birth to maturity, it is the same nature. Nonetheless, it remains the case that in the nascent state it could do none of the things it does as an adult. There is, as it were, within one and the same nature, a passage from one nature to another, that is to say a passage from one to the other within the same nature, and, he says, when animals are in the nascent state they can neither see nor walk. What training do they need? It is a radical transformation that will give them, those who are what they are, all the powers they did not have when they were born—when they were blind, stumbled, and crawled.[27*] It is the same for us, when we have not yet heard the word of God, we are blind, we stumble, we crawl. And the preparation for baptism must be similar to that transformation by which animals, by dint of exercises, failures, errors, and wounds succeed as adults in doing what they want to do and conform with their true nature. So it is this evolution that the preparation for baptism must recreate and reproduce. We must pass from imperfect infancy, unable to do anything, to full, accomplished maturity, finally capable of doing what must be done.

---

* The manuscript (folio 8) adds this quotation: "When our ears begin to drink divine words, we are like animals that have just been born: they stumble, they crawl."

This metaphor is interesting because it is opposed to the metaphor that Clement of Alexandria develops throughout his work at the same time, the idea, which is fundamental in Clement, that the Christian must consider himself as a child of God, even before he has been baptized, and even before he has become Christian. And the more Christian he is, the more he will be a child; the more Christian he is, the smaller he will be; the more Christian he is, the more he will depend on the food and nourishment given to him by God, who is *Logos*, but who at the same time is milk—or rather, the milk given to children, the milk that nourishes the child, is the very symbol of the *Logos*.[28] Consequently, the spirit of childhood, and return to the spirit of childhood is the mark of the depth of Christian experience. In Tertullian you have the exact opposite, that is to say the idea that in the sinful state into which we are born we are absolutely children, and the movement that leads us from the state of sinners to the state of Christians, good or perfect Christians [...],* is the movement from childhood to maturity. Now, it is this work of maturation, of exercise, of perfecting ourselves by ourselves that we must undertake throughout the period of preparation. We have to become ourselves adults in Christ, adults in Christendom, before God, at the same time that Clement of Alexandria was saying: if you want to become Christians, become little children before God or little children in Christ.

So much for the first aspect of sin. The second aspect of sin, which justifies the kind of preparation necessary for baptism, is the following: in sin, not only has nature been perverted, not only has it become other (well, it has remained the same and become other at the same time), but more, what characterizes sin is that the other has entered into us. That is to say, in sin, and on the basis of the original fall, Satan has found a place for himself in the soul, in the soul of every man, he has established his empire at the very heart of men's soul, and he has made of these souls, and of all of them, his own church. Each of our souls is, as it were, a little church within which Satan reigns and exercises his power. You can see how Tertullian differentiates himself here from the idea of the fall as this was understood in most religions of salvation, and equally in the Gnostics or the Neo-Platonists,[29] that is that the soul, being what

---

* Two or three unintelligible words.

it is, having its seat or its place close to God, or in the supra-celestial element, falls, and falls into matter. This means that the fall consists in the soul, in its purity, being placed within an impure element. Whereas [for] Tertullian—and this too is an important change—sin and the fall [do not consist in] falling into the element of evil and matter, but in there being an element, the element of evil within the soul, in there being something which is an other, and this other is the devil. Now the role of baptism is precisely to drive this hostile, foreign, external and other element, Satan, from the soul. Consequently, baptism involves dispossessing Satan of his empire and church, and it is understandable— put yourself in Satan's place—that he finds it difficult to put up with this and so, as Tertullian says, he "redoubles his frenzy" as the time of baptism approaches.[30]

And here too you see an important shift. Whereas in the analysis or perspective that dominated the second century you had this idea of an initiation through teaching, which meant that the individual increasingly approaches the truth and the moment of his illumination (and so we can imagine a sort of continuous progression, with nothing more dramatic than the ascent towards truth, belief, the profession of faith, and, consequently, towards illumination—the spatiality, if you like, of baptismal preparation in the second century is evidently an ascending line), in contrast, with Tertullian, you have this idea, which will also be crucial in the history of Christianity, that the more Christian one is, the more one is at risk. The more Christian one is, the more the devil rages. The closer one gets to the truth, to liberation, the more hostile, violent, furious, and dangerous the enemy. And as a result, you see in Tertullian, for the first time I think, the appearance of this idea (which he formulates moreover) that the time of baptism is the time of danger, of peril.[31] A drama of struggle and no longer a pedagogical drama of progressive illumination. Consequently you see why preparation for baptism must take on a completely different form and style here as well.

The time of baptism is both a time of radical transformation of nature, which is both the same and other and must be restored to what it is, and, on the other hand, a time of struggle and combat against the adversary.

To summarize, we can say that in his conception of preparation for baptism, Tertullian is intent on maintaining two things. First, what he calls God's "liberality," *liberalitas*, that God must remain free even within this rite that assures the purification of the soul. He must have this *liberalitas*: on the one hand, generosity, which pardons and enables men to obtain their pardon through the incarnation of the Savior and his sacrifice, and [on the other], freedom to pardon. *Liberalitas* in two senses, generosity and freedom, generosity that pardons and freedom to pardon is what has to be maintained for God's part. And what has to be maintained for man's part throughout this preparation for baptism, and up to baptism itself, and, as we shall see, after baptism? Well, it is fear, *metus*.[32] *Liberalitas* for God's part, fear, *metus*, for man's part.

So, here again, I think we have a fundamental new element with Tertullian which will be crucial for the history of the whole of Christianity. The Christian must never abandon fear when he prepares for baptism, and after he has been baptized. He must know that he is always in danger. He must always be anxious. Danger never subsides; he is never safe, he must never relax. Here again you see, of course, the contrast not only with Gnostic themes, but with all that there was behind them, with Neo-Platonist and even, to some extent, Stoic themes, all of which referred to a certain state of wisdom, of purity from which there is no return and in which one is inaccessible to danger, temptation, transgression, sin, and impurity. This idea that baptism must be prepared for with fear and maintain the Christian in a state of fear basically dismisses the theme that was so important throughout Antiquity, the Hellenistic period, and the first two and a half centuries of Christianity: the theme of the pure, the perfect, the sage. To tell the truth, it is not a definitive dismissal because the whole history of Christianity, even of Western Christianity, will be constantly traversed by the return, the recurrence of this theme, or, if you like, by nostalgia for a state of wisdom to which one might gain access through a particularly intense purification, a particularly effective ascesis, or quite simply by the fact of election and being chosen by God. The whole debate with the Gnosis, with Manichaeism, with the Cathars in the Middle Ages, with quietism in the seventeenth century, the debate, also, throughout Christianity with any form of mysticism, will be nothing other than the recurrence or reappearance in these different forms of the debate between anxiety and purity.

Even so, I think that this anxiety will be like the fundamental element in the system of salvation as Christianity conceived it in, let's say, its orthodox form, and I think that with this anxiety, this *metus*, this fear that Tertullian puts as the fundamental characteristic of the relationship that the subject must have to himself in his preparation for baptism, and in baptism itself, two things stand out. On the one hand, there can be no uncertainty with regard to access to the truth, in the sense that one must be very sure and cannot doubt for a moment that the truth is true, that what one is taught is true, that the truth really has been revealed in Scripture, and here non-anxiety, certainty without confusion is absolutely fundamental. This will be the pole of faith. But, on the other hand, there must be constant anxiety in the subject's relationship to himself, in the soul's relationship to itself, because here, on the one hand, one must never be certain that one is absolutely pure and, on the other, one must never be sure that one will be saved. [...] fundamental and necessary uncertainty, founding anxiety of the feeling of faith and the act of faith in that which concerns oneself. If one wants to have faith, one must never be certain about what one is oneself.

I am anticipating a lot, you do not find this in Tertullian, but, pushed to the extreme, it is what will be formulated in Protestantism. We can say that Protestantism, when it made the whole of Christian life revolve around what absolutely cannot be doubted in faith and the act of faith, around faith as the rock of Christian existence, and, at the same time, around the fundamental anxiety, which nothing can reassure, concerning what you are and will be, the purity you have achieved and the salvation promised you, the twinning of this certainty and uncertainty and the extreme form [that they]* take in Protestantism, and especially in Calvinism, is nothing else but the extreme version of what is formulated in embryo in Tertullian, when, in a seemingly throwaway [phrase],† he says: Preparation for baptism must be the time of *metus* and *periculi*, of fear and danger.[33] Fear, for the first time in history—well, fear in the sense of fear about oneself, of what one is, of [what may happen],‡ and not fear of destiny, not fear of the gods' decrees—this fear is, I think, anchored in Christianity from the turn of the second and third century and will obviously be of absolutely decisive importance in the whole

---

* M.F.: that this certainty and this uncertainty.
† M.F.: a passage.
‡ Hearing uncertain.

history of what we may call subjectivity, that is to say the relationship of self to self, the exercise of self on self, and the truth that the individual may discover deep within himself.

A practical consequence of this conception of the preparation for baptism in Tertullian—and here I refer you to chapter 6 of *De paenitentia*, which, together with *De baptismo*, is the most important text for understanding all this: "the sinner," he says, in this time of preparation for baptism, "must lament his sins even before the time of pardon," for, he says, and this is the text I was just talking about, "the time of repentance (*pénitence*) is that of *periculi* and *metus*, danger and fear. To those who are about to enter the water, I do not deny the effectiveness of God's benefit, but to attain it one must work, put oneself to the task"— well, "*elaborandum est*": one must work, make the effort.[34] What is this labor? It is what Tertullian calls [at the beginning of the next chapter]* "*paenitentiae disciplina*,"[35] the discipline of repentance (*pénitence*). It is the discipline of repentance that must constitute the fundamental armature of this time of preparation for baptism.

What is meant by "discipline of repentance"? First, you know that *paenitentia*, repentance (*pénitence*), is the absolutely classic Latin translation of the term *metanoia* we talked about [two weeks ago].† And what is *metanoia* in the Greek texts of the Hellenistic period and of the second Christian century, that is, in both non-Christians and Christians? You know, it is the change of the soul, that is to say essentially the movement by which the soul pivots on itself or, more precisely, the movement by which it turns away from what until then it had been looking at, and to which it was attached—shadows, matter, the world, appearances. *Metanoia* is also the movement by which the soul, by turning away from these shadows, from matter, and from the world here below, turns towards the light, towards truth, towards the truth that illuminates it, that is both the reward for this movement of the soul turning on itself, and its driving force, since it is because it is attracted by truth and inasmuch as it is attracted by truth, that the soul can thus direct itself towards the light, a light that provides it with the spectacle of what until then was hidden from it and enables it at the same time to fully

---

* M.F.: in the next sentence.
† M.F.: last week. [See the end of the lecture of 30 January, p. 87, and p. 89, note 12.]

know itself, since now it will be permeated by light. And this illumination that offers it all that is visible in the invisible, that makes the invisible visible, this movement of light that entirely permeates it and makes it transparent to itself, is also, of course, what will purify it, inasmuch as impurity is shadow, the taint, the stain. This, roughly, is what *metanoia* was in the pagan texts of the Hellenistic period, and also in the texts of the second Christian century.[36]

So, the classical Latin translation of *metanoia* is *paenitentia*, repentance (*pénitence*).[37] But in Tertullian repentance takes on a completely different meaning. We see this in chapter 10 of *De baptismo* when he questions himself about one of the most debated points of the time concerning baptism, that is to say, the meaning of John's baptism, [the fact] that the Baptist baptized even before he baptized Christ (he had to baptize before Christ, moreover, since he baptized Christ). So what was this baptism? For if we say—and Tertullian does so constantly—that this is Christian baptism, with the Holy Spirit that descends into the soul and purifies, does this mean that the Baptist who, even before the Savior, and so even before the promise of salvation is accomplished, baptized the people? This was an enormous debate at the time. If John's baptisms made Christians, and consequently saved, Christ is pointless. But if John's baptism does not save, is it then a false baptism, a pseudo-baptism, and consequently why then did Christ receive baptism from John? Tertullian's reply is that in the history of salvation—in the order of salvation, as he says—there were two baptisms. The first was John's baptism, which was *baptimus paenitentiae*, the baptism of repentance:[38] this is not a baptism in which the Holy Spirit descends; it is a specifically human baptism. John the Baptist was a man, he baptized men and there was nothing heavenly in this baptism. Consequently, there was neither illumination by the Holy Spirit nor remission of sins by God.[39] What was there? There was repentance (*pénitence*), that is to say nothing more than men's regret for their own sins, their repentance (*repentir*), their detachment from these old sins, the resolution not repeat them. This baptism of repentance had its meaning before Christ, for the whole time in which the Savior had not yet come. It was, as it were, a stepping stone, and it is when the Savior has come that this work of repentance, before salvation itself, was able to find its reward in the effective remission of sins that could only take place with Christ. Christ's baptism is precisely this turning point, for Christ receives John's baptism, not because he needs to repent, but in order to show that one must repent before receiving baptism and that true baptism for Christians will be the one he received, when the Holy Spirit came down, during baptism by John—not that John had the power to make [the Holy Spirit]* descend, because he had only the baptism of repentance; it was God who wished to transform this prior baptism of repentance into a baptism of remission and salvation by the coming of the Holy Spirit.

So, John's baptism proves that our baptism must unfold, basically, in two stages: a prior stage of repentance, which is not *metanoia* strictly speaking, which is not the illuminating turning around of the soul on itself towards the light, but which is the stage of preparation. And then, baptism strictly speaking, which will be an illumination. In other words, *metanoia* is diffracted. And this movement designated by *metanoia*, which had been at the same time both detachment from and turning towards, detachment from darkness and being illuminated, and detachment from because one is attracted by the force of the light, is now dissociated into two moments in Tertullian, one of which will be the exercise itself of repentance (*pénitence*), and then, after, the illumination that rewards it. In short, the stage of ascesis is in the process of freeing itself from the stage of illumination. Or again, the exercise of self on self must be preliminary to the movement by which one becomes subject of knowledge in the illumination that opens us up to the eternal truths.

So much for the meaning of *paenitentiae* in the *disciplina paenitentiae*. *Paenitentia*, then, is a kind of dissociation [starting] from the unified movement of *metanoia*.

Second, what is discipline? Actually, Tertullian says relatively little about this discipline of repentance. The texts—we will come back to them next week—that tell us about the nature of the ascesis prior to baptism are found in the same period as Tertullian in the Canons of Saint Hippolytus.[40] Tertullian† [first of all] gives some negative indications: if in actual fact baptism can be given only after a certain time of ascesis and exercise, after repentance, this implies, first, of course, that baptism must not be given hastily and in any old way. We don't

---

* M.F.: the baptism.
† M.F. repeats: says relatively little.

give holy things to the dogs; we don't cast pearls before swine.[41] This also means that baptism cannot be given to children and babies; it can be given only to adults.[42] This is also to say, of course, that we don't give baptism to the unmarried, for it is then that the assaults of incontinence could triumph over their virtue. When they are married, then, of course, we are more sure of their continence, and so it is more reliable to give baptism to married people.[43] So much for the negative precautions.

For the positive indications, Tertullian is equally reserved and hasty. He says: "the sinner must lament his sins before the time of the pardon"[44] and as the moment of baptism draws near, those who are going to enter into it must "call on God with fervent prayers, fasts, kneeling, and vigils."[45] At the level of prescriptions, there is not much, then, in comparison with what was said in the second century when it was still a matter of teaching. But what is interesting is the meaning Tertullian gives to these practices of fasting, vigils, kneeling, and prayer that he, like his contemporaries and predecessors, recommends. What actually is the meaning of these exercises? Of course, as always, the meaning is one of purifying, cleansing. But, the second important meaning is that not only must these practices enable faults to be erased, they must [also] give the individual the ability, the aptitude, the strength, and, we might say, the skill to struggle against evil, since, once again, Satan intensifies his attacks at the time of baptism. So we must be able to repel them, but we must also know that, after baptism, Satan will not cease to multiply his assaults and intensify their fury.[46] Consequently, the time of preparation for baptism does not simply assure or allow the purification of baptism itself. It gives the strength and ability to struggle after baptism, throughout the life of the Christian. Preparation for baptism is therefore ascesis in this strict sense: it is a gymnastics. It is a physical gymnastics, a corporal gymnastics, a spiritual gymnastics, a gymnastics of the body and the soul for this long struggle against evil, against Satan, against the Other in ourselves, against the temptation (another fundamental category to which we will return) that we will never be able to get rid of. Hence this idea that if the time of preparation for baptism must indeed be a *disciplina paenitentiae*, a discipline of repentance, then so too, the entire life of the Christian must also be a repentance.

You can see that [with this]* idea of a specific moral exercise for those preparing for baptism, and which is thus freed from the overall idea of *metanoia*, we arrive on the other hand at this idea that the whole of life must be a life of repentance (*pénitence*).[47] This is, I think, important in the new interpretation Tertullian gives of the preparation for baptism. And a second meaning is equally important. We find it in chapter 6 of *De paenitentia*, where he speaks of those, who we talked about right at the beginning, who expect automatic purification from baptism, thinking that, God having to purify the souls anyway, we can sin as much as we like, for the day will come when, through baptism, we will be freed from all this and all sins will be remitted. Faced with this, Tertullian is indignant and says: "what an insane as well as unjust calculation of not fulfilling repentance hoping for the remission of sins, that is to say, not paying the price and holding out a hand for the goods! For the Lord has put forgiveness at this price: He offers us impunity in exchange for repentance."[48] This is an absolutely interesting and, I must say, rather paradoxical idea, since it seems that Tertullian wants to say: baptism is a certain reward, the forgiving of sin, which really has to be paid for, it has to be purchased at a certain price, and one's repentance before baptism is the price one offers to be forgiven. This is a doubly paradoxical idea, first of all because it appears to establish an equivalence between the reward, which is nothing less than eternal life, and the inevitably limited time of penitential exercise in preparation for baptism. How can there be equivalence between these two things, between the finite and the infinite, Pascal will say?[49] And second, if repentance actually is the price of baptism, this means that once one has paid the price, God is obliged to give the [pardon],† and so we come back to the idea of a constraint.

However, the development of the passage shows, in fact, that this is not what Tertullian means when he says that repentance is the price one pays for baptism and the remission of sins. When he speaks of price as like money one pays to be baptized, he means the following: when one buys something, the seller begins by examining the money paid to him in order to see whether the coins have been clipped, if they bear

---

* M.F.: by separating out the idea.
† M.F.: baptism.

the legitimate stamp, or if they have been adulterated. In the same way, the Lord tests repentance as one tests a coin, in order to "accord us the reward of nothing less than the eternal truth." In the text, Tertullian calls this *paenitentiae probatio*, the test of repentance or again the truth of repentance.[50] That is to say, with this preparatory repentance the postulant does not really buy forgiveness at its just price, for the price of pardon is infinite as is the pardon itself. When the candidate for baptism gives the coin of repentance, all he does is give some elements that make possible the *probatio*, that make it possible to know whether the repentance is good money, not inauthentic, not hypocritical, but indeed true. Through this metaphor, we see emerging the idea of repentance having to display in God's sight the truth of the sinner himself, the sincerity of his feelings, the authenticity of his remorse, the reality of his intention not to sin again. Repentance therefore brings to the surface the soul's profound truth, and it is in this that we can say that repentance is a coin. It is what makes possible the *probatio*.

What we see here is a splitting of that kind of unitary movement I tried to define with regard to *metanoia*. In *metanoia* there was a unitary movement inasmuch as in turning towards the truth, the soul discovered its own truth. Now, we have two stages, two levels. On the one hand, of course, there is the truth one must learn in preparing for baptism and which enlightens you in fact in baptism itself, and then there is another truth, which is the truth of the movement itself, the truth of the soul itself moving towards the good, trying to free itself from evil, struggling against it, and training itself to defeat it. [A] truth, consequently, for the soul, that will be given at the end of the process, when, with baptism and the profession of faith, the Holy Spirit descends into the soul. So, a movement of oneself towards the truth that is God, but also a truth of the soul, a truth of self in the sight of God. And the double function of repentance is here: to prepare and ensure the progression that goes towards the truth, and to manifest, for the orthogonal gaze of God who sees all and constantly keeps watch over us, the truth of what we are. Truth for the soul, truth that will become truth in the soul, but also truth of the soul, and this is what repentance must manifest. Hence phrase which is enigmatic but which I think we can now understand: "faith," says Tertullian, "begins and is commended by *paenitentiae fides*, faith begins and is commended by the faith of repentance."[51] That is to say he [establishes a link between]* the problem of the truth of the soul, of repentance, and of the exercise of self on self that must be at every moment the guarantor and support of the progression towards the truth.

Well, I think we can stop there. Just a couple of words. You can see that with these texts of Tertullian we have the point of decoupling of what could be called the structure of teaching and the structure of test. The structure of teaching, the pedagogical structure, which dominated in the texts of the second century, is a structure in which the soul appears as the target, object, co-author, and also co-actor of a procedure that aims to form the soul as a subject of knowledge. In the structure of test we have, on the contrary, a movement by which the soul must constitute itself as the protagonist of a procedure at the end of which it becomes, and throughout which it remains, an object of knowledge. Roughly speaking, in the Apostolic Fathers and the apologists, preparation for baptism was quite similar to those forms of initiation in which the structure of teaching was dominant, or, if you like again, those forms of initiation in which teaching and test were integrated to such an extent that teaching and its progress were in themselves the test. One had, in fact, to progress in the teaching until one knew all the truths and was able to profess them. This was the fundamental pedagogical structure in Christian thought regarding baptism throughout the second century; it is what we still find in Clement of Alexandria. As it appears in Tertullian—a contemporary of Clement of Alexandria, moreover, but who marks, I think, the point of decoupling—preparation for baptism appears rather as an intertwining between a structure of acquisition of the truth by the soul and a structure of manifestation of the soul in its truth. I think that we have there the germ of that dissociation or, at any rate, of that bipolarity that appears to me to be a distinctive feature of the regime of truth of Christianity. When beginning this course,[52] I spoke to you about these two poles of the regime of truth of Christianity that stretch almost to the point of being torn apart and dissociated, the pole of faith and pole of confession, the east of faith and the west of confession. I think that the whole history of Christianity is stretched between these two poles. It seems to me that we are glimpsing,

---

* Conjecture; audition difficult.

absolutely in embryo, this dissociation of the pole of faith and the pole of confession, this dissociation of the east of faith and the west of confession, in these few texts of Tertullian, in which the idea of a *probatio fidei* comes to stress, mark, and, to tell the truth, give its profound meaning to the idea of a preparation for baptism that is relatively autonomous, or, at any rate, specific in relation to the illumination promised in baptism. Ascesis and illumination are beginning to separate. As a consequence, confession will separate from faith.

1. Clément d'Alexandrie (v. 150-215/216), *Le Protreptique*, introd., trans., and notes by C. Mondésert, revised and expanded by A. Plassart (Paris: Cerf, SC, no. 2bis, 2004 [1949]); English translation by William Wilson, Clement of Alexandria, *Exhortation to the Heathen*, in Alexander Roberts and James Donaldson, eds., revised by A. Cleveland Coxe, in *ANF, Vol. II: Fathers of the Second Century* (Grand Rapids, Michigan: W.M. Eerdmmans, 1994).

2. Clément d'Alexandrie, *Le Pédagogue*, introd. and notes by H.-I. Marrou, trans. M. Harl (Book I), C. Montdésert (Book II), C. Montdésert and C. Matray (Book III), (Paris: Cerf, SC, nos. 70, 108, and 158 1983 [1960-1970]); English translation by William Wilson as Clement of Alexandria, *The Instructor (Paedagogus)* in *ANF, Vol. II*.

3. Clément d'Alexandrie, *Stromates*, trans. C. Montdésert (Books I, II, and IV), P. Voulet (Book V), P. Descourtieux (Book VI), and A. Le Boulluec (Book VII), (Paris: Cerf, SC, nos. 30, 38, 278-279, 428, 447, and 463, 1951-2001); English translation by William Wilson as Clement of Alexandria, *The Stromata, or Miscellanies*, in *ANF, Vol. II*. See the plan announced by Clement of what was for a long time considered as his trilogy (the three stages of Christian education: conversion, education, instruction) in *Le Pédagogue*, Book I, I, 3, p. 113; *The Instructor*, Book I, ch. one, p. 209. The identification of the *Stromata* with the announced *Didascalos (The Teacher)*, however, has been challenged since the end of the nineteenth century. On this point see the introductions of C. Montdésert to the *Protreptique*, p. 14, and to the *Stromate*, I, pp. 11-22. Clement explains the title of his work at several points; see, for example, *Stromata*, p. 409: "Let these notes of ours, as we have often said for the sake of those that consult them carelessly, be of varied character—and as the name itself indicates, patched together—passing constantly from one thing to another, and in the series of discussions hinting at one thing and demonstrating another." See also H. von Campenhausen, *Les Pères grecs*, trans. O. Marbach (Paris: éd. de l'Orante, 1963; rééd. Seuil, "Livre de vie," 1969) p. 48: "As the title indicates, this book belongs to a certain literary genre cultivated by writers of antiquity. It was a matter of collections of works dealing with various subjects, often with no relation between them, and which were called 'Cloths, Embroideries, Meadows, Helicons.' They are 'miscellanies,' essays, or collections of anecdotes, drafts, which Hellenistic taste made into a veritable literary genre." For a more detailed analysis of the meaning of the title, see C. Montdésert, introduction to *Stromate*, I, pp. 6-11 and A. Méhat, *Etude sur les 'Stromates' de Clément d'Alexandrie* (Paris: Seuil, 1966, pp. 96-106).

4. Tertullien, *De paenitentia/La pénitence*, VI, 17. Foucault did not know the "Sources chétiennes" edition, which appeared in 1984. He used the translation of Father E.-A. de Genoude, in *Œuvres de Tertullien*, vol. 2 (Paris: L. Vivès, 2nd ed., 1852) pp. 197-215. The manuscript gives the citation in this form: "We are [not] bathed in the water in order to be purified, but because we are purified." It seems therefore that Foucault translated the Latin text himself, somewhat freely (*"Non ideo abluimur ut delinquere desinamus, sed quia desiimus, quoniam iam corde loti sumus"*). But in another manuscript version of the passage of this lecture, he faithfully copies de Genoude's translation: "We are not washed *in order that* we cease sinning, but *because* we have ceased, and are already washed deep in our heart" (p. 207, words underlined by Foucault). English translation by S. Thelwall as Tertullian, *On Repentance*, ch. VI, in *ANF, Vol. III*, p. 662; "We are not washed *in order that* we *may* cease sinning, but *because* we *have* ceased, since in *heart* we have *been* bathed already" (words emphasized in translation).

5. Tertullien, *De baptismo/Traité du baptême*, trans. F. Refoulé and M. Drouzy, introd. and notes by F. Refoulé (Paris: Cerf, SC, no. 35, 2002 [1952]). Foucault uses this edition alongside the translation by de Genoude in *Œuvres de Tertullien*, vol. 3, pp. 239-261; English translation by S. Thelwall as Tertullian, *On Baptism* in *ANF, Vol. III*.

6. Foucault's references to the gnosis are always very general and it is difficult to know what works he used on the subject. No doubt he drew his knowledge, in the main, from his conversations with H.-C. Puech (Professor of History of Religions at the Collège de France until 1972) and from reading his books. See already, *Sécurité, territoire, population*, lecture of 1 March 1978, pp. 198-199 and p. 221 note 6; *Security, Territory, Population*, pp. 195-196 (regarding that "sort of intoxication of religious behavior" evidenced by some Gnostic sects in the first centuries) and p. 217 note 6; see too *L'herméneutique du sujet*, lecture of 6 January 1982, First hour, p. 18, and pp. 25-26, note 49; *The Hermeneutics of the Subject*, p. 16 and pp. 23-24, note 49. On the available sources—writings of Christian refuters, original texts discovered for the most part from the middle of the 1940s (Coptic library of Nag Hammadi), various documents—and Gnostic doctrines, see: J. Doresse, "La Gnose," in H.-C. Puech, ed., *Histoire des religions* (Paris: Gallimard,

"Bibliothèque de la Pléiade," 1972; "Folio/Essais," II*, 1999), pp. 364-429, and K. Rudolph, *Die Gnosis: Wesen und Geschichte einer Spätantiken Religion* (Leipzig: Koehler & Amelang, 1977); English translation by R. McLachlan Wilson, *Gnosis: The Nature and History of Gnosticism* (New York: Harper San Francisco, 2000 [1987]), according to M. Tardieu, *Revue de l'histoire des religions*, no. 194/2, 1978, p. 200: "the best current introduction to the study of the 'gnosis'"; on the relations between Gnosticism and Christianity, an excellent synthesis by E. Trocmé, "Le christianisme jusqu'à 325," in H.-C. Puech, ed., *Histoire des religions*, pp. 241-247.

7. In the following lecture Foucault corrects: not Nicolaitans but Cainites (see below, p. 148). The confusion may be explained by the fact that Tertullian in *De praescriptione*, XXXIII, 10, presents the Cainites as another kind of Nicolaitans (cited by F. Refoulé, Introduction to *Traité du baptême*, p. 10, note 3. However, the latter clarifies later on p. 71 note 1, that Tertullian, by insisting on the fact that the water does not wash away our sins like simple filth, "has in mind the Cainites, and generally all the Gnostic dualists.") Strangely, in the manuscript Foucault first wrote "Cainites," and then replaced this with "Nicolaitans." On this Gnostic current, see J. Daniélou and H. Marrou, *Nouvelle histoire de l'Eglise*, vol. I: "Des origines à Grégoire le Grand" (Paris: Seuil, 1963), pp. 90-91.

8. Tertullien, *De baptismo/Traité du baptême*, I, 2, trans. Genoude, p. 239: "for a while a woman, or rather a most venomous viper of the Cainite sect, has seduced hereabouts a great number of our brothers by the poison of her doctrines. She attacks baptism most of all"; SC, p. 65; see F. Refoulé, Introduction, p. 11; Tertullian, *On Baptism*, ch. I, *ANF, Vol. III*, p. 669: "a viper of the Cainite heresy, lately conversant in this quarter, has carried away a great number with her most venomous doctrine, making it her first aim to destroy baptism."

9. Ibid., II, 2: Fr., Genoude, p. 240; SC, p. 66: "*nonne mirandum est lavacro dilui mortem* (is it not astonishing that a bath can dissolve death)?"; Eng., ch. II, p. 669: "Is it not wonderful, too, that death should be washed away by bathing?"

10. Ibid., III, 2: Fr., Genoude, p. 241; SC, p. 67; Eng., ch. III, p. 670 : "and the Spirit of the Lord was hovering over the waters."

11. Ibid., III, 5: Fr., Genoude, p. 240; SC, p. 68; Eng., ch. III, p. 670: "For was not the work of fashioning man himself achieved with the aid of waters? Suitable material is found in the *earth*, yet not apt for the purpose unless it be moist and juicy, which (earth) 'the waters,' separated the fourth day before into their own place, temper with their remaining moisture to a clayey consistency."

12. Ibid., V, 7: Fr., Genoude, p. 246: "Thus man is rendered to God, in the likeness of the first man who was created in the past in the image of God"; SC, p. 74; Eng., ch. V, p. 672: "Thus man will be restored for God to His '*likeness*,' who in days bygone had been *conformed* to 'the image' of God."

13. Ibid., VIII, 74: Fr., Genoude, p. 247; SC, p. 77; Eng., ch. VIII, p. 673: "the waters of the deluge, by which the old iniquity was purged."

14. Ibid., IX, 1: Fr., Genoude, p. 248; SC, p. 78; Eng., ch. IX, p. 673: "when the people, set unconditionally free, escaped the violence of the Egyptian king by crossing over *through water*, it was *water* that extinguished the king himself, with his entire forces." On the comparison of baptism with the crossing of the Red Sea, see below, lecture of 20 February 1980.

15. Ibid., IX, 3: Fr., Genoude, p. 248; SC, pp. 78-79; Eng., ch. IX, p. 673.

16. Ibid., V, 5: Fr., Genoude, p. 245; SC, p. 74; Eng., ch. V, pp. 671-672. On this "symbolism of water, in its both natural and biblical roots," see F. Refoulé, Introduction to *Traité du baptême*, pp. 19-28.

17. Ibid., I, 1: Fr., Genoude, p. 239; Eng., ch. I, p. 669: "Happy is our sacrament of water, in that, by washing away the sins of our early blindness, we are set free and admitted into eternal life!"

18. See Ibid., XVIII, 1: Fr., Genoude, p. 257; SC, p. 91; Eng., ch. XVIII, pp. 677-678.

19. Ibid., XV, 3: Fr., Genoude, pp. 255-256: "The Christian is baptized only once, so as to warn him that after this he must no longer sin"; SC, p. 88; Eng., ch. XV, p. 676: "There is to us, one and but one, baptism … We enter, then, the font *once: once* are sins washed away, because they ought never to be repeated."

20. Tertullien, *De paenitentia/La pénitence*, VI, 3, SC, p. 165: "… all these culpable tergiversations with regard to repentance are due to the fact that one receives baptism with presumption. Certain, in fact, of assured pardon of one's sins, by waiting one steals from the time that remains and accords oneself a delay to sin again, instead of learning not to sin at all"; Genoude,

p. 205: "All this slowness and criminal tergiversation with regard to repentance derive from a prejudice about the virtue of baptism. With the certainty that their sins will be remitted, the catechumens steal for themselves the time remaining to them, taking advantage of the delay to sin, instead of learning to abstain from sinning"; Tertullian, *On Repentance*, ch. VI, p. 661: "Moreover, a presumptuous confidence in baptism introduces all kind of vicious delay and ter-giversation with regard to repentance; for, feeling sure of undoubted pardon of their sins, men meanwhile steal the intervening time, and make it for themselves a holiday-time for sinning, rather than a time for learning not to sin."

21. *De baptismo/Traité du baptême*, I, 1: Genoude, p. 239; SC, p. 64; *On Baptism*, ch. 1, p. 669.

22. *De paenitentia/La pénitence*, VI, 11, SC, pp. 168-169: "*liberalitatem eius faciunt servitutem*" ("they transform His free benevolence into servitude"); Genoude, p. 206: "They make a servitude of God's generosity"; Labriolle, p. 27: "they transform His generosity into servitude"; *On Repentance*, ch. VI, p. 661: "they turn His liberality into slavery."

23. See Tertullien, *De testimonia animae*, III, PL, 1, 613 A (passage cited by A. d'Alès, *La théologie de Tertullien*, 1905, p. 265 note 2, and by A. Gaudel, "Péché originel," col. 364): "*Per [Satanam] homo a primordio circumventus ut praeceptum Dei excedere, et propterea in mortem datus, exinde totum genus de suo semine infectum suae etiam damnationis traducem fecit*"; Genoude, vol. 2, p. 121: "We too recognize [Satan] as the angel of evil, the artisan of error, the corrupter of the world, the enemy by which man letting himself be tricked in the beginning, transgressed God's precept, was given over to death as a result of this revolt, and bound to a posterity that he corrupts in his seed, the heritage of his condemnation"; English translation by S. Thelwall as Tertullian, *The Soul's Testimony* in *ANF, Vol. III*, p. 177: "the very same [Satan] we hold to be the angel of evil, the source of error, the corrupter of the whole world, by whom in the beginning man was entrapped into breaking the commandment of God. And (the man) being given over to death on account of his sin, the entire human race, tainted in their descent from him, were made a channel for transmitting his condemnation." See F. Refoulé, Introduction, *Traité du baptême*, p. 13 note 2: "His conception of original sin is found to depend on "traducianism" of which he is one of the most ardent defenders. See especially *De Anima*, 27" (see note 25 below). "For the traducianists, the soul of Adam is transmitted at the same time as the body and, in Adam, it sinned. We are all, in the testimony of the Apostle, constituted as sinners by the single fault of Adam. Now the specific seat of sin is the soul" (A Sage, "Péché originel," *Revue des Etudes Augustiniennes*, XII, 3-4 (1976), p. 227). See above, lecture of 6 February, p. 112, note 28 on original sin. On the question of generation and heredity in Tertullian, see too M. Spanneut, *Le stoïcisme des Pères de l'Eglise* (Paris: Le Seuil, "Patristica Sorbonensia I," 1957), pp. 181-188 (on the hereditary transmission of original sin, pp. 187-188).

24. So-called theory of the "pangenesis" of the sperm. The seed, according to Democritus, is a kind of shaken up foam, then propelled by a movement of the air. See Democritus B 32 in J.-P. Dumont et al., eds., *Les Présocratiques* (Paris: Gallimard, "Bibliothèque de la Pléiade," 1988), p. 861: "The sexual act is a little apoplexy. For a man comes from a man and is freed by separating from him in one go"; English translation by Jonathan Barnes in Jonathan Barnes, *Early Greek Philosophy* (Harmondsworth: Penguin Books, 1987) p, 271: "Coition is mild mad-ness; for a man rushes out of a man."

25. Tertullien, *De anima*, 27; *De l'âme*, trans. Genoude, vol. 2, p. 55: "We make life begin at concep-tion, because we maintain that the soul begins at conception. Life in fact has the same begin-ning as the soul: the substances which are separated by death are therefore equally combined in a same life. Then, if we assign priority to one, saying the other comes after, we will also have to distinguish the times of the seed, according to the nature of their degrees; and when then will we place the seed of the body, and when that of the soul? Furthermore, if the time of the seed has to be distinguished, the substances will also become different through the difference of times. Now, however we admit that there are two kinds of seed, one for the body, the other for the soul, we nevertheless declare them inseparable, and thus contemporaneous and simultane-ous"; English translation by Peter Holmes as Tertullian, *A Treatise On The Soul*, ch. XXVII, in *ANF, Vol. III*, pp. 207-208: "Now we allow that life begins with conception, because we con-tend that the soul also begins from conception; life taking its commencement at the same time and place as the soul does. Thus, then, the processes which act together to produce separation by death, also combine in a simultaneous action to produce life. If we assign priority to (the formation of) one of the natures, and a subsequent time to the other, we shall have further to

determine the precise times of the semination, according to the condition and rank of each. And that being so, what time shall we give to the seed of the body, and what to the seed of the soul? Besides, if different periods are to be assigned to the seminations then arising out of this difference in time, we shall also have different substances. For although we shall allow that there are two kinds of seed—that of the body and that of the soul—we still declare that they are inseparable, and therefore contemporaneous and simultaneous in origin." See M. Spanneut, *Le Stoïcisme*, p. 184.

26. Ibid., 41: "*Malum igitur animae, praeter quod ex obuentu spiritus nequam superstruitur, ex originis uitio antecedit, naturale quodammodo. Nam, ut diximus, naturae corruptio alia natura est*"; Genoude, p. 83: "Thus the evil of the soul, beyond that which is sown later by the arrival of the evil spirit, has its earlier source in an original corruption, in some sense inherent in nature. For, as we have said, the corruption of nature is like another nature"; *A Treatise on the Soul*, ch. XLI, p. 220: "There is, then, besides the evil which supervenes on the soul from the intervention of the evil spirit, an antecedent, and in a certain sense natural, evil which arises from its corrupt origin. For, as we have said before, the corruption of our nature is another nature."

27. See *De Paenitentia*, VI, 1-3, trans. Genoude, p. 205: "All that our weakness has striven to suggest on the need to embrace repentance and to persevere on the way, concerns all God's servants, no doubt, since they aspire to salvation by making themselves favorable to God, but it is addressed mainly to those novices, whose ears have scarcely begun to drink in divine discourses, and who, like animals just born, creep with uncertain step before their eyes are fully open, affirm that they will renounce their past life, and adopt repentance, but neglect to practice it"; *On Repentance*, ch. VI, p. 661: "Whatever, then, our poor ability has attempted to suggest with reference to laying hold of repentance once for all, and perpetually retaining it, does indeed bear upon *all* who are given up to the Lord, as being all competitors for salvation in earning the favour of God; but is chiefly urgent in the case of those young novices who are only just beginning to bedew their ears with divine discourses, and who, as whelps in yet early infancy, and with eyes not yet perfect, creep about uncertainly, and say indeed that they renounce their former deed, and assume (the profession of) repentance, but neglect to complete it."

28. See Clément d'Alexandrie, *Le Pédagogue*. This theme of childhood, which in Clement derives from the identification of the Pedagogue with the Word or Christ-Logos, recurs throughout Book I of the treatise. See the Introduction by H.-I. Marrou, pp. 23-26 ("The spirit of childhood") and especially Book I, ch. 6, p. 156 et seq., "Against those who maintain that the names "children" and "infants" symbolically designate the teaching of elementary knowledge"; Clement of Alexandria, *The Instructor (Paedagogus)* Book I, ch. VI: "The Name Children Does Not Imply Instruction In Elementary Principles." On the symbol of milk, see Book I, ch. 6: 34,3-49,3, Fr., pp. 175-199 (the *logos* milk of Christ, 35,3; 40,2; 42,1; 43,4, etcetera); Eng., pp. 215-222. I, VI, 49,3, Fr., p. 199: "If we have been regenerated for Christ, the one who has regenerated us nourishes us with his own milk, the Logos"; Eng., p. 221: "For if we have been regenerated unto Christ, He who has regenerated us nourishes us with His own milk, the Word."

29. On this theme of the soul's fall in Plotinus, for example, see *The Enneades*, I, 8, 14, trans. Stephen MacKenna and B.S. Page (London: Faber and Faber, 2nd revised edition, 1956) I, 8, 14, p. 77: "This is the fall of the Soul, this entry into Matter; thence its weakness: not all the faculties of its being retain free play, for Matter hinders their manifestation; it encroaches upon the Soul's territory and, as it were, crushes the soul back; and it turns to evil all that it has stolen, until the Soul finds strength to advance again."

30. Tertullien, *De Paenitentia/La pénitence*, VII, 7, trans. Genoude, p. 209: "But our stubborn enemy never slackens in his malice. What am I saying? His frenzy increases when he sees man escaping his bonds; the more our passions are extinguished, the more his hatred is enflamed"; Tertullian, *On Repentance*, ch. VII, p. 662: "that most stubborn foe (of ours) never gives his malice leisure; indeed, he is then most savage when he fully feels that a man is freed *from his clutches*; he then flames fiercest while he is fast becoming extinguished."

31. Ibid., VI, 8; Fr., Genoude, p. 206: "The sinner must lament his sins before the day of pardon, because the time of repentance is a time of peril and fear"; Eng., ch. VI, p. 661: "A sinner is bound to bemoan himself *before* receiving pardon, because the time of repentance is coincident with that of peril and fear."

32. Ibid., VI, 17, Fr., Genoude, p. 207: "This is the first baptism of the Listener (*Auditeur*): an absolute fear"; Eng., ch. VI, p. 662: "For the *first* baptism of a learner is *this*, a perfect fear."

33. See above, note 31.

34. Ibid., VI, 9: Fr., Genoude, p. 206: "I am far from denying to those who are about to enter the water the effectiveness of God's divine benefit, in other words, the pardon of their sins; but, to have the happiness of attaining it, effort is required"; Eng., ch. VI, p. 661: "Not that I deny the divine benefit—the putting away of sins, I mean—is in every way sure to such as are on the point of entering the (baptismal) water; but what we have to labour for is, that it may be granted us to attain that blessing" (see above, note 30).

35. Ibid., VII, 1: "*Hucusque, Christe domine, de paenitentiae disciplina servis tuis dicere vel audire contingat, quousque etiam delinquere non oportet et audientibus*"; Fr., Genoude, p. 208: "Oh Jesus Christ, my Lord, accord to your servants the favor of knowing or hearing from my mouth the rule of repentance, in the sense that it is prohibited to catechumens themselves to sin!"; Eng., ch. VII, p. 662: "So long, Lord Christ, may the blessing of learning or hearing concerning the discipline of repentance be granted to Your servants, as it likewise behooves them, while *learners*, not to sin."

36. See again below, lecture of 20 February, p. OOO. Foucault will return at greater length on the analysis of this notion, in contrast with the Platonic *epistrophē*, in his 1982 lectures, *L'Herméneutique du sujet*, lecture of 10 February, First hour, pp. 202-209; *The Hermeneutics of the Subject*, pp. 209-217, explicitly relying on P. Hadot's article, "*Epistrophè* and *métanoia*" (1953), republished in "Conversion," *Exercises spirituels et philosophie antique* (Paris: Etudes augustiniennes, 1981), pp. 175-182. See note 40 by F. Gros, Fr., p. 218; Eng., p. 226, on this "essential text" (Foucault), and his note 11, Fr., p. 216; Eng., p. 225, for the relation with the analysis of penance in the 1980 lectures.

37. See the word "Pénitence" in the appendix 1, "Naissance d'un vocabulaire chrétien," of *Ecrits des Pères apostoliques*, pp. 478-480; B. Poschmann, "Buße," *Reallexikon für Antike und Chrisentum*, vol. II (Stuttgart: A. Hiersemann, 1954), col. 805-812; J. Guillet, "Metanoia," DS, X, 1982, col. 1093-1099.

38. Tertullien, *De baptism/Traité du baptême*, X, 5-6: "*agebatur itaque baptismus paenitentiae quasi candidatae remissionis et sanctificationis in Christo subsecuturae. Nam quod legimus, praedicabat baptismum paenitentiae in remissionem peccatorum, in futuram remissionem enuntiatum est, siquidem paenitentia antecedit, remissio sequitur, et hoc est viam praeparare*"; Fr., Genoude, p. 250; SC, p. 81: "Thus baptism of repentance (*baptismus paenitentiae*) was administered as a preparation for the pardon and sanctification to be brought by Christ. We read in fact that John preached a baptism of repentance (*baptismus paenitentiae*) for the remission of sins [Mark, 1, 4: *baptisma metanoias*]: this was said of the remission to come, since repentance precedes and remission comes after"; Eng., Tertullian, On Baptism, ch. X, p. 674: "And so the '*baptism of repentance*' was dealt with as if it were a candidate for the remission and sanctification shortly about to follow in Christ: for in that John used to preach '*baptism for the remission of sins*,' the declaration was made with reference to *future* remission, if it be true (as it is,) that repentance be antecedent, remission subsequent." The expression "*baptismus paenitentiae*" (*baptisma metanoias*) also appears in the *Acts of the Apostles*, 19, 4 ["baptism of repentance" in the King James and New Standard Version translations; G.B.].

39. At the place in the manuscript that corresponds to this passage of the lecture, Foucault, citing the Genoude translation of *De baptismo*, X, 4, p. 249, added this reference by Tertullian to the *Acts of the Apostles* (19, 2-3): "Those who had received the Apostles' baptism [*sic*, instead of "John's"] did not receive the Spirit, whom they had not even heard of"; Eng., ch. X, p. 674: "we find that men who had 'John's baptism' had not received the Holy Spirit, whom they knew not even by hearing."

40. This text, composed in the first half of the fourth century, of which Haneberg (1870) and Achelis (1891) offer the first Latin translations, is known only through an Arabic translation, which itself comes from a Coptic version of the original Greek. Its attribution to Hippolytus is due to the fact that it borrows a large part of its content from the *Tradition apostolique* of the Archbishop of Rome. The first critical edition of the Arabic version is by R.-G. Coquin, *Les Canons d'Hippolyte* (Paris: Firmin-Didot, "Patrologia Orientalis," vol. 31, fasc. 2, 1966), pp. 273-444. On pre-baptismal repentance, see canon 19, "On catechumens: on the conditions that catechumens fulfill during baptism and exorcism; on the order of the liturgy of baptism

and of the consecration of the Liturgy of the body and blood," pp. 375-387. Foucault refers again to this writing below, lecture of 20 February.

41. See Tertullien, *De baptismo/Traité du baptême*, XVIII, 1: Fr., Genoude, p. 257: "Remember rather these words 'Keep from giving holy things to dogs; do not throw your pearls before swine' [Mat. 7,6]"; SC, pp. 92-93; Eng., Tertullian, *On Baptism*, ch. XVIII, p. 677: "this *precept* is rather to be looked at carefully: '*Give not the holy thing to the dogs, nor cast your pearls before swine;*' (Mathew 7,6)."

42. Ibid., XVIII, 4-5: Fr., Genoude, p. 258; SC, pp. 92-93; Eng., p. 678.

43. Ibid.,XVIII, 6: Fr., Genoude, p. 259: "The reasons for deferring who are not yet committed in marriage are no less decisive. Freedom exposes them to too many temptations, virgins by their maturity, the widowed by their deprivation; they must wait until they are married or strengthened in continence"; SC, p. 92-93; Eng., ch. XVIII, p. 678: "For no less cause must the unwedded also be deferred—in whom *the ground of* temptation is prepared, as like as *never were* wedded by means of their maturity, and in the *widowed* by means of their freedom—until they either marry, or else be more fully strengthened for continence."

44. See above, note 31.

45. Ibid., XX, 1: Fr., Genoude, p. 259-260; SC, p. 94 (Foucault uses this translation here); Eng., ch. XX, pp. 678-679: "pray with repeated prayers and fasts, and bendings of the knee, and vigils." In the article "Exorcism," DS, IV, 1961, col. 2001, J. Daniélou situates this formula of Tertullian in the continuity of rites of exorcism preparatory to baptism and refers, on the assimilation of the fast to an exorcism, to Mathew 17, 21: "This demon is cast out only by prayer and fasting."

46. See Tertullien, *De paenitentia/La pénitence*, VII, 7-9, pp. 174-175. The manuscript adds this quotation based on Genoude's translation (abridged and slightly modified) p. 109: "he intensifies his frenzy when he sees that, by the pardon granted to sins, so many works of death are destroyed in man, so many condemnations revoked" (Genoude: "so many titles of condemnation annulled"); Tertullian, *On Repentance*, ch. VII, p. 662: "Grieve and grown he [Satan] must of necessity over the fact that, by the grant of pardon, so many marks of death in man have been overthrown, so many marks of the condemnation which formerly was his own erased." Some lines lower down, after a passage crossed out, Foucault writes: "Time of the palaestra J. Chrysostom" (see below, lecture of 20 February, p. 150 and note 21).

47. On the idea of baptism as starting point for a *metanoia* extending to the whole life of the believer in the Apostolic Fathers, see A. Benoit, *Le baptême chrétien*, p. 123.

48. Tertullien, *De paenitentia/La Pénitence*, VI, 4: Fr., Genoude, p. 205; CS, p. 165; Tertullian, *On Repentance*, ch. VI, p. 661: "... how inconsistent is it to expect pardon of sins (to be granted) to a repentance which they have not fulfilled! This is to hold out your hand for merchandise, but not produce the price. For repentance is the price at which the Lord has determined to award pardon: He proposes the redemption of release from penalty at this compensating exchange of repentance."

49. Pascal, *Pensées*, Lafuma 418: "Infinity nothing," (Paris: Seuil, "Livre de vie," 1962) p. 187: "... the finite is annihilated in the presence of the infinite and becomes pure nothingness"; English translation by A.J. Krailsheimer, *Pensées* (Harmondsworth: Penguin Books, 1966) p. 149.

50. *De paenitentia/La Pénitence*, VI: Grenoude, p. 206: "If the seller begins by examining the money paid to him, in order to see whether it is clipped, without stamp, or adulterated, we must believe that the Lord tests too the repentance (*paenitentiae probationem prius inire*) before granting us a reward which is nothing less than eternal life"; *On Repentance*, ch. VI, p. 661: "If, then, sellers first examine the coin with which they make their bargains, to see whether it be cut, or scraped, or adulterated, we believe likewise that the Lord, when about to make us the grant of so costly merchandise, even of eternal life, first institutes a probation of our repentance."

51. Ibid., 16: Fr., SC, p. 169: "The baptismal bath is the seal of faith, but the faith of baptism begins by the faith of repentance (*a paenitentiae fide*) and proves by this its value"; Genoude, p. 207: "The regenerating bath is the seal of faith; this faith begins and is commended by the sincerity of the repentance"; Eng. p. 662: "That *baptismal* washing is a sealing of faith, which faith is begun and is commended by the faith of repentance."

52. See, in fact, the previous lecture, p. 102.

seven

20 FEBRUARY 1980

> *Tertullian (continued): break with the Neo-Platonist conception of metanoia.* ⌢ *Development of the institution of the catechumenate from the end of the second century. The procedures of truth at work in the catechumen's journey (non-public meeting, exorcism, profession of faith, confession of sins).* ⌢ *Importance of these practices of the catechumenate for the history of regimes of truth: a new accentuation of the theology of baptism (preparation for baptism as enterprise of mortification; the problem of sin: a permanent struggle against the other who is in us; baptism as permanent model for life).* ⌢ *Conclusion: reworking of subjectivity-truth relations around the problem of conversion. Originality of Christianity in comparison with other cultures.*

*LAST WEEK I TRIED to explain the passage in Tertullian, from chapter six of *De paenitentia*, in which he said that we are not immersed in the baptismal waters in order to be purified, but that we are already purified deep in our hearts when we arrive at baptism. I think this passage, which I have tried to clarify by other passages from *De paenitentia* or from *De baptismo*, points to a series of important distinctions in Tertullian. The idea that one must arrive at baptism already purified, and so the idea that it is not baptism that, in and by itself alone, in the effectuation of the rite, ensures purification, but that we will be able to see our sins

---

* M.F.: Am I waiting for you or are you waiting for me? [*laughter*].

remitted only if we are purified, implies a number of distinctions. First of all, there is the distinction between the work, the labor, as Tertullian says, that the soul exercises or must exercise on itself in order to purify itself—human work therefore—and the divine operation of the remission of sins. It is not the remission of sins that purifies us. So there is a distinction between these two operations. There is a distinction also between catechesis as the teaching of truths, as initiation into the truths of the faith and the fundamental rules of the Christian life, and, on the other hand, the penitential discipline, *paenitentiae disciplina*, as Tertullian says, which is understood as work, as labor by which the soul learns to free itself from evil, to resist and combat it, to throw it off now, but also to train itself in order to be able to struggle in the future, even after baptism, against the insidious assaults of the devil and all the possibilities of relapse. The idea, consequently, of a pre-baptismal discipline that is not the same as catechistic initiation into the truths, that is exercise of self on self for the future and for all future struggles. Finally, the third distinction we find in these passages, a fundamental distinction that is, I think, at the root of all the others, is the distinction between the soul's access to the saving truth, and the need, for this access itself, for a process that is different from this progressive initiation and that, as it were, both cuts across it and supports it. This other process, which is therefore not that of initiation, but which is necessary for initiation into the truth, is the manifestation of the truth of the soul by itself, that of the probationary manifestation of the soul's truth for itself. To be able to be initiated, the soul must put itself to the test. To be able to reach the truth, it must show *its*[*] truth. I think we have a fundamental distinction here. Again, this differentiation does not mean dissociation and separation. In no way do I mean that there is initiation on one side and then, completely apart, this probationary exercise [that manifests][†] the truth of the soul. The two processes are interlocked. It is precisely this interlocking that is, I think, absolutely fundamental in the history of Christianity and, more generally, in the history of subjectivity in the West. But there is a connection that leaves each of these processes its specificity.

---

* M.F. stresses the word.
† M.F.: and manifester (*manifestateur*) [although he hesitates on this word: "manifest ... er [*manifest ... ateur*]"].

In Tertullian—and here again I think there is something rather important in the history of our civilization—we see the diffraction of something that had been [conceptualized]* in an interdependent, unitary, overall way in Christian thought of the first two centuries and, more generally, in a whole, let's say, roughly, Platonizing current of Hellenistic thought. What breaks up with Tertullian's idea of a distinction between initiation into the truth and the probation of the soul's truth is, of course, that notion, experience, or form of *metanoia*, of conversion that I talked about at the end of last week's lecture. Generally speaking, we can say that [for] Platonizing Hellenistic thought *metanoia* was seen as a movement by which the soul, pivoting on itself, turned its gaze from below to above, from appearance to truth, from earth to the sky, and thus passed, in this pivoting-conversion, from darkness to light. *Metanoia* was therefore this movement of the soul revolving on itself from one direction to another. Now in this movement, as defined by Platonizing thought, in gaining access to the† truth, in gaining access to being in its truth, to the truth of being, the soul at the same time, and necessarily, discovered its own truth. That is to say, the light that fills the soul, that fills the soul's gaze, equally throws light on itself. Why is this? It is because the soul is of the same nature as the being that illuminates it. It is of the same nature, whether considered as related to it, or as a fragment or spark from it, or as a part of it that has fallen, become detached, and imprisoned in this world. In any case, there is a kinship between being and the soul and the truth is nothing other than the manifestation of the soul's kinship with being. So what is involved in *metanoia* and why, in the Platonist or Neo-Platonist perspective, is *metanoia* both access to being and access to its own truth? Quite simply because knowledge and recognition are not distinct in *metanoia*. *Metanoia* is what permits the soul to recognize, both to recognize itself in the truth and to recognize the truth deep in itself. So that, in this perspective, illumination necessarily takes place in the form of rediscoveries and memory. The soul finds again its kinship, the soul finds again what it is, and finding again what it is and being illuminated by being are one and the same thing. This then, very schematically, was *metanoia*, conversion,

---

* M.F.: thought.
† Again, M.F. stresses this word.

in a whole current which was quite dominant in the Hellenistic world at the same time as Christianity.

What I think happened, not with the appearance of Christianity strictly speaking, but with a certain inflection taken by Christianity around the turn of the second and third century, and of course in the effort it made to detach itself, to separate itself from the gnosis and all the dualist movements, is that this great unitary series—*metanoia*, or conversion, illumination, access to the truth, discovery of the truth of oneself, recognition, memory—, the unity of all this bundle of notions, which were profoundly bound up with each other in the Neo-Platonist type of *metanoia*, is breaking up with Tertullian, or that Tertullian shows that this unity is breaking up. This is what begins to be diffracted at this moment and I think that for Christian thought, for Christianity, for the whole of the West, a profoundly new and, at any rate, very complex history of the relations between subjectivity and truth begins.

Very roughly, we could say that what took place at this moment, through a series of processes that called on each other, depended upon each other, and responded to each other, is that, on the one hand, memory, through which the soul could find both its truth and the truth of being deep within itself, is in Christianity becoming a matter of institutionalized traditionality rather than of individual experience. With the idea of a tradition, guaranteed both by the text, by Scripture, and by the authority of the ecclesial institution, memory can no longer play the same kind of role as in that movement by which the soul discovers the truth by finding itself in the depths of its own memory. On the one hand, memory becomes therefore a matter of institutionalized traditionality, and, at the same time, the truth, discovery of the truth of the soul by itself, becomes the object of a number of processes, procedures, and techniques, which are also institutionalized, by which the soul is required to say, show, and manifest what it is at every moment of its move towards the truth and salvation. Between a memory institutionalized as tradition and its obligation to say and manifest what it is, the soul will indeed advance towards the truth, but it advances through a framework of powers that are completely different from what was seen in the Neo-Platonist theme of *metanoia*. There is a reorganization of memory and, as a result, a reorganization of the relationship to the truth, which will now be a relationship to the truth as dogma and, second, a relationship of self to self that

will no longer be of the order of the rediscovery of being in the depth of
oneself, but of the soul's obligation to say what it is. Believing the dogma,
on the one hand, and saying what one is, on the other, are indeed the
two poles of faith and confession I was talking about in another lecture[1]
and which constitute, I think, in the very distance that separates them,
what is fundamental, or anyway distinctive in Christian experience and
the interplay of which will no doubt have an organizing role in the long
history of subjectivity and the truth in the Christian West.

Anyway, this is how we can see that bipolarity of faith and confession I was talking about emerging around some texts from Tertullian. Of
course, I am not going to talk about faith, but about confession of self,
sketching out the preliminaries of a history of something that I do not
think has ever been completely analyzed in our society, that is the history
of "tell me who you are." The injunction, "tell me who you are," which is
fundamental in Western civilization, is what we see being formed in these
and other texts of the same time, when the soul is told: Go to the truth,
but, on the way, don't forget to tell me who you are, because if, on the
way, you do not tell me who you are, you will never arrive at the truth.
This is the point of the analysis I would like to undertake.

So, last week I referred to the analyses of Tertullian because I think
their very formulation allows us to grasp fully what is at stake in the
question. But it is evident that these analyses at the end of the second
and the beginning of the third century—*De paenintentia* is from around
200 and so exactly at the turn of the century—are not isolated or pre-
monitory. They appear simply as a more particularly elaborated form of
what is happening, evidence for which can be found not only in contemporary texts, but also and especially in the institutions of Christianity.
In fact, from the end of the second century, let's say, roughly from
170, 180, we see a new institution developing in Christian churches,
especially in Western Churches and above all at Rome. This institution, which absolutely did not exist before, is the catechumenate, the
organization of something like an order and particular category of the
life of the Christian, or rather of the life of one who is going to become
Christian: the catechumen.[2]

Of course, when I say it is a completely new institution, this is not
entirely exact. It is not so much the formation *ex abrupto* of an institution as the reorganization, the authoritarian regulation of the practices

of catechesis and preparation for baptism I have been talking about. But this institutionalization is nevertheless both very clear and has a number of very important consequences. What are the reasons for this institutionalization of the category, of the order of catechumens at the end of the second century? Historians offer a whole range of reasons which rely on a great many documents.[3] I will just indicate them rapidly. Of course, first of all, with the spread of Christianity there is the influx of postulants, and who says postulants says, of course, weakening of the intensity of religious life, and also of moral rigor. Second, the existence and strengthening of persecutions from the middle of the second century, with all that this represents in the way of the possible abandonment of Christianity by a number of Christians insufficiently prepared, trained, and armed. Third, the existence of a debate with pagans, with paganism, and as a result of this the need for Christians to be able to present pagans (with whom moreover the dialogue was not necessarily and always aggressive or confrontational) with both a well formed doctrine and rigorous morals. There was also rivalry with other, Christian or para-Christian groups or sects that prided themselves on their value and moral rigor. There was the continued importance of mystery religions with very strictly regulated initiation procedures. And finally, of course, there was the struggle within Christianity or on its immediate borders against heresies, which call for something like the organization of a catechumenate to give Christians a more rigorous training to prevent them from falling into heresy and being seduced by heretics. There was also the need for Christians to distinguish themselves from those heresies, the overwhelming majority of which were of dualist or Gnostic inspiration, whose distinctive feature was the fundamental privilege accorded the gnosis (understood in the sense, then, of knowledge), making initiation into the truth, conversion to the truth, illumination, and the soul's recollection of its true nature and origin the fundamental point of Christian existence. In relation to all these movements that privileged in a very distinctive fashion the aspect specifically to do with initiation into the truth, there was the need to organize a catechumenate in which initiation into the truth would be connected up to a whole series of moral preparations and exercises of self on self that are, precisely, those to which Tertullian referred.

Yes, incidentally, I must make a thousand apologies because the other day I found in my papers that I noted that Tertullian's *De baptismo* was a polemical text directed against a Gnostic group and I said they were Nicolaitans.[4] I am sure that you will have corrected the mistake. It was a group of Cainites.[5] I said to myself: as we do not know a great deal about the Nicolaitans, maybe after all they made the same objections to baptism as the Cainites. Anyway, they were Cainites. My apologies for this mistake.

Anyway, for all these reasons, from the end of the second century a catechumenate was organized that will constitute a regulated and controlled period of preparation for Christian existence and, more precisely, a regulated and controlled period of preparation for baptism itself. In this catechumenate, catechesis and pedagogy of the truth, on the one hand, will be associated with moral preparation and exercises, on the other, with, throughout the catechumenate, procedures intended to manifest, authenticate, and verify the process of the soul's transformation that baptism will bring to an end, sanction, and finally complete with the remission of sins.[6]

I do not want to expound on what the catechumenate was. I would just like to note what in this institution concerns the "tell me who you are," which, I was telling you, is ultimately what I would like at least to sketch the history of. What were the procedures of truth that marked out the catechumen's journey? What were the tests of truth to which he was subject between his application for baptism and the moment when he was actually baptized? We have a text that is very explicit about this by Saint Hippolytus, who left a number of rules and canons intended precisely for those who had to manage the Christian communities and who explained what had to make up the life and procedure of the catechumenate. So, two texts from Saint Hippolytus: the oldest, and the only one that is really authentic, is *The Apostolic Tradition*.[7] What are called the Canons[8] of Saint Hippolytus, which are from a bit later, give more or less the same information, only with different emphases. In the *Apostolic Tradition*, which dates from the same period as Tertullian, [at the] the turn of the second and the third century, what is said concerning the life of catechumens or rather concerning the test of truth to which they are subject?

First, when someone wants to become Christian he requests entry into the category of the catechumens. But before being accepted as catechumen, the text says he must "be brought to the doctors even before the people arrive."[9] That is to say, what now takes place must not be public. It is something that has to take place between the postulant, the doctors responsible for entry into the order of catechumens, and then, as you will see, some other persons. So, it is a semi-secret, or any rate non-public meeting. In this meeting, those applying to become catechumens are asked "the reason they seek the faith."[10] Those who introduce the postulants, that is to say, sorts of witnesses, sponsors, or patrons, also have to "testify on behalf of their subject," in order to determine whether they really will be capable of listening. "Their way of life is also examined."[11] They are asked if they have a wife, if they are slaves, if they are free. Inquiry must be made as to the occupations and professions of those who have been brought to be instructed, because a number of professional incompatibilities were very important at the time in the recruitment of Christians, or rather in the definition of the rule of Christian life (one obviously could not be Christian if one was a soldier, an actor, a prostitute, or, obviously, a teacher).[12] So, a questioning-examination procedure.[*]

It is on this and only this basis that the catechumen, well, someone who applies to become Christian, will be considered as a hearer. And for a number of months or even years—it lasted from two to three years, depending on the case[13]—the hearers, the *audients*,[14] had to lead a life that complied with a number of, if not rules, at least imperatives and injunctions. This life involved, of course, initiation into the truths of the faith and the rules of the Christian life, but it was equally necessary to do certain things that were characteristic of that preparation, that life of purification and exercises Tertullian spoke about. And it is at the end of these two or three years of preparation and exercises, of initiation into the truth and training for the Christian life, that a second examination-questioning took place that had more or less the same form as the earlier one, but that this time did not focus on the earlier life of the catechumen, but on this period itself. Still in *The Apostolic Tradition* of Hippolytus, we read the following: "When those who are set

---

[*] The manuscript adds: "A bit later, in the third century, it seems that a practice was established about which Hipp[olytus] does not speak but for which Saint Augustine [gives] evidence, namely a certain solemnity given to entry into the catechumenate, with the laying on of hands and breathing on the face, i.e., rites of exorcism, of the expulsion of spirits."

apart to receive baptism have been chosen"—that is to say, at the end of the period in which they were hearers, some are held on to as likely to be able to receive baptism—"one examines their life"[15] by asking them questions and enquiring among those who answer for them, who are so to speak their witnesses, patrons, sponsors: "did they live piously while they were catechumens? Did they honor the widows? Did they visit the sick? Did they perform good works?"[16] And at that point those who introduced them, those then who are patrons-sponsors, have to testify to the life of the hearers.[17] So, there is a new questioning-examination, a new questioning-test that will make it possible to choose those who in actual fact are to be baptized and who, ceasing to be simple hearers, are now considered as the elect or competent, the *electi* or *competentes*.[18] For a time, generally some weeks, these undergo a more intense preparation marked by a whole series of ascetic practices (prayer, fasting, vigils, kneeling),[19] the rigor of which is intended to test the authenticity of the faith.[20]

It is this particularly tough period that is generally brought to an end at Easter (it often lasts from Ash Wednesday to Easter) and that Saint John Chrysostom called the time of "the palaestra,"[21] the time of exercise during which one must become an "athlete" of the Christian life. At the end of this time of the palaestra, generally, I think, Easter Saturday or Sunday,[*] the catechumen was baptized. And in the baptismal ceremony the catechumen undergoes an exorcism. The *Apostolic Tradition* of Hippolytus explains it in the following way: when the day of baptism draws near—it seems then that this is one or two days before baptism itself—the bishop exorcizes each of the catechumens so as to determine whether they are pure. And if one is found who is impure, he must be excluded because he is not sufficiently attached to the word of the doctrine of the faith.[22] That baptism cannot take place without a test of exorcism is attested by Hippolytus, but we find it for centuries. At the beginning of the fifth century, Saint Augustine, in Sermon 216,[23] addressed precisely to the *competentes*, that is to say to those who are to receive baptism, says how things are to take place and describes the ceremony in this way: the postulant, he says—and here it seems that the exorcism was directly part of the ceremony itself, so that there was

---

* M.F. adds: you will tell me that this is, after all, important.

a shift and an integration of exorcism within baptism itself—takes off the hair shirt, he stands on the hair shirt he has removed (stripping off clothes signifies, of course, on the one hand, casting off the old man, but it is also a traditional ritual of exorcism and the eviction of spirits).[24] At this point, the bishop utters imprecations in order to drive out Satan, and the fact that the catechumen can listen to these imprecations without flinching, without moving or fidgeting, proves that the spirit of evil is no longer master of his soul and that, as a result, he may receive baptism. And the bishop utters this very characteristic phrase: "*vos nunc immunes probavimus*"—and now we have tested, we have proved, we have shown that you are pure.[25]

I think this exorcism is very important. It should not be understood as exorcism is later understood and practiced. It is not exactly a matter of freeing someone whose soul and body are possessed by evil spiritual forces that have entered into them and act in their place and against their will. It is not the same as the exorcism of maniacs, which existed at the time and was close, but even so quite different.[26] This exorcism, which is attested by Hippolytus, but also by Tertullian,[27] Quodvultdeus,[28] and all those who set out what baptism was in the first five or six centuries of Christianity, is a rite, I shall say, of dispossession, but in the quasi juridical sense. That is to say it involves driving out one power and replacing it with another. We find again here the idea that I referred to last week with regard to Tertullian: since the fall and Adam's sin, man's soul has become Satan's property, empire, seat, and even church. The soul has become his property and, as a result, correlatively, the Holy Spirit will never be able to descend into a soul so long as dispossession has not been carried out, so long as the enemy still has control, the right, the exercise of sovereignty, as it were, over man's soul. The Holy Spirit and the Evil Spirit cannot [co]exist within one and the same soul. This is what Origen explains in chapter 6 of the *Homily on Numbers*: one has to leave for the other to enter.[29] Exorcism is therefore in this sense actually a rite of eviction, of departure, of dispossession, a rite of passage of sovereignty.

But exorcism is [also] something else. It is a transfer of sovereignty, the replacement of one sovereignty by another, but it is also a test of truth, because by driving out, by expelling, exorcism purifies. It purifies, it authenticates, and it does so in two senses. On the one hand, it delivers the soul to its owner, to its authentic master and, on the other hand, it shows that the soul has in actual fact, genuinely been freed from the old attachments which held it bound. The performance of exorcism drives out the spirit and shows that it has in fact been driven out. The traditional comparison is with the test of metal by fire. The soul of the person who is to be baptized, of the catechumen, goes through exorcism as a metal through fire, which, on the one hand, enables the pure metal to be separated from its impure elements.[*30] It is an operation of division, consequently, of real purification and, at the same time, it is a test of the metal's authenticity, [enabling verification][†] that the coin, for example, submitted to this test, is indeed it what should be. Exorcism is therefore this fire as purification and fire as test of truth. We find again here, slightly transposed, combined with the difficult theme of baptism by fire,[31] Tertullian's idea in *De paenitentia*, that repentance (*pénitence*) must be a sort of coin, not by which redemption is purchased exactly, but which serves to be put to a test, the one receiving it (in the event, God) thereby being able to verify that the metal, the coin that one offers is indeed authentic.

Exorcism is therefore purification at the same time as expulsion. The names it is given proves this. Baptismal exorcism (which will be practiced up to the High Middle Ages) is called *scrutamen* or *examen*, scrutiny or examination. And in two texts from the end of the fourth century exorcism is in fact referred to in these terms. In a sermon, the bishop of Carthage, Quodvultdeus, a contemporary of Saint Augustine, says regarding exorcism: "We celebrate on you," Quodvultdeus is addressing catechumens, "the examination and the devil is rooted out from your body, while Christ, both humble and very high, is invoked." You will ask then, the bishop says to the catechumens, when exorcism is performed on you: "*Proba me, Domine, et scito cor meum*, test me, Lord, and know my heart."[32] And Saint Ambrose, in the *Explanatio symboli*, insofar as this text really is by him (but, in any case, it dates from the same period)[33] says: "In the *scrutamen*, we seek to know whether there is some impurity in the body of man"—here he employs *scrutamen* in the everyday, non-

---

* The manuscript (folio 15) clarifies: "Thus *Protocatēchesis* of Cyril of Jerus[alem], VI" (the exact title is *Procatēchesis*, PROKATECHESIS ētoi prologus tōn Katēcheseōn).
† M.F.: test.

religious sense of examination: this is the medical examination—"in the same way, in exorcism, we inquire about sanctification (*sanctificatio inquisita*, he says) not only of the body, but also the soul."[34]

So you see that there are two great series of tests in the course of this preparation for baptism that characterizes the catechumen's existence: on the one hand, the questioning-inquiry made of the postulant or his witnesses, and then this test of truth consisting of exorcism. There are still others, over which I will pass quickly, you will see why. A third test of truth, in fact, is situated at the very moment of baptism, in which it constitutes, as it were, the completion and crowning moment of the rite. At the very moment that the postulant is going to be baptized, and so when the epiclesis[35] of the three names is performed, which will ensure, effectuate the descent of the Holy Spirit, three questions are put to the catechumen: Do you believe in the Father? Do you believe in the Son? Do you believe in the Holy Spirit? And to each of these questions he must reply, of course: "Yes, I believe" and each time he is submerged in the water.[36] The cycle of tests of truth in the course of the catechumen's existence is completed in the truth act of that profession of faith. The profession of faith is the main, most constant, most archaic, and the first truth act in the organization of Christian existence. The profession of faith is that by which one becomes Christian. We find it here again as we found it even before the exercise of the catechumenate.

And then there is a fourth test of truth, a fourth procedure, the status, meaning, and existence of which is much more problematic, but we will see the importance it will have (I will explain it to you in the next lecture), and this is, of course, the problem of the confession (*confession*) of sins. Was there confession of sins in the catechumen's existence and did he have to subject himself to that practice, which will become so complex, of the examination of conscience, of the work of memory of self on self, of the recollection of faults, and of their confession (*aveu*) with the penances (*pénitences*) that are linked to all this? In fact, it is difficult to know, simply for a reason of words. On the one hand, as you know, *paenitentia* translates the Greek word *metanoia*[37] and, consequently, does not designate the ritual, canonical, ecclesial penance as it will be understood from a certain point. When we come across the word *paenitentia* in the texts of this period, we should think that it is a matter of conversion and not penance. And then, because the word *exomologēs*, translated in French as *aveu,* is a word to which we shall have to come back—I shall come back to it next week—means simply "to acknowledge." It is certain that, from Tertullian at least, the texts always say that the catechumen must recognize or acknowledge his sins: *exomologēsis*, a Greek word that the Latin authors sometimes take up as it is and which they also translate by *confessio,* but which does not necessarily mean a confession (*aveu*). It seems, in fact, that what these authors are referring to when they speak of this acknowledgement is rather an act in the form of an orison, a sort of discourse addressed to God in which the catechumen actually acknowledges, not so much the sins he has committed, but the fact that he is a sinner or that he has committed many sins. This is no doubt the meaning that should be given to the passage in chapter 20 of Tertullian's *De baptismo,* where he says that those who want access to baptism must "invoke God through fervent prayers, fasting, genuflections," and prepare themselves for it also "*cum confessione omnium retro delictorum,* with the confession of their past sins."[38] But what does this confession of all past sins mean if not the fact that one must acknowledge before God, humbly, by acts of prayer and orison, that one is in actual fact a sinner? And it is only later, precisely with the organization of penance itself as an act intended to redeem certain sins after baptism, so at the time of Saint Augustine, that we find this idea of a verbal confession addressed to the priest or bishop[39] [...].

I have dwelled on these practices of the catechumenate at such length for a number of reasons. First of all, you see that this institution of the catechumenate is basically only the implementation of those principles we saw expressed in Tertullian, that is to say the requirement not to lead the soul to the truth without it having paid, as condition or price of access to the truth, the manifestation of its own truth. The truth of the soul is the price the soul pays for access to the truth: this is the principle formulated by Tertullian and implemented here. Roughly, if you like, the theme: the being that is true will be manifested to you only if you manifest the truth of yourself. I think this is the point at which the fundamental principle is fixed of "tell me who you are."

Another reason for laying some stress on these procedures peculiar to the catechumenate is that, as you can see, this principle of "tell me who you are," or the principle "you will get to the truth only if you have manifested the truth of yourself," took shape very quickly, from the third century, within very precise, concrete techniques of the manifestation of the truth. So possibly confession (*confession*)-confession of self (but, again, we will come back to this), the profession of faith, an already traditional practice in Christianity, and also the test of the division in exorcism, and questioning-inquiry: a whole set of specific procedures for revealing the truth of the soul and which you can see are absolutely different from the pedagogical or initiatory procedures familiar to Antiquity whose function was to lead the soul to the truth and the light.

But there is a further reason why I have stressed these practices, these tests of truth in the catechumenate: this is that, starting from there and through the exercise and development of these practices, I think we can see a new way of accentuating this or that element of the theology of baptism, that is to say of the theology of the remission of sins and salvation. Very quickly, I shall say the following. You recall that from the beginning of baptismal practice we saw that baptism was linked to the theme of regeneration. Baptism brings about rebirth; it assures a palingenesy, or anagenesy.[40] It brings about rebirth, it constitutes a second birth, that is to say a second life begins with baptism, after, so to speak, a first life that was the life of death, the life of the way of death. One is born with a new father, in a filial relationship, no longer with our carnal parents, but with the Father who is master of all things, God himself. So, the idea of a second life. Baptism is situated between the first and second life. But this baptism is basically only the act of transfer from one life to another, or from one birth to another. From the third century you see a theme develop that, in one sense, appears to us as its quasi logical and natural development, at least if we refer to Scripture and to the tradition of Christian teaching, but which was not explicitly present and, in truth, was generally absent from the texts of the second century. This is quite simply that if baptism is what brings it about that one passes from one life to another (and what is baptism if not death?), then something like death is necessary between [one and the other] in order to pass from the first to the second. Let's say, if you will, that there was at least a tendency in the first and second centuries to connect one life with the other, a first life that was life of death with another life that was the true life, since it was the life of life itself. But the moment of baptism was not the moment of death. From the third century, and

by way of a return to a number of themes found in Saint Paul—this
raises the problem of the renaissance of Paulinism,[41] the lesson of Saint
Paul from the third century—we see baptism being defined as a sort of
putting to death, as a burial,[*] as a sort of repetition for man himself of
Christ's passion, his crucifixion and his burial.[42] The baptismal water,
in which the baptized is immersed, is the water of death. The bath, into
which he is put, is Christ's tomb.

You find this model, and explicitly for the first time, in Origen,
[who] employs the term tomb to designate both the baptismal water
and the baptismal bath:[†43] it is a tomb in which we must die. And so
this second life given to us by baptism is really much more a resurrection, in the strict sense of the term. Consequently, if baptism is a death,
what will preparation for baptism be if not a way, not so much of preparing us for death, as of beginning to practice this death on ourselves,
a certain way of dying voluntarily to our earlier life? The preparation
for baptism, understood as exercise, must be not so much (or not only)
a preparation for the true eternal life, as an enterprise of mortification. It is interesting to see [how] Origen, for example, [reinterprets the
crossing] of the Red Sea. You know that, [according to] the traditional
typology, baptism for the life of the Christian was like the Red Sea that
separated the Hebrews re-entering their homeland from the pursuing
Egyptians.[44] So, the typology of the Red Sea[‡] gives baptism this meaning
of the separation of one land from another, of one life from another. But
Origen takes it up again and says: Baptism is, of course, the crossing of
the Red Sea, but it is also the long crossing of the desert following the
crossing of the Red Sea, when the Hebrews almost died of hunger and
thirst in the Sinai desert.[45] Consequently, it is this mortification that
now constitutes the main meaning of baptism. The old theme found
in the *Didache*, at the end of the first and the beginning of the second
century, the old theme of the two ways, the way of life and the way of
death, splits. It is not just a matter of choosing the way of life rather

---

* The manuscript adds: "at the end of which there is resurrection".
† (a) The manuscript (folio 22) notes: "Homily on Exodus," and adds, after some illegible words: "To be buried with Christ, sacrament of the 3rd day."
  (b) M.F. also indicates on the verso of the same manuscript page: "Ambrose, *De sacramentis*, 3."
‡ M.F. adds: in relation to baptism.

than the way of death. One must die to the way of death in order to be able to come back to life.

As a result, the tests of truth take on the meaning of authenticating the mortification in which the path towards the truth must consist. One will approach the truth, the life of the truth, the truth that is life and eternal life by a path that is a mortification, and you see why the authentication of this path of mortification has to be as it were specific and autonomous with regard to the subsequent access to the truth itself. You have to know in yourself, you who apply for the truth, that which assures your mortification. Life you will know afterwards.

The second shift of accent in baptismal theology concerns, of course, the problem of sin. I have already pointed this out to you with regard to Tertullian and the fall, the stain. I think Tertullian refocuses this theme of the fall and the stain around, first, the principle of a transmission, a transmission in series, from generation to generation from Adam until now through the intermediary of the seed, and, once again, Tertullian is the inventor of original sin.[46] So, he refocuses the idea of the stain around this precise transmission of a sin through the seed and also around the idea that this original sin manifests itself, not so much by the fact that the soul is impure, stained, or tainted, but by the fact that the soul has fallen under the power of the demon and that the demon henceforth exercises his empire over the soul and must therefore be dispossessed of it. Well, in the third and fourth centuries, the theology of the sin, and so the theology of baptism, is increasingly linked to this idea of the demon's action. Here again we come across another, equally complex and fundamental process in the history of Christianity, which was the prodigious invasion of demonology into Christian thought and practice from the third century, but only from the third century. So, sin is the triumph of Satan, and in relation to sin purification cannot but assume the aspect of a battle, a permanent, ceaselessly renewed struggle against Satan who has established his power and presence in the soul and who, as the soul tries to escape him, naturally renews and redoubles his onslaughts in order to re-take possession of it. The more Christian one becomes, the more one is exposed to the devil's onslaughts. The more Christian one is, the more dangerous one's position (remember what I told you last week regarding the *metus*, about the fear that is so fundamental in Tertullian's conceptions). Consequently, not only the

life of the postulant, but also the life of the baptized must be devoted
to this endless struggle against that other who is in us, against that
other deep in the soul. And consequently, the path towards the truth
must pass by way of this expulsion of the other, and also by way of a
whole series of tests of verification in order to know whether the other
is indeed still there, what the state of the struggle against this other is,
and whether one will be able to resist his renewed attacks when he reappears in you.*[47]

Death as the form, the fundamental type of baptism, the other in
oneself and deep in oneself as fundamental source of sin, with as third
shift, as third change of accent (which is, more or less, the consequence
of these), that the effect itself of baptism has to be rethought. It is quite
certain that there was a tendency in the theology of baptism of the first
two centuries to think that, with baptism, the one who had received
it entered—definitively, once and for all—the way of life and truth.
Basically, baptism consecrated perfect beings and, at any rate, introduced
them into a life of perfection. This raises, of course, the whole problem of the elect and the perfect which, here again, intersects with other
problems and where, of course, the gnosis and dualism are encountered
as the alternative, the point of rupture, the point of dialogue, challenge,
reevaluation, and delimitation of Christianity by itself. To this problem
of baptism constituting the elect and the perfect who remained the elect
and the perfect, Christianity responded by distinguishing two things:
the redemption of past sins that is indeed, in fact, constituted, assured
by baptism itself, and then a salvation that will be given only at the end
of the Christian's life and in the event that he has not relapsed. So that
you find in Origen some formulae that are clearly very dubious from
the orthodox point of view and smell of the stake, since he speaks of
two baptisms.[48] There is the baptism one receives on earth, but this is
a sort of provisional baptism pending, as it were, a second baptism that
takes place when one is dead and really gives one access to the life of the
perfect, of the elect, which cannot happen on earth.[49] So you can see that
instead of being the solemn and definitive introduction to the true life,
baptism, with all that it comprises of mortification, on the one hand,

---

* The manuscript (unnumbered page) adds: "St. Augustine: *pia correction et vera confession*, *De Bapt[ismo]* I, 12-18."

and of struggle with and expulsion of the other, must become a sort of permanent model of life. We live, as it were, constantly and until death pending baptism, having to purify ourselves, having therefore to mortify ourselves and to struggle against the enemy deep within ourselves. Mortification and struggle against the enemy, against the other, are not transitory episodes that cease when one is baptized. Until the end of life in this world, until the end of this life, which is always a life of death, we will have to mortify ourselves and to free ourselves from Satan's grip and from his onslaughts. Even after we have been baptized, we have to mortify ourselves until death. Even after we have been baptized, we have to struggle against Satan until the moment of final deliverance. And, of course, for this we need constant tests of truth. We constantly need to authenticate what we are. We need to keep watch on ourselves, to bring the truth itself into us, and to those who look on us, who keep watch on us, judge us and guide us, to the pastors therefore, we have to offer the truth of what we are. And you see the idea becoming embedded here, much more solidly than in Tertullian's conceptions, that in this relation of subjectivity to the truth there must be two very different types of relation, and that one must engage with the other, connect up with the other, but without them being confused as if they were one and the same thing: the relation to the truth promised to us by baptism, and the relation to the truth of ourselves that we have to produce at every moment, with reference to two things, death, on the one hand, and the presence of the other, on the other.

Mortifying ourselves and struggling with the other: I believe it is with the introduction of these two elements, which are completely foreign to ancient culture—mortification and relationship to the other in oneself—that the problem of subjectivity, the theme of subjectivity and subjectivity-truth relations, completely changes from what it had been in ancient culture.

I shall add just one word. You see that this problem of subjectivity-truth relations was entirely re-elaborated, reorganized, and renewed, I believe, around the third century, around a very simple problem: [not] the problem of the individual's identity, [but] rather [that] of conversion. How to become other? How to cease being what one is? How, being what one is, can one become completely other? How, being in this world, to pass to another? How, being in error, to pass to the truth?

It is here, I believe, with this problem of conversion, that is to say of the breach of identity, that the problem of the relations between subjectivity and truth was formed for us. You will say that Christianity did not invent this problem of conversion as the fundamental form of the relationship between subjectivity and truth. It already existed, of course, as a fundamental problem of ancient culture. We could also find it in many other cultures, but I do not want to make it into a universal. I do not want to say that in all cultures the problem of the relations between subjectivity and truth inevitably take the form of conversion or is born from the problem of conversion as revelatory discontinuity of an individual. Nevertheless, it remains that this theme of conversion as the condition [on which] subjectivity may be bound to the truth, or the condition according to which subjectivity can have access to the truth, is found in a whole series of cultures. The problem is how this relationship is thought. It may be thought in the form of the trance, in the form of the individual's seizure by higher powers. It may be thought in the form of awakening. It may be thought in the form of the dream. It may be thought in the form of memory and the reunion of oneself with oneself (this is what I was saying to you with regard to Platonic themes). From a certain point—and I think there is something here that is actually unique in the field of cultures and civilizations with which we may be familiar—conversion, as establishing a relationship between subjectivity and truth, is thought in Christianity on the basis of death, of death as exercise of self on self, that is to say mortification. It is thought on the basis of the problem of the other, of the other as that which has seized power in us. And consequently and finally—and, with the relationship to death and the relationship to the other, this is the third fundamental and characteristic point of our Christian civilization—this conversion, this establishing a relationship of subjectivity to the truth requires probation, the test, bringing the truth of oneself into play.* In other words,

---

* For lack of time, M.F. does not deliver the important development extending these final remarks (immediately after "bringing the truth of oneself into play") and filling the three last (unnumbered) sheets of the lecture's manuscript:

"b. It [conversion] cannot take place without a discipline that enables the truth of this conversion to the truth to be tested and authenticated. → penitential practice.

c. Whereas ancient conversion qualifies men to govern (Plato) or puts them in a position of externality or indifference with regard to the life of the city, Christian conversion will be linked to a whole practice and a whole art of governing men, to the exercise of a pastoral power.

we cannot get to the truth, there cannot be any relationship between subjectivity and truth, subjectivity cannot get as far as the truth, the truth cannot produce its effects in subjectivity except on condition of mortification, on condition of struggle and combat with the other, and only on condition that one manifests to oneself and to others the truth of what one knows. All of this—relationship to self, to death, and to the other—is what is being formed in these texts of Tertullian and these new practices of the catechumenate. Good, well that's it for today.

The paradox of a form of power with the intended purpose of being exercised universally over all men insofar as they have to convert, i.e., gain access to the truth by a radical and [fundamental]* change that must be authenticated by manifesting the truth of the soul. Governing the being-other through the manifestation of the truth of the soul, so that each can earn his salvation.

Which really is the reversal of Oedipus's problem, where it was a matter of saving the whole city, by returning to the king's identity through [a lengthy]* procedure of inquiry. Identity in the strong sense: murderer and son, husband and son, king and culprit, the one who consults the oracle and the one the oracle speaks about, the one who goes from Thebes to Corinth and the one who returns, the one who flees his parents of Corinth and meets his parents in Thebes.

The king was all this. And it is [through] the discovery of this identity of the royal individual that the salvation of all is brought about.

Christianity assures the salvation of each by authenticating that they have in fact become completely other. The relation government of men/manifestation of the truth is entirely recast. Government by the manifestation of the Completely Other in each.

We say that Christianity takes hold of men by promising them an illusory other world → sleep and ideology.

In fact Christianity governs by posing the question of the truth with regard to the becoming other of each."

*Conjecture; reading uncertain.

1. See above, lectures of 30 January and 6 February.
2. See A. Turck, "Aux origines du catéchuménat," *Revue des sciences philosophiques et théologiques*, 48 (1964), pp. 20-31; reprinted in E. Ferguson, ed., *Conversion, Catechumenate and Baptism in the Early Church* (New York and London: Garland, 1993), pp. 266-278.
3. Ibid., p. 29: "[The institutionalization of the catechumenate] is due…to a whole series of conjugated causes: weakening of the initial fervor, the apostasy of some, the always active offensive against paganism, the influence of heresies."
4. See above, lecture 6.
5. On the Cainites (or Cainians), see the Introduction by F. Refoulé to *De baptismo*, pp. 10-11: "[They pushed] the fundamental principles of Gnosticism to the extreme limit: the opposition of the creator god and the redeemer god, that of the soul and the body. It was in this way that they did not hesitate to rehabilitate the most abominable characters of the Old Testament, beginning with Cain (hence their name) …."
6. See A. Turck, "Aux origines du catéchuménat," p. 27, who defines this "very precise institution" in this way: "institution of the Church that aims to prepare for collective baptism those who, precisely, are called catechumens, first by a structured teaching called catechesis, but also by a whole set of disciplines and rites."
7. Hippolyte de Rome, *La tradition apostolique*, ed., B. Botte, SC, no. 11, 1946; English translation in *The Apostolic Tradition of Hippolytus*, translation with Introduction and notes by Burton Scott Easton (Cambridge: Cambridge University Press, 1934). This text and its critical apparatus have been republished in a corrected and expanded edition: Münster Westfalen, Liturgiewissenschaftliche Quellen und Forschungen, Heft 39, 1963. The SC edition, 1968, reproduces the latter, without the critical apparatus. Our references will be to the first edition used by Foucault. The authenticity of this text is still debated. It is claimed that it was originally the work of at least two authors from the "Hippolytian" community of Rome, and was expanded later. For a critical survey of the discussion, see A. Brent, *Hippolytus and the Roman Church in the Third Century: Communities in Tension before the Emergence of a Monarch-Bishop* (Leyde: Brill, 1995), ch. 4 and 5. In the opinion of most of the commentators, however, the section relating to Christian initiation seems to form a unified whole. See A. Dondeyne, "La discipline des scrutins dans l'Eglise latine avant Charlemagne," *Revue d'Histoire ecclésiastique*, t. 28 (1932), pp. 8-10 (source indicated in the "green notebook": see P. Chevallier, "Foucault et les sources patristiques," pp. 139-140).
8. See above, lecture of 13 February.
9. Hippolyte de Rome, *La tradition apostolique*, 16, p. 44; *The Apostolic Tradition of Hippolytus*, p. 41: "New converts to the faith, who are to be admitted as hearers of the word, shall first be brought to the teachers before the people assemble." See the Introduction by F. Refoulé to *De baptismo*, p. 32.
10. Ibid.; Eng.: "their reason for embracing the faith."
11. Ibid.; Eng.: "Inquiry shall then be made as to the nature of their life."
12. Ibid., pp. 45-46. In the text, the list of activities incompatible with aspiration to the catechumenate is the following: manager of a house of prostitutes, actor, teacher (someone "who teaches the profane sciences to children"), charioteer, gladiator, guardian of idols, soldier, prostitute, sodomite, magus, sorcerer, astrologer, seer, or dream interpreter ; Eng., pp. 42-43: a "pander," an actor, a teacher "of young children," a charioteer, a gladiator, "anyone who tends idols," a soldier, a "harlot or licentious man," an "enchanter, an astrologer, a diviner, a soothsayer, a user of magic verses," etcetera.
13. Ibid., 17, p. 46; Eng., p. 43.
14. The original Greek version of the text has been lost. It has been reconstructed on the basis of fragments of a Latin translation and Greek or Eastern adaptations (see the Introduction by B. Botte, p. 12). The Latin translation corresponding to the pages cited by Foucault having disappeared, the word *audients* is not to be found in them therefore. As P. Chevallier clarifies in his thesis, *Michel Foucault et le christianisme*, Université de Paris XII-Val de Marne, 2009, t. I, pp. 239-240 note 781, "the application to Hippolytus seems guided by a passage from the article by Dondeyne in which the latter clarifies that the distinction between *auditores* and *competentes* was applied 'in Africa, just as in Rome at the time of Hippolytus' ('La discipline des scrutins dans l'Eglise latine avant Charlemagne,' p. 11) … The category of *audients* is mentioned several times by Tertullian in *De Paenitentia* (VI, 15,17, 20; VII, 1). Foucault has therefore crossed several references."

15. *La Tradition apostolique*, 20, p. 47; *The Apostolic Tradition*, p. 44.

16. Ibid., pp. 47-48; Eng., p. 44: "whether they have lived soberly, whether they have honoured the widows, whether they have visited the sick, whether they have been active in well-doing."

17. Ibid., p. 48; Eng., p. 44.

18. On these Latin words, see above note 14. See F. Refoulé, Introduction to *De baptismo*, p. 35: "As Easter approaches, if the priest or deacon responsible for the instruction of the catechumen judged his preparation sufficient, the latter could put in his application. He then took his place among those who will soon be called the *electi* in Rome, the *competentes* in Africa and elsewhere."

19. See Tertullien, *De baptismo/Traité du baptême*, 20, 1, p. 94; Tertullian, *On Baptism*, ch. 20 (see already above, lecture of 13 February).

20. Hippolyte de Rome, *La tradition apostolique*, 20, pp. 48-49; Hippolytus, *The Apostolic Tradition*, p. 44.

21. Jean Chrysostom, *Trois catéchèses baptismales*, trans., introd., and notes A. Piédagnel with the collaboration of L. Doutreleau (Paris: Cerf, SC no. 366, 1990), Catéchèse I, I, 16, p. 145: "falls are not dangerous for athletes in the palaestra: they struggle with comrades and exercise methodically body to body with their trainers. But when the time of the games arrives and the stadium is open ... one must either fall, if one gives way, and withdraw with great shame, or, if one has stood firm, carry off the crowns and prizes. That is how it is for you also: these thirty days [which precede baptism] are in a way like a palaestra with its gymnasium and training. Learn now therefore to triumph over the Evil One, the Devil, for it is against him that we must prepare ourselves to struggle after baptism ...."

22. Hippolyte de Rome, *La tradition apostolique*, 20, p. 48: "As the day of their baptism draws near, may the bishop exorcise each of them, to test if they are pure. If there is one who is not pure, may he be excluded, for he has not heard the word with faith ..."; *The Apostolic Tradition of Hippolytus*, p. 44: "... as the day of their baptism draws near, the bishop himself shall exorcise each of them that he may be personally assured of their purity. Then, if there is any of them who is not good or pure, he shall be put aside as not having heard the word in faith ...."

23. Augustine, Sermon 216: "*Ad competentes*," PL 38, col. 1076-1082. See A. Dondeyne, "La discipline des scrutins dans l'Eglise latine avant Charlemagne," pp. 15-16. In Augustine, the reference to exorcism is accompanied by an appeal to the *competentes* to undertake the *scrutamen* of their own heart: "What we do in entreating you in the name of your Redeemer, complete it by examining and shaking your heart (*cordis scrutatione et contribulation*)" (§ 6, col. 1080; translation under direction of abbé Raulx, in *Œuvres complètes de saint Augustin*, t. 6 (Bar-Le-Duc: Ed. L. Guérin, 1868), p. 227.

24. Ibid., § 10, col. 82, trans. p. 228: "... at the moment of your examination (*cum scrutaremini*), when in the All Powerful and awesome name of the majestic Trinity, some deserved imprecations were made over this renegade which brought about flight and desertion, you were not covered by the cilice: but your feet walked as it were on it (*non estis induti cilicio: sed tamen vestri pedes in eodem mystice constiterunt*)."

25. Ibid., § 11, col. 82; trans. p. 229: "... we have established that you were not under the empire of those spirits (*vos immunes probavimus*): therefore, congratulating you, we advise you to preserve in your hearts the exemption from evil that we have seen in your bodies (*ut sanitas quae apparuit in vestro corpore, haec in vestris cordibus conservetur*)."

26. On the practice of expelling demons in the first centuries, see F. J. Dölger, *Der Exorzismus*, p. 25 et seq.; J. Daniélou, "Exorcisme," DS, IV, 1961, col. 1997-2000, which refers in particular to H. Vey, *Die Funktionen der bösen Geister bei den griechischen Apologeten des zweiten Jahrhunderts nach Christus* (Winterthur: Keller, 1957, pp. 166-168. On the importance of baptismal exorcism in the early development of Christianity, see J. Daniélou, "Le symbolisme des rites baptismaux," in *Dieu vivant*, I, 1945, pp. 17-43, and E. A. Leeper, "The role of exorcism in Early Christianity," *Studia Patristica*, 26, 1993, pp. 56-62.

27. See F. Refoulé, Introduction to Tertullian's *De baptismo*, p. 36: "These exercises [prayers, fasts, genuflections, vigils] testify to the sincerity of repentance (*repentir*) and their aim is to attract God's mercy. They also have a value of exorcism, for ...the catechumenate was not seen only as a period of teaching, but first of all as the expulsion of the demon installed in pagan man." On fasting, in particular, as ritual of exorcism preparatory to baptism in the first centuries, see J. Daniélou, "Exorcisme," col. 2001.

28. See below, notes 31 and 32.

29. Origène [Origen], *Homélie sur les Nombres*, VI, 3, trans., L. Doutreleau (Paris: Cerf, SC no. 415, 1996), p. 149: ""The spirit of God...dwells in the pure in heart" [see Mathew, 5, 8], and in those who purify their soul of sin; on the other hand, it does not dwell in those given over to sin, even if it has dwelt there some time; for the Holy Spirit cannot tolerate either sharing or community with the spirit of evil." The editor also refers to the *Commentaire sur Saint Jean*, 32, 8, 86-88, Introduction, translation and notes C. Blanc (Paris: Cerf, t. V, SC no. 385, 1982), p. 225, and notes, p. 149, note 1, that "we already find in *The Pastor* of Hermas (33, 3) the idea that the Holy Spirit is confined in an impure soul and seeks to separate from it"; English translation by Alan Menzies, *Origen's Commentary on the Gospel of John*, Book I, ch. XXXII, in *ANF*, Vol. IX, ed. Allan Menzies (Grand Rapids, Mich.: Eerdmans Publishing, 1994) p. 314. See A. Dondeyn, "La discipline des scrutins dans l'Eglise latine avant Charlemagne," p. 10 note 3.

30. See Saint Cyrille [Cyril] de Jérusalem, *Catéchèse préliminaire ou Prologue des catéchèses*, in *Catéchèses baptismales et mystagogiques*, trans. Canon J. Bouvet (Namur: Éditions du Soleil levant, 1962), pp. 23-39, (§ 9: "Hasten your steps to catechesis. Eagerly welcome the exorcisms: under the insufflations, under the exorcisms your salvation is brought about. Keep in mind that you are a gold without value, falsified, mixed with various materials: bronze, tin, iron, lead. We are after the possession of the gold without alloy. Without fire, gold cannot be purified of foreign elements. Similarly, the soul cannot be purified without exorcisms; they are divine prayers, drawn from the divine Scriptures"); English translation by Edwin Hamilton Gifford, *Procatechesis, or Prologue to the Catechetical Lectures of our Holy Father, Cyril, Archbishop of Jerusalem*, in Philip Schaff and Henry Wace, eds., *NPNF2*, Vol. VII (Grand Rapids, Mich.: Eerdmans Publishing, 1994), p. 3:"Let your feet hasten to the catechisings; receive with earnestness the exorcisms : whether thou be breathed upon or exorcised, the act is to you salvation. Suppose you have gold unwrought and alloyed, mixed with various substances, copper, and tin, and iron, and lead: we seek to have the gold alone; can gold be purified from the foreign substances without fire? Even so without exorcisms the soul cannot be purified; and these exorcisms are divine, having been collected out of the divine Scriptures."

31. See E. Ferguson, *Baptism in the Early Church: History, Theology, and Liturgy in the First Five Centuries*, (Grand Rapids, Mich.: W. B. Eerdmans Publishing, 2009), pp. 90-91, p. 288, pp. 297-298, pp. 408-410 (on Origen and eschatological baptism of fire), p. 417, p. 730, and especially C.-M. Edsman, *Le baptême de feu* (Leipzig-Uppsala: A. Lorentz-A. B. Lundequistskan, 1940), and the very detailed review of this by A. Guillaumont, *Revue de l'histoire des religions*, vol. 131, no. 1, 1946, pp. 182-186. See below, note 49, regarding baptism of fire in Origen and the passage from the latter in *Homelies on Saint Luke*, XXIV, cited by Daniélou, *Origène*, p. 73. The mention of baptism as passage through fire, as well as the reference to Sermon 3 of Quodvultdeus are found in the article by A. Dondeyne, *La discipline des scrutins*, pp. 16-17 (see P. Chevallier, "Foucault et les sources patristiques," p. 140).

32. Quodvultdeus, *Sermones 1-3*, "De symbolo ad catechumenos 1-3," ed. R. Braun, Corpus Christianorum, Series Latina (CCSL) 60, Turnhout, Brepols, 1953, pp. 305-63. These three sermons were attributed—not without reservations on the part of Migne—to Saint Augustine in editions of the latter's works until the beginning of the twentieth century (see PL 40, col. 637, et seq.). Dom Germain Morin, "Pour une future edition des opuscules de S. Quodvultdeus, évêque de Carthage au Ve siècle," *Revue Benedictine*, 31, 1914, pp. 156-162, was the first to restore them to their real author. The passage quoted by Foucault is in PL 40, col. 637 (verses from Psalm 138, 23).

33. Saint Ambroise of Milan, *Explanatio symboli/Explication du symbole*, 1, introduction, translation, and notes by B. Botte (Paris: Cerf, SC no. 25bis, 1994 [1961]) p. 48: "We have celebrated up to here the mysteries of the scrutinies. We have made an inquiry from fear that an impurity remains attached to the body of someone. By exorcism we have sought for and applied a means of sanctifying not only the body, but also the soul." On the question of the authenticity of the work, see the Introduction pp. 21-25. English translation by R. H. Connolly, *The Explanation Symboli Ad Initiandos: A Work of Saint Ambrose*, Cambridge: Cambridge University Press, 1952), p. 19: "Thus far the mysteries of the Scrutinies have been celebrated. Therein search was made lest some uncleanness should still cling to the body of any one of you. By exorcism was sought and applied a sanctifying not only of the body, but of the soul as well."

34. Ibid., pp. 46-47: "We have celebrated up to here the mysteries of the scrutinies (*mysteria scru-taminum*). We have made an inquiry (*inquisitum est*) from fear that an impurity remains attached to the body of someone. By exorcism we have sought for and applied a means of sanctifying (*quaesita et adhibita sanctificatio*) not only the body, but also the soul"; English translation, see previous note. See A. Dondeyne, "La discipline des scrutins," p. 27.

35. From the Greek, *epiklēsis*, which means "action of appealing to" hence "invocation." R. Bultmann, *Theology of the New Testament*, vol. I (London: SCM Press, 1952), p. 137, defines epiclesis, or "calling of the Name," in this way: "... a special prayer which summons the power of Christ into the water to give it the ability to purify and sanctify"; see to J. W. Tyrer, "The meaning of ἐπίκλησις," *Journal of Theological Studies*, 25, 1923-1924, pp. 139-150.

36. This is the moment of "the baptismal rite strictly speaking: the triple submersion with the triple profession of faith" (R.-F. Refoulé, Introduction to Tertullian's *Traité du baptême*, p. 37).

37. See above, lecture of 13 February.

38. Tertullien, *De baptismo/Traité du baptême*, XX, 1, SC, p. 94. The manuscript completes the quotation: "in memory of the baptism of John of whom it is said that he received him confessing his sins"; Tertullian, *On Baptism*, ch. XX, pp. 678-679: "They who are about to enter baptism ought to pray with repeated prayers, fasts, and bendings of the knee, and vigils all the night through, and with the confession of all by-gone sins, that they may express *the meaning* even of the baptism of John: They were baptized, says (the Scripture), confessing their own sins."

39. The manuscript here, (verso of folio 18), cites these two references: "*Protocatachesis* of Cyril of J[erusalem]: 'Strip off the old man by confession of your sins,' Canons of Hipp[olytus]: confession to the bishop." The phrase attributed to Cyril of Jerusalem, however, is not in the *Procatechesis, or Prologue to the Catechetical Lectures* (see above p. 000, footnote *). See *Canons d'Hippolyte*, canon 19, p. 377: "... may he [the catechumen, after having been baptized] confess to the bishop that he takes his responsibility on himself alone, so that the bishop be satisfied with him and judge him worthy of the mysteries."

40. See above, lecture of 6 February, pp. 105-107 with reference to Justin's *Apology*.

41. On this phenomenon, see A. Benoit, *Le baptême chrétien au second siècle*, p. 228: "... we are indeed forced to note that Paulinism underwent a sort of decline in the second century...Pauline conceptions strictly speaking are completely foreign to the thought of the Fathers of the second century; and anyway, even implicitly, these conceptions cannot form the foundation of their baptismal doctrine"; L. Padovese, "L'antipaulinisme chrétien au IIe siècle," *Recherches de science religieuse*, t. 90, 2002-2003, pp. 399-422; see too A. Lindemann, *Paulus im ältesten Christentum. Das Bild des Apostels und die Rezeption der paulinischen Theologie in der frühchristlichen Literatur bis Marcion* (Tübingen: J.C. Mohr, 1979), pp. 6-10, which presents a detailed inventory of research since the end of the nineteenth century on the actual influence of Saint Paul in the second century.

42. On the parallel between baptism and burial, see Romans 6, 4: "We were buried with him therefore by baptism into death, so that as Christ was raised from the dead by the glory of the Father, we too might walk in newness of life"; Colossians 2, 12: "and you were buried with him in baptism, in which you were also raised with him through faith in the working of God, who raised him from the dead." This idea of the death and resurrection of the believer with Christ in baptism is specifically Pauline. See A. Benoit, *Le baptême chrétien*, p. 54. On the presence of this symbolism in the Fathers, see G. Bareille, "Baptême (d'après les Pères grecs et latins)," col. 199-200.

43. (a) See Origène [Origen], *Homélies sur l'Exode*, trans., P. Fortier (Paris: Cerf, SC no. 16, 1947) V, 2, p. 139 [commenting on Hosea 6, 2] "If...the Apostle is right to teach us that these words contain the mystery of baptism, it is necessary that 'all of us who were baptized into Christ be baptized into his death and buried with him' [Romans, 6, 3], and with him resurrected from the dead those who, as again says the Apostle, 'raised us up with him, and made us sit with him in the heavenly places' [Ephesians, 2, 6]"; but there is no mention of the baptismal bath (text cited with commentary by J. Daniélou, *Origène* (Paris: La Table ronde, 1948), pp. 68-69). See *Commentaire sur saint Jean*, V, 8, with regard to the need for repentance (*pénitence*) to gain access to baptism: "You must first die to sin in order to be buried with Christ"; and *Commentaire sur l'Épître aux Romains*, VIII, 5: "Those who are baptized are baptized into the death of Christ and are buried with him by baptism into death" (cited by J. Daniélou, ibid., p. 68).

(b) See Ambroise [Ambrose] de Milan, *De sacramentis/Des sacraments*, III, 1, introduction, translation, and notes by B. Botte (Paris: Cerf, SC, no. 25bis, 1994 [1961]), p. 91: "Yesterday [see II, 16-24] we dealt with the fountain, which is apparently like a sort of tomb. We are taken in there and immersed, believing in the Father, Son, and Holy Spirit, then we rise up again, that is to say we rise from the dead."

44. See above, lecture of 13 February, with regard to Tertullian (*On Baptism*, ch. IX). The reference to the crossing of the Red Sea as a prefiguration of baptism constitutes, along with the mysticism of death and resurrection with Christ (see the previous note), an essential theme of Saint Paul's thought (I, Corinthians, 10, 1-2: "our fathers were all under the cloud, and all passed through the sea, and all were baptized into Moses in the cloud and in the sea"). See F.J. Dölger, "Der Durchzug durch das rote Meer als Sinnbild der christlichen Taufe," in ibid., *Antike und Christentum*, (Münster: Aschendorff, 1930), t. II, pp. 63-69 ("The author," writes A. Benoit, *Le baptême chrétien*, p. 89, "shows how this typology of baptism is found in Origen, Tertullian, Chrysostom, Ephraim, Ambrose, Augustine ..."); J. Daniélou, "Traversée de la Mer rouge et baptême aux premiers siècles," *Recherches de science religieuse*, t. 33, 1946, pp. 402-430, and A. Benoit, *Le baptême chrétien*, p. 55, who cites the preceding article at length; see too G. Bareille, "Baptême (d'après les Pères grecs et latins)," col. 197-198 (numerous references).

45. See J. Daniélou, *Origène*, p. 71: "... on this point [the two traditional figures of baptism, the crossing of the Red Sea and of Jordan], Origen, while using a traditional theme, gives it a particular form... Here [*Homilies on Joshua*, IV, 1 and I, 4] the whole itinerary, from leaving Egypt to entry into the Promised Land, figures the stages of initiation. This is typical of Origen's way. He alludes to the common interpretation, but develops it in a personal direction."

46. See above, lectures of 6 February, p. 107 (and note 28) and of 13 February, pp. 122-123.

47. See Saint Augustine, *De baptismo contra donatistas*, in *Traités anti-donatistes*, II, trans. and ed. G. Finaert (Paris: Desclée de Brower, "Bibliothèque augustinienne," 1964), p. 97: "One who has approached (baptism) with dissimulation, is not re-baptized, but a filial amendment and a loyal confession (*aveu*) (*sed ipsa pia correctione et veraci confessione*) purifies him, which would not be possible without baptism"; English translation by J.R. King revised by Chester D. Hartranft, *On Baptism, Against the Donatists*, Book I, ch. 12, 18, in Philip Schaff, ed., *NPNF1*, Vol. IV (Grand Rapids, Michigan: W.M. Eerdmans Publishing,), p. 418: "as in the case of him who had approached the sacrament in deceit there is no second baptism, but he is purged by faithful discipline and truthful confession, which he could not be without baptism."

48. See Origène, *Commentaire sur saint Jean* (SC no. 157, 1970), t.II: VI (23), 125, p. 227; VI (37), 159, p. 251; VI, (33), 168, p. 257;

49. Origen even speaks of a triple baptism: "the pure figurative baptism, that of the Old Testament and John, Christian baptism, which is both reality in relation to the figure and figure in relation to future reality, and finally the baptism of fire of entry into glory" (J. Daniélou, *Origène*, pp. 71-72): "One must first have been baptized in the water and spirit, so that when one arrives at the river of fire one shows that one has kept the purifications of the water and spirit and that one deserves then to receive the baptism of fire into Jesus Christ" (*Homélies sur saint Luc*, XXIV; cited by J. Daniélou, *Origène*, p. 73). See E. Ferguson, *Baptism*, p. 400. On this third baptism (eschatological baptism distinct from baptism of water), see above, in this lecture, p. 000. This conception, which makes baptismal regeneration the prefiguration of total purification, does not seem to be at all contrary to Christian orthodoxy. See Daniélou, *Origène*, p. 74: "[Origen] gives the theology of baptism its eschatological extension and ends by making it the perfect expression of the common faith of the Church."

eight

27 FEBRUARY 1980

(II) Practices of canonical and ecclesial penance, from the second to the fifth century. ∽ Hermas, The Pastor. Scholarly interpretations to which it has given rise, from the end of the ninteenth to the beginning of the twentieth century (Tauftheorie, Jubiläumstheorie). Meaning of the repetition of repentance (pénitence) after baptism ∽ Early Christianity, a religion of the perfect? Arguments against this conception: ritual forms, texts, various practices. New status of metanoïa on the basis of Hermas: no longer simple state extending the baptismal break, but repetition itself of redemption. ∽ The problem of relapse. The system of law (repeatability of sin) and the system of salvation (irreversibility of knowledge) before Christianity. Effort of Greek wisdom to find a way to accomodate these two systems (Pythagoreans and Stoic examples). Why and how the problem arises for Christianity: the question of the relapsed (relaps) and the debate with the gnosis. ∽ Concluding comment: Christianity did not introduce the meaning of sin into Greco-Roman culture, but was the first to think the repercussions of the subject breaking with the truth.

TODAY I WOULD LIKE to begin to study something of the practices of penance (pénitence), post-baptismal penance, canonical and ecclesial penance between the end of the second and the fifth Christian century. I will begin by reading you a text from the middle of the second century, around the 140s: it is a text by Hermas, *The Pastor*.[1] In a part of this book Hermas represents himself engaging in dialogue with an angel

who is the angel of repentance (*pénitence*). And he says to him: "I still
have one question.—Speak, says [the angel].—I have heard [, Hermas
replies,] some doctors say that there is no other repentance than that of
the day on which we went down in the water and received forgiveness
for our former sins." So, a clear proposition: some doctors say that there
is repentance only on the day on which we go down into the water,
which means that there is repentance only through and with baptism.
To which the angel replies: "What you have heard is correct. That is
how it is. The person who has received forgiveness should in fact sin no
more, but live in holiness. But since you need all the details, I will point
out to you this too, not [however] to give pretext for sin to those who
will believe, or those who are now beginning to believe in the Lord, for
both the one and the other do not have to repent their sins: they have
absolution for their former sins. It is therefore solely for those who were
called before these last days that the Lord has established a repentance.
For the Lord knows the heart and, knowing all in advance, he knew the
weakness of man and the manifold schemes of the devil, who will do
harm to the servants of God and exercise his malice against them. In his
great mercy, the Lord was moved for his creature and [he] established
this repentance, and he bestowed its direction on me. But I say to you:
if, after this important and solemn call, someone, seduced by the devil,
commits a sin, he has only one chance of repentance; but if he sins time
and again ... repentance is useless to such a man; it will be difficult for
him to enjoy eternal life."[2]

This text is a classic of scholarly discussion concerning the history
of Christian penance (*pénitence*).[3] Straightaway you see that in this passage we can locate the distinction between two teachings: that of "certain doctors," *tines didaskaloi*, who say: "there is no other repentance
than that of baptism. Once baptism is carried out, there will be no
other repentance"; and then the angel of repentance adds to this teaching, which he does not refute (he says: "that's right, that's how it is"),
something that is his own, the angel's lesson, and says: "but however,
there is something else." A second distinction appears clearly in this
passage which is that there are not only two teachings, but there are also
two categories of hearers or two categories of persons addressed by the
angel and to whom also repentance is addressed. There are those who
are said to be now beginning to believe in the Lord, or those who will

soon believe in the Lord, that is to say those whose conversion is current or future. And for these, the passage seems to say, there will be one
and only one repentance. On the other hand, for those who are already
converted, for those already baptized, those who were called to believe
in former times or in the past, there is another lesson, another teaching
and the possibility of repentance. Finally, the third important element
to emphasize in this passage: God is said to have established a repentance for this second category, and the reason for this repentance is to
be sought in man's weakness, the devil's schemes, and the greatness of
divine mercy. But this repentance, foreseen for these reasons, can only be
a unique repentance. It cannot be repeated indefinitely. One will have
only one repentance, but if one starts to sin time and again, even if one
repents (*se repentir*) it will have no effect.

From the end of the nineteenth century until around 1910, 1920, this
passage was interpreted in a very simple way that became authoritative:
[it] shows that there was a teaching of these famous "certain doctors"
that represented the old and rigoristic tradition. In the early Church,
there would have been one and only one repentance, that of baptism,
and after that nothing more, baptism being the sole and unique possibility of repenting. No repentance outside of baptism. This is what the
German scholars call quite simply "*Tauftheorie*," that is to say the theory
of baptism as the sole possibility of repentance.[4] With regard to this, the
Angel that Hermas gets to speak, or Hermas speaking through the angel,
would say: Yes, it is true, there is only this form of repentance, that
of baptism. However, there is the possibility for some to be redeemed
anew by a new repentance, but of course this cannot be offered to those
who are presently on the path of baptism or who have only just been
baptized. It can be a second repentance only for those who have been
baptized for a certain length of time and who have fallen again due to
human weakness and the devil's schemes. For these, a collective, simultaneous repentance has been established that will be valid for all those
who, presently, will repent (*se repentir*) in this collective repentance,
which is that of a jubilee: a collective jubilee enabling each to repent
and, as a result, see his sins remitted once again. And, if the text speaks
of those who are currently baptized and do not have the possibility of
repentance anew, it is because this jubilee, obviously, can have no meaning for them. It can be a jubilee only for those who have already been

baptized for a certain length of time. This is what is called the theory of the jubilee,[5] which corrects the theory of baptism, the *Tauftheorie*, and which is a sort of step forward that then leads, later, to the conception of an indefinitely renewable repentance. So, there would be a first stage: there is repentance only in baptism; a second stage: there will be a once only collective repentance for all those who really wish to repent; and then, finally, a third stage, renewable repentance for all.

This conception of the *Tauftheorie* [and] the *[Jubiläumstheorie]** gives rise, obviously, to marvelous scholarly discussions. [It] was criticized by d'Alès around 1910, 1920,[6] and in particular by Poschmann in a big book published in 1940[7]—even so, this is the marvelous and magnificent folly of erudition: to think that in 1940 a book of hundreds and hundreds of pages was written on the problem of the meaning of this text by Hermas. So, Poschmann, in the *Paenitentia secunda*, criticized *Tauftheorie* and *[Jubiläumstheorie]*,† and he showed, first, that even in early Christianity there are elements proving that repentance could be either renewed or, at any rate, continued, reactivated, even after baptism—there was not therefore any early phase of absolute rigorism—and that in fact, in this text Hermas does not refer to a practice of Jubilee, but merely wanted to say: Hurry up, Christ's Parousia is imminent and you will no longer have the chance to repent on Earth; it will be too late to repent when Christ has returned because one does not repent in heaven. So, for those already baptized,‡ there is still, not a first, but a final possibility of repentance. As for those who have just been baptized, a second repentance is not necessary, since their baptism will coincide with the Parousia of Christ, which will take place in the days in which we are living. This is Poschmann's theory, which was authoritative for a number of years, and, more recently, Joly, in his edition of *Le Pasteur* for the "Sources chrétiennes," returns to the theory of the jubilee saying: even if it is true that there is an eschatological vision in Hermas that means that he is speaking of Christ's Parousia when he speaks of the present days during which one must repent (*se repentir*), it is precisely as a function of this Parousia that there has to be a jubilee in the course of

---

* M.F.: *Jubilee-Theory* (*Jubilé-Theorie*) [see below, p. 188, note 5].
† M.F.: *Jubilee-Theory*.
‡ M.F. adds: and for those who had the opportunity before Christ's imminent Parousia.

which those who have been baptized for a certain length of time will be able to repent (*faire pénitence*).[8]

Quite simply for reasons of incompetence I leave aside this discussion, which is, as you see, utterly gripping. The problem I would like to pose is this: within a conception of salvation, that is to say within a conception of illumination, of redemption obtained by men on the basis of their first baptism, what meaning can the repetition of repentance have, or even the repetition of sin? I think that on this we need to go back over some elements concerning, let's say, early Christianity, anyway, the Christianity for which we have evidence from earlier than *The Pastor* of Hermas, that is to say prior to the middle of the second century, to the years 140-150. In fact, if we accept, as did the old *Tauftheorie*, that Christianity accepted repentance only in baptism, with baptism, and through baptism, and if it is true that it is simply later, during the second century, maybe with Hermas, that the possibility of a second recourse began to be added, this means that throughout this early period of Christianity, until more or less the middle of the second century, Christianity considered itself as a religion of the perfect, of the pure, of people incapable of falling into sin. If, in fact, there is no recourse to repentance after baptism, this means that baptism in itself gave those who received it access to the truth, the light, and perfection so that it was impossible for those to whom this light and truth were opened to go back and fall again. Either one receives illumination, and then remains enlightened, or one does not remain in the illumination, which means that one was not really enlightened. You can see that it is the whole problem of the subject's relationship to the truth, of the form of the subject's link to the truth, of the form of the subject's insertion in the truth and the truth's insertion in the subject, of the reciprocal anchorage of the subject and the truth, that is raised by this problem of whether one can sin after having received baptism and whether, as a result, one can and must foresee a post-baptismal repentance that recommences and resumes the procedure of purification, conversion, *metanoia*, remission, *aphesis*[9] by which the individual is assured of his salvation and finds again the way of eternal life, of the truth, and of salvation.

It is, of course, solely from this point of view of the forms of relationship, anchorage, and linkage of the truth and subjectivity that I would like at least to cross this field of scholarly questions. Of course, and you know better than me, there is a whole series of texts in Christianity that do seem to indicate that once one has actually received baptism, there is no longer any question of committing a sin, of falling away, or of obtaining a second repentance as a result. One cannot obtain repentance quite simply because, basically, one does not need it. It is the text of the Epistle to the Hebrews that says: "it is impossible for those who were once enlightened, who have tasted the heavenly gift, have become partakers of the Holy Ghost, and have tasted the good word of God, and the powers to come, if they shall fall away, to renew them again by bringing them to repentance while they themselves crucify the Son of God afresh, and scorn him openly."[10] A bit further on, in the same *Epistle to the Hebrews*, it is said: "For if we sin willfully after having received the knowledge of the truth, there remains no more sacrifice for sins, but a certain fearful perspective of judgment and fiery indignation, which shall devour the rebels."[11] These texts from Scripture are echoed in a whole series of texts from the apostolic period, that is to say the period going, roughly, from the end of the first to the middle of the second century. For example, Ignatius of Antioch, who writes around 100-110, says: "No one, if he professes the faith sins, nor, if he possesses charity, hates. 'The tree is known by its fruit.'[12] Those who make profession of being of Christ shall be recognized by their works."[13] And in the Epistle of Barnabas, which is from the years 120, 130, it is said also: "It is by receiving the remission of our sins, it is by hoping in his name that we have become new men, that we have been recreated from top to bottom" (you find again here the themes I spoke about last week). "It is in this way that God"—after baptism, after we have been recreated from top to bottom—"really dwells in us ... He accords repentance (*repentir*) to us who were subject to death, and in that way introduces us into incorruptible time."[14] So we really do enter the world of non-corruption, of incorruptibility with baptism. How could one conceive of sin under these conditions? And, if someone falls again, how could we imagine that he can be redeemed anew? In other words, the subjectivity-truth bond is acquired once in baptism, but it is acquired once and for all. There can no longer be any dissociation of the bond between subjectivity and truth. And this is what we find again in Hermas himself, moreover, in a passage in the third precept preceding the fourth that I just read to you and in which the angel of repentance says to Hermas: "Love the truth, that it alone may come from your mouth; so that the spirit that God has lodged in your flesh [may be found true] (*alethēs*) in the eyes of all men and thus the Lord, who dwells in you, will be glorified, for the Lord is true"—well, he is *alethinos*, the text says, he is truthful—"[the Lord is truthful] in all his words and there is no falsehood in him."[15]

You see here what could be called the cycle of the truth in the person who has been enlightened, in the person whose sins have been remitted, in someone once he has entered the truth. First, he is bound to the truth because he loves the truth. Second, once he loves the truth, all the words from his mouth are true words. "Only the truth can come from your mouth." If the truth alone can come from the mouth of someone who believes, that is to say if the person who believes, when he speaks, can say only the truth, it is because the spirit of God dwells in him. The spirit of God manifests itself as true spirit, to the same extent that the words of those who believe in him are true. And it is in this way that God manifests himself as truthful, since it is God who speaks the truth through the words of the person speaking, of the person who is speaking after having loved the truth. So that the subject going to the truth and attaching himself to it through love manifests in his own words a truth that is nothing other than the manifestation in him of the true presence of a God who can only speak the truth, for he never lies, [he] is truthful. So once baptism has manifested, authenticated, and sacralized the relationship between the subject and the truth, there is an essential relationship that cannot be broken and undone. This anyway is one of the main themes, one of the lines of Christian thought in these texts of the first centuries.

However, it remains the case that there are a number of texts in the same period that, while not taking a completely different direction—well, this is what I will try to show you—nonetheless prevent us from thinking that Christianity, in its early forms, was a religion of the perfect, the pure, and that the Christian Church thought of itself as a community of perfect, pure individuals unable to fall again by virtue of the essential and definitive character of the relationship to salvation and the truth. A number of things prove that the early Christian Church did not consider itself a religion of the perfect. In the first place, a number of ritual forms have been attested from very early on, from the end of the first and the beginning of the second century, that show

that for baptized Christians, members of the community, there is still
and always a possibility of sinning, but of sinning without leaving the
Church, without losing their status as Christians, without being driven
out, or at least not definitively. There is the possibility of sinning and
the need to repent (*se repentir*) of one's sins, to break away from them by
a movement of *metanoia*, but this is no longer the movement of *metanoia*
by which one enters the Church, by which one has access to the truth,
but a *metanoia* that is internal to that relationship to the truth. That is to
say that *metanoia*, conversion, continues to work, so to speak, within the
subject–truth relationship.

These ritual forms are well known. The specifically individual ritual
form, in individual prayer, the famous text of the Lord's Prayer which
you find in the *Didache*, at the beginning of the second century, and
which has to be recited three times a day, says this: "Remit our debt"
and "deliver us* from the Evil One."[16] "In the Assembly," that is to
say at the meeting of believers for daily prayer, the *Didache* prescribes
also: "you shall confess your faults[17] and not go to prayer with a bad
conscience"†—well, *ponēra suneidesei*: conscious of having done wrong,
uneasy conscience, as it were.[18] This passage from the *Didache* is found
in almost the identical form in the *Epistle of Barnabas* where it says that
one must make the public confession of one's sins:[19] "do not go to prayer
with a bad conscience. Such is the way of light."[20] I leave aside the
problem—because we will come back to it later at greater length—of the
nature of this public confession (*confession*) this famous exomolegesis,
which clearly should not be understood as a detailed enunciation in
the form of a public confession (*aveu*) of the sins one has committed. It
is much more likely that this public confession is a formulation in the
form of an orison and supplication made collectively to ask for God's
forgiveness of sins, without their being a precise procedure of confession
of self (*aveu*).[21] Another ritual form that clearly indicates that, for all
that he is a Christian, and for all that he is a subject who has received
the light through baptism, the Christian may and does in fact sin. For
the Sunday meeting, the weekly meeting in the course of which the
Eucharist is celebrated, the *Didache* says again: "Every dominical Lord's

---

* M.F. adds: from the devil.
† The manuscript adds: "(confession = *exomologein*)".

day meet together, break bread, and give thanks after first having confessed your sins so that your sacrifice is pure."[22] So, in prayer, every day, in the group meeting where one prays, every week, at the moment of the Eucharist, there is an act by which the Christian acknowledges that he is a sinner.

In the texts of the same period we also find the paraenetic theme of a repentance that should take place in the Christian's life itself, in the form of a constant detestation of sin and a supplication to God to obtain from his kindness the forgiveness of sins. In the first epistle of Clement [of Rome], at the end of the century, we read in chapter 9: "Let us submit to [the] magnificent and glorious will [of the Lord], making ourselves supplicants, asking on bended knees for his pity and kindness, and, having recourse to his mercies, let us abandon the vain concerns and jealousies that lead to death."[23] This is not a discourse addressed to catechumens or candidates for entry into the ecclesiastical community, but to those who already belong to it. In the same sense, the same epistle of [Clement]* says: "For all our falls and the sins we have committed at the instigation of one of the enemy's fiends, let us implore forgiveness ... For it is better to confess (*confesser*) one's sins publicly"—the same remark as before with regard to this public confession—"than to harden the heart."[24]

Finally, we have the evidence of a number of particular practices concerning the manner of repenting (*se repentir*) and the manner of, as it were, reacting when a sin has been committed, either on the part of the person who committed it, or on the part of the community with regard to the sinner. It seems that very early on there were practices of provisional exclusion, of provisional suspension from the community, so to speak, of those who had committed a sin. In chapter 10 of the *Didache* (concerning the Eucharist and the Sunday meeting at which it was celebrated), after giving the formula of the rituals that have to be observed, the text adds: "If any one is holy, let him come! [If he is not holy], let him repent (*fasse pénitence*)!"[25] This seems to suggest that he should not come and instead of participating should do something called "repentance (*la pénitence*)" which, of course, cannot apply to people who had not received baptism, but to those who, normally, should participate

---

* M.F.: Barnabas.

in the Eucharist and [consequently] are baptized. So, something like exclusion or suspension of individuals from certain rituals. It also seems that some form of collective participation in the act of repentance was foreseen. In [his] first epistle, addressing a community which had to deal with sinners, Clement tells them: "You struggled day and night for the whole group of brothers ... You mourned your neighbor's faults; you considered his lapses to be your own."[26] A collective participation of which Polycarp also gives an example in his *Epistle to the Philippians*. It concerns a priest named Valens who had committed I don't know what sin—I think it was avarice, but it's not important—and Polycarp says: "I am much distressed for him and his wife; 'may the Lord give them true repentance (*vrai repentir*).' Be then very moderate yourselves also [on this point]. "Do not regard them as enemies," but call them back as suffering and straying members in order to save your whole body."[27] Finally, a number of very specific acts are prescribed to obtain redemption of sins, when one is a Christian and part of the community. In the *Didache*, chapter 4: "If you possess something thanks to the work of your hands, give [it] to redeem your sins."[28] Once again, this is advice, a prescription given to those who are already Christians and which indicates that almsgiving appeared, very early therefore, as an act by which sins can be redeemed, sins that were probably committed after baptism, since those committed before baptism no longer need to be redeemed, having already been redeemed by baptism itself. And in a text from a bit later, contemporary with *The Pastor* of Hermas, that is to say in the second epistle attributed to Clement, it is said: "Almsgiving is an excellent repentance for sin; fasting is better than prayer, but almsgiving is better than both."[29] So we have the trilogy that will be found for more than a thousand, almost two thousand years, in the practices of satisfaction in penance, that is to say prayers, fasting, and almsgiving.

All this shows therefore that the Christian communities did not consider themselves to be a society of the perfect, of the pure, of people who having once gained access to the light and to eternal life could never be dispossessed of this and could never fall again. We see that sin and weakness, may be, are in actual fact present in the Christian communities and that awareness of these sins and weaknesses, and repenting (*repentir*) them, are characteristic of the Christian life, of the life of individuals and of communities. This implies therefore that *metanoia*—which, with regard to baptism, was the movement by which the soul was turned towards the light, gained access to the light, by which it entered into the truth and truth entered it—in some way continues to be at work in the Christian's life, to be present in and part of it.

Where the text of Hermas represents a difference and a break is not that previously there was *metanoia* only in baptism and then no more after, but that *metanoia*, which must continue to produce its effects in the Christian's life, changes its nature or takes on a new status from the years or period in which Hermas wrote his *Pastor*. Let's say roughly that, before, it seems that the *metanoia* in question in the texts I have just quoted is entirely dependent on the *metanoia* of baptism, that it is like its continuation or extension. It is not, basically, a new act of *metanoia* with a different principle, a different system, and possibly different effects that is required after baptism. The *metanoia* of baptism must be not only a moment during which the soul turns round, but a sort of constant effort, on the part of the soul, to remain turned towards the light and the truth. There is the idea that with baptism one enters into the truth and has access to it. But we must understand (and the texts say so moreover) that with baptism one also enters into *metanoia*. That is to say that *metanoia* is a constant dimension of the life of the Christian. This movement by which one turns round must be maintained. It is not only a break, but a state. It is a state of break by which one detaches oneself from one's past, one's faults, and from the world in order to turn around towards the light, the truth, and the other world. *Metanoia* seems to be defined, or at any rate its principle as a state-break seems to be sketched in the texts I have been talking about.

I think something new emerges with the *Pastor*, that is to say the establishment of a post-baptismal repentance that, to start with, is a quite specific and delimited institution, and then has a system, and soon a ritual, as well as effects that are very specific and to a certain extent different from or not assimilable to baptism. In other words, what is involved is transition from a *metanoia* that already spanned the whole life of baptized Christians, but was basically only the same *metanoia* of baptism in its echoes and extensions, to a second *metanoia*. It is no longer the extension of baptismal *metanoia*. It is the problem of the repetition of this *metanoia*, of the recommencement of the entire act by which one is purified of the sins one has committed. In other words, from the middle of the second century Christianity had to think about something that, basically, it had not yet considered, and I think *The Pastor* is the first manifestation of this, which is the problem of relapse, of the recommencement of *metanoia*, of the repetition of redemption. If this problem was so important, so difficult, and gave rise to so many problems and discussions in Christianity, practically up until Saint Augustine, I think it is basically because the very notion, the very idea of relapse was foreign to Greek, Hellenistic and Roman culture as well as to the Jewish religion. Thinking the relapse, is, I believe, one of the fundamental features of Christianity and one of its stakes with regard to both the Hellenistic milieu in which it developed and the Jewish tradition in which it was rooted.

That relapse is an extremely difficult and, it seems to me, new problem could be explained—very simply, in a kind of overview—by saying the following. Basically, the Mediterranean world before Christianity was familiar with two things, a system and a schema: the system of the law and the schema of salvation. The system of the law, which you find in the Hebrews and also the Greeks, is a system that permits a division between good and evil, that is to say a system that makes possible the definition and characterization of what is a good action and what is a bad action. Either the law defines the good action in the form of prescription and, as a result, the rest is thus negatively left on the side of evil, or it defines the bad action, the infraction, and the rest is, if not good, at least acceptable. In any case, it is this type of division that the law carries out. That is to say the law defines the form of the action, and it carries out this division on actions, on the form, components, and possibly the effects of the action. The law does not take into consideration the quality of the person who commits the action. It does not take the actor, the author, the subject into consideration. You will say: yes it does, without cease. Yes, it takes the subject, actor, or author into consideration, but how? It takes it as modifying element of the action. The same action will not be considered good or bad according to whether it was committed by this or that person, because the subject of the action appears as a circumstance modifying the very form of the action, making good what may be and generally is bad, or conversely. That is to say the subject intervenes only as a distinctive element of the action that is as it were the basic unit, the grain on which the law focuses. When the law is a principle of division between good and evil, between good and bad, a principle of division that is concerned with the action and distinctive elements of the action, you can see that the transgression as bad action is by definition indefinitely repeatable. It is a possible form of action and repeatability is inscribed in the very functioning of the law.

On the other hand, the schema of salvation, of perfection, initiation, and illumination, is entirely different. It consists in focusing the division on subjects rather than actions. Salvation, perfection, illumination, and initiation select between those who are saved and those who are not, those who have received the light and those who have not, those who are initiated and those who are not. And it is the quality of the subject that determines the quality of the action. This appears very clearly in the conception of philosophical wisdom [of the] first Stoicism, which accepted that someone who has attained perfection can no longer do evil. He can no longer do evil, not because he has interiorized the law and obeys the law so much that the idea of breaking it does not even enter his mind; it does not enter into the field of his possible actions. His action is inevitably good because he is wise.[30] It is the quality of the subject that necessarily and inevitably brings about the quality of the actions. The same action—this is the paradox of the Stoic sage, but it is ultimately the paradox also of holiness, of perfection, and of illumination—does not have the same value when committed by one or the other, by someone who is wise or by someone who is not, by someone who is perfect or by someone who is not.

Now this clearly implies a division that is not only concerned with individuals, but with the life of individuals, the time of their life. It is a temporal division: before and after, before initiation and after, before receiving the light and after, before attaining the stage of wisdom and after. This is a temporal division that the law, by definition, must ignore. It is a temporal division that also implies irreversibility. Having actually reached the point of wisdom or enlightenment, how can one go back, since time, the time of individuals anyway, does not turn back on itself? If, according to some philosophies or cosmologies, the world may well in fact turn in one or the other direction, in the life of individuals time [has only]* one direction. So, it is irreversible. The division of salvation is not repeatable.

So, on one side we have the system of the law that is concerned with the division of actions in their specific form, with, of course, repeatability of the transgression, and, [on the other], the division of salvation that is concerned with the life and time of individuals and entails irreversibility. It [should be added] that the subjects on whom this division is carried out are subjects of knowledge, since knowledge is precisely a temporal process such that when one has acquired knowledge, when one is in the truth, one has seen, one has received the light, and one can no longer be deprived of it. One knows. One has seen. Knowledge is irreversible. On the other hand, the subject to which the law refers is a subject of will, and not a subject of knowledge; a subject of will can ceaselessly will anew, sometimes good and sometimes evil. Well, I think that the system of the law, which focuses on actions and refers to a subject of will, consequently presupposing the indefinite repeatability of the transgression, and the schema of salvation and perfection, which focuses on subjects and entails a temporal scanning and irreversibility, cannot be integrated—or, at any rate, that they have not been integrated and that one of the major dimensions and tensions of Greek thought was to try to find something like an adjustment and composition between the system of law and the system of perfection. In a sense, this was in fact the problem of Greek wisdom.

We can say, to take only two examples, that the Pythagoreans—[for whom] goodness knows nevertheless [how] important the schema of salvation, purity, and illumination was—did all they could to integrate the elements of law and those of salvation by considering that the life of the pure man, someone who had achieved salvation and had reached the stage at which one achieved salvation, had to be framed in an extremely tight, detailed, finicky regulation giving as it were a permanent legal armature, an almost indefinite regulatory armature to the life of the perfect.[31] We find the same problem, but in other terms and with other solutions, with the Stoics, since in the first Stoicism there was the idea that the sage, once he had reached the stage of wisdom, could not do evil, could not experience evil, and in the final analysis was indifferent, in his

---

* Conjecture: inaudible passage.

quality as sage, to all the real forms of action he might commit.[32] For this idea of a sage for whom it is as if he is indifferent, as a sage, to whatever he might do, the second Stoicism and the Stoicism of the Roman period substituted, of course, the idea of a sage who is to be only a sort of regulating principle of behavior. No one, of course, can really be a sage. No one, of course, in this conception, can in actual fact find himself in that unfailing and irreversible status of wisdom. One may always fall again. In this Stoicism, therefore, there is the idea of a repeatability of fault, but this is because the sage has become an ideal regulator of behavior, that is to say, a sort of law imposed on individuals, which is imposed on their conduct and which makes it possible to sort out, as it were, which of their actions are good and which are bad.[33] So you see again here, but functioning in a different way, this tension between law and salvation, which are, I believe, two forms that remained profoundly incompatible in all Greek, Roman, Hellenistic thought before Christianity.

Christianity—and in a sense this has been one of its great historical problems, one of the great historical challenges it had to confront—had to think this law-perfection relation, or, if you like, this problem of the irreversibility of the subject-truth relationship and of the repeatability of sin. If the subject-truth bond is irreversible, how is sin still possible? Consequently, how can one repeat the sin and is it legitimate, is it possible to reconstitute, can one conceive of reconstituting this subject-truth relationship within the Christian, someone who has already attained this stage, who has first acquired this relationship and then, it seems, lost it by the sin? Christianity was forced to think the repeatability of *metanoia*, the recommencement of establishing an essential relationship of the subject and the truth, for two reasons, one internal and the other both internal and external, at its borders.

The internal problem was, of course, [that of] the relapsed.[34] That is to say [that] Christianity had the "good fortune"* to be persecuted: for more than two centuries, from the end of the first century until the Constantine peace, the recurrence of persecutions constantly raised the problem of those who renounced their faith or agreed to a number of compromises with those who demanded signs of them having abandoned their faith. What was to be done about these people? Should

---

* In quotation marks in the manuscript.

they be abandoned? Have they broken definitively with Christianity or should they be readmitted? You can see that this is a problem that, in its altogether complex form, is different from [that of] sins internal to the Christian community for which, without too much difficulty it seems, it was thought that the *metanoia* of baptism had to be extended and had to produce its effects up [to the end].* This is no longer a matter of avarice, dispute, or rivalry within the community, of all those petty weaknesses for which it was foreseen that every Sunday, every day, three times a day one had to repent (*se repentir*) solemnly in prayer. This is something else. With the relapsed, what is at issue is people who have effectively abandoned their profession of faith and agreed to break their relationship with the truth. Can they revive it? Can the subject take up again that fundamental relationship he had once entered into and that he had entered into because God had indeed wanted to give him the grace to do so? This is one of the problems.

The other problem, on the borders of Christianity, both within and outside, was, of course, the great debate with the gnosis, with Gnostic movements, that is to say with the whole series of movements that, inside or outside Christianity, in any case close to it, made salvation, and salvation through knowledge, an absolutely definitive deliverance and an absolutely irreversible state.[35] In the gnosis we have forms of thought in which the [schema of] salvation, with all that this comprises of the radical thesis of the irreversibility of the truth-subject relationship, is pushed to its end. For the gnosis, no relapse is possible. Deliverance, which is deliverance through knowledge, is acquired once and for all, and if the subject apparently falls back it is in fact because he had never been delivered. And this [idea], typical of a religious conception of salvation through knowledge, clearly implied a radical rejection of the system of the law. Pushed to the limit, the schema of salvation cannot fail to exclude any division in terms of law. With the gnosis we have a pure system of deliverance, a pure system of salvation and perfection, and the law cannot but be rejected. In a couple words let's say the following: in the gnosis, the world is not to be considered as a place in which good and evil are regulated, with law as the internal principle for dividing good and evil in this world. For the gnosis, the entire world is bad. It is

---

* Conjecture: inaudible words.

intrinsically bad in every particle; it is wholly bad, without mixture or division. It is bad because the creative act itself that gave birth to it is bad. And this creative act is bad because the god who created the world is himself bad.[36] So, everything belonging to the world being bad, the law, as order of the world, as principle that claims to divide what is good from what is not in the world, that claims to say what in human actions is bad and what is good, this law, inasmuch as it is intrinsic to the world [and] tries to divide this and that in the world, arises from evil itself, like the world. The law, as principle of division within the world, is part of evil and therefore cannot claim to make the division between good and evil. The difference between good and evil as established by the law is in itself evil.

To tell the truth, this conception that the law is evil because it belongs to the world, and that there can no longer be any evil in the realm of salvation, is not entirely foreign to Christianity, and Christianity had to wrestle with it. We find it in Saint Paul, of course, in that enigmatic text with which Christianity has battled we can say until now, and which is: "it is by the law that we know sin."[37] Should this not be understood in the following way: it is the law, the very existence of a law dividing good and evil, that reveals sin? [Without] law, there would be no sin. This anyway is the meaning that a large number, most of the Gnostic movements gave to Saint Paul's text, and it was against this meaning that orthodox Christianity was obliged to construct an extraordinarily subtle and complex conception to which we will have to return.[38] We also find this tendency to reject the law in everything in Christianity that invalidated or rejected the Old Testament. Christianity was forced to connect the Old and New Testaments through a whole series of games or analogies, relations, and prophecies precisely in order to steer clear of one of its original tendencies, [which consisted] in saying: insofar as it is the Jewish text, Jewish scripture and, as a result, Jewish law, the Old Testament is evil, and the New Testament, as opposed to the book of the law, is the book of salvation.*[39] It is in this opposition between the Old Testament as book of the law and the New Testament as book of salvation that a whole line of Christian thought developed, of which Saint

---

* The manuscript (folio 18) adds: "Marcion: Jehovah as [author][a] of the creature, is the evil God."
[a] Reading uncertain.

Paul, of course, was the first representative to whom one always referred afterwards, a line internal to Christianity for making Christianity a religion not of the law, but of salvation.

On the basis of this rejection of the law, the kernel of which is found in Christianity and which is absolutely fundamental in the gnosis, two attitudes develop. One was that of an extreme asceticism that does not take the form of observance of the law, but whose function and meaning is to cross over, to go beyond the domain of the law in order to arrive at a perfection that no longer knows the evil of the division of good and evil. An extreme asceticism and, on the other hand, antinomianism: since the law is bad and one must be delivered from this evil of the law, one must systematically defy the domain of the law; the law is made to be violated, to be broken, and deliverance will be obtained when one has in fact broken all the laws. Hence the idea, those themes found in the gnosis of the systematic practice of everything prohibited by the Decalogue understood as law, as law of the Old Testament, as law of the Hebrew religion and, consequently, as law of evil.

So, Christianity is confronted with persecution, on the one hand, and, on the other, with the gnosis, with the problem of the re-evaluation, the re-elaboration of the relations between law and salvation, of the relation between irreversible perfection reached by a single act of salvation, and the constant and indefinitely repeatable division of good and evil. What I think made possible, not the solution to this problem, because there isn't one, but its elaboration, is basically that Christianity did not pose the question of Greek philosophy, namely: what type of observation of the law will lead us to perfection? Nor did it seek to know, like the Gnostics, what might remain of the law once one became perfect. For the reasons I have given, Christianity was forced to pose concretely the question: what to do with those who have, in actual fact, fallen? What to do with those who, in actual fact, at a given moment, have said no to the truth, to that truth to which they said yes at baptism? What to do with those who have gone back on the *metanoia* that they manifested, authenticated, and professed in baptism? In other words, Christianity was forced to think the problem of relapse and of those who fell after having arrived at the truth and the light.

One word more, if you will. It is often said that Christianity introduced the meaning of the transgression, of sin into a Greco-Roman culture that did not possess it. I do not think this is right for a very simple reason. This is that if there truly was a world, a civilization, a culture, which knew, codified, reflected on, and analyzed the nature of transgression, infraction, and its possible consequences, it is indeed the Greek world and Roman world. The rules of right, the judicial institutions and practices, the idea of a philosophy that principally would be morality, a morality of everyday life, with rules of existence, the codification of conducts, the permanent definition of good and evil, correct or incorrect, the dividing up of every human conduct in terms of good and evil, just and unjust, legal or illegal, are all absolutely typical of Greek and Roman civilization. Consequently, definition of the transgression was absolutely central, important, and extremely particular in them. And let's not say that it was a matter of some kind of objective definition of the transgression and that the subject was not questioned. The problem of the subject, as I told you, as particular circumstance modifying the value of the act and figuring as it were in the objective characteristics of the act, was absolutely fundamental both in Greek and Roman morality and in Greek and Roman law. The Greco-Roman world is a world of the transgression: it is a world of transgression, responsibility, and guilt. In a sense, it is nothing but a question of this from Greek tragedy to Roman law. And Greek philosophy, Hellenistic philosophy, is a philosophy of the fault, of transgression, of responsibility, of the subject's relationship to his transgression. So Christianity is not a religion that introduced the transgression, sin, the *peccatum* into the innocence of a world without guilt. It did something else. It did not introduce the problem of the *peccatum*, sin, transgression into innocence, but in relation to it. It introduced the problem of the *peccatum* in relation to the light, deliverance, and salvation. That is to say: what is the situation regarding transgression, and how can one transgress when one has had access to the truth? It is here, therefore, [with] the *peccatum* inserting itself into the essential and fundamental relationship between subject and truth, that Christianity posed its problem and this was the point of its work and of the successive and indefinite elaborations to which it gave rise. Christianity thought transgression, not so much in terms of the fall, for this is no longer the main thing—the fall, basically, was a very common theme in Greek philosophy, in the Hebrew religion, and in most of the religions of initiation and salvation that pre-existed

Christianity. Christianity thought the *re*lapse (*rechute*).* It battled with the problem of how the subject, having arrived at the truth, could lose it, how, in this relationship, which is after all conceived of as a fundamentally irreversible relationship of knowledge, something can take place that is like falling back from knowledge to non-knowledge, from light to darkness, and from perfection to imperfection and sin.

In bringing this problem together with the problem we encountered regarding baptism, we can say the following: basically Christianity (and this is no doubt what ensured that its both institutional and theoretical, practical and speculative work was so fundamental) did not struggle fundamentally with the problem of subject-truth relationships, it did not raise [the question] of what the situation of the subject was when he was in the truth. It did not raise [the question] of what the situation was regarding the truth when the subject was enlightened by it. This is the problem of Buddhism, for example.[40] What is the situation of the subject in its positive relationship with the truth? When the subject is enlightened by the truth, is it still subject? Christianity did not pose this problem, but it posed two other problems. With baptism, the problem: what is the situation regarding the truth of the subject when the subject goes to the truth—[this is] all those problems of authentication and probation I talked about last week with regard to baptism. And then it posed the other, opposite problem: what is the situation of the subject when, having established its fundamental relationship to the truth through baptism, it has fallen away from this relationship, when it has fallen back, not so much according to an original fall—although this will be referred to, since it is so to speak the general explanatory principle—but how do things stand when the subject falls back, personally and individually, into its own transgression? In other word what is the situation of the subject when it breaks with this truth? The problem of baptism was: what is the situation regarding the subject when, breaking with itself, it goes to the truth? And the problem of penance, now, will be: what is the situation of the subject when, breaking with the truth, it turns back to the very thing with which it was forced to break at the moment of baptism?

---

* M.F. stresses the first syllable.

It is therefore this problem of the double break that is posed. It is not the subject's belonging to the truth or the truth's belonging to the subject, it is their distance that creates the problem. And this is not the question of the subject's identity; it is the question of the break that creates the problem. The break of the subject in the relation of distance it has with the truth: I think this is what Christian practice, institutions, theories, and speculation struggled with, and this is the problem of penance (*pénitence*), of penance after baptism, of penance in the strict, narrow sense of the word. This is what I will try to explain next week so as to try to show you how Christianity gave form to this problem of the relationships [between] truth and subject in the repurcussions of the subject breaking with the truth.

1. Hermas, *Le Pasteur*, Introduction, translation and notes by R. Joly (Paris: Cerf, SC, no. 53 bis, 2nd, revised and expanded ed., 1968, re-ed., 1997); English translation by F. Crombie as, *The Pastor Of Hermas*, in Alexander Roberts and James Donaldson, eds., revised by A. Cleveland Coxe, *ANF, Vol. II: Fathers of the Second Century* (Grand Rapids, Michigan: Eerdmans Publishing, 1994).

2. Hermas, *Le Pasteur*, Précepte IV, 31 (3), pp. 159-161. This translation is also reproduced in *EPA* (Paris: Cerf, 1963); for the passage quoted, see pp. 341-342; *The Pastor*, Book II, Commandment 4, ch. 3, p. 22: "And I said to him, I should like to continue my questions. Speak on, said he. And I said, I heard, sir, some teachers maintain that there is no other repentance than that which takes place, when we descended into the water and received remission of our former sins. He said to me, That was sound doctrine which you heard; for that is really the case. For he who has received remission of his sins ought not to sin any more, but to live in purity. Since, however, you inquire diligently into all things, I will point this also out to you, not as giving occasion for error to those who are to believe, or have lately believed, in the Lord. For those who have now believed, and those who are to believe, have not repentance for their sins; but they have remission of their previous sins. For to those who have been called before these days, the Lord has set repentance. For the Lord, knowing the heart, and foreknowing all things, knew the weakness of men and the manifold wiles of the devil, that he would inflict some evil on the servants of God, and would act wickedly towards them. The Lord, therefore, being merciful, has had mercy on the work of His hand, and has set repentance for them; and He has entrusted to me power over this repentance. And therefore I say to you, that if any one is tempted by the devil, and sins after that great and holy calling in which the Lord has called His people to everlasting life, he has opportunity to repent but once. But if he should sin frequently after this, and then repent, to such a man his repentance will be of no avail; for with difficulty will he live."

3. See, for example, the commentary on this passage by E. Amann, "Pénitence," DTC, XII, 1933, col. 760-763; A. Benoit, *La Baptême chrétien au second siècle*, pp. 115-124.

4. Or "*Sündlosigkeitstheorie*" (theory of impeccability). The theory is expounded, not without raising objections to it, by H. Windish, *Taufe und Sünde im ältesten Christentum bis auf Origenes. Ein Beitrag zur altchristlichen Dogmengeschichte* (Tübingen: J.C.B. Mohr, 1908). See p. 507: "Christen sind ihrem wirklichen Wesen nach sündlose Menschen." Impetus was no doubt given to this discussion by P. Battifol, "L'Eglise Naissante—Hermas et le problème moral au second siècle," *Revue biblique*, 10, 1901, pp. 337-351 (see his conclusion, p. 351, according to which early Christianity was understood as "a communion of saints"). On this theory, see B. Joly, Introduction to Hermas, *Le Pasteur*, pp. 22-23, which summarizes it in this way: "baptism remits earlier sins, but the early Church then requires perfect purity of Christians. If one sins (gravely) after baptism, one no longer has any terrestrial recourse: one must await God's judgment in complete uncertainty, if not in the certainty of hell. There is no post-baptismal repentance."

5. R. Joly, ibid., p. 23: "the [post-baptismal] repentance of Hermas is an exceptional repentance, on a fixed date, a *jubilee* after which one will return to the previous rigorism, waiting for the imminent Parousia."

6. A. d'Alès, *L'Édit de Calliste* (Paris: Beauchesne, 1914), pp. 52-113.

7. B. Poschmann, *Paenitentia secunda: die kirchliche Busse im ältesen Christentum bis Cyprian und Origenes: eine dogmengeschichtliche Untersuchung* (Bonn: P. Hanstein, "Theophaneia," 1940). On Hermas, *The Pastor*, see pp. 134-205. For a synthetic presentation of this interpretation, see B. Joly, "La doctrine pénitentielle du Pasteur d'Hermas et l'exégès récente," *Revue de l'histoire des religions*, vol. 147, no. 1, 1955, pp. 32-49, which discusses it at length (p. 37 et seq.).

8. See B. Joly, Introduction to Hermas, *Le Pasteur*, p. 25: "... it seems to us ... that Hermas is incomprehensible if we do not accept, with those who hold the first theory set out here [= the theory of the jubilee], that he is struggling against rigorism. In our view, his repentance is indeed an exceptional jubilee ...."

9. The *aphesis amartiōn* designates the remission of sins that follows baptismal repentance. On this expression, see already Acts, 13, 38: "Let it be known to you therefore, brethren, that through this man forgiveness of sins [*aphesis amartiōn*] is proclaimed to you." See A. Méhat, "'Pénitence seconde' and 'péché involontaire' in Clément d'Alexandrie," *Vigiliae Christianae*, 8, 1954, pp. 225-233, and A. d'Alès, *La théologie de Tertullien* (Paris: Beauchesne, 1905), p. 340, note 1: "... Hermas reserves the noun *aphesis* (*ignoscentia*) for baptismal forgiveness." He cites the passage

from *Le Pasteur* (Précepte IV, 31 (3)) commented on by Foucault at the beginning of the session: "for both the one and the other do not have to repent their sins: they have absolution (*aphesis*) for their former sins"; *The Pastor*, Book II, Commandment IV, chapter III, p. 22: "For those who have now believed, and those who are to believe, have not repentance for their sins; but they have remission of their previous sins."

10. *Epistle to the Hebrews*, 6, 4-8, B.J, p. 1732; SRV: "For it is impossible to restore again to repentance those who have once been enlightened, who have tasted the heavenly gift, and have become partakers of the Holy Spirit, and have tasted the goodness of the word of God and the powers of the age to come, if they then commit apostasy, since they crucify the Son of God on their own account and hold him up to contempt." Foucault says "savored" instead of "tasted." The authenticity of this Epistle, for long attributed to Paul, has been discussed since the first centuries. The text, which presents in fact the oratorical character of a sermon, is thought to be the work of a Jewish companion of Paul with Hellenistic training.

11. Ibid., 10, 26-27; RSV: "For if we sin deliberately after receiving the knowledge of the truth, there no longer remains a sacrifice for sins, but a fearful prospect of judgment, and a fury of fire which will consume the adversaries."

12. Mathew, 12, 33.

13. Ignace d'Antioche, *Lettres*, Aux Ephésians, XIV, 1, Introduction, translation and notes by P. T. Camelot (Paris: Cerf, SC, no. 10 bis, 4th ed., 1969), p. 71. The French translation quoted here is that of P.-T. Camelot, "Lettres d'Ignace d'Antioche," in *EPA*, pp. 147-148; English translation by Alexander Roberts and James Donaldson, as Ignatius of Antioch, "The Epistle of Ignatius to the Ephesians," ch. XIV, in *ANF, Vol. I*, p. 55: "No man truly making a profession of faith sinneth; nor does he that possesses love hate any one. The tree is made manifest by its fruit; so those that profess themselves to be Christians shall be recognised by their conduct."

14. *Epître de Barnabé* [Barnabus] (see above, lecture of 6 February, pp. 112-113, note 29), XVI, 8-9, trans. M.A. Laurent, revised by H. Hemmer in *Les Pères apostoliques*, I-II (Paris: Librairie A. Picard et fils, 1907) p. 91; quoted by A. Benoit, *Le baptême chrétien*, p. 42. "Repentance (*repentir*)" in this quotation translates the Greek word *metanoia*. On the conception in Barnabas of baptism as new creation, Benoit, ibid., p. 42, emphasizes the eschatological dimension of this "new creation," the anticipation of what will take place in the Aeon to come. English translation by Alexander Roberts and James Donaldson, *Epistle of Barnabas*, ch. XVI, in *ANF*, Vol. 1, p. 147: "Having received the forgiveness of sins, and placed our trust in the name of the Lord, we have become new creatures, formed again from the beginning. Wherefore in our habitation God truly dwells in us ... opening to us who were enslaved by death the doors of the temple, that is, the mouth; and by giving us repentance introduced us into the incorruptible temple."

15. Hermas, *Le Pasteur*, Précepte III, 28, pp. 149-151; *EPA*, p. 337 (the words in square brackets correspond to Foucault's modifications of the translation by R. Joly. Joly: "the spirit that God has lodged in your flesh will be found genuine"); *The Pastor*, Third Commandment, p. 21: "'Love the truth, and let nothing but truth proceed from your mouth, that the spirit which God has placed in your flesh may be found truthful before all men; and the Lord, who dwelleth in you, will be glorified, because the Lord is truthful in every word, and in Him is no falsehood.'"

16. *La doctrine des douze apôtres (Didachè)*, 8, 2, trans. R.-F. Refoulé, *EPA*, p. 45; English translation by Maxwell Staniforth, *The Didache* in *Early Christian Writings*, p. 231: "forgive us our debt...deliver us from the Evil One."

17. Hemmer, *Les Pères apostoliques*, translates the verb literally: "You will make an exomolegesis of your sins (*exomologēsē ta paraptōmata sou*)" (*Épître de Barnabé*, XIX, 97, 12). To it bring closer with *Didache*, 14, 1, where confession (*confession*) of sins is related to the Eucharist sacrifice.

18. *Didachè*, 4, 14, p. 43; Greek text in Hemmer, *Les Pères apostoliques*, p. 12; *The Didache*, 4, p. 229: "In church, make confession of your faults, and do not come to your prayers with a bad conscience."

19. *Lettre de Barnabé* (pseudo-Barnabé), XIX, 12, trans., Sister Suzanne-Dominique, in *EPA*, p. 285: "Make the public confession (*confession*) of your sins." The Laurent-Hemmer version in *Les Pères apostoliques*, which Foucault does not use here, again stays closer to the original text, p. 97: "You will make the exomologesis of your sins (*exomologēsē epi amartiais sou*)"; *The Epistle of Barnabas*, 19, ANF, Vol. I, pp. 148-149: "Thou shalt confess thy sins." See A. d'Alès, *La théologie de Tertullian*, 1905, p. 342 note 2, who also brings the two texts together on this point.

20. *Lettre de Barnabé* ; *The Epistle of Barnabas*, ANF, *vol. I*, pp. 148-149: "Thou shalt not go to prayer with an evil conscience. This is the way of light." The final phrase—"This is the way of light"—is a variant of some manuscripts, not retained by the *Sources chrétiennes* edition (see p. 210 note 3). F. Louvel, *EPA*, note 114, clarifies that "chapter 19 of the *Epistle of Barnabas* corresponds to chapters 2, 3, and 4 of the *Didache.*"

21. The same remark is made by C. Vogel, *Le pêcheur et la pénitence dans l'Eglise ancienne* (Paris: Cerf, "Traditions chétiennes," 1962, 1982 2nd ed.), p. 15: "The confession (*aveu*) of sins referred to in the *Didache* is not a 'sacramental confession (*confession*),' but a sort of collective prayer, performed by all the members in meetings of the community ..."; see also Hemmer's Introduction, p. XL.

22. *La doctrine des douze apôtres (Didaché)*, 14, 1, p. 53; *The Didache*, 14, p. 234: "Assemble on the Lord's Day, and break bread and offer the Eucharist; but first make confession of your faults, so that your sacrifice may be a pure one."

23. Clément de Rome, *Epitre aux Corinthiens*, IX, 1, trans., Sister Suzanne-Dominique, in *EPA*, p. 53; English translation by John Keith as Clement of Rome, *Letter to the Corinthians*, ch. IX, in *ANF*, Vol. IX, (Grand Rapids, Michigan: W. Eerdmans, 1994), pp. 231-232: "Wherefore, let us yield obedience to His excellent and glorious will; and imploring His mercy and loving-kindness, while we forsake all fruitless labours and strife, and envy, which leads to death, let us turn and have recourse to His compassions."

24. Ibid., LI, 1 and 3, pp. 99-100; Eng., ibid., ch. LI, p. 244: "Let us therefore implore forgiveness for all those transgressions which through any [suggestion] of the adversary we have committed...For it is better that a man should acknowledge his transgressions than that he should harden his heart." See too LII, 1-2, p. 100: "The Master of all things, brothers, has need of nothing, he asks nothing of any one, except the confession (*aveu*) of sins. For David, his elect, says: 'I will confess my sins to God, this will please the Lord more than any young bullock with horns and hoofs. On seeing this, the humble will rejoice [Psalms, 69, 31-33]'"; Eng., ch. LII, p. 245: "The Lord, brethren, stands in need of nothing; and He desires nothing of any one except that confession be made to Him. For, says the elect David, 'I will confess unto the Lord; and that will please Him more than a young bullock that has horns and hoofs. Let the poor see it, and be glad.'"

25. *La doctrine des douze apôtres (Didaché)*, 10, 6, p. 49 (passage modified by Foucault: "If any one is not so"); *The Didache*, 10, p. 232: "Whosoever is holy, let him approach. Whoso is not, let him repent."

26. Clément de Rome, *Epitre aux Corinthiens*, II, 4 and 6, trans. H. Hemmer in *Les Pères apostoliques*, II (Paris: Librairie A. Picard et fils, 1909), p. 9: "you cried over the sins of your neighbor; you considered his lapses were yours"; Clement of Rome, *Letter to the Corinthians*, ch. II, *ANF*, Vol. IX, pp. 229-230: "Day and night ye were anxious for the whole brotherhood ... Ye mourned over the transgressions of your neighbours: their deficiencies you deemed your own."

27. Polycarpe de Smyrne, *Lettre aux Philippiens*, XI, 4, trans., P.-T. Camelot, in *Les écrits des Pères apostoliques*, p. 215. The quotation is slightly modified by Foucault: "on this point" instead of "in this." The verses inserted in the quotation correspond to 2, Timothy, 2, 25 and 2, Thessalonians, 3, 15. The presbyter Valens was in fact guilty of avarice. English translation by Alexander Roberts and James Donaldson, *Epistle of Polycarp to the Philippians*, in *ANF*, Vol. I, p. 35: "I am deeply grieved, therefore, brethren, for him (Valens) and his wife; to whom may the Lord grant true repentance! And be ye then moderate in regard to this matter, and 'do not count such as enemies,' but call them back as suffering and straying members, that you may save your whole body."

28. *La doctrine des douze apôtres (Didaché)*, 4, 6, p. 42; *The Didache*, 4, p. 229: "If the labour of your hands has been productive, make an offering as a ransom for your sins."

29. *Homélie du IIe siècle* (formerly called *Deuxième épitre de Clément de Rome aux Corinthiens*), CVI, 4, in EPA, p. 130; English translation by John Keith, The "Second Epistle" of St. Clement, ch. XVI, in *ANF*, Vol. IX, p. 255: "Good, then, is alms as repentance from sin; better is fasting than prayer, and alms than both."

30. See Diogène Laërce [Diogenes Laertius], *Vie et opinions des philosophes*, VII, § 117-131, trans. L. Bréhier, revised by V. Goldschmidt and P. Kucharski, in *Les Stoïciens* (Paris: Gallimard, Bibliothèque de la Pléiade, 1962), pp. 53-58, on the doctrines of Zeno, Cleanthes, and Chrysippus: "[Sages] are without sin because they cannot fall into sin (§ 122, p. 55); "... the

sage possesses a soul that is perfect at every moment" (§ 128, p. 57); English translation by R.D. Hicks as Diogenes Laertius, *Lives of Eminent Philosophers*, Vol. II, Book VII (Cambridge, MA, and London: Harvard University Press and William Heinemann Ltd., The Loeb Classical Library, 1979 [1925]), p. 227: "the wise are infallible, not being liable to error"; p. 233: "the good man is always exercising his mind, which is perfect." Foucault returns to this point below.

31. On this Pythagorean regulation, see the old but still interesting work of A.E. Chaignet, *Pythagore et la philosophie pythagoricienne* (Paris: Didier, 1873), vol. I, ch. 4: "The Pythagorean order—Its organization, constitution, and regulations" (pp. 97-154). See in particular pp. 117-118: "A cleverly contrived and strict discipline presided over the organization of the [Pythagorean] Institute ... Members of the Order had their fixed, specific function, determined according to their character and aptitudes. But they were nevertheless subject to general and meticulous rules governing all the details and all the duties of common life. These regulations, these constitutions, these laws, *nomoi*, were fixed in writing; ... these rules were venerated by everyone as having a sacred, divine character ... In these truly monastic rules, often expressed in symbols, we see the taste for a both internal and external discipline, the need for obedience, of forgetfulness of self, of renunciation of the government of one's soul and its own conscience, which goes so far as to give its direction to someone else ..." (an analysis marked, one can see, by the critical perspective of the author who recognized "the Roman Church already" in the religious organization of the Institute (p. 113)). See the details of these rules, pp. 119-123.

32. See A.-J. Voelke, *L'idée de volonté dans le stoïcisme*, p. 76: "[In Ariston of Chios and Herillus, the first disciples of Zeno] the supremacy of virtue over all other objects is such that it deprives the very idea of making a choice between them of all foundation, at the risk of removing all matter from virtue itself. This indifferentism that does not recognize any intermediary between the absolute good and the axiological nothingness renounces any attempt at regulating the life of the average man ...."

33. On this evolution from the middle Stoicism and the Stoicism of the imperial period in relation to the first Stoicism, see among other numerous references, E. Bréhier, *Histoire de la philosophie* (Paris: PUF, 1931, republished 1981, "Quadrige"), vol. 1, pp. 348-359. Cicero, *On Duties*, trans. Margaret Atkins, eds. M.T. Griffin and E.M. Atkins (Cambridge: Cambridge University Press, 1991), Book I, 110, p. 43, faithfully follows the doctrine of Panaetius, when he writes: "... we must act in such a way that we attempt nothing contrary to universal nature; but while conserving that, let us follow our own nature, so that ... we should measure our own by the rule of our own nature." See also A.-J. Voelke, *L'idée de volonté dans le stoïcisme*, pp. 76-79.

34. On the problem of the *lapsi*, "that is to say those who 'failed' at the time of persecution and who, regretting their action, wanted to be reintegrated into the Church" (R. Gryson, Introduction to Ambrose of Milan, *La Pénitence* (Paris: Cerf, SC no. 179, 1971, p. 16), see *Sécurité, territoire, population*, lecture of 22 February 1978, p. 189 note 16; *Security, territory, population*, p. 187. On the attitude of Cyprian towards the *lapsi*, see the Introduction by the Canon Bayard to Saint Cyprien, *Correspondance*, pp. XVIII-XIX and G. Bardy, "Saint Cyprien," DS, II, 1953, col. 2665-2666, and below lecture of 5 March, p. 000 note 12. While Foucault used the word *lapsi* in the 1978 lectures, he improperly replaces it here, and throughout the next lecture, with "*relaps* (relapsed)" which, strictly speaking, does not designate an apostate, but someone who has fallen back into a heresy after having solemnly renounced it ("heretic who falls back into an error that he had abjured," N.S. Bergier, *Dictionnaire de théologie* (Toulouse, 1817), vol. 7, col. 125). In *Mal faire, dire vrai*, lecture of 29 April 1981, p. 107, where he returns briefly to this point, he speaks, quoting Cyprian's *De lapsis*, of "apostates."

35. On the gnosis, see above lecture of 13 February 1980, p. 118 and note 6.

36. On this Gnostic conception of the Demiurge (distinct from the absolute and immutable Being), see, for example, Plotinus, *Ennéades*, II, 9, trans., E. Bréhier (Paris: Les Belles Lettres, CUF, 1924), pp. 111-138: "Against those who say that the demiurge of the world is wicked and that the world is evil"; English translation by S. Mackenna, Plotinus, *Enneads*, I, IX (London: Faber, 1956), p. 132: "Against the Gnostics; or Against those that Affirm the Creator of the Cosmos and the Cosmos Itself to be Evil" (a formula which, according to J. Doresse, "La Gnose," p. 422, "summarizes the essential of what the Symbols of faith and Christian anathemas will condemn in all the Gnostics").

37. Saint Paul, *Romans*, 7, 6-7: "But now we are discharged from the law, dead to that which held us captive, so that we serve not under the old written code but in the new life of the Spirit. What then shall we say? That the law is sin? By no means! Yet, if it had not been for the law, I should not have known sin. I should not have known what it is to covet if the law had not said, 'You shall not covet.'"

38. Foucault does not return to this question in the rest of the course.

39. On Marcion, see Tertullien, *Contre Marcion*, Introduction and trans. R. Braun, 5 vols., SC, Nos. 365, 368, 369, 456, and 483 (1990-2004); English translation by Peter Holmes, Tertullian, *Against Marcion*, Books I to V, in *ANF*, Vol. III. See also E.C. Blackman, *Marcion and his Influence* (London: SPCK, 1948); E. Trocmé, "Le christianisme jusqu'à 325, pp. 247-250 (p. 248: "Marcion was at first only a Pauline extremist, who, from the opposition between the Law and the Gospel ... drew the conclusion that the Old Testament was completely abrogated and no longer had any authority for Christians"); P. Brown, *The Body and Society. Men, Women and Sexual Renunciation in Early Christianity* (New York and London: Columbia University Press/ Faber and Faber,1988), pp. 88-89: "For Marcion, the 'present age' was the visible world, subject in its entirety to the rule of a Creator-God, to whom the true God of love was unknown. A chasm separated the present world from the heaven from which Christ came to save mankind ... The present universe, in his opinion, had been brought about by a forming power that was far removed from the radiant tranquility of the highest God. Human life was lived out under the shadow of an unreliable and oppressive force that maintained and guided the material world ... The Creator-God was the God of the Jewish Law ... Mankind as a whole, and not merely the Jews, lived 'under the Law.'"

40. See M. Foucault, "Sexuality and Solitude," (talk given in English, 1981) in *The Essential Works of Michel Foucault, 1954-1984, vol. 1: Ethics: Subjectivity and Truth*, ed. Paul Rabinow (New York: The New Press, 1997), p. 178: "The Buddhist, too, must go to the light and discover the truth about himself; but the relation between these two obligations is quite different in Buddhism and in Christianity. In Buddhism, it is the same type of enlightenment which leads you to discover what you are and what is the truth. In this simultaneous enlightenment of yourself and the truth, you discover that your self was only an illusion. I would like to underline that the Christian discovery of the self does not reveal the self as an illusion."

nine

5 March 1980

> *Canonical penance (continued): not a second baptism, but a second penance. Characteristics of this second penance: it is unique; it is a status and an all-encompassing status.* ∽ *Truth acts entailed by entry into this status: objective acts and subjective acts. (a) Analysis of objective acts on the basis of the* Letters *of Saint Cyprian: an individual, detailed, public examination. (b) Subjective acts: the sinner's obligation to manifest his own truth (*exomologēsis*). Exomologesis: evolution of the word from the first to the third century. The three moments of penitential procedure:* expositio casus, *exomologesis strictly speaking (*publicatio sui*), and the act of reconciliation (*impositio manus*). Analysis of the second episode (Tertullian; other examples). Two usages of the word "exomologesis": episode and all-encompassing act.* ∽ *Three remarks: (1) the* expositio casus/publicatio sui *relationship in the history of penance from the twelfth century; (2) difference between exomologesis and* expositio casus; *(3) exomologesis and the liar's paradox.*

LAST WEEK I TRIED to show you that the problem of Christian penance was the problem of whether the act that saves, that brings about the passage from death to life, the act that brings light, can actually be repeated. It was to this question, the theological implications of which are obviously enormous, that the organization of what we have called canonical penance replied. What is canonical penance? Is it a second baptism? Can we view canonical penance as a way of purely and simply, or entirely, repeating baptism? We sometimes come across the expression second baptism to designate canonical penance. For example, in Clement of Alexandria, in the text on the salvation of the rich, with regard to a particularly intense and dramatic penitential act, you find the expression that it was "like a second baptism."[1] In fact, the expression "second baptism" to designate canonical penance is rare and, as the phrase of Clement of Alexandria proves moreover, it has a metaphorical much more than canonical value. Because, in fact, in the Christian conception from the first century, baptism is unique and cannot in itself be repeated. On the other hand, what can be repeated is a certain part of baptism, or a certain element that was linked with baptism, associated with it, and this was, precisely, the penance, the *disciplina paenitentiae* Tertullian spoke about, which is indispensable to baptism and comes to be what can be repeated once baptism has been given. So that canonical penance is not defined as a second baptism, except, again, as a quasi metaphorical indication. Canonical penance is seen as a second penance, that is to say as that which repeats the penitential accompaniment of baptism, the penitential discipline linked to it.

I would like to talk to you about this second penance because it is connected to a whole series of procedures of truth that seems to me to mark a considerable inflection in what could be called the relationships of subjectivity and the truth, not only in Christianity, but in the whole of Western civilization.

What is second penance? In what does it consist? First, and this is important, *paenitentia secunda*, this second penance, which repeats the penitential part of baptism, is just as unique as baptism.[2] It is, as Tertullian says, "another plank of salvation."[3] It is a way for Christ to open for a second time the doors of forgiveness previously opened by baptism, but closed again immediately after. The doors are opened for a second time, but they will not be opened again. Quite simply, after baptism one can do penance once, but not twice. Penance, therefore, turns out to be an unrepeatable repetition of something that, in any case, cannot be repeatable. We are dealing with uniqueness. It is the splitting of uniqueness, and nothing more. Baptism was a unique event; penance too will be a unique event, although in a way it is a sort of at least partial repetition of baptism. This will remain in force in Christianity until at least the sixth and seventh centuries, and even at this time we do not see the principle of only one penance disappear, but coupled with a practice of what will become repeatable penance.[4] This tells you how difficult it was, in Christian thought, in the institution of Christianity, and, it seems, in the whole of Western culture, to pass from a binary system of salvation, in which the individual's lifespan is divided by the one event of conversion and access to the truth, to a juridical system of the law, of a law that indefinitely sanctions the repeatable events of transgression. To pass from this binary system of salvation to the repeatable system of the law and transgression required a whole series of transformations which I may or may not have time to refer to, no matter. Essentially, it required the conjunction of two processes. On the one hand, there was the organization, the institutionalization of a monastic discipline putting itself forward as a rule of life, and so as a continuous control of individuals, with, of course, the definition, listing, and sanction of every possible infraction of this rule. So, it required the organization of monastic life and the monastic rule that gave a certain legal relation to sin, and, on the other hand, from outside Christianity, it needed the arrival in Europe of the Germanic system of law, which made the sanction for the transgression appear as a sort of redemption.[5] The sanction as redemption of the transgression will be, if you like, the secular and external juridical form in which the whole system of penance is able to be rethought from the Middle Ages. And it is the combination of the monastic rule, on the one hand, and the conception of Germanic law, [on the other], that will make possible the organization of penance with which we are now familiar, that Christianity has known for more than a millennium, and which is the penance one does for every act and in order to redeem every act. At this point, penance no longer focuses so much on the individual's status and is not so much what redeems the individual overall and totally; it is an objective penance, defined in relation to what an act is, to what an action is, and which defines that by which one can redeem that act and that action.

So, the first thing about *paenitentia secunda* is that it is not repeatable; like baptism, it is a unique event. The second characteristic of *paenitentia secunda* is that it is a status. It is not just a number of acts that one must perform after having sinned; it is a status. It is a status that concerns the whole individual: doing penance—the Latin expression is *paenitentia agere*[6]—carrying out penance basically means entering an order. The texts of the third and fourth centuries say this clearly. Pacian, for example, says that there are three orders of Christians. There are the catechumens, who are those, so to speak, at the door of Christianity and who will enter it. There are the fully practicing Christians. And then there are the penitents.[7] Penitents form an intermediary order between catechumens and fully practicing Christians, and it may well be that this order had gradations and that there were sub-orders within this order of penance. I say "may well be." In the East there is clear evidence for the existence of grades in the order of penance according to the seriousness of the sin. It is much less certain for the West. There is just one passage in the *De Paenitentia* of Saint Ambrose where, concerning someone who had sinned, he says it was decided in what order of penitents he would be placed.[8] This would seem to indicate that there was, in the West, an order of penitents, but as this is the only testimony ... Good, well, endless discussion on this. One enters this order of penitents because in fact one asks to be admitted, and one does so because, as a Christian sinner one feels that one has sinned and risks losing the promise of salvation accorded with baptism and, as a result, one asks to do penance again. One requests it because one feels the need for it or again because one has been pushed, threatened, or exhorted by the leaders of the Church, and Pacian explains that one of the roles of the bishop is precisely to exhort, to objurgate all sinners to penance.[9] It is therefore, as it were, at the point where individual will and group pressure, or the pressure of authority come together that one acquires the status of penitent. One enters the order of penitents after a ceremony that to some extent recalls that of baptism, at least in some of its elements. The main element being the laying on of hands, which as you know, on the one hand has a meaning and value of exorcism[10] and, on the other, also has a function and role of an appeal to the Holy Spirit. One drives out the evil spirit, which is both substantially and etiologically linked to the sin, and at the same time one appeals to the other spirit of holiness, which has to replace it: this is the role of the laying on of hands. This is the ritual of entry to the status of the penitents, [which] lasts for months, years, and it is simply at the end of this long placement in the order of penitents, sometimes even just at the end of life, when one is just about to die, that one has the right to reconciliation, which is also marked by a ceremony, symmetrical to the ceremony of entry into the order of penitents: here too there is the laying on of hands and reconciliation.

Penance, therefore, is unique, a status, and finally, an all-encompassing status. It is an all-encompassing status inasmuch as it concerns every aspect of existence. In penance an individual is not asked to do this or that or to renounce this or that; every aspect of his existence is at stake in the penitential status. Religious existence, in the first place, inasmuch as the penitent has to perform a number of religious obligations but is excluded from a number of practices—here too there is discussion about what he was excluded from. It is certain that he no longer had a right to *communio* or to *communicatio*. He is therefore deprived of the Eucharist. He is no doubt also excluded from a number of other ceremonies—the difficulty is knowing which ones. There are also a number of prohibitions and obligations concerning the penitent's personal, private life. If he or she is married, for example, having sexual relations with one's spouse is prohibited. There is the obligation to fast, the prohibition against caring for one's body or, if you prefer, an obligation of dirtiness.[11] At the level of civil, social, collective life there is the obligation also to perform a number of works: charitable works, visiting the sick, almsgiving. There are prohibitions too of a purely juridical order inasmuch as the penitent does not have the right to institute legal proceedings, to take part in a dispute, at least as plaintiff, inasmuch as someone who asks for the forgiveness of others cannot accuse someone else and demand an apology and reparation. Finally, what is no doubt most remarkable in this penitent status is that, even after reconciliation, even after leaving the order of penitents, the fact of having been a penitent for a part of one's life will never be entirely erased. Until the end of one's days, the old penitent will be marked out in the middle of the community of Christians by a number of impossibilities and prohibitions: the impossibility of becoming a priest or deacon, the impossibility of exercising certain jobs that are particularly dangerous because they provide too many opportunities for falling, and the fact of having fallen once and the impossibility of being able to do penance a second time means that some jobs would represent too many dangers. For example, to become a merchant would expose one too easily to theft, and consequently an old penitent will not be able to become a merchant, just as he cannot marry.

This, very schematically, roughly, without going into any detail and without providing any precision, is how this second penance appeared by which someone, once in his life but no more, could obtain, not remission exactly, but forgiveness for a sin or series of sins that he may have committed after baptism. But obviously it is not this that I would like to talk about, but rather, within this penitent status, the truth acts entailed either by entry into penitent status or by the unfolding of penance itself. These truth acts, these truth procedures, are of two orders: if you like, objective procedures and reflexive procedures. Objective procedures: these are those procedures of which the penitent is the object, but the operator or operators of which is not the penitent himself, in other words the truth procedures by which others, either the whole community, or the bishop, or the leaders, are able to know the penitent and make him the object of a truth inquiry. And then, reflexive acts: these are the acts by which the penitent himself becomes operator of the manifestation of his own truth. Reflexive acts: [those] by which the penitent himself manifests his truth as sinner or his truth as penitent.

Let us begin with the objective acts. They are not very different from those we encountered in baptism, when it was a matter of testing the postulant's will to become Christian or the way in which, during his catechumenate, he gave proof of his progress and his *metanoia*. Anyway, these objective acts involve an examination of the sinner's conduct. This examination or these examinations rather, take place at two moments. First, they take place at the time the sinner asks for penance. And at this point the question is whether or not it will be granted. Whether the sin really is sufficiently serious and important to warrant penitent status, or whether the person asking for penance has committed such big, serious, heavy sins that forgiveness or redemption is not possible. Here again, there is the problem of whether in fact, up to what point, and which sins can or cannot be remitted. Fine, let's leave this. In any case, there is a first examination that takes place at this point. And there is a second examination that takes place at the end of the penitential procedure, at the end of the whole penitential action. Just before he is going to be reconciled, the penitent is examined to find out whether, in fact, he deserves to be.

Historically, these acts had their greatest importance and the point of their maximum development [in] a relatively precise period, [in] the third century—the middle and end of the third century—at the time or just after the great persecution,[12] that is to say at the time when the number of those who had rejected Christianity or who had ceded to the injunctions of the civil power to sacrifice or sign a certificate of sacrifice was very large and when there was also a large number of those who, after having fallen, having engaged in sacrifice or signed a certificate, asked to be reintegrated. So there were numerous requests for reintegration and the procedures by which these requests were made were equally numerous, varied, and uncertain. One of the major means utilized, and which was foreseen by the texts and councils moreover, was the possibility of getting oneself recommended by a confessor, "confessor" understood here, of course, not in the sense of the person who hears the confession, but in the sense of the person who has confessed, who has professed Christ, that is to say who refused to cede to the injunctions either to sacrifice or to sign a certificate of sacrifice. These, inasmuch as they had professed Christ and had therefore affirmed, guaranteed their faith in the face of persecution, had the right to guarantee the faith of others and to recommend the reintegration of those who had fallen due to their weakness.

All this obviously gave rise to a great deal of confusion and, no doubt, abuse, and throughout the end of the third century—the correspondence of Saint Cyprian[13] attests to this—one tried to filter somewhat all these requests for the reintegration of the relapsed. The principles that emerge from the correspondence of Saint Cyprian are relatively clear.

First, there can be no reintegration without examination. Second, these examinations cannot be collective, [but] must take place case by case. In fact, in these procedures of recommendations by confessors, not just a relapsed, but often the whole family of the relapsed was recommended, with the view, in accordance with well-known and familiar juridical ideas of the time, that responsibility was shared. Hence the idea that, no, examination has to take place case by case. And this is not because a relapsed will have been considered as able to be reintegrated inasmuch as all his family will. Case by case, individually and taking account of the circumstances of the act. In letter 55 [epistle 51], Saint Cyprian says: We must distinguish between "someone who, of his own will, straightaway committed the abominable sacrifice and someone who, after long resistance and struggle, is forced to commit the appalling act. [We must distinguish between] someone who has betrayed himself and his relations and someone who, on the contrary, facing the danger alone on behalf of all, protected his wife, children, and household."[14] So, individual examination.

Second, this individual examination must be undertaken collectively or, at any rate, as far as possible the whole community, directed by the bishop, should decide by means of this individual examination whether or not to reintegrate the one who has fallen. In a letter addressed to Saint Cyprian by the priests of Rome, we read: "It is an important responsibility and heavy burden to examine the faults of a great many without being many and to pronounce the sentence alone ... A decision cannot carry great weight if it does not appear to have been approved by a large number."[15]

So there is the idea of the practice of individual examination, itemized in terms of acts, but which is carried out collectively, and therefore in public. This public examination of individual cases seems to have been governed by the decisions of synods or councils and to have been drawn up in a small manual of examination to which Saint Cyprian refers,[16] but which has unfortunately been lost.

Behind all this, behind the idea that the relapsed must be examined case by case, Saint Cyprian and his contemporaries are not saying that by such means one will be able to reach into the recesses of the soul of the relapsed and penitent, that one will be able find out how things really stand and whether or not his repentance is sincere and he will in fact be forgiven by God. In fact, letter 57 [Epistle 53] says, "so far as seeing and judging is granted us, we see only the outside of each one. As for probing the heart—*cor scrutari*—and penetrating the soul, we cannot do so."[17] So there is no question here of a procedure of the kind soon to be found, that is to say from the fourth century, in the monastic practice of the examination of conscience, there is absolutely no question of a scrutiny of the recesses of the heart. It is simply a matter of judging as best one can from the outside and remaining on the outside. It being understood, consequently, since one cannot judge in truth and in the depths of the penitent's soul, [that] the decision one is able to take on whether or not to reintegrate him remains an improbable decision, I mean a decision that will not bind, with certainty, God and his forgiveness. Here again, unlike what will be found in the sacrament of penance as defined in the medieval Church, no one knows if the decision of the one who grants penance and reconciles corresponds to an analogous decision, an analogous will on Heaven's part. Saint Cyprian says in one of his letters: "We make our decisions as best we can, but it is the Lord's right to correct the decisions of his servant."[18] The principle—what we bind on Earth will be bound in Heaven—is evoked in the text, but it is never interpreted as [signifying]* that the decision of a penitential order taken by priests is God's own decision. This is something that arises much later.

So much for the core of the external, objective examination which, once again, although its effects are different and the procedure in which it is inscribed is not the same, is even so, roughly speaking, of the same type as that *probatio animae*, that examination that was required in baptism, that was indispensable for access to baptism. What is involved therefore is someone or a group knowing, as far as this is possible from the outside, what the situation is regarding someone's soul.

What, on the other hand, is quite specific to this *paenitentia secunda*, and which is not found, except indirectly and discretely—in short, which did not yet have any true status in the procedure of baptism—is the sinner's obligation to manifest his own truth. Once again, we must be very prudent. When, in the baptismal rites, one spoke of the *probatio animae*, when one spoke of the *disciplina paenitentiae*, when Tertullian said that the catechumen must train his soul, this did involve the latter manifesting his own truth and giving others the possibility of grasping how things were with his soul and his progress, with his ability to receive the rites. But this obligation to show *oneself*, to manifest *oneself*,† did not have any specific status within the catechumenal institution. In penance, on the other hand, there is a whole series of acts and procedures explicitly intended to invite, exhort, or constrain the person doing penance to show his own truth. It is to these acts that the Greeks apply the terms *exomologein* or *exomologēsis*. *Omologein* means to say the same thing; *omologein* is to be in agreement, to give one's assent, to agree something with someone. *Exomologein*, the verb designating these acts—the substantive is *exomologēsis*—is not to be in agreement, it is to manifest one's

---

* M.F.: the fact.
† Stressed by M.F. (*se* montrer soi-même, *se* manifester).

agreement. And so *exomologēsis* will be the manifestation of one's agreement, the acknowledgment, the fact of admitting something, namely
one's sin and the fact of being a sinner. It is this *exomologēsis*, roughly,
that is demanded of the penitent.

The Latin authors translate this term *exomologēsis* by *confessio*, and
exomologein by *confiteri* or sometimes *fateri*. The equivalence, you will see,
is only approximate, because, on the one hand, it often happens that
the Latin authors employ the Greek word in Latin, *exomologesis*, as if
it designated something that the common Latin word *confessio* failed to
catch fully. At the beginning of the third century, Tertullian says that the
term *exomologesis* is now familiar in Latin and in current use.[19] And then,
on the other hand, you will see also that the word *confessio*, which more
or less covers the set of significations of *exomologein*, is also employed for
something that is designated by neither *exomologesis* nor *exomologein*. So
that, if you like, we have two circles: that of *confessio*, of *confiteri*, and that
of *exomologesis* and *exomologein*, which overlap, but with small lunes on
both sides that do not coincide and for which, on one side, the word
confessio is employed exclusively and, at the other, the word *exomologesis*
is employed generally, and which is not covered by the word *confessio*.

Well, let's take the central core and leave to one side, for the moment,
these particular and somewhat divergent elements. What is the meaning of *exomologein* and *exomologēsis*? In fact, the word *exomologein* was not
simply applied to the acts of canonical penance, of the *paenitentia secunda*
I am talking about. In the texts of the end of the first century, like the
Didache, for example, you see the word employed to designate in fact a
certain way of acknowledging one's sins. Thus, in chapter 4, paragraph
14, we read: "In the assembly, the *ekklēsia*, you will confess your faults
and you will not go to your prayers with a bad conscience."[20] So, at the
assembly where one prays collectively, one must confess, *exomologein*, the
amartiais, faults, transgressions. Again in the *Didache*, chapter 14, paragraph 1: "Meet on the Lord's day"—here it is not a matter of daily prayer,
but of the weekly meeting, that of the Eucharist—"break bread and give
thanks after first having confessed—*exomologesantes*—your sins so that
your sacrifice is pure."[21] Here again, then, one must confess. What kind
of confession is involved in this exomologesis? It does appear, it is even
certain, that this exomologesis required every day in prayer and once
a week for the Eucharist, does not involve something like a detailed,

verbal, and public personal confession (*aveu*) by every faithful of the sins he or she has committed. It is much more, and in line moreover with a Jewish practice, a matter of a collective prayer, but in which also, at the same time, each on his own account affirms and acknowledges before God and, consequently, before the others that he has sinned and is a sinner; a collective prayer, recited by each and in which each says individually, but also in which all say collectively: I am a sinner, we are sinners. So it does not involve a confession (*aveu*) of what one has done, but of a collective profession or supplication concerning what one is, namely a sinner: we have all sinned, each of us is a sinner. It is this core, so to speak, and nothing else that is designated in the exomologesis referred to in the *Didache* and texts at the end of the first and the beginning of the second century.

On the other hand, exomologesis has a more precise meaning in the canonical penance that is organized at the end of the second and the beginning of the third century—at the end of the second century, certainly. In fact, here too, there are a great many discussions that broadly speaking are always turned in the same direction: some, inevitably the Catholics, try to bring together penitential exomologesis and auricular confession (*confession*), the confession (*aveu*) from mouth to ear that will become canonical from the twelfth century, and others, of Protestant inspiration, tend rather to say that there was nothing like confession (*aveu*) in the old exomologesis and that the word designated rather the set of all the acts characteristic of penitential status.[22] Let's leave all these discussions, which are important but we are not going to enter into them, and [say] somewhat schematically that three things need to be distinguished in these truth procedures peculiar to penitential status.

First, there is something—I am now speaking of the Latin texts—that is not designated by the word *exomologesis* (the Greek word, then, transferred into Latin), for which rather the word *confessio* is reserved, or, if you like, you have this word *confessio* which has a general meaning, but which is also used, and to designate something that is exclusive of *exomologesis*. This is the following: when the penitent—well, the person who is not yet penitent, the person who has sinned—goes to ask for penance and asks the authority, the leaders, the bishops to accord him penitent status, he is obliged to say why he wishes to receive penitent status. He is obliged to set out his case. This is what is called precisely *expositio casus* in the texts of Saint Cyprian.[23] Setting out the case to the bishop: he declares verbally, and no doubt privately, so more or less secretly or in any case discreetly, the sin he has committed. It is to [this setting out of the case]* that a text from the end of the fourth century refers. The life of Saint Ambrose by Paulinus[24] says that when one confessed (*avouait*) one's sins to Saint Ambrose, he wept with the sinner and "spoke of them to no one but the Lord with whom he interceded." The which, the biographer of Ambrose says, is "a good example for priests, who should be intercessors rather than [public†] accusers."[25] Here then we see quite clearly both the distinction of the practices and the pastoral discussion to which all this gives rise. So the penitent comes to set out his case to the bishop and at this point the bishop decides if in actual fact the person who has sinned must and can receive penitent status, that is to say a status that, once again, takes over his whole life, will last for years and years, possibly until his death, or if much more discreet measures are sufficient to make amends for the sin committed. His biographer says that Saint Ambrose was not in favor of the generalized or, at any rate, too frequent imposition of penitent status and preferred to settle the question in secret, as it were, between the sinner, God, and himself. This shows how much, already at this time, penitent status, the publicity it was given, and its overall implications, raised problems and that pastoral practice was already tending towards a sort of direct accommodation or arrangement, without penitential status, between the sinner and God.

Whether of not penitent status was decreed or decided after this, there was in any case this moment of the *expositio casus*. We do not know a great deal about this confession (*confession*). In any case, one thing is certain, which is that, as you can see, this verbal, secret setting out of the sin itself, and no doubt of a number of other circumstances of the sin, was not part of penance. It is prior to it, it is the basis for being able to say: yes, you will do penance, or there is no need to do penance. What will later become one of the central components of the penitential procedure, the *confessio*, the detailed, verbal confession (*aveu*) is an

---

* Crackling on the recording: two or three inaudible words.
† Uncertain audition.

external element in the institution of this *paenitentia secunda*, a condition no doubt, but a prior condition. It does not form a part of penance.

What kind of truth act, what truth procedure is there within penance? We find a certain, relatively precise episode for which, precisely, the word *exomologēsis*, exomologesis is reserved. Just as the Latin authors tend to employ only *confessio* for the episode I have just been talking about, the *expositio casus*, so they tend to employ the Greek word *exomologēsis* exclusively for the episode I shall now talk about. I say they tend to do so, which means that they are not absolutely consistent. But, generally, exomologesis designates this episode. We can see clearly how [the latter] is situated, according to the texts of Saint Cyprian in which, very regularly, in his correspondence regarding penance, he lists the following series: *paenitentiam agere, exomologesim facere, impositio manus*[26]—*impositio manus*, of course, is the laying on of hands, that is to say the act of reconciliation. It is the end. *Paenitentiam agere*, on the other hand, is the fact of leading the life of a penitent, having penitent status, fulfilling all its obligations and commitments. And so, between *paenitentiam agere*, the first stage, and *impositio manus*, the last stage, we have *exomologesim facere*, doing exomologesis, which is therefore an episode that is indispensable for being reconciled. Penitent status has come to its end. One does exomologesis, and then at that point one is finally reconciled.

In what does this episode consist exactly? Saint Cyprian's correspondence, so at the end of the third century, does not tell us a great deal. There is simply an, as it were, spatial indication concerning the ritual and symbolic place where the exomologesis of sins must take place: this is, of course, the door, the threshold. Those who make exomologesis, Saint Cyprian says, are "those who knock on the door."[27] They are in the vestibule, they request to enter and knock on the church door with their staff. This is both a real and a symbolic indication therefore: it designates the actual spot where the penitents are standing at the moment of this exomologesis and situates them in relation to the community. They are outside, or partially outside the community; they are on the threshold, they are waiting to be readmitted and have the right to the *communio*, to the *communicatio*. This is all we can find in Saint Cyprian, but we have much more detail through either older or later texts.

On this precise episode of exomologesis, so between the fact of *paenitentam agere* and the moment one is reconciled, we have first of all the texts of Tertullian. I will begin with one of the latest, which he wrote when he was a Montanist (but despite this it is interesting for, let's say, orthodox, non-heretical practice). In *De pudicitia*,[28] then, Tertullian has become a Montanist.[29] Being a Montanist is not, as is sometimes said, a rejection of a second penance. The Montanists were indeed rigorists, but their rigorism did not consist in saying: once the baptized has sinned, he is lost and cannot be reconciled. The Montanists said: once the baptized has sinned, he must repent, but the Church cannot reconcile him. It is God who will decide whether or not he is to be saved. The Church cannot take this decision for God.[30] While Saint Cyprian, a bit later, will say: It is true that we cannot know what decision God will make, but we, ourselves, can and must reconcile, the Montanist position consists in saying: We cannot reconcile. So that in the paragraph 3 of *Du pudicitia*, Tertullian gives the specifically Montanist ritual which seems to be, basically, the first part of the orthodox ritual, of the non-heretical ritual accepted and practiced by the entire Church, that is to say that this was the moment at which the penitent performed exomologesis outside the Church. This is the only part of the ritual that the Montanists, who do not accept reconciliation, can accept. And it is likely that it is a ritual that was therefore common to non-heretics and to Montanists.

What does this episode consist of? The penitent, explains Tertullian's *De pudicitia*, is at the church door: "[He] prefers to blush before the Church than to remain in communion with it. Look! [he] remains standing at the door, [he] serves as warning to others by the example of his humiliation, [he] calls the tears of his brothers to his aid."[31] So, ritual of supplication at the church door. Paragraph 13 of the same *De pudicitia*: here Tertullian gets enraged. Just as he admits this first rite, so he rages against the other, or the other part of the ritual, which is precisely the moment when the penitent who is going to be reconciled is led within the church. Addressing those bad shepherds, those bad bishops, those bad priests who re-admit the penitent into the church, he says: "… you bring into the church the repentance of a fornicator in order to soothe the indignation of the Christian assembly. [You take] by the hand the guilty person hidden beneath his haircloth, covered with ashes and announcing his grief and dejection by his appearance. [You oblige him] to prostrate himself before the widows and priests. [You oblige him] to implore the aid of his brothers. [You oblige him] to kiss the steps of each of them and to roll humbly at their feet!"[32] This then is the maybe somewhat emphatic, exaggerated, because critical description Tertullian gives of a ritual that he rejects, but that does seem to have been practiced by the Church, since this is precisely what he reproaches it for doing: bringing the penitent into the church and forcing him to these supplications, which Tertullian does not criticize for their intensity, dramatic character, and emphasis, [but] which he objects to for taking place inside the church, when the penitent, since he has sinned, basically no longer has a right to communion, and which he reproaches for signifying that it is to the community, to the Christians, that the penitent makes supplication, that he throws himself at their feet, and that they are the ones who can reconcile and have the power to reconcile, whereas for him, Tertullian, only God can do that. So, through these criticisms we get an image of the ritual of exomologesis, one which is echoed down the centuries, moreover. At the end of the fourth century, in a letter of Saint Jerome, letter 77, and so at a time when the Montanist episode leaves no more than some after-effects, which are relatively less important than at the time of the great debate at the beginning of the third century, Saint Jerome gives a description of penance in a Christianity that is now in the majority, triumphant, and accepted by more or less everyone— this is the penance of Fabiola. Fabiola was a very wicked woman: she divorced her first husband and married another man before this first husband had died; after this she experienced remorse and so repented. So, this is how she did penance, according to Jerome: "In the eyes of all Rome, in the days before Easter"—and, in fact, the reconciliation of penitents generally took place at Easter—"Fabiola stood in the ranks of the penitents"—so, they are grouped together, probably standing at the church door in ranks—"the bishop, priests, and people weep with her, her hair disheveled, her face pale, her hands unwashed, her head soiled with ashes and humbly bowed...She wounded her bared breast and the face with which had seduced her second husband, she revealed to all her wound and Rome in tears contemplated the wounds on her pale body."[33]

So, at the beginning of the third and the end of the fourth century we have the description of an ultimately fairly constant, fairly precise ritual that had a definite place in the penitential procedures and that comprised, not at all a verbal confession (*aveu*) of sins, but a manifestation, a spectacular manifestation of what? Not so much of the sin as of the fact of having sinned, a spectacular manifestation of the fact that one recognized that one was a sinner, of the consciousness one had of being a sinner, a manifestation of the remorse one felt and of the desire to be reintegrated. We will have to come back to all this, of course, but I would like now to move on to another meaning of the word exomologesis. Or rather, the word exomologesis, therefore, designates this very precise ritual that takes place at the end of the penitential procedure and before reconciliation, but [it] is also employed fairly constantly to designate the entire penitential procedure, everything that happens, from the moment one begins to repent up to the end. We have examples of this comprehensive usage of the word exomologesis, rather than its employment for the precise designation of a particular episode, some of which are early and others from later.

For example, early on, in the second century, in Saint Iranaeus, in *Adversus haereses* (*Against Heresies*), Book I, chapter XIII, paragraph 5, concerning a woman who had been converted by the Gnostics and who, after this conversion to the gnosis, returned to the Church, we read: "She passed all her life in *exomologein tas amartias*, in doing exomologesis of her sins."[34] In Book 3, chapter 4, paragraph 3, a Gnostic called Cerdon is said to be a character of great hypocrisy, since he spends his life sometimes teaching heresy, sometimes confessing his transgression.[35] In this case, then, it is less than the previous woman who spent her whole life exercising *exomologēsis*. Here it is half of his life, but still a half ... So you can see that this does not [concern]* the episode I was talking about a short while ago. In Tertullian's *De paenitentia*, in chapter 12, you also find it said that "God has instituted *exomologēsis* to restore the sinner to grace"[36]—it is clear here that this is not the episode of exomologesis strictly speaking, but that Tertullian employs the word to designate the general institution of penance. And he confirms this a few lines later by saying that a king of Babylon, "continued the exomologesis of his transgressions for seven years."[37] So it is actually the whole of the penitential procedure that is designated here.

---

* M.F.: designate.

Now how and why can we say that the entire penitential procedure is an exomologesis? Why this slippage of meaning from the precise episode I was just talking about to the designation of penance in its entirety? Unless, for that matter, it is rather the general meaning that is gradually crystallized around a rite. Here again there is discussion and I won't go into it. On this point, chapter 9 of *De paenitentia* is, I think, rather illuminating for understanding why penance in its entirety can also be called and is fairly constantly called exomologesis. The first paragraph of this chapter is the following: "The more the second repentance"—*paenitentia secunda*, so this is what we are talking about now—"the more this second and unique repentance is necessary, the more difficult, laborious" (*laboriosior*, the text says) "its proof, its proofs (*laboriosior probatio*)."[38] So, penance must be a laborious proof, a laborious probation. What does Tertullian understand by this? The rest of the paragraph develops it very clearly. He says the following: penance, to be a good penance and to have the effects one expects from it, must not take place merely in thought, *in conscientia sola*. The *metanoia* characteristic of repentance must not be merely a conversion of thought, in thought, and for thought itself. Not merely *in conscientia sola*, repentance must also be *actus*, it must be an act. What is this act? It is the externalization of the conversion of thought, it is its transcription in comportment, and exomologesis is this repentance as act. Hence the overall description of exomologesis which Tertullian gives in this paragraph: "Exomologesis is the discipline that prescribes man's prostration and humiliation (*disciplina prosternandi et humiliandi* [sic]), imposing a regime of a kind to attract mercy. In what concerns clothing and food ..."[39]—then, I am not very strong in Latin, but I am not entirely in agreement with the translation. It says: "*de ipso habitu atque victu.*"[40] *Habitu[s]* is much more likely the general mode of life than clothes. Exomologesis is concerned with a way of living and not just a way of dressing oneself at a given moment. It is a way of living, a way of being, a way of feeding oneself. Moreover, the text says a bit before, it is a *conversatio*,[41] a way of existing and of relating to others, to oneself. So, with regard to mode of life, exomologesis "wishes one to lie down under sackcloth and ashes, to cover one's body in somber rags, to abandon one's soul to sadness, to correct one's sinful members with harsh treatment. Exomologesis, on the other hand, knows only simple food and drink, such as the soul's good demands, and not the belly's pleasure. The penitent usually feeds his prayers with fasting. He groans, he weeps, he cries out day and night to the Lord his God, he grovels at the feet of the priests, kneels before those who are dear to God, he calls on all the brothers to be his intercessors in order to obtain his forgiveness. Exomologesis does all this to give credit to the repentance."[42]

The first thing we can take from this is that we have in this description of exomologesis, no longer as an episode at the end of penance, but as the overall act translating, expressing, manifesting *metanoia*, exactly the same elements as those of the exomologesis-episode. We must therefore think that there was, on the one hand, a precise ritual of exomologesis making the transition between the penitential procedure and the laying of hands, the exomologesis-episode. But, basically, this exomologesis-episode was only the intensification, the tightening, the dramatization in a public episode, at the church door, and at the moment of reconciliation, of what was basically the permanent drama of repentance, that kind of theatrical dramatization (I say this without any pejorative connotation) of *metanoia* that was characteristic and fundamental in all repentance.

So, in sum we can say that the truth procedures in canonical penance, in ecclesial penance, these truth rites, these truth procedures are three in number. First, there is the *expositio casus*, the *confessio*, which has a verbal form and the juridical form of which is clearly suggested by the term itself, *expositio casus*, a juridical term. Here we have a juridical, verbal episode that is of the same type as the one we will find later in medieval penance. But here, in the first centuries, it is an external, preliminary procedure that does not form part of penance. And then, second, we have exomologesis as permanent dimension of penance, as way of constantly manifesting it for the seven, fifteen, or twenty years that the status of penitent lasts. And finally, [third], we have exomologesis as dramatization, as intensification of the dramatic character necessary for all penance and which is the exomologesis-episode between the end of the penitential action and before the laying on of hands. In a few words, if you like, a juridical-verbal truth procedure prior to penance and a dramatic dimension peculiar to penance, for which Tertullian has a word which I think is fundamental: *publicatio sui*, one must expose oneself publicly (*se publier*).[43] *Exposition casus*, juridical form; *publicatio sui*, well, this is precisely exomologesis strictly speaking. Here again, I think that just as we should distinguish the *expositio casus* from the *publicatio sui*, we should also distinguish the *probatio animae*, that test of the soul I talked about with regard to baptism, from this *publicatio sui*.

If you will allow me five or ten more minutes ... yes? a few words on this *publicatio sui*. The history of penance will be the history of the way in which the *expositio casus*, this juridical-verbal form prior to penance, [will be] reintroduced over the centuries (but not before the twelfth century, finally) within penance, will replace the *publicatio sui*, and a day will come when the *publicatio sui*, the making public of what one is as a sinner will no longer take place except through the verbal [filter]* and juridical grid of an *expositio casus*. It is at that point, I think, that the relation of subjectivity to the truth, codified in terms of law, filtered through a discursive practice, will give Christian penance the form that we now [know]† and will also entail, for Western subjectivity, a relation to discourse and a relation to confession (*aveu*) that is absolutely characteristic of our civilization. But confession (*aveu*), that is to say *publicatio sui* by way of *expositio casus*, exomologesis transformed into a juridical-verbal practice, is something that takes place slowly, that required almost a millennium or, at any rate, seven or eight centuries to be accomplished. In early penance, the manifestation of self did not pass through language and did not have the form of law. The whole pivoting of Western culture on the problem of the practice of discourse and forms of law is involved in this history of penance; right, the law, discourse, and, as a result, all the types of relationship between truth and subjectivity. It is quite clear that the relationship of the truth to subjectivity will be completely modified when it comes to be codified in terms of law and filtered through the thread of a discursive practice. This was the first remark.

The second remark is only the development of this. I would like, by this, to bring out what is specific in this exomologesis in contrast with the *expositio casus*, with the juridical-verbal framework. Let's take the axis of the secret and the public. The *confessio*, the *expositio casus*, this verbal act prior to penance is evidently on the secret side. On the other hand, the acts of exomologesis only have meaning because they are public; they

---

* M.F.: thread (*fil*).
† M.F.: have given it.

are entirely, wholly on the side of public action. Exomologesis is under-taken in order to be public. Tertullian, chapter 10: "I presume that most avoid this duty,"—of penance—"or defer it[44] because they fear to display themselves in public. They are more concerned about shame than about their salvation."[45] So, exomologesis is on the public side.

Second, the verbal-non-verbal axis. The *confessio* is obviously on the side of verbal formulation. When one seeks out the priest, one exposes one's sin to him only through words. Exomologesis, you can see, is entirely on the side of non-verbal expressive elements, or, if one uses words, if one prays, if one implores, it is not at all to speak of the sin one has committed, it is to affirm that one is a sinner. That is to say that speech here has the value of the cry, an expressive value, and not at all the value of the precise designation of a sin. In this exomologesis it is the ashes, the hair shirt, the clothes, the mortifications, and the tears that speak, and the verbal has only an expressive function. Saint Ambrose, in his *De paenitentia*, chapter 1, will say that the tears, groans, and humilia-tions are necessary for Jesus to return in turn to grace.[46] This is moreover what is called confession (*confession*) by tears, or baptism by tears.[47]

Third, on the axis of the analytic and the synthetic, we can say that the role of the *confessio*, of the *expositio casus* before penance is to deter-mine, for the bishop's or leader's information, what the fault is, in what it consists, and what its circumstances are. Exomologesis, on the other hand, does not have any analytical or descriptive function. It refers to the sins en bloc, en masse. Fabiola manifests herself as sinner with the interesting feature, however, that there are sometimes symbolic relations to the sin itself in this dramaturgy of penance. You recall what Saint Jerome said: "Before the eyes of the public, she wounded the face with which she had seduced her second husband."[48] That is to say, in this case there is an expressive and symbolic relationship between the body and the sin that is manifested in penance, but which has nothing to do with the kind of [detailed] analysis of the act involved in the *expositio casus*.

Finally, the axis of the subjective and the objective. The role of *confes-sio*, of the setting out of the case, is clearly to tell of the sin itself. What, on the other hand, is the function of exomologesis? It is not at all to say what the sin was. Its function is to show the sinner, to show the sinner himself, to manifest who he is. Now, how does it manifest the sinner? It manifests him essentially through the rites of ashes, entreaties, the hair shirt, cries, tears, kneeling—that is to say essentially the elements with which, in Greek, Hellenistic, and Roman societies one manifested supplication. There is nothing new, basically, in this Christian exomologesis. The dramaturgy, the elements anyway of the dramaturgy, what I will call, if you will, the substratum of the penitential drama, is that of the supplication.

But what is different—and it is here, I think, that a history begins that is a history of the relationships of subject and truth in Western Christian civilization—lies in this: what is involved when the ancient supplicant arrives with his head covered with ashes and with torn clothes, when he cries out, weeps, and kneels before those he entreats? Basically, it is a matter of creating an obligation between himself and the person he entreats, an obligation the burden of responsibility for which, the weight of which will fall on the one being entreated. It consists in saying: I show myself. In what do I show myself? It is true, I show myself in my truth, in my truth as someone who has suffered misfortune. And from the moment that I show myself with this emphasis on my misfortune, I create an obligation in you. Look at the end of Oedipus: Oedipus has committed every sin on earth, he arrives a blind and bloody supplicant, and as a result it is up to Thebes, to Creon, to his family to take care of him and the obligation is handed over to them. Ancient supplication operates as the transfer of obligation through the manifestation of misfortune.

Christian exomologesis functions quite differently and the alethurgy, the manifestation of what the sinner is in truth has quite different functions. By spreading ashes on one's head, wounding oneself, crying out, weeping one shows what one is, that is to say a sinner—not, once again, the sin—one shows oneself to be a sinner. One shows oneself to be a sinner, that is to say to be on the way of death, to belong to the kingdom of death, to be on the side of the dead. But from the moment one shows oneself in this way, by fasting, renouncing everything, and wearing the clothes of poverty, one shows that one renounces the world, that none of its possible pleasures, wealth, and satisfactions matter. The death one manifests in Christian exomologesis is both the death one is and represents because one has sinned, but also that death one seeks with regard the world. One wants to die to death. It is this double meaning of death as state of the sinner and as will to die to sin that is present in the rite of exomologesis, in the set of practices characteristic of exomologesis. And, as a result, by doing this, that is to say by using the vocabulary of supplication to manifest both that one is dead and that one is dying to death, on the one hand one brings out the truth of oneself—this is what I am, man of flesh who is nothing other than death—and, on the other, at the same time one erases death, since by dying to death one can be reborn. Consequently, this exomologetic expression does not consist in transferring or creating an obligation in the person one entreats. It does not involve this transfer of duty. In this supplication it is a matter of manifesting what one is and, at the same time, erasing what one is.

You see that here, as for baptism, we find again the problem of death, but of death as mortification at the very heart of the manifestation of truth. Mortification and manifestation of truth, mortification and alethurgy are absolutely at the heart of the Christian practice of exomologesis, of the practice of the Christian obligation of the manifestation of one's truth. One can manifest one's truth only in a certain relation to death which is that of mortification.

Finally, I shall add—I shall try to explain all this later—[a] third and final remark: when one manifests what one is, that is to say a sinner, that is to say a being of death, but at the same manifests that one dies to this state of sinner and dies to death, and therefore one shows one's truth and erases it at the same time, you can see that there is something in Christian exomologesis that is like the echo of the liar's paradox. The Cretan who lied, and who lied by saying, "I lie," was a cynic, not in the philosophical sense of the word, but when he lied he had the insolence to say that he was lying. And you know that in boasting of lying he could speak neither truth nor falsehood, since when one says "I lie," it is impossible to say whether this proposition is true or false. This is the paradox of the effect of the enunciation on the statement. The Cretan liar is therefore a cynic who can speak neither truth nor falsehood. But the Christian, who is not a liar, who is truthful, who is truthful in his exomologesis, and who in his humility says, "I am a sinner," also cannot speak either truth or falsehood. Or rather he speaks both truth and falsehood, since he says something true, namely that he is in fact a sinner, and of this there is absolutely no doubt. But what is the effect of the enunciation itself, in the form at least of its dramatic exomologetic character? Precisely that of showing, and not only of showing, but of actually carrying out that kind of detachment with regard to the state of sinner, since it is through the exomologesis that one effectuates *in actu*, really, *metanoia*, detachment from sin. And I am all the less a sinner as I affirm that I am a sinner. Paradox of the Christian's truthful humility as opposed to the Cretan's cynical lie. And this will be the whole problem of the paradox of Christian humility that affirms a truth and at the same time erases it, that qualifies the Christian as a sinner and at the same time qualifies him as being no longer a sinner, this is what is at the heart of the paradoxes of Christian humility and of Christian asceticism. And it will be—we will see next week or the week after[49]— one of the great problems of ascetic life, of monastic life, of the humility of the ascetic, when this humility is flaunted, as it were, and like a cynical (in the non-philosophical sense) manifestation of the sinner's state, the effect of which is that one equally flaunts, one manifests that one is not a sinner. So what is this humility worth if it says at once: I am a sinner and see how little I am a sinner since I say that I am a sinner? "Yes, brother, I am a wicked, guilty, wretched sinner, full of iniquity, the greatest villain that has walked on earth": as you will have recognized, this is a statement by Tartuffe[50]—well, I do not say this in a polemical sense, but this is the paradox of humility.

1. Clément d'Alexandrie, *Tis o sōxomenos plousios/"Quis dives salvetur*, 41, PG, 9, col. 650 d: "… *lacrymis velut altero quodam baptismo expiabatur*"; trans. Genoude, "Quel riche peut être sauvé?" in *Défense du christianisme par le Pères des premiers siècles de l'Eglise*, 2nd series, "Œuvres choisies de Clément d'Alexandrie" (Paris: Librairie de Perrodil, 1846), pp. 249-289: "baptized (βαπτιζόμενος) a second time by tears." A new translation by P. Descourtieux has recently appeared in the collection of Sources chrétiennes, *Quel riche sera sauvé?* (Paris: Cerf, SC no. 537, 2011). Foucault was familiar with, but used freely, the translation by F. Quére-Jaulmes, revised by Dom Juglar, in G. Hamman, ed., *Riches et pauvres dans l'Eglise ancienne* (Paris: Grasset, "Lettres chrétiennes," 1962, republished Paris: Desclée de Brower, "Ichtus," 1982); see p. 54: "With his sobs he expiated as much as he could his crimes, and his tears baptized him a second time" (the case concerns a young man who had fallen back into banditry and who the apostle John brings back to the faith. On this story, see below lecture of 19 March, pp. 255-257); English translation by William Wilson as, Clement of Alexandria, "Who is the Rich Man who Shall be Saved?" in *ANF*, Vol. II, XLII, p. 603: "and baptized a second time with tears."
2. See, for example, Ambroise of Milan, *De Paenitentia/La pénitence*, II, 10, 95, Introduction, trans. and notes by R. Gryson (Paris: Cerf, SC no. 179, 1971), p. 193: "Just as there is only one baptism, there is only one penance—at least that which is performed publicly; for every day we must repent our sins …"; English translation by H. de Romestin, E. de Romestin and H.T.F. Duckworth, Ambrose, "Concerning Repentance" in *NPNF2*, Vol. X, eds. Philip Schaff and Henry Wace (Grand Rapids, Michigan: W.B. Eerdmans Publishing, 1994), Book II, ch. X, 95, p. 357: "for as there is but one baptism, so there is but one course of penance, so far as the outward practice goes, for we must repent of our daily faults." On this "unrepeatable" character of ancient canonic penance, see P. Adnès, "Pénitence," DS, XII, 1984, col. 963, which refers to Clement of Alexandria, Tertullian, Origen, and Ambrose.
3. Tertullien (Tertullian), *De paenitentia/La pénitence*, XII, 9, p. 191: "But why speak more of these planks, if I can put it like that, of the salvation of man (*istis duabus humanae salutis quasi plancis*)…?" i.e., "penance and exomologesis, its instrument"; Tertullian, *On Repentance*, in *ANF*, vol. 3, ch. XII, p. 666: "Why should I add more touching these two planks (as it were) of human salvation …." See VII, 2, p. 173: post-baptismal penance is presented as a "second or rather … last hope (*secondae, immo iam ultimae spei*); Eng., ch. VII, p. 662: "a second—nay, in that case, the *last*—hope." See also XII, 5, p. 189: "there is still a second refuge (*seconda subsidia*) in exomologesis"; Eng., ch. XII, p. 665: "there still remains for you, in *exomologesis* a second reserve of aid." P. Adnès, "Pénitence," col. 964, notes: "The expression 'second plank after the shipwreck,' whose paternity goes back to Tertullian, … will become a traditional expression for designating ecclesiastical post-baptismal penance." Adnès refers notably to Saint Jerome, *Letters*, 84, 6 and 130, 9.
4. This is "tariffed" penance. Foucault referred to this practice in his 1975 course, *Les anormaux*, the lecture of 19 February 1975, pp. 159-160; *Abnormal*, p. 172, already connecting it to the German penal model. He returns to it in more detail in 1981, in *Mal faire, dire vrai*, lecture of 13 May, pp. 000-000, describing it as "the first major juridification of penance." See C. Vogel, *Le pécheur et la pénitence au Moyen-Âge* (Paris: Cerf, "Traditions chrétiennes," 1969), pp. 17-23.
5. See "La vérité et les formes juridiques," 3rd lecture, DE II, p. 573; English translation by Robert Hurley, "Truth and Juridical Forms" in *Essential Works of Foucault 1954-1984. Vol. 3. Power*, ed. James D. Faubion (New York: The New Press, 2000), p. 56: "[In ancient Germanic law the] series of vengeful actions could be broken with a pact. In that event, the two adversaries would appeal to an arbiter who, in harmony with them, and with their mutual consent, would set a sum of money that would constitute the compensation—not compensation for a transgression, for there was no transgression but only a wrong and a vengeance. In this procedure of Germanic law, one of the two adversaries would buy back the right to have peace, to escape the possible revenge of his adversary." The source for this analysis is *Germania* by Tacitus.
6. See for example Saint Ambroise, *De Paenitentia/La Pénitence*, II, 95, p. 193: "There are some who think they can do penance several times (*saepius agendam paenitentiam*). These 'give themselves up to debauchery in Christ.' For if they performed their penance seriously (*si vere agerent paenitentiam*), they would not think they could renew it afterwards"; Saint Ambrose, *On Repentance*, Book II, ch. X, 95, p. 357: "Deservedly are they blamed who think that they often do penance, for they are wanton against Christ. For if they went through their penance in truth, they would not think that it could be repeated again." See below, note 26 (Saint Cyprian).

7. Pacien (bishop of Barcelona, end of the fourth century), *Parænesis, sive Exhortatorius, ad poeni-tentiam*, PL 13, col. 1082 d; trans. C. Vogel, "Exhortation à la pénitence," in *Le pécheur et la pénitence dans l'Eglise ancienne*, p. 89: "Let no one think that my remarks concerning the peni-tential institution are addressed only to penitents. No one should feel bored, thinking that it does not concern him and that my discourse was addressed only to the next person, whereas penance is like the bond that holds together the discipline of the entire Church. It is a mat-ter of acting so that catechumens never have to enter this state [penance] and the faithful no longer have to return to it." See the translation of C. Epitalon and M. Lestienne: Pacien de Barcelone, *Ecrits*, "Sources chrétiennes" no. 410, 1995, p. 121; English translation by Rev. C.H. Collyns, *Saint Pacian, Paraenesis, or, Treatise of Exhortation unto Penance* in *The Extant Works of Saint Pacian* (Library of Fathers of the Holy Church, 1842), p. 365: "Moreover let no man imagine that this very discourse on the institution of penance is framed for penitents only, lest for this reason whoever is placed without that rank, despise what shall be spoken as intended for others; whereas the discipline of the whole Church is tied as it were into this fastening, since Catechumens must be careful that they pass not into this state, and the faithful that they return not to it." On Pacian's debt to Tertullian, see J.-C. Fredouille, "Du *De Paenitentia* de Tertullien au *De Paenitentiae* de Pacien", *Revue des Études Augustiniennes*, 44, 1988, pp. 13-23.

8. Saint Ambroise, *La Pénitence*, II, 7, 54, p. 169: "In what situation is he among the guilty, in what class of penitents (*in quo paenitentium ordine*)?"; Saint Ambrose, *On Repentance*, Book II, ch. VI, 54, p. 352: "... in what condition of guilt is he? In which rank of penitents?" See p. 168 note 1 of *La Pénitence*, which notes that "the Asian Churches in the fourth century [had] a system of public penance of several grades, in which penitents pass[ed] successively, in principle, from one class to another and [were] progressively re-integrated into the liturgi-cal community," but nothing of this existed in Milan, where Ambrose was bishop. See also P. Adnès, "Pénitence," col. 961: "In the East, at least in Asian Minor, different classes of peni-tents were established ... There were four and, in principle, one had to pass successively from one to the other. For the West, we have no indication as to the existence of similar classes. J. Grotz (*Die Entwicklung des Bußstufenwesens in der vornicänischen Kirche*, Fribourg, Herder, 1953) has tried to prove this existence from the oldest times, but has not been followed by everyone. Nor does it seem that in the West the penitents were generally sent back with the catechumens before the offertory." Foucault notes the reference to Grotz's thesis in his "green notebook" (see P. Chevalier, "Foucault et les sources patristiques," p. 140). The question of different classes of penitents is distinct from that of the existence of an *ordo paenitentium*, which is attested very early in the West (see P. Adnès, "Pénitence," col. 960: "[In the fourth and fifth centuries] penitents form a special category of Christians whose obligations and rights are not the same as those of the other faithful"). See also E. Amann, "Pénitence," col. 803-804.

9. See above, note 7.

10. See F.-J. Dölger, *Der Exorzismus im altchristlichen Taufritual*, pp. 77-78; J. Daniélou, "Exorcisme," col. 2002. On baptism as a ritual of exorcism, see above, lecture of 20 February, pp. 150-153.

11. On these obligations, see R. Gryson, Introduction to Ambroise, *La Pénitence*, p. 39, which refers notably to Book I, ch. XXVI, 91 (on fasting); Book II, ch. X, 96 (on continence); Book I, ch. VII, 37, Book II, ch. IX, 88 (on coarse clothing and abstaining for care of the body).

12. The persecution to which the problem of apostates or *lapsi* is linked historically is that under-taken by the emperor Decius in 250. The title "Great persecution" is usually reserved for Diocletian's much more violent persecution, which took place from 303 to 311 (see, for exam-ple, J. Daniélou and H. Marrou, *Nouvelle histoire de l'Eglise*, t. I: "Des origines à Grégoire le Grand," p. 263, 272 and passim). R. Gryson, in his Introduction to Ambroise, *La Pénitence*, p. 16, also speaks of the "great persecution of Decius," but E.R. Dodds, in *Pagan and Christian in an Age of Anxiety: Some Aspects of Religious Experience from Marcus Aurelius to Constantine* (Cambridge: Cambridge University Press, 1965), p. 108, describes the Decian persecution as the "first systematic attempt to exterminate Christianity" but distinguishes it from the "Great Persecution under Diocletian and Galeris" See C. Lepelley, *L'empire romain et le chris-tianisme* (Paris: Flammarion, "Questions d'histoire," 1969), pp. 47-48, for the first persecution and pp. 51-53 for the second; see also C. Vogel, *Le pécheur et la pénitence dans l'Eglise ancienne*, pp. 24-25, and for a synthetic approach, J. Liébaert, *Les Pères de l'Eglise, Ier-IVe siècles* (Paris:

Desclée, "Bibliothèque d'histoire du christianisme," no. 10, 2000 [1986]) ch. 3: "Au vent de la persécution et des conflits dans l'Eglise: saint Cyprien," pp. 103-114.

13. Saint Cyprien, *Correspondence*, trans. Canon Bayard (Paris: Les Belles Lettres, CUF, 1962 [1925]) in two volumes; English translation by Robert Ernest Wallis, *Epistles of Cyprian of Carthage*, in *ANF*, Vol. V, eds. Alexander Roberts, James Donaldson, and A. Cleveland Coxe (Grand Rapids, Michigan: W.B. Eerdmans Publishing, 1994).

14. Ibid., letter LV, 13, 1, vol. 2, p. 139 (words in brackets added by Foucault); the original (French) text ends with the words: "by a convention which exposed him alone"; Eng., ibid., Epistle LI, 13, p. 330: "For we must not place on a level one who has at once leapt forward with good-will to the abominable sacrifice, and one who, after long struggle and resistance, has reached that fatal result under compulsion; one who has betrayed both himself and all his connections, and one who, himself approaching the trial in behalf of all, has protected his wife and his children, and his whole family, by himself undergoing the danger."

15. Ibid., letter XXX, 5, 2, vol. 1, pp. 74-75; Eng., ibid., Epistle XXX, 5, p. 311: "For it seems extremely invidious and burdensome to examine into what seems to have been committed by many, except by the advice of many; or that one should give a sentence when so great a crime is known to have gone forth, and to be diffused among so many; since that cannot be a firm decree which shall not appear to have had the consent of very many."

16. Ibid., letter LV, 6, vol. 2, p. 134: "with the regret for sins, paternal benevolence will be asked for, the cases, intentions, and extenuating circumstances will be examined one by one in accordance with the little work, which I believe you have received, in which the points of the ruling are itemized (*secundum quod libello continetur quem ad te pervenisse confido*)"; Eng., ibid., Epistle LI, 6, p. 328: "repentance should be long protracted, and the paternal clemency be sorrowfully besought, and the cases, and the wishes, and the necessities of individuals be examined into, according to what is contained in a little book, which I trust has come to you, in which the several heads of our decisions are collected." The French translator notes: "This ruling has not come down to us. It was no doubt joined to *De Lapsis* by Saint Cyprian."

17. Ibid., letter LVII, 3, 2, vol. 2, p. 157; Eng., ibid., Epistle LIII, 3, p. 337: "We, so far as it is allowed to us to see and to judge, look upon the face of each one; we are not able to scrutinize the heart and to inspect the mind."

18. Ibid., letter LV, 18, 1, vol. 2, p. 142: "We do not with a prior judgment prevent the Lord's Judgment, and if he finds the sinner's penance full and sufficient he may ratify what we have decided here on Earth"; Eng., ibid., Epistle LI, 18, p. 331: "Moreover, we do not prejudge when the Lord is to be the judge; save that if He shall find the repentance of the sinners full and sound, He will then ratify what shall have been here determined by us." See H.C. Lea, *A History of Auricular Confession and Indulgences in the Latin Church*, vol. 1 (London: Swan Sonnenschein, 1896) p. 10, to which Foucault seems very close here, as much by the quotation as by the commentary: "[The Church] could grant the penitent 'peace' and reconciliation, but it did not pretend to absolve him, and by reconciliation he only gained the opportunity of being judged by God. St. Cyprian, who tells us of this, had evidently never heard of the power of the keys, or that what the Church loosed on earth would be loosed in heaven; it cannot, he says, prejudge the judgment of God, for it is fallible and easily deceived."

19. Tertullien, *De paenitentia/La pénitence*, IX, 1, p. 181: "This act [which manifests second penance], which is more commonly designated by a Greek term, is *exomologēsis*"; Tertullian, *On Repentance*, ch. IX, p. 664: "This act, which is more usually expressed and commonly spoken of under a Greek name, is ἐξομολόγησις [*exomologēsis*] whereby we confess our sins to the Lord." See G.G. Stroumsa, "Du repentir à la pénitence: l'exemple de Tertullien," in A. Charles-Saget, ed., *Retour, repentir et constitution de soi* (Paris: Vrin, 1998), p. 82: "As has often been noted [previously], this is the first mention of *exomologēsis* in Christian literature."

20. *La doctrine des douze apôtres (Didachè)*, 4, 14, trans., R.-F. Refoulé, p. 43; *The Didache*, ch. 4, in *Early Christian Writings*, p. 229: "In church, make confession of your faults, and do not come to your prayers with a bad conscience." This phrase was quoted in the previous lecture, p. 174 (see note 19 regarding the translation). "*epi amartiais*" is a variant of the manuscript translation, not accepted by the editions of Hemmer (p. 12) and *Sources chrétiennes* (p. 164), which replace it with: "*ta paraptōmata*."

21. Ibid., 14, 1, p. 53: "*proexomologēsamenoi ta paraptōmata*" (Foucault quotes the Latinized form of the word here); Eng., ibid., ch. 14, p. 234: "Assemble on the Lord's Day, and break bread and

offer the Eucharist; but first make confession of your faults, so that your sacrifice may be a pure one."

22. See, for example, A. d'Alès, *La théologie de Tertullien* (Paris: Beauchesne, 3rd ed., 1905), p. 343: "In this sacerdotal inquiry, preliminary to public penance, we grasp the origin of private penance, destined to such a great development later," and p. 344, note 1, his criticism of the interpretation of H.C. Lea, for whom, "the early Church did not claim to exercise any jurisdiction in the internal forum of conscience." As the latter wrote, in fact, calling upon the testimony of F. Suarez, "the early penance was not sacramental, but wholly in the *forum externum*, regulating the relations of the sinner with the Church but not with God" (*A History of Auricular Confession and Indulgences in the Latin Church*, vol. I, p. 9 note 8). See also, in the bibliography indicated by J.H. Taylor, "St. Cyprian and the reconciliation of apostates," *Theological Studies*, 3, 1942, p. 27, the work by C. Mortimer, *The Origins of Private Penance in the Western Church* (Oxford: Clarendon Press, 1939) directed against the arguments of P. Galtier, *L'Eglise et la rémission des péchés aux premiers siècles* (Paris: Beauchesne, 1932), in favor of the existence of private penance from the first centuries.

23. In *Mal faire, dire vrai*, lecture of 29 April 1981, p. 104, Foucault more correctly attributes to Saint Cyprian the expression "*expositio causae*" (the setting out of the case). See Saint Cyprian, *Correspondance*, Letter XXII, 2, p. 61 where he relates *expositio causae* before the bishop to *exomologesis*: "... after their case will have been examined before the bishop and they will have confessed their sin ... (*exposita causa apud episcopum et facta exomologesi habeant pacem*)"; *Epistles of Cyprian*, XXI, 2, p. 299: "the case being set forth before the bishop, and confession being made."

24. Paulin [Paulinus] de Milan, *Vita S. Ambrosii*, PL, col. 27-50. First French translation by E. Lamirande, *Paulin de Milan et la "Vita Ambrosii": Aspects de la religion sous le Bas-Empire* (Paris: Desclée-Montréal, "Recherches Théologie" no. 30, Bellarmin, 1983). This text, which dates from 412-413, was written on the request of Saint Augustine. English translation by F.R. Hoare, in *The Western Fathers* (New York: Harper and Row, 1954).

25. Ibid., 39, col. 40 C. Passage translated by R. Gryson, Introduction to Ambroise de Milan, *La Pénitence*, p. 35: "He was joyful with those who rejoiced, and in tears with those who wept. Whenever someone had confessed (*avoué*) his sins to him in order to receive penance, he wept in such a way that he forced him to weep as well ... With regard to the sins that one confessed (*avouait*) to him, he spoke of them to no one other than to the Lord, with whom he interceded. In this way he left a good example to future priests, so that they may be more intercessors with God than accusers of men." The biographer, as R. Gryson clarifies, is inspired here by *De Paenitentia*, II, 73, p. 181; *Concerning Repentance*, Book II, ch. VIII, 73, p. 354.

26. Saint Cyprien, *Correspondance*, letter XV, 1, vol. I, p. 43: "... before any penance, before confession of the greatest and most serious sins, before the laying on of hands by the bishop and the clergy for reconciliation (*ante actam paenitentiam, ante exomologesim gravissimi atque extremi delicti factam, ante manum ab episcopo et clero in paenitentiam impositam*)" (translator's note, p. 43: "This is here the whole process of penitential discipline"); Eng., Saint Cyprian, *Epistles of Cyprian*, Epistle X, 1, p. 291: "... before penitence was fulfilled, before confession even of the gravest and most heinous sin was made, before hands were placed upon the repentant by the bishops and clergy"; Fr., letter XVI, 2, pp. 46-47: "When it is a matter of lesser sins, the sinners do penance for the prescribed time (*agant peccatores poenitentiam*), and, according to the order of discipline, are admitted to confession (*ad exomologesim veniant*), then by the laying on of hands of the bishop and clergy, (*per manus impositionem episcopi et cleri*) they re-enter communion"; Eng., Epistle IX, 2, p. 290: "... in smaller sins sinners may do penance for a set time, and according to the rules of discipline come to public confession, and by imposition of the hand of the bishop and clergy receive the right of communion"; see also Fr., letter XVIII, 1, p. 51; Eng., Epistle, XII, 1, p. 293. On penitential discipline in Cyprian, there is a good synthesis in V. Saxer, *Vie liturgique et quotidienne à Carthage vers le milieu du IIIe siècle: le témoignage de saint Cyprien et de ses contemporains d'Afrique* (Rome: Pontificio Istituto de archeologia cristiana, 1969), pp. 145-188; on the *ordo disciplinae (paenitentia, exomologesis, manus impositio)*, see pp. 160-161 (numerous citations in notes); on exomologesis (which designates "the public confession of the penitent before receiving the laying on of hands and ... has nothing to do with private confession [*aveu*]"), pp. 169-171; on the rite of laying on of hands, sign of God's forgiveness, pp. 171-172.

27. See, ibid., Fr., Letter XXX, 6, vol. 3, p. 75: "Let them [the *lapsi*] knock on the door, but not break it down"; Eng., Epistle XXX, 6, p. 310: "Let them indeed knock at the doors, but assuredly let them not break them down." On the *vestibulum* in the rite of canonical penance, see Tertullien, *De paenitentia/La pénitence*, VII, 10, SC, p. 175: "[God] has placed the second penance in the vestibule, to open for those who would knock," and the explanations of C. Munier, Introduction, pp. 60-62 (see p. 75, the plan of the Roman *domus* serving as model for the *domus ecclesiae*); Tertullian, *Of Repentance*, ch. VII, p. 663: "In the vestibule He has stationed the second repentance for opening to such as knock."

28. Tertullien, *De pudicitia/La pudicité*, trans., C. Munier, with Introduction by C. Micaelli (Paris: Cerf, SC, no. 394-395, 1993), but, as we will see, in this lecture Foucault uses the old translation of the abbot de Genoude; English translation by the Rev. S. Thelwall as Tertullian, *On Modesty*, in *ANF*, Vol. IV, ed., Philip Schaff (Grand Rapids, Michigan: W.B. Eerdmands Publishing, 1994).

29. On this movement, born in Phrygia (Asia Minor) in the second half of the second century, see H. von Campenhausen, *Les Pères latins*, trans., C.A. Moreau (Ed. de l'Orante, "Livre de vie," 1967) p. 40: "Its prophets—Montanos and the women who escorted him—presented themselves as the instruments of a new outpouring of the Spirit, that is to say of the 'Comforter' promised in John's gospel. At the same time, they announced the next coming of the Kingdom of God in the mountains of their homeland. They advocated repentance (*pénitence*), conversion, an intensification of severity in morals, and distinguished themselves by a burning disposition for martyrdom. The movement underwent a rapid spread: at the beginning of the third century they had reached Africa. Tertullian adhered to it and quickly became the most fiery militant of the 'new prophecy.'" See also J. Daniélou and H. Marrou, *Nouvelle histoire de l'Eglise*, vol. I: *Des origines à Grégoire le Grand*," pp. 131-134; E. Trocmé, "Le christianisme jusqu'à 325," pp. 250-252. On the evolution of Tertullian regarding penitential matters, starting from his conversion to Montanism around 207, see C. Munier, Introduction to *De paenitentia*, pp. 93-98. See also P. de Labriolle, *La crise montaniste* (Paris: E. Leroux, 1913), Book III, pp. 294-467: "Tertullien et le montanisme" and, more recently, T.D. Barnes, *Tertullian: a Historical and Literary Study* (Oxford: Clarendon Press, 2004 [1971]) pp. 130-142: "The New Prophecy."

30. See Tertullien, *De pudicitia/La pudicité*, III, 3-4; Tertullian, *On Modesty*, ch. III. The sins involved in this book are adultery and fornication.

31. Ibid., III, 4-5, Genoude translation, *Œuvres de Tertullien* (Paris: 1852). vol. 3, p. 450. In the original text the subject of the sentence is "penitence." The Latin text says: "*quod ecclesiae mauult erubescere quam communicare.*" P. de Labriolle's translation in Tertullien, *De paenitentia. De pudicitia* (Paris: P.A. Picard et Fils, "Textes et documents pour l'étude historique du christianisme, 1906), p. 69, is more correct with "to re-enter in communion." C. Munier's translation, SC, 1993, p. 161 has: "it calls to its aid the tears of its brothers and returns, more enriched for having obtained their compassion that it would have been re-entering into communion with them"; English trans., Tertullian, *On Modesty*, ch. III, p. 77: "it [repentance] prefers the blush of shame to the privilege of communion. For before her doors it stands, and by the example of its own stigma admonishes all others, and calls at the same time to its own aid the brethren's tears and returns with an even richer merchandise—their compassion, namely—than their communion."

32. Ibid., XIII, 7, p. 473 (the brackets indicate Foucault's modifications or additions); Eng., ibid., p. 86: "Why, do you yourself, when introducing into the church, for the purpose of melting the brotherhood by his prayers, the repentant adulterer, lead into the midst and prostrate him, all in haircloth and ashes, a compound of disgrace and horror, before the widows, before the elders, suing for the tears of all, licking the footprints of all, clasping the knees of all?"

33. Saint Jérôme, *Lettres*, Letter LXXVII to Oceanus, on the death of Fabiola, trans. J. Labourt (Paris: Les Belles Lettres, CUF, 2nd edition revised and corrected by M. Testard, 1989), vol. 4, p. 43 and pp. 44-45, § 4-5; English translation by W. H. Fremantle with the Rev. G. Lewis and the Rev. W.G. Martley, Letter LXXVII, 4-5, in Saint Jerome, *Letters*, in Phillip Schaff and Henry Wace, eds., *NPNF2*, Vol. VI (Grand Rapids, Michigan: W.B. Eerdmans Publishing Company, 1994), pp. 159-160: "It was then that in the presence of all Rome (in the basilica which formerly belonged to that Lateranus who perished by the sword of Cæsar) she stood in the ranks of the penitents and exposed before bishop, presbyters, and people—all of whom

wept when they saw her weep—her dishevelled hair, pale features, soiled hands and unwashed neck … She laid bare her wound to the gaze of all, and Rome beheld with tears the disfiguring scar which marred her beauty … That face by which she had once pleased her second husband she now smote with blows." See H.C. Lea, *History of Auricular Confession and Indulgences*, vol. I, p. 20, for whom, contrary to what Foucault says, "such spontaneous manifestations of repentance must have been uncommon indeed thus to excite [Jerome's] admiration."

34. Saint Irénée (Iraneaus of Lyons), *Adversus haereses/Contre les hérésies*, I, 13, 5, critical ed. A. Rousseau and L. Doutreleau (Paris: Cerf, SC, no. 264, 1979), vol. 2, p. 201. The words *tas amartias* ("her sins") do not appear in the Greek text of this edition (nor in that of U. Mannucci [Rome: Forzani & Socii, "Bibliotheca Sanctorum Patrum et Scriptorum ecclesiasticorum, 1907], p. 178) which contains: *ton apanta*, "her transgression." As P. Chevallier has shown, "Foucault et les sources patristiques," p. 140, basing himself on Foucault's notebook, the latter takes his quotations from the article of H. Holstein, "L'exhomologèse dans l'Adversus Haereses' de saint Irénée," *Recherches de Science Religieuse*, 35, 1948, p. 282. The error of transcription would be explained by a confusion with the text of the *Didache*. English translation by Alexander Roberts and William Rambaut, Iraneaus of Lyons, *Against Heresies*, Book I, ch. XIII, 5, in Alexander Roberts, James Donaldson, and A. Cleveland Coxe, eds., *ANF*, Vol. 1, p. 335: "she spent her whole time in the exercise of public confession."

35. Ibid., III, 4 (Paris: Cerf, SC, no. 211, 2nd revised and corrected ed., 2002), p. 51; *Against Heresies*, Book III, ch. IV, 5, p. 417.

36. Tertullien, *De paenitentia/La pénitence*, XII, 7, trans. Labriolle (see above, note 31), p. 51: "The sinner … knows that God has instituted exomologesis to restore him in grace; SC, p. 189: "*Peccator restituendo sibi institutam a Domino exomologesin sciens*"; Tertullian, *On Repentance*, ch. XII, p. 665: "*exomologesis* has been instituted by the Lord for his [the sinner's] restoration."

37. Ibid., Fr.: "For a long time, this king [the king of Babylon (see Daniel, 4, 29-33)] offered to God the sacrifice of his penance (*paenitentiam immolarat*); he fulfilled the exomologesis (*exomologesin operatus*) in a sordid humiliation of seven years; his nails, grown wildly, were like those of the eagles, and his disordered hair recalled the bristling mane of the lion. Hard treatment!"; Eng.: "Long time had he [the king of Babylon] offered to the Lord his repentance, working out his *exomologesis* by a seven years' squalor, with his nails wildly growing after the eagle's fashion, and his unkempt hair wearing the shagginess of a lion. Hard handling!"

38. Ibid., IX, 1, trans. Labariolle, p. 41. All the editions (PL, Hemmer, and SC) contain the words "*operosior probatio*." It is therefore likely that the variant "*laboriosior probatio*" is Foucault's (who directly translates the Latin text here); Eng., ibid., ch. IX, 1, p. 664: "The narrower, then, the sphere of action of this second and only (remaining) repentance, the more laborious is its probation."

39. Ibid., IX, 3. Latin text of the SC edition, p. 180: "*exomologesis prosternendi et humilificandi hominis disciplina est*"; Eng., ibid.: "And thus *exomologesis* is a discipline for man's prostration and humiliation, enjoining a demeanor calculated to move mercy. With regard also to the very dress and food …."

40. Ibid.: "*conversationem iniungens misericordiae inlicem, de ipso quoque habitu atque victu.*" Genoude, p. 212 translates: "his appearance and his table," and Mounier, in the SC edition, p. 181: "the way he dresses and feeds himself"; Eng.: "the very dress and food."

41. See the previous note. Munier, like Genoude, translates this as "a conduct"; Eng., "a demeanor."

42. Ibid., trans. Labriolle, p. 41; Eng., ibid.: "commands (the penitent) to lie in sackcloth and ashes, to cover his body in mourning, to lay his spirit low in sorrows, to exchange for severe treatment the sins which he has committed; moreover, to know no food and drink but such as is plain,—not for the stomach's sake, to wit, but the soul's; for the most part, however, to feed prayers on fastings, to groan, to weep and make outcries unto the Lord your God; to bow before the feet of the presbyters, and kneel to God's dear ones; to enjoin on all the brethren to be ambassadors to bear his deprecatory supplication (before God). All this *exomologesis* (does), that it may enhance repentance."

43. Ibid., X, 1, p. 43: "And yet, I presume that most avoid this duty, or defer it from day to day, because they fear to display themselves in public (*ut publicationem sui*)"; Eng., ibid., ch. X, p. 664: "Yet most men either shun this work, as being a public exposure of themselves, or else defer it from day to day." See Munier, Introduction, p. 90: "[Exomologesis] was established

through a humiliating approach, which, for the penitent, was equivalent to a confession (*aveu*) of his sinful condition before the whole Christian community (*publicationem sui*)."

44. Foucault omits the words: "from day to day."

45. Ibid.; Eng., ibid.: "Yet most men either shun this work, as being a public exposure of themselves, or else defer it from day to day. I presume (as being) more mindful of modesty than of salvation."

46. St. Ambroise, *De paenitentia/La pénitence*, I, 16, 90, pp. 125-127: "I wish that the guilty hopes for forgiveness and requests it with tears, that he requests it with groans, that he request it with the tears of all the people, that he implore to be forgiven. And when for the second or third time communion has been deferred, that he consider he has implored too weakly; that he increase his tears; that he returns making himself even more pitiable; that he embrace with his arms the feet (of Jesus), cover them with kisses, wash them with his tears, not release them so that Jesus may say of him too: 'His many sins are forgiven, for he loved much.'"; Saint Ambrose, *Concerning Repentance*, Book I, ch. XVI, 90, p. 343: "I am willing, indeed, that the guilty man should hope for pardon, should seek it with tears and groans, should seek it with the aid of the tears of all the people, should implore forgiveness; and if communion be postponed two or three times, that he should believe that his entreaties have not been urgent enough, that he must increase his tears, must come again even in greater trouble, clasp the feet of the faithful with his arms, kiss them, wash them with tears, and not let them go, so that the Lord Jesus may say of him too: 'His sins which are many are forgiven, for he loved much.'"

47. See P. Adnès, "Larmes," DS, IX, 1976, col. 293, for the Eastern tradition: "It is the purifying power of tears that the great Eastern spirituals generally emphasize [quotations from John Chrysostom, Barsanuphius, and John Climacus]...Gregory Nazienzen speaks of tears as of a fifth baptism, the four others being, in order of increasing perfection, allegorical baptism, of Moses in the water of the Red Sea, John the Baptist, which was purely of repentance, of Christ in the Spirit, of the martyr in blood. The baptism of tears is in a sense more painful than that of the martyr (*Oratio* 39, 17, PG, 36, 353-356)"; and 298 for the less frequent occurrence of the theme in the West; B. Müller, *Der Weg des Weinens. Die Tradition des "Penthos" in den Apophthgegmata Patrum* (Göttingen: Vandenhoeck und Ruprecht, 2000), ch. 10: "Die Tränentaufe." See also above note 1 (with reference to *Quis dives salvetur?*).

48. See above, p. 207 and note 33.

49. See below, lecture of 26 March 1980, with regard to *discretio* in monastic spiritual direction.

50. Molière, *Le Tartuffe* (1664), Act III, scene 6, 1074-1076. The last line actually finishes with the words: "there has ever been." It is at the beginning of *Dom Juan*, I, 1, in the mouth of Sganarelle, that we find the expression: "the greatest villain that has ever walked on earth."

ten

12 MARCH 1980

> *The coupling of the detailed verbalization of fault and exploration of oneself. Its origin: neither the procedures of baptism nor those of penance, but the monastic institution.* ∽ *Techniques of testing the soul and public manifestation (*publication*) of oneself before Christianity. Verbalization of fault and exploration of oneself in Greek and Roman Antiquity. Difference from Christianity.* ∽ *(*III*) The practice of spiritual direction (*direction de conscience*). Its main characteristics: a free, voluntary, unlimited bond aiming at access to a certain relationship of self to self. Comment on the relation between the structure of political authority and the practice of direction. Non-institutional and institutional practices (*philosophical schools*) of direction in Greece and Rome. A fundamental technique: examination of conscience. How it differs from Christian examination of conscience. Two examples of ancient examination of conscience: the Pythagorean* Carmen aureum; *Seneca's* De ira, III, 36.

WE HAVE SEEN THAT in the Christianity of the first centuries, the believer was obliged to manifest his truth in two clearly defined and ritualized circumstances. First, when he is on the path that should lead him to the truth, that is, broadly speaking, [during] preparation for baptism, he is subject to a series, a set of procedures that constitute the test of the soul, the *probatio animae*.[1] Second, when he has become a Christian, once baptized, if he happens to fall again and commit a sin, at any rate a sin sufficiently grave to create a problem about his membership of the Church, then he has a procedure available to him that does not exactly assure him of God's forgiveness but enables him to make out the possibility of that forgiveness. This procedure is penance, and here, in the course of this penance, he has the obligation to manifest, in a partially different way, his own truth, and this is what Tertullian called *publicatio sui*, which I talked about last week, that public manifestation (*publication*) of self that may be characterized by the term exomologesis that was used in the second and third centuries to designate the manifestation of the sinner's state during penance.

I think there are two things to note with regard to these two series of tests, these two types of manifestation of truth, *probatio animae, publicatio sui*. First, the quite limited part of verbalization. Of course, you remember, there is a verbal part in the *probatio animae* as well as in the *publicatio sui*, in the tests in preparation for baptism, the tests of the catechumenate, as well as in the tests of exomologesis. For example, in the catechumenate there is recourse to questioning of the candidate, the postulant, as well as to testimony. In penance [also], there is recourse to testimony, [and] even to written certificates. And we know that in exomologesis, the great dramatic exomologesis to which the penitent was urged at the moment of his reconciliation, he had to proclaim his faults, to declare himself sinner, to cry out his sin and his sinful state. But what we do not observe in these rites of the *probatio* or in the rites of exomologesis, is the presence of the verbalization of sins understood as the analytical description of the sin with its characteristics and circumstances. What we do not observe is the presence of a definition, an assignation of the subject's responsibility in his sin. What is involved, in short, are all-encompassing and dramatic expressions of the sinner's state. There is not a self-accusatory verbalization of the sin by the sinner himself.

So, verbalization plays a limited part and, second, there is no procedure of knowledge of self. That is to say the subject is not asked, either in these tests or in the exomologesis, to know himself. He is asked to show himself. He is asked to manifest himself. But there is no self-exploration, no journey to the interior of oneself, no discovery by the subject of things that he does not know deep within himself. He has nothing else to do but manifest what he is, to manifest his state. There is no question, either in the catechumen's *probatio* or the penitent's exomologesis, of searching deep within oneself for some kind of knowledge of self that one does not yet possess.

[I think that] the appearance of these two procedures, first, the detailed verbalization of the sin by the subject who committed it and, second, the procedures of knowledge, discovery, and exploration of oneself, and the coupling of these two procedures, that of the detailed verbalization of the sin and that of the exploration of oneself, is an important phenomenon, [the] appearance [of which] in Christianity and, generally, in the Western world, marks, I believe, the beginning of an ultimately very lengthy process in which the subjectivity of Western man is developed—and by subjectivity I understand the mode of relation of self to self. What is important and, I think, decisive—anyway, it is something of the history [of this] that I would like to sketch out, to see at least some of its main reference points—is this coupling of "truth-telling about oneself" whose function is to erase the evil and "transit of self"* from the unknown to the known, giving oneself to oneself and in one's own eyes a status of object to be known at the same time as one verbalizes the sins in order to erase them, getting oneself to exist as object of knowledge at the moment that, through verbalization, one provides oneself with the means to bring it about that the sin no longer exists or at any rate is erased, is forgivable. It seems to me that this interplay between the inexistence or the erasure of the sin and the emergence of self in a process of knowledge of self by self is an important phenomenon and one that appears in Christianity. It appears in Christianity relatively late on, for if I have emphasized both the procedures that accompanied preparation for baptism and those of penance, it is precisely in order to show you that if, both in one and the other, the necessity for the subject to manifest himself in truth did in actual fact exist, if it was well marked, emphatic, ritualized, and had its rules and codes, this manifestation of self did not take the form of a coupling between the verbalization of the sin for the purpose of its erasure and the exploration of oneself for the purpose of passing from the unknown to the known.

When do we find the coupling of these two procedures, verbalization of oneself and passage of self from the unknown to the known, self-exploration? We do not find it in baptism. As paradoxical as it may

---

* The quotation marks correspond to the written form in the manuscript.

be—at least, as surprising as it may be for us now—we do not find it in penance. It is during the seventh and eighth centuries, and following a number of episodes, which I may or may not have the time to recount, but no matter, that [the coupling is brought about]* and the exploration of oneself and the detailed verbalization of sin becomes one of the main components of penance. But this is late on: [in the] seventh and eighth centuries; ultimately it requires a whole change in, I shall say, the juridical functioning of penance. Above all it requires that penance cease to be a unique status, granted to the penitent once and once only, and become a sort of recurrent and repeated behavior that has to be deployed, prompted, encouraged whenever one has sinned.[2]

The coupling of the detailed verbalization of sin by the subject who committed it with exploration of oneself in order to know oneself is due neither to the institution of baptism nor to that of penance. We owe this coupling to a third type of institution, the monastic institution, and its addition of a third theme, that of ascesis and continuous improvement in ascesis, to the Christian themes of access to the truth and relapse in baptism and penance. Roughly speaking, the appearance of this coupling of verbalization of sin and self-exploration is not found in baptism and it is not found in penance. It seems to me that the reason for this is that in baptism and in penance and forgiveness it is not a question of grasping the subject as he is, deep down, in his identity and continuity, but rather of making the manifestation of the truth a sort of de-identification of the subject, since it involves turning someone who was a sinner into someone who is no longer a sinner. It is the break in the subject that calls for the, so to speak, paradoxical necessity of a manifestation of the truth. There is a text that is characteristic on this subject in Saint [Ambrose],† in which, to describe *metanoia*, repentance (*pénitence*), he cites the following anecdote: a young man has a relationship with a young woman and loves her; he leaves for a long voyage and returns a convert; he returns a convert and, of course, no longer sees his old fiancé; one day he meets her in the street; she approaches him and says: But don't you recognize me? "It's me, *ego sum*," and the young man replies: "*Sed ego non sum ego*, but I am no longer me."[3] It is this break in

---

* M.F.: it takes place.
† M.F.: John Chrysostom.

the subject's identity in repentance and baptism that is the point that makes necessary the manifestation of the truth, because the manifestation of the truth of the subject is what frees the subject from his own truth.

On the other hand, there will be a strongly continuous structure in monastic life and monastic ascesis, since it involves the subject advancing every day, every moment, every instant towards a continuously greater perfection, and at this point the subject's relationship of truth to himself will necessarily have to be structured in a completely different way than that of the break and the *ego non sum ego* that characterized the other manifestations of truth of baptism and penance.

This, then, is what I would like to talk about now, that is to say the relationship between the verbalization of sin and exploration of oneself. A retroactive comment, however. [With regard to] the catechumenate, the test of the soul, exomologesis and the public manifestation of oneself, I was, of course, talking only of phenomena absolutely internal and specific to Christianity and I proceeded as if all these things arose with Christianity. It is clear that this is not true, that this is not what happened, and that there was, of course, already a long history in paganism behind techniques of the test of the soul as well as those of public self-manifestation. For example, the test of catechumens, the *probation animae* that characterizes catechumenate depended on a long historical tradition of initiatory methods and rites. In the ancient religions, there was no initiation, and so no access to the truth, without purification of the subject and testing that authenticated him. So you have there a whole kind of prehistory of the Christian catechumenate. In the same way, with regard to penance, the obligation to manifest oneself publicly, to manifest oneself as a sinner, to make exomologesis, also has a long history behind it. In pagan religion, in Greek and Roman religion, when one has sinned, the need for, or in any case the effectiveness of a solemn public self-manifestation (*publication*) to the god is quite normal, not only in order to manifest one's wretchedness, according to the rite of supplication to which someone submits when misfortune befalls him, but also* when one has committed an offence and, a fortiori, when fault and misfortune go together. This is clear in Sophocles' *Oedipus*: when he

---

* M.F. adds: solemn supplication.

arrives blind and supplicant, Oedipus manifests both his wretchedness and his sin. A sort of exomologesis: I am a criminal, I have committed a sin and I am wretched.

We also find practices of manifestation of oneself of a more popular kind. For example, in a series of temples, and in particular in the temple of Knidos, which was the temple of both healing and repentance, a series of stele dating from the Hellenistic period have been found on which those who have committed sins acknowledge, confess (*avouent*) their sins and engrave their name, the acknowledgment [of their] sin and, possibly, the nature [of the latter]. And this was called, precisely, exomologesis.[4] [So,] to obtain forgiveness, one engraved a stele with one's sin and one's name. In Eastern religions also, of course, we find a whole series of procedures of redemption and pardon, obtained by declaring, manifesting, and as if exalting one's own transgression. In Juvenal, for example, we [read] a description [of] the practice of the priests of Anubis who, as a condition for granting pardon to those who had transgressed, demanded that they solemnly confess (*aveu*) their misdeeds. Juvenal recounts: "It is the priest who intercedes for the wife when, on the holy day of strict obedience, she illicitly lays with her husband. This violation of the conjugal bed deserves a severe penalty. The silver serpent was seen to move its head. But thanks to his tears and learned gibberish, the priest obtains the pardon of Osiris. A fat goose and a small cake, and he will let himself be bribed."[5]

So, there is a whole non-Christian history of these truth rites. But if there is a prehistory of the *probatio animae* and of the *publicatio sui*, the pre-Christian history of the verbalization of sin and of the exploration of oneself is on a quite different scale, and I do not think we can understand the verbalization of sin in Christianity unless we go back a bit and look at what happened in Greek and Roman philosophy, in Greek and Roman thought and morality. Actually, the relationship between paganism and Christianity raises a number of problems from every point of view, and from this point of view in particular, inasmuch as there is a bit of a temptation to trace something like a direct descent of Christian practice from some major precepts of ancient philosophy and moral philosophy. We have the impression that we can draw a direct line from the *gnothi seauton* to the obligation of the examination of conscience in Evagrius Ponticus, Cassian, Saint Jerome, and Saint Augustine.[6] Now what I would like to show you is that, if it is true that there is a line of descent, if it is true that, roughly speaking, the same type of practices are transmitted over the centuries and take root at the very heart of Christianity, in actual fact, the forms of verbalization, the forms of self-exploration, and the way in which verbalization and self-exploration are coupled are completely different in paganism and, in truth, in different forms of pagan religion or philosophy, and in Christianity.

I do not think that the coupling of verbalization of sin and exploration of oneself can really be understood unless it is situated within the practice in which it originated or, at any rate, in which it found its maximum form of development, in Antiquity as well as in Christianity: this is what is called direction, spiritual direction (*direction de conscience*), the direction of souls, the direction of individuals. I think that the practice, the technique of direction, is something very important whose history, sadly, has never been studied, or at any rate, not directly and for itself.[7]

What is the direction of individuals? What is this direction of souls, of conscience, which is traditionally called, well, in Greek especially, the government of souls, *kubernai*? A definition which seems obvious and immediately comes to mind is that in direction an individual submits to and leaves to another a whole series of decisions of a private kind in the sense that they normally, usually, and statutorily fall outside the domains of political constraint and legal obligation. In the domain where political constraint and legal obligation do not apply, direction requires one to rely on the will of the other. Where one is free as an individual, one leaves the decision to another person.

Rely on, submit to: I think we need to reflect on this a bit, because I do not think this submission of will to the will of someone else in direction should be understood as a transfer of sovereignty. What I mean is that it is not a matter of the process described by jurists when they try to analyze the way in which someone who is free, who has his sovereign will, not subject to anyone, agrees to cede this will and transfer it to someone else. In fact, in direction there is no transfer of sovereignty. I will even say: there is no renunciation of will by the individual. In direction one does not renounce one's own will. One simply wants one's will to be subject to the will of someone else. That is to say that the person directed is the one who says: I want the other to tell me what I must will. I refer myself to the other's will as the principle of my own will, but I must myself will this other's will. In the juridical transfer of sovereignty, one ceases to will, one transfers all or a part of one's will to someone else who, as a result, takes the place of your will, and is, as it were, its lieutenant or representative. The political power wills in my place and imposes its will on me, whether I will it or not. All I can say is that I willed it, provided that there was, at a given moment, a social contract in the course of which I was able to say: I want someone to will in my place. There is no social contract in direction because there is no transfer of a part of will to another. There is someone who guides my will, who wants my will to want this or that. And I do not cede my own will, I continue to will, I continue to will to the end, but to will in every detail and at every moment what the other wants me to will. The two wills remain continuously present. One does not disappear to the advantage of the other. The two wills coexist, but they coexist with a bond between them in which one does not replace the other, in which one does not limit the other, but a bond that binds the two wills in such a way that they remain intact and permanent, but also in such a way that one wills wholly and always what the other wills. It is therefore, in the strict sense, a subordination of the will to the other, in which the two wills remain intact, but one willing always what the other wills.

The consequence of this is, of course, that this bond is one that in itself is free, voluntary and unlimited. In direction—and this is what distinguishes spiritual direction, or the direction of souls or individuals from any political or juridical structure—there is no sanction or coercion. The one directed always wants to be directed, and the direction will last, function, and unfold only insofar as the one directed still wants to be directed. And he is always free to cease wanting to be directed. If at any time a threat or sanction were to be introduced that meant that the person directed was thereby constrained, by whatever coercive means, to let himself be directed, then this would no longer be direction. The game of full freedom, in the acceptance of the bond of direction, is, I think, fundamental. And we see the proof of this by studying the history of this institution, by considering it for example—since it is maybe here that it has been most evident—in the organization of seminaries at the time of the Counter Reformation, in which, of course, confession is obligatory for seminarians, in which confession is a statutory, juridical obligation or, at any rate, arises from the internal law of the Church (such that sanctions can be imposed on someone who does not confess regularly, which he is obliged to do at least once a year). Seminarians are bound by confession, but they are also bound by direction.[8] That is to say all one can do is recommend that they have a director. One cannot impose any sanction on those who do not have a director, or on those who break off or change their direction. At the most one can give them advice. Furthermore, direction has no definite content. Direction is unlimited. It can go as far as either side wishes. It may concern absolutely every or only some aspects of existence. In other words, there is never any codification of direction; it does not have a juridical structure. There are techniques of direction, which are means for correlating the two wills that remain entirely intact, but the interplay of which is such that one of them always wills what the other wants it to will.

The third characteristic of direction then—the first being that it does not comprise any transfer of will, the second that it does not have a juridical structure and, consequently, neither sanctions nor limits—is the aim of direction: what is the point of direction and why would one get oneself directed, why does one get oneself or let oneself be directed, why does one want to be directed? Apparently, the answer could be: one wants to be directed simply so as to obtain something like happiness, wealth, [or] health. This is not the reason in fact, because if direction were obeying someone else as a means for obtaining wealth or health, then there would be an external aim of direction. There would be an external finalization and at least technical conditions for attaining that goal. In other words, there would be a sort of codification of direction in terms of that objective end. I think the true relationship of direction is that it fixes as its goal, not something like the wealth or health of the person who is directed, but something like perfection, or tranquility of the soul, or the absence of passions, self-control, beatitude, that is to say a certain relationship of self to self. That is to say the person directed does not seek an external end in direction, but an internal end understood as a modality of the relationship of self to self. Basically, the formula of direction is this: I freely obey what you will for me, I freely obey what you will that I will so that in this way I may establish a certain relationship to myself. And as a result, if we call subjectivation the formation of a definite relationship of self to self, then we can say that direction is a technique that consists in binding two wills in such a way that they are always free in relation to each other, in binding them in such a way that one wills what the other wills, for the purpose of subjectivation, that is to say access to a certain relationship of self to self. The other and the other's will are freely accepted by me so that I may establish a certain relationship of myself to myself. This seems to me to be the general meaning we can give to this notion of direction.

Of course, this is only a very general formula that involves a whole range of variations, modulations, and diverse integrations in institutional fields and multiple practices. Direction, of course, is not a specifically Christian practice. We find it in Ancient Greece and Rome, we find it in other civilizations, and here again, the West is far from having a privileged claim to it. You find highly developed practices of direction in Chinese, Japanese, and Hindu civilizations.

One more word of a general nature concerning direction. We are accustomed to seeing in direction a religious practice as opposed to coercion or the exercise of political power. In a way this is true, and I have stressed the structural difference between political subordination, the exercise of political authority, and the specific form of subordination in direction. Nevertheless, it would be completely wrong to imagine that there is no relation, no connection between the structure of political authority and the practice of direction. After all, most, if not all, well, a great many political utopias are precisely dreams of the exercise of a political power that takes the form of, or at any rate is extended to the real and effective direction of individuals. The Platonic city[9] or Thomas More's city[10] are political structures developed to the point at which they end up with the complete and exhaustive direction of individuals. We could also say that in the political functioning of both Catholic and Protestant societies at the end of the sixteenth and the beginning of the seventeenth century, we had very subtle, thought out, and organized combinations of the development of an administrative political power and a whole series of institutions of spiritual direction, of the direction of souls and individuals, again both Protestant and Catholic. So forms of direction and forms of political functioning may well be heterogeneous, but their coexistence, linkages, and reciprocal supports are no less evident.

With regard to religious institutions, we should note that it is true that the direction of individuals is a practice that, to a not inconsiderable extent, is of religious inspiration, or at any rate develops within religious institutions. But we should not forget that direction in Antiquity, for example, which we will talk about in a moment, was absolutely not of a religious order. It was fundamentally of a philosophical character and, to a degree, we can say that it was not anti-religious but had only relatively distant relations with religion. Medicine in Antiquity, and still today to some extent, is composed, is combined with a whole series of activities of direction. We could say that it would be interesting to study the organization of political parties in the contemporary world inasmuch as a whole part comprises institutions and practices of direction in addition to the specifically political structure of the organization.[*][11]

Now, let's take a look at this in Greek and Roman Antiquity to see how, on the one hand, direction was practiced and how, within this direction, the coupling of the verbalization of faults with the exploration of oneself might take place. In Greek and Roman Antiquity we find practices of direction in different forms. Roughly speaking there are, if you like, two major forms. Spiritual direction, [first of all], in what could be called the free state, as it were, in the form of discontinuous, episodic relationships that are absolutely individual and with no precise institutional context. Quite simply, relatively early on, in the fifth and at the beginning of the fourth century there were, for example, consultations for a fee. Antiphon the sophist,[12] for example, had an office for consultations in Athens, where those who found themselves going through a bad patch in their life—adversity, misfortune, bereavement, or whatever—came to consult him and, for a fee, Antiphon gave them advice on the conduct to adopt to face up to these difficult situations. Generally speaking, this was one of the activities of physicians. Galen[13] gave advice not only to those who suffered physical ills, but also to those who had moral ills and who, at a particular point in their life, felt the need to be guided and advised in their daily [life]. But beyond these consultations for a fee, which, in that respect, were regular and part of a market, direction could also take the form of a purely free and benevolent act of friendship. Conversations, exchange of correspondence, long letters written in the form of short treatises of consolation

---

* Manuscript: "It is not doubt more interesting to study the organization of political parties as institutions of direction than as ideologies akin to religion."

or encouragement to someone who was a friend or just someone with whom one had a relationship and who asked you to help him: all of this constituted sorts of little episodes, fragments of the activity of direction. It involved occasional relationships, generally responding to a definite situation, concerning a setback, exile, bereavement, or a more general crisis. For example, Serenus writes to Seneca telling him: Yes, presently I am changing philosophy, Epicureanism no longer satisfies me; I am becoming initiated into Stoicism. Only I am making no headway, it's not working and you must help me. And Seneca gives him a consultation and, for a certain time, acts as his spiritual guide.[14]

So much for forms of direction that are not immediately institutional. You also have continuous, dense, strongly institutionalized forms of direction: those, of course, that are found in the schools of philosophy. In these the individual was committed for a relatively long period, and sometimes until the end of his life. And the problem was no longer just a crisis or an aspect of his existence for which he sought the aid of direction, it was every aspect of his life that was taken into account in the life of the philosophical school: his food, clothing, sexual relations, whether or not he should marry, his passions, his political attitude, were all subjects for advice or prescriptions of direction. A general regimen of existence was imposed, or rather proposed to those who really wanted to practice this philosophy and become integrated in this school of philosophy. This activity of guidance was carried out within what were often strict and hierarchical institutional structures. For example, in the Epicureans there was a whole activity of spiritual guidance, with the hierarchy of those who were not thought to need guidance themselves, as being able to guide but not needing, never having needed to be guided—and, in truth, there was only one in this position, Epicurus himself; then there were those who had needed a guide at a particular moment—this was Epicurus' successor, Metrodorus; then there were those who had needed a guide at some time and who needed the continuous assistance of direction to support them throughout their life.[*15] There was also a system of consultations. Group consultations, [with] the *kathēgētēs* who was able to direct a group, to give indications valid for a certain number of individuals [as] a regimen of life. But,

---

* The manuscript specifies: Hermarchus.

much more developed and learned were those who had the right to be a *kathēgemōn*.[16] The *kathēgemōn* was someone with the right to practice individual direction. He addressed himself individually to individuals or individuals approached him and asked for advice, and regularly, each month, each week, there was a discussion in the course of which the *kathēgemōn* directed the person for whom he was responsible.[17]

These practices of direction, whether in the dense and continuous institutional form of schools of philosophy, or in the form of those simple episodes I was talking about before, employed many and varied processes and techniques, and I think that, precisely here, verbal techniques, the different processes of discourse—debate, demonstration, refutation, exhortation—were very important and developed within these practices. In other words, it is true that, as Vernant has shown,[18] in the Greek world all these discursive forms were to a large extent developed in the public arena, and on the basis of the public arena, whether in the judicial space or in the space of political debate, but they were also developed within these practices of direction in relationships between individuals.

Now in these verbal practices of direction and in the middle of these many techniques—advice, exhortation, refutation, demonstration— there was an essential, fundamental component, which was precisely examination of conscience. [In Greco-Roman direction it constituted]* the hinge, inasmuch as it was the means by which the director's hold over the one being directed could take effect and the element through which the one being directed could take up on his own account the operation of the director. Tell me what you are so that I can tell you what you should do: the director could not direct if the directed did not examine his conscience and display it before his director. Conversely, the one being directed said: See what I am, look at what I am able to do so that I may be what you tell me it is necessary to be. I cannot understand your lesson, I cannot will what you want unless I have a clear and distinct consciousness of what I am and what I can do. The hinge between the director's will and the will of the one being directed, the need for this hinge in order that the will of the one being directed does

---

* Part of sentence reconstructed on the basis of the manuscript (folio 20). This passage of the recording, which corresponds to the changing sides of the cassette, presents in fact a short gap.

indeed reproduce the director's will and freely wills what the director wills, entailed, at the center of the mechanism, the practice of examination of conscience.

But I do not think it is sufficient to situate the examination of conscience in this way, because, in truth, there are many ways of [practicing it].* And I think—this is what I would like to stress—it would be completely mistaken to say that, since the examination of conscience existed in Greek and Roman direction, then this is what we find again in Christianity. In fact, examination of conscience in Greek and Roman direction and examination of conscience in Christianity are significantly different from and cannot be assimilated to each other. Greek and Roman examination of conscience brings with it a number of effects of knowledge (*connaissance*), a number of effects of subjectivation. Christian examination of conscience brings with it, I believe, quite different effects of knowledge and quite different modes of subjectivation. From this point of view, the subjectivation of Western man is Christian, not Greco-Roman. Because, after all, one can examine one's conscience in many ways. One can change the very nature of what one examines. One may examine, for example, what one has done, but one may also examine what one has to do and what one is going to do. One may examine the situation in which one finds oneself. One may also examine possible situations in which one might find oneself. One may ask oneself, for example: What should I do if I were exiled? What should I do were I to know that I was going to die? What should I do if someone close to me were to die? So, the field on which examination of conscience focuses is completely variable, and you will see that in Greco-Roman philosophy it is by no means the same as in Christianity. The instruments used to perform this examination of conscience may also change. One may use concentration, the immediate and present attention of self to self. One may concentrate on oneself and, as it were, try to see oneself or grasp oneself, either in one's immobility or, on the contrary, in one's change. One may use memory and try to know everything one has done or said or thought during the day (or in the week, the month, the year, or since birth). One may use the virtual discourse one delivers to oneself. One may use explicit

_____

* M.F.: of making the examination of conscience.

verbalization, with a confession (*aveu*) to the other person. One may use writing, either writing for oneself or for others. And then, finally, there may be completely different and varied objectives. Why does one examine oneself? To discover something unknown, an explanation we lack, the reason for doing or feeling certain things. But one may also pursue other aims. One may examine oneself in order to assure mastery of oneself and to drive out anything, passion for example, that would risk weakening this self-control. One may examine oneself in order to gauge one's progress. One may examine oneself to try to purify oneself of one's faults. In short, you can see that the practices of examination of conscience, their aim, their instrument, and their object may change profoundly. I think this appears clearly when we compare Greco-Roman and Christian examination.

Greco-Roman examination first of all (well, no doubt I will only have time to talk about this today, and no more). I will take two or three examples, or rather one very old example, the oldest testimony we have of the practice in Greek culture, that is to say Pythagorean examination of conscience. And then, in contrast, I will take examination of conscience at the end of the day in the Stoic philosopher spiritual directors of the Roman epoch, principally Seneca and Epictetus—well, Seneca in particular.

First, the Pythagoreans. You know that the invention of examination of conscience is attributed to the Pythagoreans. This is quite traditional. You find it constantly in the Greek and Roman authors, and also in Christian authors, and Saint Chrysostom will still cite Pythagoras and his verses as evidence of the importance of the examination of conscience.[19] In fact, the text available to us now is the one that was transmitted by the famous *Carmen aureum*,[20] a late text which seems to have contributed some, if you like, modernist elements—or elements specific to the Hellenistic or Roman period—to the old Pythagorean tradition. Well, here is the whole text as passed on in the *Carmen aureum*: "Do not allow gentle sleep to creep into your eyes before having examined every action of your day: In what have I sinned? What have I done? What have I failed to do that ought to have been done? Start with the first"—the first of these actions—"and go through them all. And then, if you have sinned, rebuke yourself; but if you have acted well, rejoice."[21] So, the experts (of which I am not one, for sure) have distinguished the old part in this text from the modern part, or that part added in the Hellenistic period. The old part is certainly in the first two lines: "Do not allow gentle sleep to creep into your eyes before having examined every action of your day." The middle part of the text—"In what have I sinned? What have I done? What have I failed to do that ought to have been done?"—seems doubtful. The end—"Start with the first and go through them all. And then, if you have sinned ..."—is certainly a recent addition.[22]

Let's take the first nucleus, simply to point out two or three features. You see that—"Do not allow gentle sleep to creep into your eyes before having examined every action of your day"—involves a retrospective examination. Once again, examination of conscience does not have to be retrospective. We will see that with the Stoics it is very often prospective; examination of what one is going to do. So, it is regular, it must take place every evening, and, second, it focuses on actions. It does not focus on feelings, states of the soul, or intentions, but well and truly on what one has done. Third, although this is not in the first two lines, but in the third [and] fourth—and it is not certain that they are absolutely authentic—it does seem that, even in the ancient form, the function of this retrospective and regular examination focusing on actions was to sift and discriminate between good and bad actions.

What was the meaning of this retrospective exercise of the examination of good or bad actions? Inasmuch as we know that Pythagoreanism presented itself as a rule of life, a regimen of life shared by a number of people and practiced in closed and institutionalized communities, and that the aim of this Pythagorean life was for the individual to gain access to a certain state of purity and perfection, it may be thought that the function of this examination was to gauge the progress made each day: more or less good actions, more or less bad actions. No doubt. But it also seems that it had two other important and interesting functions. First, the pure exercise of memory, inasmuch as memory, remembering, and remembering as much as possible, was fundamental for the Pythagoreans. There was a fundamental, radical affiliation between knowledge (*savoir*) and memory: knowing and remembering have the same nature, and the pure exercise of memory, pure mnemotechnics was both a spiritual and intellectual exercise. It was an instrument of knowledge (*connaissance*).[23] In a passage where Cicero is talking about this [Pythagorean]* examination, he says that it was "*memoriae exercendae gratia*,"† to exercise his memory.[24]

Another aspect of the [Pythagorean] examination is the purificatory preparation for sleep. Because for the Pythagoreans sleeping was not just sleeping. It was opening one's soul to an absolutely material reality that was manifested to you by the dream, and the quality of the dream indicated both the state of the soul's purity and was like its reward or sanction. Insofar as the dream put you in communication with a world that was, as it were, representative of your state of purity, it was clear that the quality of the dream was absolutely essential, as sign or as reward. One prepared one's dreams moreover by listening to music or by inhaling perfumes. It seems that for the [Pythagoreans] the function of the evening examination of the day was to purify, to classify the good and bad, to rejoice for good actions one had been able to perform and, as a result, to prepare well the good dream.[25] And finally, sleep—this was the other aspect of the meaning of sleep for the [Pythagoreans]—prefigures death. In preparing for one's sleep, one prepared as it were for one's death, or one prepared the prefiguration of one's death.[26] So this preparation for sleep was undoubtedly one of the fundamental components of the [Pythagorean] examination.

So, memory exercise on the one hand, preparation for sleep [on the other]. [Far from the]‡ problem of making the individual feel guilty, [of] the individual's knowledge of his own faults and the reason for them, there was clearly a prospective intention in relation to sleep, although the examination was retrospective with regard to the day.

Let us now take a quite different example, from much later, that of Roman Stoicism. Here I would like to give you two examples, but since I do not have the time, I will take just one§: it is found in Seneca, in *De ira*, Book III, 36.[27] This is a very famous text that is also frequently

---

* M.F.: Stoic.

† Foucault adds: In *De senectute*, I think ... no, I no longer know where he says it.

‡ M.F.: much less than the.

§ M.F. leaves out here pp. 24-27 of the manuscript devoted to the letter of Serenus to Seneca at the beginning of *De tranquillitate animi*, I, 1-18 (we put the references in brackets):

  "Sen[eca], *De tranquillitate animi*. [The examination] made by the disciple when he has not arrived at autonomy. Serenus. General examination, i.e., on the state of his soul

  —at a particular moment of crisis, uncertainty,

  —and in order to confide in his interlocutor, or rather in the form of a confidence, a letter.

  a. The form: consultation, clearly medical

cited by Christian authors, and this is what Seneca says. First of all, he invokes the example of the philosopher Sextius who, at the end of the day, before retiring to his nightly rest, questioned his soul. And he asked his soul: "Of what fault have you cured yourself today? What vice have you struggled against? In what way have you become better?" Commenting on this example, Seneca says: I do the same thing. "What is finer than this habit of surveying one's day?" (he uses the word *executer* which means "to shake out, to shake so as to make fall": as one shakes a tree to make the fruit fall, or shakes clothes to get the dust out, so, as it were, one shakes one's day).[28] "What sleep after this review of these actions![29] How peaceful and deep it is,[30] when the soul has received its portion of praise or blame and, subject to its own control, when it has become," the text says, "*speculator sui*"—*speculator* is in fact a kind of inspector, controller, sometimes in the military sense of scout.* So, one is the scout, the controller, the inspector of oneself, one

---

"Why should I not tell you the truth, as to a physician?" [I, 2; Eng., "for why should I not admit the truth to you as to a physician?" p. 203]
request for remedy, and for this I will tell you my state so that you find the name of the malady (*tu morbo nomen invenies* [I, 4]).

But this medical consultation constitutes a sort of stage, a point one arrives at in a pedagogical process. Serenus is becoming initiated into Stoic philosophy. He learns, he advances: he exercises and strengthens his virtue. But he is not yet at the end of his difficulties. He feels that the exercise must continue. Now in the progress there is a moment of uncertainty. Stabilization. He does not know if habit does not bind him in an increasingly constraining way both to good and evil [I, 3]. He does not know if he is advancing or standing still. He will therefore expose his "*habitus*" [I, 2], the state in which he exists.

b. The object of the examination
His state: "distressing and tiresome," "neither sick nor in good health" [I, 1-2; Eng.: "I am complaining and fretful—I am neither sick nor well" p. 203].
Drawing up a balance sheet of forces: that which allows him to remain master of himself, that is to say that which pleases him without shaking his soul, without forcing it outside of itself; that which on the other carries it away, makes it escape its own control, draws it outside of itself. Test of "*placere*" [I, 5, 5, 7, 8, 10, 12] (tranquility)/*praestringer* [1,8] *concutere* [I, 9; II, 3] (movement).

Two domains, two axes:
—poverty-wealth, moderation-luxury
He is pleased with his modest fortune, does not seek to enrich himself, etc. But when he sees the wealth of others, his mind resists, but not his senses.
—private-public
As a Stoic who applies himself, he is concerned with public affairs, but in order to do good for others, not for himself. When he returns from the forum, he is happy at home, has no [ambition].
But sometimes, reading some[thing],[a] he gets carried away; he dreams [of immortality].[a]"
[a] Uncertain reading.

* The manuscript (folio 28) adds this reference: "Seneca (qu. naturelles, VI, 4): scouts of the hailstorm" [see *Quaestiones naturales*, IV, 6: "*speculatores futurae grandinis*"].

is subject to one's own censor—*censor*, of course[31]—and at this point the soul undertakes the trial of its own conduct.[32] It puts itself on trial, it takes cognizance of its own conduct, it catches hold of itself and investigates its own conduct: judicial metaphor. "I have taken this authority over myself, *utor hac potestate*, and every day I summon myself before myself, *causam dico**—again, juridical vocabulary. "When the light is lowered and my wife, familiar with my habit, has become silent, I examine with myself my whole day, *totum diem mecum scrutor*, and I take the measure again of my words and deeds, I measure them anew. I dissimulate nothing, I leave nothing out. Why would I fear any of my errors, when I can tell myself: See that you do not do it again, I forgive you today? Thus, in that discussion," Seneca says, "you spoke too aggressively, you reproached someone with too little reserve and you did not correct him. On the contrary, instead of correcting him, you offended him. See to it that in the future what you say is not only true, but that the person to whom you speak can bear the truth you tell him."[33]

This then is the Stoic examination. You can see that it has a quite different form from the Pythagorean examination, with, however, an important point in common: the remarkable identity of the immediate objective proposed. Like the Pythagoreans, Seneca says: If you want a good sleep, examine your conscience. Examination of conscience is therefore prospective; it is preparation for a good sleep. Examination of the day constitutes, as it were, an indispensable component in the regimen of life. One must be good when one is awake, but one must also be good when one sleeps. You will judge yourselves, although I am not very keen on these comparisons, concerning the possible relation between this Stoic examination and the Freudian conception of the censor (the word is in Seneca moreover), since it is the Freudian censor that, at the point where sleep and waking meet, prevents the drive or libido from waking you and, in order to keep you in sleep, elaborates what will become the dream.[34] In Seneca there is the idea of a censor that is also exercised at the seam of wakefulness and sleep, but in the other direction. It is a matter of exercising a censor when one is still awake in order to filter, as it were, the good and bad elements of the day, and minding that only the good will be able to figure in sleep [and] ensure the quality of a good

---

* The manuscript adds in the margin: "I plead my own cause."

sleep. The quality of a good sleep has physical and moral effects that are absolutely central for the regimen of life. So much for what concerns the aspect of preparation for sleep in the Stoic examination.

I have picked out the words regarding the second thing to note: the judicial form. But here we need to be a bit careful. It is certainly a judicial form. The text says that one exercises a *potestas* over oneself, that is to say an institutional power. Second, this *potestas* takes on the appearance of what? Well, of the functions of censor, of the investigating judge: I plead my own cause, *causam meam dico*, I investigate, I make investigations, search through my day, I take the measure again, he says, of my actions and gestures (that is to say I weigh up whether they are good or bad). A sort of judicial splitting: is not conscience becoming a sort of tribunal in which the subject has to become both accused and judge? In actual fact, I do not think this is entirely [the case], because you know that in Roman judicial practice there is not just a judge and an accused. There must be a judge, an accused, and an accuser. There cannot be an accused without an accuser. Now it is noticeable that there is no accuser in Seneca. We will see the character of the accuser arrive later, precisely in Christianity. You know who this will be: it will, of course, be Satan. We will then have a ternary structure. But [this is not the case] in Seneca. So there is indeed this judicial metaphor—one pleads one's own case, one investigates. But I think that the set of terms employed, the series of metaphors, with these words like censor, *scrutator, speculator* refer much more to an administrative procedure of inspection and verification, than to a judicial procedure of accusation with a verdict and sentence. Basically, we are in the world of administration. One has to become, not so much the judge of oneself, or the accused of oneself, or the accuser of oneself, or the accused who is going to reply to an accuser before oneself—I do not think this is the real scene represented by Seneca's Stoic examination of conscience. It is the scene of the auditor. It is the scene of the functionary inspector who, as it were, looks over the shoulder of the daily functionary to see whether he has done what he had to do. And the expression "I take the measure again of my faults and actions" does indeed indicate this exercise of verification characteristic of an administration that is split. One is the functionary of oneself, or rather the inspector of oneself—myself, who is the functionary of my own life. In the examination of conscience one has to be the official in charge of the correction of the operations that have been carried out—*scrutator, observator, censor*—and one discovers precisely *errores*, mistakes of management, of administration. It is less a matter of a judge condemning infractions than of an administrator who has to supervise the faults of management, the mistakes of management, and who, as a result, has to rectify them.

Now, what is involved in these mistakes of management? I think the two examples Seneca gives at the end of the passage are typical. He gives two examples of faults he could have made during the day. First, "you argued too sharply with ignorant people." This is what Seneca says to his soul, that is to say, if you like, what the inspector says to the manager. "You argued too sharply with ignorant people. You did not convince them or teach them anything. You wasted your time." First example. The second example is the following: "You wanted to correct someone, but you did so with such anger, so sharply, that in the end you did not correct him at all. He was offended and you achieved nothing." You see that [what is involved] here is, strictly speaking, not so much faults in the sense of infractions of a moral law, as of *errores*, mistakes. That is to say one set oneself a certain aim—to teach something to an ignorant person, to argue with someone so as to convince him of something and to correct his manner of doing or being—and then one bungled it, it didn't work. The mistake is defined in terms of the aim one set for oneself and not in terms of a moral law, as it were, behind us. And this matches up with, but I am not stressing this, the Stoic conception, very marked in Epictetus, that the fault can be defined only in terms of the aim one sets for oneself. Epictetus says: "Ask yourself first of all what you want to be. Wrestlers decide what they want to be and act accordingly." It is this alignment with the end that can define what counts as a fault.[35]

So, the aim of examination of conscience is to inspect, looking over the shoulder of the manager soul of life as it were, the aims that have been set and the way in which they have or have not been achieved. Hence, [the] important [point] in Seneca's text: what happens when one has discovered, when one knows that one has not done what one ought to have done? Is there repentance, self-punishment, and allocation of one's own guilt? Absolutely not. [Rather,] straight away, once the mistake has been discovered, there is the formulation of a rule of conduct for the future, a rule of conduct that has to enable one henceforth to attain the aim sought. There is not even an attempt to find the causes or roots of the fault; no etiological exploration of the fault committed. There is the effort to constitute straightaway a sort of operational schema for the future. It is a question of programming one's future conduct. For example: you disputed with ignorant people and wasted your time. But why did you waste your time? You wasted your time because you forgot a rule (well, here I am spelling out the text), a general rule that you did not but should have had in your mind: that those who have not yet learned anything in their life will learn nothing. And, consequently, rather than waste your time trying to teach people who are incapable of [learning], people who are now too old to be able to learn, you would do better to keep quiet and not waste your time. Examination of conscience therefore leads to this principle, which is in Seneca's text: those who have learned nothing will never learn anything. That is to say that examination of conscience enables one to establish and formulate a rational and constant principle for future circumstances. In the same way: You reproached someone too sharply, you wanted to correct him and you spoke so sharply that you offended him. What does pinpointing this fault lead to? It is not remorse, and it is not an etiological investigation. Simply, it leads to the formulation of the following rule: when one tells someone the truth, when one speaks the truth to someone, one must not [only]* be concerned that what one says is true. One must also be concerned about whether the person who hears it and to whom one is speaking is actually capable of receiving and accepting this truth. For to tell the truth to someone who is not capable of receiving the truth is to waste one's time. You see that, here again, the outcome of examination of conscience is the formulation of a rule of conduct, a programming of behavior.

In a sense, we have here the opposite of what will later be casuistry. The problem for casuistry is the following: take some general laws given by tradition, by authority; how can they be applied to a precise and particular case? Here, we have the opposite. We have a particular situation in the course of which one has not conducted oneself correctly (not having conducted oneself correctly means not attaining the objective one set for oneself). What will examination of conscience do on the basis of

---

* M.F.: simply.

that particular situation? It will enable one to formulate a general rule, or a more general rule, for the whole series of events or situations of the same type that may [arise].*

In conclusion we can say the following: [first], this Stoic examination is, of course, retrospective, since it goes through the day that has just gone by. It is evening, one is going to sleep, the wife is quiet, the light is dimmed, and one goes over the whole of the day. Retrospective examination. But you see that it is fundamentally turned towards the future, be it the future anterior, in the sense that one asks oneself: what was the aim that I set for myself? Towards what goal was I heading while doing this or that, and was my action actually in line with that goal, with that future? So, use of analysis in the future anterior and directed towards an aim in the simple future, since, starting from there, it now involves determining what one has to do. Second, you see that this examination, focused on the future therefore, is not so much focused on acts to be judged in terms of a code, permitted/prohibited, good/evil. It is focused on the organization of new, more rational, more apt, and more certain schemas of conduct. It involves therefore an exercise, in the strict sense of the term, what the Greeks call *askēsis*, ascesis, an exercise thanks to which, from now on, one will be stronger and better adapted in one's comportment, more in tune with the circumstances that present themselves.[36] As in the example of the athlete, it is a question of henceforth being able to attain the goals one has set. And what does examination of conscience have to discover for one to be able to achieve these goals? Once again, one does not have to drag out internal secrets deposited in the recesses of the heart because these explain one's bad conduct. Not at all. If one examines what one has done in this way, and if one examines oneself in the course of the day that has gone by, it is to discover, to extract rational principles of conduct which are indeed in our soul, but which are in our soul as seeds, as germs of all the rational principles that, according to the Stoics, are deposited in the soul. Examination of conscience involves bringing forth these germs of rationality that will enable one to confront any circumstance and so conduct oneself both autonomously, since these are the germs of my own reason, and at the same time as this being an autonomous conduct, it will also be a conduct

---

* M.F.: be proposed.

properly in line with the whole world, since the principles of rationality are universal and since rational conduct is what enables me to be autonomous in connection with the whole world. An essential end of Stoic examination is therefore autonomy: I examine myself in order to be autonomous, in order to be able to be guided by myself and my own reason. The other side of this aim of autonomy is the fact that if I am in actual fact autonomous by managing myself by my own reason, I will as a result be able to bring my own actions into line with the principles of the general and universal reason that governs the world.

You see then that this has nothing to do—well, little to do with an examination of conscience whose function would be the exploration of the secrets of the heart, the mysteries of the heart in which the roots of sin are to be found. It is a matter of an examination of oneself as a rational subject, that is to say as a subject who sets goals for himself and whose actions can be considered good or bad in terms of whether or not they attain their end. It is a matter of an examination of oneself as rational subject who can actually attain his ends only by making an autonomous use of the reason that he shares with the whole world. You may well think Christian examination of conscience, which we will examine next week, has a quite different structure, a quite different object, and quite different [ends].*

---

* inaudible.

1. See above, lecture of 13 February, pp. 132-135.
2. At the turn of the seventh and eighth century—the moment when "what may be called the first great juridification of penance appears in Christian institutions, that is to say tariffed penance" (*Mal faire, dire vrai*, lecture of 13 May 1981, p. 176)—see above, lecture of 5 March, p. 216, note 4.
3. Ambroise de Milan, *De paenitentia/De la pénitence*, II, X, p. 193: "We must live by dying to our usual way of life. Man must deny himself and change entirely, like the young man whose story the fables recount. After illicit love affairs, he left for foreign lands, and when he returned, his love was extinguished. He later happened to meet his former love, who was surprised that he did not speak to her. She thought he had not recognized her and, approaching him, said: 'It is me'—'But,' he replied, 'I am no longer me.'"; Saint Ambrose, *Concerning Repentance*, Book II, ch. X, 96, p. 357: "... the mode of life must be such that we die to the usual habits of life. Let the man deny himself and be wholly changed, as in the fable they relate of a certain youth, who left his home because of his love for a harlot, and, having subdued his love, returned; then one day meeting his old favourite and not speaking to her, she, being surprised and supposing that he had not recognized her, said, when they met again, 'It is I.' 'But,' was his answer, 'I am not the former I.'" The anecdote is also recounted by Francois de Sales, *Introduction à la vie dévote*, III, 21 (Paris: F. Aubier, 1931), p. 221, with regard to the "boy about whom Saint Ambrose spoke in the second book of *Concerning Repentance*."
4. This is the Sanctuary of Demeter at Knidos (Asia Minor). See R. Pettazzoni, *La confessione dei peccati*, Part Two, vol. 3 (Bologna: Zanichelli, 1936), pp. 74-76 ("Iscrizioni imprecatorie di Knido). "Also in the *arai* [imprecatory inscriptions] of Knidos, alongside the *exomologein*— usually in the forma media *exomologeisthai*—and *omologein* of the Phrygian and Lydian confessional inscriptions, the verb *exagoreuein* recurs more frequently to express the act of confessing" (p. 76).
5. Juvénal, *Satires*, VI, 565-574. The translation read by Foucault is close, at the beginning, to that of P. de Labriolle and F. Villeneuve (Paris: CUF, 1941 [1921]), p. 80 (quoted by C. Vogel, *Le pécheur et la pénitence au Moyen-Age*, p. 225) and, at the end, to that of H. Clouard, *Juvénal et Perse* in *Œuvres* (Paris: Classiques Garnier, 1934), p. 107: "But the highest honors go to that man who, with a cortege of priests in linen tunics and shaven heads, passes through the town, laughing to himself at the credulous people who venerate Anubis. He intercedes for the wife who has made love on the holy days of continence, a grave fault which deserves severe penalty, and the silver serpent's head has been seen to stir! But the worthy priest weeps and prays; he will obtain the pardon: a fat goose, a little cake, and Osiris will let himself be bribed!"; English translation by Susanna Morton Braund, *Satire 6*, 534-541, in *Juvenal and Persius*, (Cambridge, Massachusetts, and London: Harvard University Press, Loeb Classical Library 91, 2004), pp. 284-285: "Consequently, the highest, most exceptional honour is awarded to Anubis who runs along, mocking the wailing populace, surrounded by his creatures in linen garments and with shaved heads. He's the one that asks for a pardon whenever your wife does not refrain from sex on the days which should be kept sacred and a large fine is due for violation of the quilt. When the silver snake has been seen to move its head, it's his tears and his practised mumblings which ensure that Osiris will not refuse to pardon her fault—provided, of course, he's bribed by a fat goose and a slice of sacrificial cake."
6. An allusion, perhaps, to P. Courcelle's book, *Connais-toi toi-même de Socrate à Saint Bernard* (Paris: Etudes augustiniennes, 1974) in two volumes. A specialist in Saint Augustine, Courcelle was the first to recount the history of the Delphic precept "from pagan Antiquity up to the pre-Scholastic Christians," striving "within this continuity" to "discern the main mental families, the themes, and the progress of reflection on the poverty and greatness of man" (Preface, vol. I, p. 7).
7. See, however, the work already cited by I. Hausherr, *Spiritual Direction in the Early Christian East*, which Foucault had read and from which he takes a number of references. See also the books of Paul Rabbow, *Seelenführung. Methodik der Exerzitien in der Antike* (Munich: Kösel-Verlag, 1954), which goes back from the *Spiritual Exercises* of Ignatius Loyola to the ancient tradition, and Ilsetraut Hadot, *Seneca und die griechich-römische Tradition der Seelenleitung* (Berlin: Walter de Gruyter, 1969). Foucault never refers to the former in the lectures of the following years or his last books. On the other hand, he uses the second in 1982, in *The Hermeneutics of the Subject* and, in 1984, in *The Care of the Self*.

8. See *Les anormaux*, lecture of 19 February 1975, pp. 170-171; *Abnormal*, pp. 183-184, and the citations, which Foucault comments on, of F. Vialart, *Règlements faits pour la direction spirituelle du séminaire … établi dans la ville de Châlons* (Châlons, 1664).

9. See Platon, *Peri politeias/La République*, trans. E. Chambry (Paris: Les Belles Lettres, CUF, 1973 [1934]), vol. VII, Part 2, pp. 80-81. On the utopian character of the ideal city, see Book IX, 592 b where Socrates defines it as a city in thought "a model in heaven for he who wishes to contemplate it and have it rule his government of himself," and which "it doesn't matter if it is or will be realized." English translation by Desmond Lee, Plato, *The Republic* (London: Penguin Books, 2nd revised ed., 1987), p. 420: "'Perhaps,' I said, 'it is laid up as a pattern in heaven, where he who wishes can see it and found it in his own heart. But it doesn't matter whether it exists or ever will exist ….'"

10. Thomas More, *Utopia (De optimo rei publicae statu, deque nova insula Utopia)* (Louvain: Thierry Martens, 1516); English translation by Robert M. Adams, *Utopia*, ed. George M. Logan and Robert M. Adams (Cambridge: Cambridge University Press, "Cambridge texts in the history of political thought," 2002 revised edition).

11. This comment is an extension of the project of studying "party governmentality" Foucault formulated the previous year in the lectures, *Naissance de la biopolitique*, lecture of 7 March 1979, pp. 196-197; *The Birth of Biopolitics*, pp. 190-191.

12. See Plutarque [Plutarch], *Vie des dix orateurs* (Antiphon, 18), in *Discours, suivi des fragments d'Antiphon le sophiste*, trans. L. Gernet (Paris: Les Belles Lettres, CUF, 1923), p. 28: "At the time when he devoted himself to poetry, he established an art of healing distress, analogous to that which doctors apply to diseases: in Corinth, near the agora, he set up premises with a sign where he became strong in treating moral pain by means of discourse; he enquired as to the causes of the distress and comforted his patients. But, finding this profession beneath him, he turned to rhetoric." Exegetes are divided as to whether Antiphon the Sophist, papyrus fragments of whose writing were found in 1915, is the same person as Antiphon the orator (born around 479 or 470 and died around 411 B.C.E.) whose life Plutarch traces.

13. Galen, Greek physician (?131-?201). On this activity of direction, see his *On the Passions and Errors of the Soul*, trans. P. W. Harkins (Columbus: Ohio State University Press, 1963), to which Foucault devoted a part of the lecture of 10 March 1982 of the course *L'herméneutique du sujet*, pp. 378-382; *The Hermeneutics of the Subject*, pp. 395-399. See also *Le souci de soi* (Paris: Gallimard, "Bibliothèque des Histoires," 1984), p. 72; English translation by Robert Hurley, *The Care of the Self* (New York: Pantheon Books, 1986) pp. 55-56.

14. See Seneca, *De Tranquillitate Animi/On Tranquility of Mind*, trans., John W. Basore, in *Moral Essays*, vol. II (Cambridge, Massachusetts: Harvard University Press, Loeb Classical Library, 1979), pp. 202-213. Here again Foucault returns at some length to this example in *L'herméneutique du sujet*, p. 86, p. 126-129, and p. 151; *The Hermeneutiques of the Subject*, p. 89, pp. 130-134, pp. 156-157.

15. See Seneca, *Ad Lucilium Epistulae Morales/The Epistles of Seneca*, vol. I, trans. Richard M. Gummere (Cambridge, Massachusetts: Harvard University Press, Loeb Classical Library, 1979), Letter 52, 3-4, pp. 344-347 on the "distinction between the different leaders of the school" (manuscript, folio 17), that is to say between its founder and the disciples of the first generation, Metrodorus and Hermarchus. This letter is cited by I. Hadot, *Seneca und die grieschich-römische Tradition der Seelenleitung* (Berlin: W. de Gruyter and Co., 1969), p. 49.

16. See I. Hadot, ibid., p. 51: "Die nächsten im Rang nach Epikur waren Metrodor, Hermarch und Polyainos. Diese drei hatten den Titel eines *kathēgemōn* inne, was nach De Witt [see following note] soviel bedeutet wie "beigeordneter Führer," aber es ist nachdem Zitat aus Seneca klar, daß Epikur diese drei Männer der Führung nur insoweit fähig hielt, als er ihnen den Weg bereits gezeigt hatte."

17. See N.W. de Witt, "Organization and Procedure in Epicurean Groups," *Classical Philology*, vol. 31, no. 3, July 1936, pp. 205-211; reprinted in *Epicurus and his Philosophy* (Minneapolis: University of Minnesota Press, 1954). Foucault refers explicitly to this article in *L'herméneutique du sujet*, lecture of 27 January 1982, pp. 131-132; *The Hermeneutics of the Subject*, pp. 136-137, adding "it seems that the hierarchy proposed by people like De Witt does not entirely correspond to reality" and referring to the proceedings of the Association Guillaume Budé devoted to Greek and Roman Epicureanism (Paris: Les Belles Lettres, 1970).

18. J.-P. Vernant, *The Origins of Greek Thought* (London: Methuen, 1982), ch. 4: "The Spiritual Universe of the *Polis*."
19. St Jean Chrysostome [John Chrysostom], *In ps.*, 4, 8, PG 55, col. 51-52; cited by J.-C. Guy, "Examen de conscience. III. Chez les Pères de l'Eglise," DS, IV, 1961, col. 1805: "This examination must become daily: never go to sleep before having recapitulated (*analogisē*) the faults of the day ...." See the translation of *Œuvres complètes*, ed. Jean-Baptiste Jeanin with the collaboration of the priests of the Immaculate Conception of Saint-Dizier (Bar-le-Duc: Guérin & Cie, 1865), vol. V, "Explication sur le psaume IV," p. 534: "Make your secret thoughts of the day, the evil designs you have conceived feel the goad, chastise them, punish them in your beds at the hour of rest; when no friend will disturb you, no servant will excite your wrath, when you will be free from the worries of affairs, then weigh up your actions of the day. And why not speak at all of words and actions, but solely of bad thoughts? This precept presupposes the other." There is the same exposition, J.-C. Guy notes, in *Non esse ad gratiam concionandum*, 4, 5, PG 50, col. 659-660 and in *In Mattaeum* 42 (43), 4, PG 57, col. 455.
20. Latin title of *Krusa Epē*, a compilation of extracts of Pythagorean *Discours sacrés* (*Hieroi Logoi*). The first modern critical edition was established by A. Nauck, following his edition of the *Life of Pythagoras* by Iamblichus: *De Vita Pythagorica* (St. Petersbourg: 1884, reprinted Amsterdam: A.M. Hakkert, 1965); English translation by Thomas Taylor in, *Iamblichus' Life of Pythagoras* (Rochester, Vermont: Inner Tradition, 1986 [1818]). Nauck's dating of the text as from the beginning of the fourth century has been challenged by A. Delatte, *Etudes sur la littérature pythagoricienne* (Paris: E. Champion, 1915), p. 45, who situates its publication around the middle of the third century. See H. Jaeger, "L'examen de conscience dans les religions non chrétiennes et avant le christianisme," *Numen*, vol. 6, fasc. 3, December 1959—who is Foucault's main source here—p. 191: "Classical or Christian tradition has always presented the examination of conscience practiced by the Pythagoreans as the most perfect example offered by Antiquity. We can identify its first appearance in the *Hieros Logos* which goes back to the third century before our era, then in the *Life of Pythagoras* by Diogenes Laertius, that by Porphyry, that by Iamblichus, and especially in the most successful literary synthesis of Pythagorean wisdom, the *Carmen aureum* of Hierocles, a convinced pagan of the sixth century" (see also the abridged version of this article in DS, IV, 1961, col. 1792). See also *Le souci de soi*, p. 77; *The Care of the Self*, pp. 60-61 (Foucault refers in notes to Diogenes Laertius, *Lives of Eminent Philosophers*, VIII, 1, 27, and Porphyry, *Life of Pythagoras*, 40).
21. *Pythagore, Les Vers d'or. Hiéroclès, Commentaire sur les Vers d'or des pythagoriciens*, trans. M. Meunier (Paris: L'Artisan du livre, 1925; republished Paris: Ed. de la Maisnie, 1979), p. 30 (the author notes, p. 18, note 1, that he translated the text "according to the interpretation given to us by the pious Hierocles in his eloquent commentary"; see the latter, pp. 220-230); cited by H. Jaeger, "L'examen de conscience dans les religions non chrétiennes et avant le christianisme," p. 192 (DS. col. 1792-1793). Foucault returns briefly to this text in *L'herméneutique du sujet*, lecture of 24 March 1982, p. 460; *The Hermeneutics of the Subject*, p. 480.
22. See A. Delatte, *Etudes sur la littérature pythagoricienne*, Part I, ch. 3, pp. 45-82; H. Jaeger, "L'examen de conscience dans les religions non chrétiennes et avant le christianisme," p. 192. The manuscript, folio 22, notes in the margin: "Stoic influence."
23. See J.-P. Vernant, "Mythical Aspects of Memory," in *Myth and Thought Among the Greeks* (London: Routledge & Kegan Paul, 1983), p. 86: "The obligation laid on the members of the [Pythagorean] fraternity to recall all the events of the day gone by, each evening, had more than the moral value of an exercise in soul-searching [*examen de conscience*]. The effort involved in remembering, if undertaken following the example of the sect's founder so as to encompass the story of the soul throughout ten or even twenty different lives, would make it possible for us to learn who we are and to know our own *psyche*—that daemon which has become incarnate in us."
24. Cicéron [Cicero], *De Senectute (De la vieillesse)*, XI, 38, trans. P. Wuilleumier (Paris: Les Belles Lettres, CUF, 1955), p. 152: "*multum etiam Graecis litteris utor; Pythagoreorumque more, exercendae memoriae gratia, quid quoque die dixerim, audierim, egerim, commemoro vesperi. Hae sunt exercitationes ingenii, haec curricula mentis, in his desudans atqe elaborans corporis vires non magnopere desidero*" ("I also devote a lot of time to Greek literature; and, in the manner of the Pythagoreans, to exercise my memory I recollect in the evening what I have said, heard, or done each day. Such are the exercises of my mind, such are the courses of my thought; while sweating and struggling with

them, I scarcely experience the loss of my physical forces"; English translation by William Armistead Falconer as Cicero, *Cato Maior de Senectute/ Cato the Elder on Old Age*, in *Cicero* Vol. XX (Cambridge, Massachusetts, and London: Harvard University Press/William Heinemann, Loeb Classical Library, 1923) p. 47: "I also devote much of my time to Greek literature; and in order to exercise my memory, I follow the practice of the Pythagoreans and run over in my mind every evening all that I have said, heard, or done during the day. These employments are my intellectual gymnastics; these the race-courses of my mind; and while I sweat and toil with them I do not greatly feel the loss of bodily strength." According to Wuilleumier, "Cicero ... reduced to a mnemotechnic exercise a moral examination of conscience, which also tended, according to Herocles [*sic*], to give a feeling of immortality by recalling previous lives" (ibid., note 4). The reference to this passage is given by H. Jaeger, "L'examen de conscience dans les religions non chrétiennes," p. 193, following P.C. Van der Horst, *Les Vers d'or pythagoriciens* (Leyde: E.J. Brill, 1932).

25. On this theme of preparation for sleep in ancient Pythagoreanism, see H. Jaeger, "L'examen de conscience dans les religions non chrétiennes," pp. 193-194, which cites at length G. Meautis, *Recherches sur le Pythagorisme* (Neuchâtel: Société académique, 1922), p. 31 *et seq.* Foucault returns briefly to the subject in *L'herméneutique du sujet*, lecture of 13 January, First hour, p. 48 (see p. 61 note 8 for more clarifications); *The Hermeneutics of the Subject*, p. 48 and p. 62 note 8.

26. See H Jaeger, ibid., pp. 195-196: "Examination of conscience is so integrated into the spiritual exercise of the *meletē thanatou* [the exercise of death (see Plato, *Phaedo*, 81 A; 67 D)] that in the *Vers d'or* it represents the preparation for sleep, prefiguration of death, according to the ideas current in Hellenism (see for example, P. Boyancé, "Le sommeil et l'immortalité," in *Mélanges de l'Ecole de Rome*, XLV, 1928, p. 99 ss. ...)." There follows a long quotation from F. Cumont, *Recherches sur le symbolisme funéraire des Romans* (Paris: P. Geuthner, 1942), p. 365 *et seq.*

27. Sénèque, *De ira (De la colère)*, III, 36, in *Dialogues*, vol. I, trans., A. Bourgery (Paris: CUF, 1951), pp. 102-103; English translation by John W. Basore, Seneca, *De ira/On Anger*, in *Moral Essays*, Vol. I (Cambridge, Mass.: Harvard University Press, LCL 214, 2003), pp. 338-341. At the beginning Foucault uses, and quotes fairly faithfully, the old translation of the Panckoucke collection, revised by M. Charpentier and F. Lemaistre, *Œuvres complètes de Sénèque*, vol. 2 (Paris: Garnier, 1860, republished in "Classiques Garnier," no date), pp. 360-361. He devotes a long exposition of this text in *L'herméneutique du sujet*, lecture of 24 March 1982, pp. 461-464 (see p. 469 note 17 for a comparison of this analysis with that presented in the 1980 course); *The Hermeneutics of the Subject*, pp. 481-484, and p. 489 note 17. See too *Le souci de soi*, pp. 77-78; *The Care of the Self*, pp. 61-62.

28. Ibid., p. 370: "*Quid ergo pulchrius hac consuetudine excutiendi totum diem?*"; Eng., ibid., p. 341: "Can anything be more excellent than this practice of thoroughly sifting the whole day?"

29. Ibid., "... which follows this examination"; Eng., ibid.: "And how delightful the sleep that follows this examination of conscience."

30. Foucault omits here a first adjective, "free"; Eng., ibid.: "how tranquil it is, how deep and untroubled."

31. Ibid., "... *et speculator sui censorque secretus cognoscit de moribus suis*"; Eng., ibid.: "this secret examiner and critic of self." On the specifically Roman sense of *censura* as examination of morals, see C. Nicolet, *Le Métier de citoyen dans la Rome républicaine* (Paris: Gallimard, "Bibliothèque des Histoires," 1976), ch. II, pp. 103-112. See also B. Kübler, "Censura," *Reallexikon für Antike und Christentum* (Stuttgart: A. Hiersemann, 1954), t. II, col. 965-969; A. Fontana, "Censura," *Enciclopedia* (Turin: Einaudi, 1977) t. II, pp. 877-878. The censor, like the law, dealt with morality, but was related to it in a different way. According to Cicero, it was established by the ancients in such a way that it may bring a certain fear, and not a penalty: Cicero, *Pro Cluentio/ In Defence of Aulus Cluentius Habitus*, trans., H. Grose Hodge, in *Cicero*, Vol. IX, *Orations* (Cambridge, Massachusetts, and London: Harvard University Press/William Heinemann, LCL 198, 1927), XLIII, pp. 348-349: "*timoris enim causam, non vitae poenam in illa potestate esse voluerunt*"; "our forefathers intended to invest the censor's office with the power of inspiring fear, not of punishing for life." It was in this that it differed from legal justice. Cicéron, *La République*, IV, 7, fragment 5, trans. E. Bréguet (Paris: Gallimard, "Tel," 1994), p. 119: "The censor's verdict inflicted hardly more than the blush of shame (*ruborem*). That is why, just as this way of judging only concerns reputation, the penalty with which it strikes is called

ignominia, loss of reputation"; English translation by Clinton Walker Keyes as Cicero, *De Re Publica/On the Republic* in *Cicero*, Vol. XVI (Cambridge, Massachusetts, and London: Harvard University Press/William Heinemann, Loeb Classical Library, 213, 1928), Book IV, V pp. 234-237: "... The censor's judgment imposes almost no penalty except a blush upon the man he condemns. Therefore, as his decision affects nothing but the reputation, his condemnation is called 'ignominy.'"

32. Ibid.: "... when the soul has received its portion of praise or blame, and that, censor of its own conduct, it has secretly informed against itself"; Eng., ibid.: "when the soul has either praised or admonished itself, and when this secret examiner and critic has given report of its own character."

33. Foucault translates the last part of the text more freely. Ibid.: "Such is my rule: each day I summon myself before my tribunal. When the light has gone from my room, and my wife, familiar with my custom, respects my silence with her own, I begin the inspection of my entire day, and go over, to weigh them, my words and my actions. I hide nothing from myself and neglect nothing: why, in fact, would I fear to view just one of my faults, when I can say: Try not to do it again; for now I forgive you. You were sharp in that discussion; in the future avoid verbal disputes with ignorance; it does not wish to learn, because it has never learned. You gave that warning more freely than was appropriate, and you did not correct, but shocked. Another time look less to the justice of your views than to the ability of the one you are addressing to suffer the truth"; Eng., ibid.: "When the light has been removed from sight, and my wife, long aware of my habit, has become silent, I scan the whole of my day and retrace all my deeds and words. I conceal nothing from myself, I omit nothing. For why should I shrink from any of my mistakes, when I may commune thus with myself? 'See that you never do that again; I will pardon you this time. In that dispute, you spoke too offensively; after this don't have encounters with ignorant people; those who have never learned do not want to learn. You reproved that man more frankly than you ought, and consequently you not so much mended him as offended him. In the future, consider not only the truth of what you say, but also whether the man to whom you are speaking can endure the truth.'"

34. See J. Laplanche and J.B. Pontalis, *The Language of Psycho-Analysis*, trans. Donald Nicholson-Smith (London: The Hogarth Press and the Institute of Psycho-Analysis, 1973), p. 66: "Freud holds the censorship to be a permanent function: it constitutes a selective barrier between the unconscious system on the one hand and the preconscious-conscious one on the other, and it is thus placed at the point of origin of repression. Its effects are more clearly discernible when it is partially relaxed, as it is in dreaming: the sleeping state prevents the contents of the unconscious from breaking through on to the level of motor activity; since they are liable to come into conflict with the wish for sleep, however, the censorship continues to operate in an attenuated way." For a first elaboration of this notion, see S. Freud, *The Interpretation of Dreams*, in *Complete Psychological Works of Sigmund Freud*, Vol. 4 (London: Vintage Books, 2001).

35. See Epictète, *Entretiens*, vol. 3, trans., J. Souilhé (Paris: CUF, 1963), III, 25, pp. 112-113: "To those who are unfaithful to their resolutions": English translation by W.A. Oldfather as Epictetus, *The Discourses*, in *Epictetus II* (Cambridge, Massachusetts: Harvard University Press, LCL 218, 2000), Book III, 25, pp. 222-227: "To those who fail to achieve their purposes."

36. On this notion of *askēsis*, ascesis, in the Ancients, which, unlike in Christianity, does not imply any self-renunciation, but finds its end in "the constitution of a full, perfect, and complete relation of self to self," see *L'herméneutique du sujet*, lecture of 24 February, Second hour, pp. 301-313; *The Hermeneutics of the Subject*, pp. 301-313. See also: H. Strathmann, "Askese," *Reallexikon für Antike und Christentum*, vol. I (Stuttgart: A. Hiersemann, 1950), col. 756-757, on the meaning of *askēsis* in Stoic philosophers; P. Hadot, "Exercices spirituels," *Exercices spirituels et philosophie antique*, p. 17 note 17 (republished Paris: Albin Michel, 2002, p. 25 note 1); English translation by Michael Chase, "Spiritual Exercises" in Pierre Hadot, *Philosophy as a Way of Life. Spiritual Exercises from Socrates to Foucault*, ed. and introd. Arnold I. Davidson (Oxford: Blackwell, 1995), p. 111 note 18: "Many Stoic treatises entitled *On Exercises* have been lost; cf. the list of titles in Diogenes Laertius, 7, 166-7. One chapter of Epictetus' *Discourses* is dedicated to *askesis* (3, 12, 1-7) ['Of exercise (Eng., training),' *Peri askēseōs*. He classifies the exercises from the point of view of philosophical *topoi* which are related to the three faculties of the soul: the faculty of desire, the faculty of action, and the faculty of thought.]" [The words in square brackets are omitted from the footnote in the English translation; G.B.]

eleven

19 MARCH 1980

> *Examination of conscience in the practice of direction (contin-*
> *ued). Its late appearance in Christianity, in the fourth century;*
> *a phenomenon linked to the spread of the monastic institution.* ⌒
> *The problem of the relations between salvation and perfection.*
> *The double Christian reply: penance (system of salvation in non-*
> *perfection) and monasticism (search for perfection in a system of*
> *salvation).* ⌒ *Monasticism as philosophical life. Development in*
> *Christianity of the techniques peculiar to ancient philosophy.* ⌒
> *The example of Cassian. First principle: no monastic life with-*
> *out direction. Necessity of direction for the anchorite as for the*
> *cenobite. The three phases of preparation for entry into a cenoby.*
> *Two correlative obligations: to obey in everything and to conceal*
> *nothing. Importance of this coupling in the history of Christian*
> *subjectivity. Characteristics of this obedience according to Cassian*
> (subditio, patientia, humilitas). *A direction poles apart from*
> *ancient direction.*

LAST WEEK I TRIED to give you some very brief and schematic indications regarding the practice of direction in Antiquity, then [of] examination of conscience, with, you recall, its pivotal position between the
director and the person being directed, examination of conscience basically being intended to give the director a hold on the directed and to offer
the director a knowledge of the individual that only the individual can
bring to bear on himself and on the basis of himself. So, the examination
of conscience occupies a pivotal position in the practice of direction.

What is strange, and what I would like to begin with today, is this. Whereas the themes of ancient philosophy, whether Platonic or Stoic, whether they take the form of a structure of speculative, theoretical, theological thought, or are themes of morality, or everyday morality, whereas then these themes penetrated Christian thought very early on and we see evident traces of them in Saint Paul,[1] the practice of direction, on the other hand, the practice of examination of conscience, everything we might call techniques of the philosophical life, penetrated Christianity only rather late on. We have to wait until the fourth century to see these practices of the philosophical life taken up again by Christianity. First observation, therefore: you find practically no reference to the examination of conscience in Christian literature before the fourth century. Of course, we see a certain number themes, reflections, and analyses concerning knowledge of oneself, or the necessity to reflect on what one is doing or has done. But this is not examination of conscience in the strict sense.[2]

I will give you just two examples, [the first] is taken from Clement of Alexandria, in *The Instructor*: it is the famous passage of the first chapter of the third book—right at the beginning, the first sentence. Clement of Alexandria says: "It appears that the greatest knowledge is knowledge of self"—or knowing oneself (*to gnōnai auton*)—"for the one who knows himself will have knowledge of God and, having this knowledge, will be made like God."[3] It is clear that what is affirmed here is without doubt the fundamental, essential necessity of "knowing oneself." But it has nothing to do with a technique of investigating oneself, of the retrospective and systematic examination of one's actions, nothing to do with their classification and relative valorization into good or bad, a bit better, a bit worse. There is nothing of that sort of judicature or inspection that we saw in Seneca, for example, in Book Three of *De ira* and which I spoke about last week. It has nothing to do with all that. What is this passage of Clement of Alexandria about? What is the purpose of knowing oneself? One knows oneself so that one can have access to knowledge of God, that is to say so that one can recognize what is divine in oneself, so that one can recognize the part or element in the soul that is of divine form, principle, origin, or at any rate in contact with God. The proof that this is the meaning of the necessity to know oneself in Clement of Alexandria is found in what follows in the text, where, after having asserted that one must know oneself, Clement of Alexandria develops his intention by referring to the Platonic tripartition—the *logi[sti]kon*, the *thumikon*, and the *epithum[ēt]ikon*[4]—saying that in the *logi[sti]kon*, in the *logos* and through it, one can in actual fact know the divine Logos. So it is not so much oneself that one knows in the *gnōnai heauton*. What one knows is God or the divine in oneself,[5] or what enables you to know the divine itself.

Another example, which is quite different, but which also does not lead us to examination of conscience. It is from a bit later than Clement of Alexandria, who was from the end of the second and beginning of the third century. Now, in Saint Ambrose, in the second half of the third century, we find a similar reflection—it concerns the commentary on the famous psalm 118 [119],* the psalm, precisely, that will later serve as reference to the practice of examination of conscience: it is *"cogitavi vias meas,* I have reflected on my ways, on my own paths."[6] From the fourth century it is always cited with regard to examination of conscience. Now, what does Ambrose make of it? With regard to this text of Psalm 118 [119], he says simply: "We must think of what we must do, *quid geramus.* When reflection, *cogitation,* precedes, then at that point actions can attain their perfection."[7] What is involved here is not the need to pay attention to what one does. There is absolutely no question of a retrospective analysis of what one has in actual fact done. What is involved is the prospective consideration of what one is going to do, and of the way of reflecting on these actions to be performed with enough maturity, in a sufficiently reasonable manner, in order that they conform to the law or to divine prescriptions. While in Clement we had a reflection on the necessity of knowing oneself in a very Platonic style, with Ambrose, in contrast, we have, let us say, rather Stoic type instructions or prescriptions. But in neither case do we find anything resembling that examination of conscience, not only the evidence for which, but also the organization, manner of performance, and technique of which we saw in Seneca.

We could say the same regarding direction. The fact itself of direction, or rather the institutionalization of direction, the establishment

---

* [The psalm cited is 118 according to Ambrose's numbering, but it appears in the Bible as Psalm 119; G.B.]

of a technique for direction, appears late in Christianity. Of course, very soon, from the beginning we find the theme of pastoral power, that is to say the fact that at the head of the flock there must be a guide who leads it to salvation. This shepherd is responsible for the flock itself and he is responsible not only for the flock, but also for each of the sheep, and he must save each sheep and bring it aid as soon as it falls.[8] This pastoral theme is therefore important and evident, but it does not coincide with the idea or technique of direction. It does not coincide with the idea of a permanent intervention of one individual on another with the goal of observing him, knowing him, guiding him, conducting him in every detail throughout his existence within a relationship of uninterrupted obedience. The theme of pastoral power does not entail a technique of direction, even if, later, when this technique is developed within Christianity, it is situated within the realm of the pastorate.

Let us take, for example, another text of Clement of Alexandria. This time it is in the *Quis dives salvetur* (*Who is the Rich Man who shall be saved?*), chapter 41,[9] in which he is in fact speaking about something like the need for direction. Anyway, he says that when a man is rich and powerful, that is to say when he has against him all the difficulties and obstacles that may prevent him earning his salvation, he needs, he says, a governor, a *kubernētēs*, someone who directs him, he needs an *aleiptēs*, who is his gymnastics teacher.[10] This governor, this gymnastics teacher must exercise over him what Clement defines as supervision, *epistēsastai*,[11] the word that will become the technical term designating direction.[12] But when we look at what Clement—at the end of the second century—puts under this need to have a governor, a director, when one is rich and powerful, so when it is difficult to earn one's salvation, we see that it is not at all something like ancient direction. He says: If the rich and powerful wishes to be saved, then he must listen to his director. He must fear him, he must respect him. Be there only one person to fear and respect, he says, let it be this director, this governor. And he will speak with frankness and harshness. He will have to accept this frankness and harshness.[13] But this is not all, and to tell the truth, it is not the main thing. The essential role of this *kubernētēs* in Clement of Alexandria will be that he himself must practice a number of ascetic, sacrificial, and probation exercises. This *kubernētēs*, this governor will himself have to keep vigil (not in the sense of supervision, but of depriving himself of sleep). He will have to pray, of course. He will have to fast also and in this way be an intercessor between the person he directs, and represents in fact, and God himself.[14] Basically, this governor is [not so much] someone who guides the conduct of the one being directed according to a precise and considered technique, [as] his alter ego, his representative, witness, guarantor, and surety before God and with regard to God. And this is why rather than supervising the conduct of the person he directs, he shares with him the mortifications he imposes and, if need be, he imposes more on himself than on the person he directs, for it is his mortifications that have to obtain God's forgiveness in the procedure of intercession. It is therefore a sharing of mortification rather than a direction of conduct. And we have an example of this in the story Clement of Alexandria recounts right after this passage—a story traditionally attributed to the apostle John.[15] The apostle John [had] baptized a young man in whom he put all his hopes and confidence and, after having baptized him, [he] had to set out again to continue his task of evangelization. So he entrusts the young man to the local bishop and, when he returns after some time, the young man had fallen again, he had even fallen to the lowest point since he had become a highway bandit. Indignant, John addresses the bishop and says to him: "I have given the soul of my brother to a fine guardian!"[16] And in his anger, [he] goes in search of his protégé who had fallen and for whom the bishop had not served as, precisely, a sufficient and effective intercessor. He finally finds him (on the highway, since he is a highway robber) and tells him: "I will defend you to Christ. If necessary I will die in your place and with good heart, following the example of our Lord, I will sacrifice my life for yours."[17] At this point the young man is gripped by repentance. He falls, weeping, to his knees. Saint John also falls to his knees weeping. He clasps his hands, leads him back to the church and, for a time, shares his fasting and has long conversations with him.[18]

So in this procedure, which we can say is, in a sense, actually one of guidance, you can see that what is important is not the technique by which the director uses methods of observation, analysis, and exhortation in view of the nature and needs of the one being directed, (there is a reference to long conversations, but that is all). The most important thing in the procedure [is] the fact that Saint John offers himself as a substitute victim, shares in the purifying exercises, or rather begins them himself, getting upset, weeping, offering himself as victim. And it is within this process of sacrificial substitution that the young man, whose soul Saint John wished to be offered to God, is saved.[19] The most important thing here then does not concern a technique of direction. It concerns a sacrificial substitute, that is to say the Christ-like model. It is inasmuch as John is Christ in relation to this young man and inasmuch as he makes the same type of sacrifice as Christ in relation to humanity, that the salvation of the other can be brought about by the one who guides him, who directs him, who, once again, is rather his guarantor, his surety.

So, in all these cases I have cited, whether concerning examination of conscience or direction, we are far from the ancient model I talked about last week with reference to Seneca and Stoic philosophers, we are also far from what direction, spiritual direction, the direction of conscience will be in the centuries to come, even though a number of these themes will not disappear, even though, for example, the idea of responsibility, of the sharing of mortifications, of sacrificial substitution will continue to haunt, at least in principle, the practice of direction up to and including the seventeenth century. In fact, in the fourth century there will be a significant and abrupt change of accent. You see the appearance, then, of the technique of examination of conscience fairly close to that found in Seneca, and also fairly close to what is found later in the Christian tradition until the seventeenth and eighteenth centuries, possibly until now. Thus, in the Life of Saint Antony written by Saint Athanasius there is this precept, which is attributed to Saint Antony but that commentators think is from a bit later, but it doesn't matter, the text being from the fourth century. He attributes this principle to Saint Antony: "Let each one keep a daily record of what he does night and day. Let each note in writing his actions and his soul's impulses, as if he had to make them known to others. Let the written letter play the role of our companions."[20] This is an important text because we are far from Clement of Alexandria's simple recall of the *gnōthi seauton*, and thus close to a technique, an exercise similar to that of Seneca, with even, you can see, what is found in some ancient philosophers—Seneca does not mention it, but [there is] also the idea in some Stoics that not only must one examine one's conscience, but one should write it down, one should keep a kind of accounting.[21] We could also cite Saint John Chrysostom who said: "We ask the servant what has been spent well or at the wrong time, what we have left...We must proceed in the same way for the conduct of our life. Let us call on our conscience, let us get it to give an account of actions, words, and thoughts. Let us examine what profits us or harms us, what evil we have spoken, what thought has led us to cast glances that are too free, what harmful fate we have prepared. Let us cease spending at the wrong time. Let us endeavor to replace harmful expenses with useful investment."[22] You have here a definition, a description of examination of conscience in a style extraordinarily close to that of Seneca, you recall, who compared the examination of conscience to a sort of inspection one makes of the management of life and of the day. How have we managed our day? Well, we take the measure of all the past actions, of what has been done and said during the day, and we see whether what we have done is in fact in line with the goal we set ourselves. John Chrysostom proposes the same work of inspection that is very close to Seneca.

Similarly, we could say that direction, in its strict and precise institutional form, reappears, is inserted, is transferred and imported into Christianity from the fourth century, and not before.

Let's summarize this. There is a sort of paradoxical phenomenon, since on the one hand, as I was saying at the start, the themes of Platonic and Stoic philosophy penetrated Christianity very early on. On the other hand, the techniques of the philosophical life scarcely appear before the fourth century. You will have guessed the very simple reason for this: they are reinserted, reactivated, and taken up again in Christianity only within and because of the monastic institution. It is in monasticism, precisely, and not in Christianity in general, that these techniques of the philosophical life were reactivated or—because they never ceased being active in pagan philosophy at this time—were transferred into Christianity.

Why in monasticism? I'll say just a couple of words, because obviously I do not want to go into this immense and complex history. Let's just say this—with all the randomness it may involve, inasmuch as we are here at a level of generality in which maybe the facts no longer have a very precise place—well, we could simplify by saying that, basically, one of the fundamental problems of Christianity, of Christian theology, of the Christian pastorate was [that of] the relations between salvation and perfection. Does salvation imply perfection? Does the act that saves us make us perfect, or do we have to be perfect to be saved? Once again, this was one of the most fundamental points of debate of Christianity, not only with regard to other religious movements that were developing in this period (it was the major point of friction and confrontation with the Gnostic movements), [but] it was [also] a question within Christianity. How was a religion of salvation constructed that does not entail the perfection of those who are saved? Christianity is a religion of salvation in non-perfection. This was an extraordinarily difficult endeavor to realize at a time when, precisely, for most of the religious movements of the ancient world, of the Hellenistic and Roman world, the promise of salvation and access to perfection were profoundly and fundamentally linked. I think that the great effort and historical singularity of Christianity, which no doubt explains a great many of the features of its development and endurance, is that it succeeded in dissociating salvation and perfection. It was a separation that was difficult to maintain against the gnosis, against the religious movements of the time, and against a whole range of temptations internal [to] Christianity. But, in any case, it is in this divergence between salvation and perfection, it is [according] to this principle that one can be saved without being perfect, that two institutions developed that are both close and in a sense parallel, but that go in opposite and opposed directions. First, the institution I have already talked about, that is to say penance, since penance is precisely that by which one can maintain the effects of salvation, of the saving act, of Christ's saving sacrifice, the effects of baptism as sign of salvation, through a life that is however a life threatened by sin and that falls into sin. Penance is what enables the effects of salvation to be maintained in the non-perfection of existence.

Monasticism will also develop in this same divergence between perfection and salvation, but with an opposite function: no longer that of maintaining the effects of salvation despite sin, but that of seeing whether and how one can develop a life of perfection, or rather a life of working at perfection, in a system of salvation in which Christ's sacrifice has already been accomplished, once and for all and for everyone who recognizes it. What does it mean to still want perfection in a system of salvation? You can see that this question is opposite and symmetrical to the question: how can one preserve salvation if one continues to sin?

Penance and monasticism: two parallel and neighboring institutions, therefore, which will interact with each other a great deal. To a certain extent, monasticism will be a life of penance. Throughout its history, the practice of penance itself will borrow many elements from monasticism. But I think that both are lodged in that divergence introduced into the history of Christianity, by the history of Christianity, between perfection and salvation.

Monasticism is then the life of perfection, or of working at perfection, it is the way towards a perfect life. What characterizes this perfect life? A text of Saint Nilus says: "This perfect life involves establishing the *ēthōn katorthōsis*, the rectification, the perfecting of morals, of the way of being, with the *tou ontos gnōs[i]s alēth[ēs]*, the true knowledge of what is."[23] It is when morals have been purified, when the way of living has been rectified and conforms to the law and, at the same time and thereby, one arrives at the true knowledge of what is, that constitutes perfection and is the objective of monastic life: *ēthōn katorthōsis, tou ontos gnōsis*, rectification of morals, knowledge of being. This is the object of monastic life, the aim of the perfect life, and, you will also recognize that it is the definition of the philosophical life as this was understood by ancient philosophers. And this is why, quite naturally, and without raising many problems, monasticism was defined straightaway as the philosophical life. To be a monk was to be a philosopher; it was the same thing. And then we have a cross-over, a chiasmus that is very interesting: if, on the one hand, it is true that the themes of philosophy penetrated Christianity very early, [that] the debate with ancient philosophy, the double movement of development of, rejection of, and differentiation from ancient philosophy developed constantly, so that in the fourth century there was a whole anti-philosophical discussion, a discussion directed against the themes of Platonic [and] Stoic philosophy, at the same time, or rather from the fourth century, there is an as it were immediate recuperation, not of the philosophical themes one is struggling against, but of the philosophical life, of the principle that one must lead a philosophical life.[24] With monasticism there is the clear objective of a truly philosophical life, with the same techniques of the philosophical life. Monastic life is defined by John Chrysostom, and then by Saint Nilus, as, for example, "the philosophy *kata Kriston*,"[25] philosophy in accordance with Christ, or "philosophy *dia ergōn*,"[26] philosophy through works; and the monasteries will be called, and moreover to a large extent will be organized as, philosophical schools. So it is not surprising that these techniques of the philosophical life, of philosophical practice, are not found before the fourth century but are developed very quickly and intensely from the fourth century within the monastic institution as a specifically philosophical institution, an institution of the philosophical life.[27]

It is on the existence, development, and transformations within Christianity of these techniques of the ancient philosophical life that I would now like to focus a little. Because there is obviously a vast literature on this, I will take the texts of Cassian as reference and guideline. Cassian, as you know, was probably of Scythian origin[28] and spent a fair amount of time in the Middle East in the monastic communities, both cenobite and anchorite, in Palestine and Lower Egypt. After this long journey through the monastic life of the Middle East, Cassian returns to Europe and settles in the French Midi where he proposes the implantation of monastic institutions in Western Christianity.[29] He makes plans for the foundation of a monastery that he sends to his bishop—who incidentally will become pope[30]—and writes two major works on this subject: one is called *The Institutes of the Cenobia*,[31] which is the presentation of monastic life, of the cenoby of the Middle East, and another, much longer collection [entitled] *The Conferences*,[32] which is the memory, the recollection of his conversations with important and famous monks from the time when he was in the Middle East. I will refer to these texts for a number of reasons. Once again, [Cassian] is far from being the only one, but, on the one hand, he is significant because it was through the *Institutes* and the *Conferences* that Eastern monasticism became known in the West and as a result it is from these texts that the great monastic institutions of the West derive, principally, of course, Benedictine monasticism, the monasticism [stemming]* from Saint Benedict.[33] So, in a sense, the main part of Western monasticism comes from these texts. And, on the other hand, [they] are interesting because, unlike the other texts, they are basically a compendium of practices. In both the East and the West there was a whole series of compendia in circulation concerning the life of the ascetics or monks, but these were mainly collections

---

* M.F.: which will derive from.

of sayings, like the *Apophtegmata patrum*,[34] or examples of miracles, of particularly intense acts of ascesis practiced by this or that monk, [like] the *Lausiac History* written by Palladius.[35] There are also the collections of rules in the strict sense. The *Rule* of Saint Pachomius[36] was translated into Latin by Saint Jerome[37] and known as such. But between the examples of what could be called monastic heroism, on the one hand, and then the simple schema of rules or regulations, Cassian's texts are interesting because they refer to these examples, certainly, and he also sets out the rules, but he shows how it works, how one lives in the monastery, the point of this system of rules and how it operates in such a way that one arrives at these summits of monastic heroism. What he wants [to explain],[*] he says in the Preface to the *Institutes*, is "the simple life of the saints,"[38] as he had personally experienced and practiced it. He wants to set out "the institutions and the rules of the monasteries and, above all, the cause of the principal vices[39] as well as the way to remedy them."[40] And he will not display, he says, "God's miracles," that is to say the exploits of the ascetics and monks, but "the correction of our morals and the way to lead the perfect life."[41] So, it is quite precisely a regime of life or the regime of life of the monastic communities or of the anchorites that he will set out in his works and from this point of view I think it is undoubtedly the best document for understanding how the practices of the philosophical life, already defined by the ancients, were elaborated and transformed within the monastic institution.

The first principle is, of course, the following: there can be no monastic life without direction. A word of explanation, and I apologize to those who already know all this. I remind you that at the time when Cassian is writing "monastic life" should be understood in two senses: it refers to *anachōrēsis*, that is to say to the monastic life of hermits or semi-hermits who live in the desert and conduct their ascesis individually, as it were, and then there is the monastic community or cenoby, in which the monks live in common, under direction and with a rule. But—and this is what is important—as a result [of a series] of episodes, with which historians of religion are familiar, *anachōrēsis* (that is to say individual, isolated asceticism, totally isolated in the case of Upper Egypt, relatively isolated in the case of Lower Egypt) was at this

---

* M.F.: to show.

time the object of a number of criticisms or gave rise to a number of somewhat suspicious reactions [owing to] excesses, wanderings, or even aberrations of this both intense and spectacular asceticism oriented towards thaumaturgy.[42] Against these divagations of spontaneous asceticism, the entire undertaking of the great theologians and pastors of the Middle East in the fourth century was to define a system of rules that would enable a regime of monastic life to be established in the forms of either *anachōrēsis* or the cenoby.[43] All the authors of this period are in agreement: one cannot become a monk, one cannot be a good monk, one cannot avoid the danger of falling and relapsing if one is not directed and if one does not have a fundamental relationship with a director. No monastic life without direction, and *The Lausiac History* recalls the passage from *Proverbs* which will then be recorded endlessly: "Those who are not directed fall like dead leaves."[44]

What do we see in Cassian? First, with regard to the anchorites, that is to say those who live in the desert, he says that there is no question of them leaving for the desert without having undergone prior training under the direction of a teacher. One tradition would have it that this prior training was generally to be undertaken by just one teacher, that is to say that one set out to practice *anachōrēsis* alongside an already established anchorite well-known for his virtue, and that under his direction one learned to become an anchorite oneself. With [regard] to which Cassian—and other authors, Saint Jerome speaks in the same vein[*45]— says that this is, of course, fine, but that it is not sufficient to see a single teacher, for there are drawbacks in having just one teacher and it does not allow sufficient control. One should not attach oneself to just one teacher, however great he may be. "The monk"—this is in the Fifth Book of *The Institutes*, chapter IV—"who desires to make provision of spiritual honey must, like a most prudent bee, gather each virtue from those for whom it has become second nature."[46] So, one needs to take examples from all round and to pass through the hands of several successive directors, each one renowned for a particular virtue.[47] Still in the same vein, Cassian would have it also that when one wants to become an anchorite

* Manuscript, sheet 15: "Similarly St. Jerome, letter 12 [5], 15: place yourself under the direction of a single Father, but learn lessons from the Ancients: humility from one, patience from another, silence from another, and leniency from another."

and withdraw to the desert, [one begin]* with a period of training in
the cenoby, that is to say in a community.[48]

What takes place in the cenoby and in these communities, and how
does Cassian depict the training and direction of those who apply to enter
them? When one wishes to enter a cenoby, Cassian says, one must pass
through three successive stages. First—this is in Book IV of the *Institutes*,
the book that is most explicit about the rules of the monk's training[49]—
one remains at the door of the monastery for ten days, "systematically
repulsed and despised by everyone, as if one wished to enter the monastery, not with a pious intention, but out of necessity. One is heaped with
abuse and reproaches."[50] So, ten days at the monastery door, [during]
which the other monks reject, repulse, and despise you. You remember
the position of the penitent at the church door when he performs exomologesis and in which he proclaims his sins, throws himself at the feet
of the faithful, and asks them to let him enter the church. After these ten
days of training in humiliation, dust, and abjection, and if he has proved
that he really can withstand this, the postulant is accepted. At this point
he is stripped of his clothes, renounces his wealth, and puts on the dress
of the monastery.[51] After this—and this is the second major phase of the
preparation—he will stay for one year, not exactly in the monastery, but
in the house or rooms for receiving strangers and guests at the entrance
of the monastery, and, under the guidance of an elder, he is charged with
caring for strangers and passing guests.[52] And then, at the end of just
one year of this period of training, he is admitted to the monastery, but
again entrusted to an elder who is in charge of ten young persons whom
he must "*instituer et gubernare*,"[53] instruct, direct, and govern, ensure their
education, training, and government.

Between these three phases of preparation—the ten days before entry
into the monastery, the year at the door of the monastery, and finally
the undetermined period during which [the novice]† will be part of
a group of ten governed by a person in charge—you can see the difference of form, but also the convergence of objectives. At the monastery door he requests admittance and is met with rebuffs, humiliations,
refusal, and rejection, all practices close to those of penance with (as

* M.F.: it is good, basically, to begin.
† M.F.: he.

with penance moreover) the function of tests: will he in actual fact be able to withstand them? He must show his capacity for endurance, he must demonstrate his will to enter the monastery despite everything. It is a matter, Cassian says, of an *experimentum*,[54] of probation. But what does one experiment, what does one test? One tests [the postulant's] patience* in receiving insults, his ability to accept everything imposed on him, one tests his submission. The words employed by Cassian are *patientia, oboedientia, humilitas*.[55] Afterwards, therefore, comes the point when he is about to enter the monastery, and Cassian explains that the reason he is stripped is first of all to test his agreement to detach himself from the world, but it is also to make him entirely dependent upon the monastery. Cassian notes that he will never be able to get back the wealth he gives up, it will never be returned to him,[56] like the clothes of which he has been stripped, for he must no longer be able to be independent.[57] And, Cassian says, "if he runs away, he will have to flee like a thief in the night,"[58] for he is no longer free to leave and rediscover his identity, his goods, his clothes. What must he show, then, in the guest house where he must stay for a year under the direction of a governor, a director? He must show, Cassian says, his *famulatus*,[59] that is to say his ability to be a servant, a slave, to be *famulus*. He must show his *humilitas*, he must show his *patientia*. And finally, what will he do and what type of training will he undergo in the period in which he is being directed by a teacher, in this indefinite period of training (indefinite not in the sense of it being endless, but of it not being precisely delimited like the year in which he must remain in the guest house), during this training period of variable length? The object of the "teacher's solicitude," says Cassian, his concern, his *eruditio*—he speaks of the teacher's *eruditio*, which should be understood in the sense of way of teaching, art of teaching—must focus principally on two points. First, "to teach the novice to vanquish his wishes."[60] The novice will be taught to conquer his wishes by being given orders, by being given a great many orders, and orders that are, as far as possible, contrary to his inclinations. Going then against the current of his inclinations so that he obeys and in this way his wishes are conquered.[61] So he is taught obedience. [And,] Cassian [says]† in

---

* M.F.: his patience.
† Passage reconstructed from the manuscript, folio 18. Gap in the recording due to changing cassette.

this famous Book IV of the *Institutes*: to obtain this result (obedience), "we teach beginners not to hide with false shame any of the thoughts that gnaw at their heart, but as soon as such thoughts arise," they must "reveal them to the elder."[62]

Here I think we are at the heart of what is distinctive about Christian direction and that was, to tell the truth, the object of this year's lectures. That is to say: we are at the point where we find joined together, coupled, connected up to each other, two fundamental obligations that, in a way, recall a number of elements that we talked about regarding ancient repentance, certain elements also that bring together again what we said about penance and baptism, but with a different emphasis and organization, a different apparatus (*dispositif*). What is involved, in fact, is the joining together of the two following obligations: to obey in everything and to hide nothing. Or, joining together the principle of willing nothing by oneself with the principle of telling all about oneself. Telling all about oneself, hiding nothing, willing nothing by oneself, obeying in everything; the junction between these two principles is, I think, at the very heart of not only the Christian monastic institution, but of a whole series of practices, of apparatuses (*dispositifs*) that will inform what constitutes Christian and, as a result, Western subjectivity. To obey and to tell, to obey exhaustively and exhaustively tell what one is, to be under the will of the other and to make all the secrets of one's soul pass through discourse, so that the secrets of one's soul come to light and so that, in the ascent of the soul's secrets to the light, obedience to the other is total, exhaustive, and perfect; we have here an absolutely fundamental set of arrangements, a quite specific relationship between the subject, the other, the will, and enunciation. In this and the next lecture I would like to say something about this technique for establishing and setting to work—between self, other, will, and enunciation—obedience to the other and telling all about oneself.

First, obeying in everything. Christian direction, monastic direction, thus entails that one obeys. You will tell me that the idea that direction passes by way of the student's obedience to the teacher is clearly an old idea and one does not imagine that there could be a direction in which the person directed did not obey the person who directs—of course. It seems to me that direction, as it is found in ancient philosophical life, or in ancient pedagogy, is profoundly different from the direction that develops in monastic institutions and in Christianity.[63]

In fact, direction in ancient philosophical life and ancient pedagogy has three characteristics. First, it is limited and instrumental. What I mean is that obedience has a definite end that is external to it. One obeys a teacher, a director insofar as he is able to enable us to free ourselves from a passion, to overcome a sorrow, to dominate the vexation of exile or ruin, [or] to get out of a state of uncertainty—you recall Serenus asking Seneca: Things aren't going well presently, I am not making much progress, help me take the plunge.[64] What is involved therefore is a precise or definite goal external to the relationship of obedience, and the relationship of obedience must be simply instrumental [in view of] this goal. Second, ancient direction presupposes a certain competence on the part of the master. This competence is not necessarily a form of knowledge, a technical knowledge. It has been said enough since Socrates and the debates with the Sophists. But it may be an experience, or a particular wisdom, or a kind of divine mark: the *theios anēr* is the one who is able to guide you because he is *theios anēr*.[65] So between the one who directs and the one directed there needs to be a sort of difference of nature. Finally, third, ancient, non-Christian, non-monastic direction is provisional, that is to say the most important thing about its aim is to lead to a stage at which one no longer needs a director and is able to conduct oneself and be the sovereign director of oneself. This is moreover what Seneca was able to do when he, a philosopher, examined his day in the evening, being his own censor, his own scrutinizer, his own inspector. In this sense he was master of himself and he said so quite clearly, since he said that with regard to himself he made use of his *potestas*, his power.[66] Those are the three characteristics of non-Christian, pagan direction.

Now I think a completely different form of relationship is involved in Christian direction. Let's go over these three characteristics. I told you that [ancient, non-Christian direction] was provisional, entailed the competence of the master, and that it was limited and instrumental. So, let's take its provisional character. Christian direction is not, in fact, provisional. Of course, you will tell me that there is a difference between novices and those who are not novices. Of course, there are elders, and these may direct, whereas novices may not. But first of all we should note that the notion of elder is not at all a chronological notion. The term elder, the term old man actually designates someone who is sufficiently advanced to direct others or someone thought sufficiently endowed with holiness to be asked for help and protection.[67] We should also note that the person who directs—and this is fundamental in Christianity—even if he is an elder, in the sense that he is thought to have already travelled a long way towards perfection, even in this case, he is never exempt from relapsing. He is unstable to the end. Right until the end he is exposed to temptation and, possibly, to the fall. The devil is always present in him (we will come back to this with regard to the problem of the examination of conscience). No one is safe, in the sense of absolutely free of all possibility of relapse. "Those without direction fall like the leaves," but anyone may fall like a leaf, even those who direct. Precisely with regard to directors, Cassian says: "These admirable men recognize that it is the height of wisdom to conduct others well and let oneself be conducted well. They say openly that in this single point consist the great gift of God and the effect of the grace of the Holy Spirit."[68] That is to say: conducting and being conducted, conducting and letting oneself be conducted must be two, as it were, correlative aspects. There is not exactly the phase during which one is conducted and the phase during which one conducts because one no longer needs to be conducted. Basically, ultimately one always needs to be conducted, even and especially when one conducts. Hence a series of anecdotes (which I pass to you) of distinguished figures very advanced in holiness, recognized directors, about whom Cassian recounts that, in actual fact, they fell as a result of a number of faults, generally those of pride, presumption, etcetera.[*]

So you can see that obedience is not a transitional period in life. There is not a period of life during which one obeys and then a period in which one no longer has to obey. Obedience is not a transitional period, it is a state.[69] It is a state in which one must remain until the end of one's life and with regard to anyone. This is why one of the figures most highly prized by Cassian is the abbot Pinufius,[70] whose example is cited in both the *Institutes* and the *Conferences* and who was of such holiness that, until the end of his life, he could not accept being a director and no longer being in a position of obedience, so that no sooner was his

---

[*] Anecdotes not mentioned in the manuscript.

holiness recognized in a convent than he escaped and presented himself as a novice at another convent in order to be quite sure that he would always be in the position of obedience. His virtue of obedience was such that it could not fail to be recognized so that he was unmasked by his very obedience. He was sought out therefore so that he could be put back among the most holy characters able to direct, and he wept for not being able to end his life in submission, in the *subjectio* that he had acquired. He thought himself to be a great sinner, since God did not accord him the possibility of ending his life in endless submission.[71] So, the principle of the universality, the indefinite permanence of direction: one is made to be directed until the last day.

Second, Christian direction is not founded on the master's competence and Cassian, like the authors of his time, emphasizes the fact that the director is frequently an uneducated monk, lacking erudition, a *rusticus*, a peasant without knowledge.[72] But, after all, this is not a feature that is peculiar to Christianity; since Socrates we know that in order to direct and guide someone, one does not need knowledge, in the theoretical and speculative sense, in the sense of abilities strictly speaking. What is more interesting is that in monasticism direction does not even really entail a precise qualification of the master in that, for example, he may be, or anyway appear to be cantankerous, unpleasant, unjust, and giving the most detestable orders. For the one who obeys, the fact of obedience on its own will be a merit and have a positive effect. In other words, what gives the relationship of obedience its value is neither the quality of the order nor the quality of the person who gives it. It is not an as it were homogeneous transfer of the master's value or competence, of his quality, to the disciple through the quality of the order given. It is just the fact that one obeys whatever the order. And so there is the series of examples of absurd orders and appalling obedience without protest that Cassian cites following the *Lausiac History*. For example, as well as Pinufius, there is the most revered example of obedience: the famous abbot John of whom it was recounted that his director ordered him to go every day, twice a day, to water a dried stick that his master had planted in the desert, so that it might flower, he told him. For a year the abbot John went to water the stick, and at the end of the year, the master said to him: "What, hasn't the stick flowered? You haven't watered it enough." And the abbot John begins again to water it until—Cassian does not say this, but it is in the *Lausiac History*—the stick, of course, [flowers].[73] There is also the story of Patermucius, who enters the monastery with his eight years old son. The monks of the monastery at which he is a guest persecute his son in front of him, beat him, cover him with filth, insult him, and deprive him of food.[74] Of course, Patermucius accepts this, and does so with more joy than if he had seen his son well cared for and honored. And when Patermucius is asked to throw his son in the river, he seizes his son and runs to the river to throw him in. And, of course, Abraham is there—well, the example of Abraham,[75] and everything is sorted out.[76]

A theme as important as the latter; it is the relationship of obedience in its formal structure that possesses in itself an operational value. The distinction found already in *Socrates' Apology*, between *didaskalia* and *ōpheleia*, that is between *didaskalia* as the content of the teaching, and *ōpheleia* as the useful effect of the relationship of direction,*[77] still functions.† But what is useful in the direction relationship is the very form of the relationship of obedience. Any order, however absurd, simply by the fact that it is given and that one obeys it, is what constitutes the useful effect of the direction relationship. But useful for what? What does such obedience have to produce? Why is it necessary and sufficient that orders be given, however absurd we may think them, and that they be followed and obeyed, for there to be a useful effect in the relationship of direction? What does obedience produce? This is not difficult: obedience produces obedience. That is to say that if one must obey—and this is the big difference—it is not for an external objective, it is not, as in the case of ancient direction, in order to recover one's health, or to arrive at a state of happiness, or to overcome a pain or grief. One obeys in order to become obedient, in order to produce a state of obedience, a state of obedience so permanent and definitive that it subsists even where there is not exactly anyone that one has to obey and even before anyone has formulated an order. One must be in a state of obedience. That is to

---

* The manuscript, folio 24, is a bit more precise: "*didaskalia*: this is the procedure of transmission of knowledge from the teacher who possesses it to the disciple who desires it. The *ōphelia* is useful, produces an effect. It is the activation of something on the basis of the teacher's behavior and which in one way or another (often, in an enigmatic fashion) produces a positive effect on the disciple, it shakes him, impresses him, works in him."

† The manuscript, sheet 24, adds: "In the realm of philosophy the teacher is not only someone who teaches. He also *acts* on the disciple. He produces a useful effect in him."

say, obedience is not a way of reacting to an order. Obedience is not a response to the other. Obedience is and must be a way of being, prior to any order, more fundamental than any situation of command and, consequently, the state of obedience in a way anticipates relationships with the other person. Even before the other is present and gives you an order, you are already in a state of obedience and what direction has to produce is obedience. Or let us say again that obedience is at once the condition for direction to function and its end. Obedience and direction must therefore coincide, or rather there is a circularity of obedience and direction. If there is direction it is of course because one is obedient. The *probatio* at the monastery door proves it: one has shown that one is able to obey. Throughout the time of training, one obeys. And, at the end of the training, one is obedient. This direction-obedience circle is fundamental. There is no need to say how far this is from the effects peculiar to ancient direction.

In a few words, let us say this.* This obedience, which is therefore condition, permanent substratum, and effect of direction, is characterized by Cassian in three ways. First, by what he calls *subditio*,[78] submission, the fact of being subject. What does *subditio* mean exactly? It means two things. First, in everything he does the monk must be subject to the rule, or to his superiors, or his companions, or to events that may occur. He not only receives orders, but he sees to it† that everything takes on the form and value of an order. Basically, the monk lives in a world filled with orders.‡ Every event§ must function as an order given and the monk must react to it as to an order. Everything must be order for him, but also every act he makes must be inscribed within this structure of order (in the sense of order given, of command). There can be no act in the monk's life that is not a response to an order or, at the least, a reaction to permission given. In any case, whether imperative or permissive, the other's will must be there. This is the principle stated by Cassian: "The young not only must not leave their cell without the knowledge of

---

* Foucault adds: "Yes, I would have liked to speak to you ..."—he leafs through his notes—"... well fine, let's pass over this a little ... Ah, all the same! You give me five minutes? Thanks!" The end of the lecture faithfully follows the manuscript.
† Manuscript: it is necessary as it were.
‡ The manuscript adds: "and which must be taken as such. An ordering world."
§ "Every other, every event" is heard.

the person in charge, but they must not even presume his authorization to satisfy their natural needs."[79] A nobler example is that of Dositheus, who was the student, the disciple of Saint Barsanuphius.[80] Dositheus was a young man who was dying from tuberculosis but who obviously could not die without the permission of Saint Barsanuphius. Saint Barsanuphius refused permission for a time, at the end of which he told him: "I now authorize you to die," at which point, relieved, Dositheus passed into the other world.[81] "Any action not ordered or permitted by the superior is a theft," says the text of Saint [Basil].[*] "It is a theft and sacrilege that leads to death and not to advantage, even if it seems good to you."[82] So, any action not part of this general web of orders given or permissions granted constitutes a veritable theft. The monk's world must be a web in which each of his deeds and gestures must be inscribed as response to either an order or permission.[†83] This is *subditio*. The whole world is order, every action must have the value and form of a response to an order or a permission.

Second, obedience is also *patientia*.[84] *Patientia* is a difficult notion which means, I think, two things. On the one hand, *patientia* is of course passivity, non-resistance, non-inertia to orders. One has to respond to orders in a completely passive way, without the least inertial resistance. The *perinde ac cadaver* will come much later,[85] but already in the *Logos askētikos* of Saint Nilus we read this: "It is necessary not to differ in any way from an inanimate body or from the raw material used by an artist…And as the artist shows his skill without the material, of whatever kind, preventing him from the pursuit of his end," so the director must be an artist who manipulates in his hands the inert material absolutely as he wishes and, as a result, in the physical mythology of Saint Nilus, without resistance.[86] So, no resistance, absolute passivity: this is *patientia*. But if *patientia* is this absolute passivity, this ability to respond immediately, it is also a certain endurance, an ability to resist or, at any rate, to withstand. A veritable inflexibility is required in the face

---

* M.F., after a hesitation: Nothing (*Nil*). The manuscript does not clarify the author's name (which is no doubt why M.F. says: "I have forgotten the most important thing"), but refers to PG 31, i.e. the writings of Saint Basil. In *Mal faire, dire vrai*, lecture of 6 May 1981, p. 137, the same quotation is correctly attributed to Saint Basil.
† The manuscript adds this quotation from Saint Jerome: "*Prima apud eos confederation est obedire majoribus et quidquid jusserint facere.*"

of everything that is not the order, or is contrary to it, or is its unbearable consequence. When, for example, Patermucius puts up with seeing his son slapped, scorned, trampled underfoot, deprived of everything, and beaten, he bears it with a *patientia*[87] that, in a sense, is immediate docility with regard to the order, but that is also the ability to resist absolutely and with utter inflexibility the possible impulses of his heart, to resist all that might be opposed to the order.* Total plasticity, total inflexibility: this is what *patientia* means.

Finally, the third characteristic of obedience is *humilitas*, humility[88]— and what is humility? It is a relationship to oneself that consists in placing oneself as low as possible in relation to anyone else; one must be inferior to any other; consequently, one must obey and serve him in everything. It is the principle that the monk must consider himself more humble than any of his companions, put himself below them and accept their wishes as orders. And then *humilitas* is not only putting oneself lower than anyone else; at the same time, because one judges oneself to be less than nothing, it means disqualifying one's own will as having no right to want anything. My will has no right to will anything, since I am worthless, I am nothing, I am a sinner. There is no justification, no natural or other right for me to will anything: that is what the will must tell itself. I am the lowest of beings and it is not permissible to will anything at all.

So, in this structure of *oboedientia* we have three things. *Subditio*, submission, which means: I want what the other wills; *patientia*, which means: I want not to will anything different from the other; and *humilitas*, which consists in saying: I do not want to will. Wanting what the other wills, wanting not to will, not wanting to will, are the three aspects of obedience as, at the same time, condition, substratum, and effect of direction. In short, *subditio* is the general form of the relationship to others; *patientia* is an attitude towards the external world; and *humilitas* is the relation to self. You can see that these three distinctive elements of obedience, of an obedience that is itself fundamental, distinctive, central, and focal in the relationship of direction, you can see

---

* The manuscript, which does not cite this example, adds: "Far from having to make oneself indifferent to this, one must rather take it 'full on.' Expose oneself to it without hesitation. Avoid prevarication."

that, in a sense, all this and ancient direction are poles apart. What
was the goal of ancient direction in fact? Ancient direction, as seen
at work in the Stoics, for example, involved getting the individual to
be able to free himself in relation to his teachers, to others, and to
events. It involved the individual establishing himself in a position of
self-sufficiency and autonomy in relation to everything else, to others, or to the world. This autonomy is the exact opposite of *subditio*, of
submission that means that one is subject to everything that happens
and that everything becomes an order on which one depends. Ancient
direction involved ensuring that the individual was no longer subject
to the impulses of his passions, that is to say that he no longer experi-
ences anything that may agitate or affect him in one way or another.
Now the *patientia* of Christian direction does not say this. The *patientia*
one must attain is rather the immediacy with which one reacts to the
order given by others and also the possibility of accepting the sharpest,
keenest suffering and ordeal coming from others or from the world.
The more one suffers, the more *patientia* will be tested and, as a result,
the more the relationship of obedience, of *subditio*, submission, will be
strengthened. You can see that there is a radical difference between the
ancient *apatheia*[89] that ancient direction aims for in Stoic philosophy,
and the *patientia* that Christian direction aims for. Finally, through this
self-mastery, ancient direction involved getting the individual to be
able communicate with the order of the world and that by obeying his
own reason, he complied at the same time with the reason that rules
the world, so that, being master of himself, he is in a certain way master of the universe.[90] This typical mastery of Stoic autonomy, is [thus]
the exact opposite of *humilitas*, or rather *humilitas*, which puts me below
everyone and makes me want nothing, is the opposite of this autonomy
through which, by willing rationally what I will, I will what the entire
world itself may will.

So, from the fourth century, within monastic institutions there is the
transfer of a number of fundamental techniques of ancient philosophical
life into Christianity. But this transfer of techniques, and in particular
of the technique of direction, is brought about, principally around the
relationship of obedience, with a veritable inversion of all the effects
produced by this technique. In other words, the procedure of direction, the technique of direction, is now inscribed in a general apparatus

(*dispositif*) or, if you like, in a technology of direction that alters and inverts all its effects.

That is what I wanted to say [about] direction. So, next week we will talk about the other aspect of the philosophical or monastic life, that is to say the obligation to tell all and the techniques of examination.

1. On the question, much debated for more than a century, of the influence of Greek philosophy on Pauline theology, see already the review of the discussion by A. Schweitzer, *Geschichte der paulinischen Forschung von der Reformation bis auf der Gegenwort* (Tübingen: J.C.B. Mohr, 1911), pp. 50-82; English translation by W. Montgomery, *Paul and his Interpreters* (London: Adam & Charles Black, 1912/New York: The Macmillan Company, 1951) pp. 63-78.

2. On this question see J.-C. Guy, "Examen de conscience. III. Chez le Pères de l'Eglise," col. 1806-1807: "… it is quite remarkable that, during this period of Stoic influence [= the first three centuries], the examination of conscience is practically never mentioned among the practices proposed to Christians to keep up the fervor of their faith." The example of Clement of Alexandria, *The Instructor (Paedagogus)*, Book III, I, 1, is examined following this passage: "Clement of Alexandria certainly knew the Stoic moralists well. He uses and comments on the *gnothi seauton* at several points (*The Instructor*, III, I, 1; *Stromata*, I, 174, 2; III, 44, 3; IV, 27, 3) However, this sentence is always interpreted in the sense of a *permanent state* of attention to oneself and internal vigilance, never in that of a *periodic act* of turning in on oneself" (col. 1802).

3. Clément d'Alexandrie, *Le Pédagogue*, III, 1, 1, p. 13; Clement of Alexandria, *The Instructor (Paedagogus)*, Book III, ch. 1, ANF, Vol. I, p. 271: "It is then, as appears, the greatest of all lessons to know one's self. For if one knows himself, he will know God; and knowing God, he will be made like God."

4. Plato, *The Republic*, Book IV, 439d-441a. Foucault says (and writes in the manuscript) "*logikon*" (instead of *logistikon*)—the first form being acceptable moreover (see, for example, Cassien, *Conférences*, 24, 15, vol. 3, p. 187)—and "*epithumikon*" (instead of *epithumētikon*).

5. On the theme of the Logos common to man and God, "mediator, both son of God and savior of men," who resides in the soul of the Christian, see Clément d'Alexandrie, *La Pédagogue*, III, 1, 4, p. 15; Clement of Alexandria, *The Instructor*, Book III, ch. I, p. 271: "for the Mediator is the Word, who is common to both—the Son of God, the Saviour of men." See also the general introduction [to the French] by H.-I. Marrou, SC 70, 1960, p. 40: "The one in whom this divine Word lives models himself progressively in and finishing realizing his resemblance 'becomes god, *theos gietai*, for such is God's will.' (III, 1, 5)"

6. Psalm 119, v. 59: "*Cogitavi vias meas, et averti pedes meos in testimonio tuo*" (passage quoted by Saint Ambrose—see the following note—col. 1306 c. The Vulgate translation has "… *et converti pedes meos*." [RSV: "I will meditate on thy precepts, and fix my eyes on thy ways"; Robert Alter: "I have reckoned my ways, and turned back my feet to your Precepts."]

7. St Ambroise [St Ambrose], PL, 15, 1308 c, *In Psalmum David CXCIII expositio: "Cogitandum est igitur quid geramus; ubi enim praecidi cogitation, maturitas operationis adhibetur*" (quoted by J.-C. Guy, "Examen de conscience. III. Chez les Pères d l'Eglise," col. 1803). Opposite the quotation of Ambrose, Foucault adds in the manuscript: "the same thing in Saint Hilaire, PL IX, 556 ab." See *Tractatus super Psalmos*, Littera VIII (Heth), PL 9, 556 ab: "10. Agenda quisque debet praemeditari.—*Ex his quae Propheta se gerere, vel gessisse commemorat, quid nos quoque facere oporteat docet. Vias enim suas cogitat, et cogitatis his pedem in testimonia Dei refert. Nihil egit, quod non antea cogitatione pervolverit. Non linguam in officium suum movit, non pedem in aliquod quod acturus esset opus protulit, non manum ad agendum aliquid exseruit, nisi antea super his omnibus cogitasset, et cum operationem atque effectum cogitatio rebus attulerit."*

8. See *Sécurité, territoire, population*, lecture of 22 February 1978, pp. 172-173; *Security, Territory, Population*, pp. 167-169.

9. Clément d'Alexandrie, *Quis dives salvetur*, 41, PG 9, col. 645-648. On the translation used freely by Foucault, see above, lecture of 5 March, p. 216, note 1; English translation by William Wilson, Clement of Alexandria, *Who is the Rich Man who shall be saved?* in ANF, Vol. II, p. 602.

10. Ibid., col. 645 c: "*aleiptēn kai kubernētēn*" (Latin translation: *rector ac gubernator*). Quéré-Jaulmes translation, pp. 51-52: "It is thus indispensable that you who boast of your power and wealth choose a man of God for a director who will serve as gymnastics teacher and helmsman"; P. Descourtieux translation, p. 207: "a man of God who will train you and steer you"; English, p. 602: "Wherefore it is by all means necessary for thee, who art pompous, and powerful, and rich, to set over thyself some man of God as a trainer and governor." On the first word, see I. Hausherr, *Spiritual Direction in the Early Christian East*, p. 191, quoting Saint Basil: "One must give the new monk the spiritual *aleiptēn* (trainer) for whom he may ask."

11. Ibid.
12. See I. Hausherr, *Spritual Direction in the Early Christian East*, p. 4, who indicates, among the multiple ways of designating the spiritual director, the following: *"diorthōtēs* (one who sets right), *paideutēs* (teacher), *aleiptēs* (trainer)," and adds: "Especially among the cenobites they used *prostates* (leader), *epistatēs* (master), and *ephestos* (director)." On epistates (*epistatēs*) (Christ called "master" by Simon) see Luke, 5, 5; 8, 24. *Epistateia,* which in classical Greek designates the function of epistate, magistrate of the city (in Athens notably responsible for looking after the State seals and keys of the public archives), took on, by extension, the sense of direction, supervision. See too, *epistatein*: to supervise, oversee, direct and care for something.
13. Clément d'Alexandrie, *Quis dives salvetur,* col. 645 d. F. Quéré-Jaulmes trans., p. 52: "Would you respect, would you fear him alone, this would already be very good. Get used to hearing him speak to you with frankness, let him treat you harshly and also pity you"; Clement of Alexandria, *Who is the Rich Man who shall be saved?* p. 602: "Reverence, though it be but one man; fear, though it be but one man. Give yourself to hearing, though it be but one speaking freely, using harshness, and at the same time healing."
14. Ibid.: "He will pass long sleepless nights to defend you before God, and he will end by touching the Father by dint of insistence. For God does not refuse his compassion to those who pray to him. And your director will pray fervently, if you honor him as God's envoy, and do not cause him pain, at least willingly"; Eng., ibid., p. 603: "Let him pass many sleepless nights for thee, interceding for thee with God, influencing the Father with the magic of familiar litanies. For He does not hold out against His children when they beg His pity. And for you he will pray purely, held in high honour as an angel of God, and grieved not by you, but for you."
15. Ibid., 42, col. 647-652; Fr.: pp. 52-54; Eng., pp. 603-604. See E. Amnann, "Pénitence," col. 759, which summarizes this "charming anecdote": "… Clement presents it as a story religiously handed down and confided to the memory of the faithful. Whatever its relationship with reality, the tale had existed for some time when the Alexandrian priest recorded it …"; B. Poshmann, *Paenitentia secunda,* pp. 252-256; E. Junod, "Un écho d'un controverse autour de la pénitence: l'histoire de l'Apôtre Jean et du chef des brigands chez Clément d'Alexandrie (Quis Dives Salvetur 41, 1-150)," *Revue d'Histoire et de Philosophie religieuse,* 60, April-June 1980, pp. 153-160.
16. Ibid., col. 650 bc; Fr., p. 54: "At these words, John rent his clothes and struck his head, moaning: 'Ah! I have given a fine guardian to the soul of your brother!'"; Eng., p. 603: "Rending, therefore, his clothes, and striking his head with great lamentation, the apostle said, 'It was a fine guard of a brother's soul I left!'"
17. Ibid., Foucault here quotes the Quére-Jaulmes translation literally; Eng., ibid.: "I will give account to Christ for thee. If need be, I will willingly endure thy death, as the Lord did death for us. For thee I will surrender my life."
18. Ibid., col. 650 cd; Fr., ibid.: "… he takes him back to the church. There … he shared his continual fasting and won over his mind with ceaseless discourses"; Eng., ibid.: "… led him back to the church. Then by supplicating with copious prayers, and striving along with him in continual fastings, and subduing his mind by various utterances."
19. The story can also be read as a defense and illustration of Clement's position in favor of post-baptismal penance (the bishop representing the rigorist position). See above, the reference to penance as "second baptism" according to Clement at the beginning of the lecture of 5 March; E. Junod, "Un écho d'un controverse autour de la pénitence," p. 159.
20. Saint Athanase, *Vie d'Antoine,* 55, PG, 26, 924 ab; ed. and trans. G.J.M. Bartelinck, *Vie d'Antoine,* 55, 7-9, SC 400 (Paris: Cerf, 1994), p. 286; English translation by Cardinal Newman, revised by J.H. Lupton as Saint Athanasius, *Life of Antony* in NPNF2, Vol. IV, ed. Archibald Robertson (Grand Rapids, Michigan: W.B. Eerdmans Publishing, 1994), 55, p. 211: "Daily, therefore, let each one take from himself the tale of his actions both by day and night … Let us each one note and write down our actions and the impulses of our soul as though we were going to relate them to each other … Wherefore let that which is written be to us in place of the eyes of our fellow hermits." The passage is quoted by J.-C. Guy, "Examen de conscience. III. Chez les Pères de l'Eglise," col. 1805, who notes that "such a teaching is very rare in monastic literature of the fourth century" and "scarcely finds an echo in Basilian monasticism" (ibid., col. 1806). Saint Athanasius bases himself on 2, Corinthians, 13, 5. This text is also quoted in P. Hadot, "Exercices spirituels antiques et 'philosohie chrétienne,'" in

Exercices spirituels et philosophie antique, p. 69 (Albin Michel ed., p. 90); "Ancient Spiritual Exercises and 'Christian Philosophy,'" in Philosophy as a Way of Life, p. 135. For examination of conscience, this article refers to I. Hadot, Seneca und die griechisch-römische Tradition der Seelenleitung, p. 70.

21. See I. Hadot, Seneca und die griechisch-römische Tradition, p. 70: "Man bediente sich sogar schriftlicher Tabellen, um eine genaue Überprüfung zu gewährleisten." Epictetus, Discourses, Book II, 18, 12 et seq. is cited as an example of this practice.

22. St Jean Chrysostome [St John Chrysostom], Œuvres complètes, Vol. III, homily "That it is dangerous for the orator and the auditor to speak in order to please, that it is of much greater utility and more rigorous justice to accuse one's sins," 4, p. 401: "Immediately after rising, before appearing in public and concerning ourselves with any business, we summon our servant and ask him for an account of what has been spent, in order to know what has been spent well or at the wrong time, and what we have left. If there is little left, we search our minds for new resources so as not to risk dying of hunger. We must proceed in the same way for the conduct of our life. Let us call on our conscience, let us get it to give an account of actions, words, and thoughts. Let us examine what profits us or harms us; what evil we have spoken, the malicious, clownish, offensive remarks we have permitted ourselves, what thought has led us to glances that are too free; what plan we have carried out to our detriment, whether of the hand, the tongue, or even the eyes. Let us cease spending at the wrong time, and endeavor to replace harmful expenses with useful investment, indiscreet words with prayers, brazen glances with fasting and almsgiving. If we spend regardless, without putting anything in its place, without storing up for heaven, we will fall insensibly into extreme poverty, and we will be delivered up to tortures as unbearable for their duration as much as for their intensity."

23. Saint Nil [Nilus], Logos askētikos/De monastica exercitatione, PG, col. 721 B: "Est quippe philosophia morum emendatio (ēthōn katorthōsis), cum laude verae cognitionis illius que est (meta doxēs tēs peri tou ontos gnōseōs alēthous)." See M.-G. Guérard, "Nil d'Ancyre," DS, XI, 1981, col. 353, concerning his spiritual doctrine: "monasticism is defined as the true philosophy ([PG 79], 732 c, 720 a, 721 c) that leads to the true knowledge of being (721 b) ... ascesis is not sufficient by itself (721 b, 1028 b), it is a pedagogical stage towards contemplation (728 b, 748 a)."

24. On the identification of Christianity with true philosophy in the Cappadocians and John Chrysostom ("philosophy according to Christ"), see P. Hadot, "Exercises spirituels antiques et 'philosophie chrétienne'" in Exercises spirituels, (pp. 61-62) pp. 79-80; "Ancient Spiritual Exercises and 'Christian Philosophy'" in Philosophy as a Way of Life, p. 129, which refers to A.N. Malingrey, "Philosophia." Étude d'un groupe de mots dans la littérature grecque, des Présocratiques au IVe siècle ap. J.-C. (Paris: Klincksieck, 1961).

25. P. Hadot, ibid., Fr., [p. 62] p. 80; Eng., p. 129: "When ... monasticism came to represent the culmination of Christian perfection, it, too, could be portrayed as a philosophia ... by ... such as ... John Chrysostom" (reference to Adversus oppugnatores vitae monasticae, III, 13, PG, 47, 372). According to A. N. Malingrey (see previous note), "we owe Clement of Alexandria the honor of being the first to link Christ's name to the word philosophia in the expression: ē kata Kriston philosophia" (p. 292; see p. 150 for the quotation of Stromates, VI, viii, 67, I, SC no. 446, 1999, p. 196; The Stromata, Book VI, ch. VIII, ANF, Vol. II, p. 495). See also G. Bardy, "'Philosophe' et 'philosophie' dans le vocabulaire chrétien des premiers siècles," Revue d'ascétique et de mystique, 25, 1949, pp. 97-108; I. Hausherr, Spiritual Direction, pp. 52-53; P. Miquel, "Monachisme," DS, X, 1979, col. 1555-1556 ("Vie monastique, vraie philosophie") and the bibliography, col. 1557; reprinted in A. de Solignac, ed., Le monachisme. Histoire et spiritualité (Paris: Beauchesne, 1980), pp. 53-75.

26. See Saint Nil [Nilus], Epist. 54, PG, 79, 224 c, where the monk is defined as "imitator of Christ, who showed us the true philosophy by action and words (tou paradeixantos ergo kai logō tēn alētē philosophia) trans., P. Miquel, "Monachisme," col. 1555-1556; see also, Grégoire de Nazianze (Gregory Nazienzen), Oratio VI, PG, 35, 721, "who identifies the life of the monks with di'ergōn philosophia" (I. Hausherr, Spiritual Direction, p. 52).

27. See P. Hadot, "Exercises spirituels antiques et 'philosophie chrétienne'" [p. 63] p. 81; "Ancient Spiritual Exercises and 'Christian Philosophy'" p. 129: the result of "this [monastic] tendency [linked ... to the tradition of the Apologists and of Origen] ... was the introduction of philosophical spiritual exercises into Christianity."

28. "*[N]atione Scytha*" according to his first biographer, Gennadius (Gennade of Marseilee), c.
470, *De viris illustribus*, 62, ed. E.C. Richardson (Leipzig: J.C. Hinrich, 1896). On the dis-
cussions to which this testimony has given rise, see O. Chadwick, *John Cassian* (Cambridge:
Cambridge University Press, 1950, 2nd ed., 1968), p. 9; J.-C. Guy, *Jean Cassien. Vie et doctrine spirituelle* (Paris: P. Lethellieux, "Théologie, pastorale et spiritualité," 1961), pp. 13-14.
According to the most probable hypothesis, Cassian would have come from a part of present
Romania, close to the town of Constantza (see the argument of H.-I. Marrou, "La patrie de
Jean Cassien," in *Miscellanea G. de Jerphanion* (Rome: 1947), p. 588 and p. 596, cited by J.-C.
Guy, *Jean Cassien*, p. 14).
29. John Cassian (?360-435) spent several years, with his companion Germain—older than him
and to whom he often gives the title *abba*, "father"—in a monastery at Bethlehem ("it seems
... that he lived there in a 'sanctuary monastery,' as if he were at Rome and Jerusalem close
to big basilicas," E. Pichery, Introduction to the *Conférences*, p. 57; see *Institutions* [and below,
note 31] 3, 4, p. 102 ; 4, 31, p. 171; 17, 6, p. 253 [There are only twelve Books of *The Institutes*;
it may be that the French reference is to *The Conferences*, Conference XVII, ch. VI; G.B.];
English translation Boniface Ramsey, *The Institutes* (New York/Mahwah, NJ: Newman Press,
"Ancient Christian Writers," No. 58, 2000), Book III, ch. IV, pp. 62-63; IV, ch. XXXI,
p. 96; [*Conferences*, XVII, ch. VI, p. 589, see above]), then with monks in Egypt: "This was
when we were living in our monastery in Syria. After having received the first elements of the
faith and made some advance, we felt the desire for a higher perfection and resolved to go forth-
with to Egypt. We wished to penetrate as far as the distant desert of the Thebaid, to visit the
greatest number of holy men whose fame had spread glory throughout the world, pushed by
the zeal, if not to emulate them, at least to learn to know them" (Cassien, *Conférences*, 11, 1, t. 2,
p. 101); "When we were living in a cenobium in Syria and, after an initial training in the faith,
had gradually and increasingly begun to desire a greater grace of perfection, we at once decided
to go to Egypt and, after having penetrated the remote desert of the Thebaid, to visit many
of the holy ones, whose reputation had made them glorious everywhere, if not for the sake of
imitating them, then at least for the sake of becoming acquainted with them." (John Cassian,
The Conferences, trans. Boniface Ramsey (New York/Mahwah, NJ: Newman Press, "Ancient
Christian Writers," No. 57, 1997), Conference XI, chapter I, p. 409. Forced to leave Egypt,
following the anti-Origenist campaign unleashed by the Patriarch of Alexandria, Theophilus,
in 399, he was ordained deacon by John Chrysostom at Constantinople in the first years of the
century (the later ordination to the priesthood is uncertain), stayed at Rome, then founded
and directed two convents, one for men and the other for women, in the Marseille region. See
M. Olphe-Galliard, "Cassien," *DS*, II, 1937, col. 214-276, and the books of O. Chadwick and
J.-C. Guy cited in the previous note. Foucault, who had already referred to this author in his
1978 lectures (see *Sécurité, territoire, population*, lecture of 22 February 1978, p. 170 and passim;
Security, Territory, Population, p. 165 and passim) and in 1979 ("*Omnes et Singulatim*': Toward
a Critique of Political Reason" in *The Essential Works of Foucault, 1954-1984. Volume Three.
Power*, ed. James D. Faubion (New York: The New Press, 2000), pp. 308-309, with regard
to obedience: the relationship between the pastor and his flock conceived of, in Christianity,
as a relationship of individual and complete dependence), returns to him frequently afterwards: see *Mal faire, dire vrai*, lecture of 6 May 1981, pp. 126-150; "Sexuality and Solitude,"
The Essential Works of Foucault, 1954-1984. Volume One. Ethics, Subjectivity, and Truth, ed. Paul
Rabinow (New York: The New Press, 1997); "Le combat de la chasteté" (1982)—a chapter
from the unpublished work *Les Aveux de la chair*, appeared in *Communications*, no. 35, 1982,
pp. 15-25, republished in *Dits et écrits*, IV, pp. 295-308/ Quarto, Vol. II, pp. 1114-1127 (on
the spirit of fornication and the ascesis of chastity); English translation by Anthony Forster,
amended, as "The Battle for Chastity" in *Essential Works of Foucault*, Vol. One, pp. 184-197; the
Résumé du cours de 1981-1982, "L'Herméneutique du sujet," *Dits et écrits*, IV, p. 364/Quarto,
Vol. II, p. 1183; English translation by Graham Burchell, "Course Summary," *The Hermeneutics
of the Subject*, p. 503; "L'écriture de soi" (1983), *Dits et écrits*, IV, p. 416/Quarto, Vol. II, p. 1255;
English translation by Robert Hurley, as "Self Writing" in *Essential Works of Foucault*, Vol. One,
p. 208; "Technologies of the Self" in Luther H. Martin, Huck Gutman, and Patrick H. Hutton,
eds., *Technologies of the Self. A Seminar with Michel Foucault* (London: University of Massachusetts
Press/Tavistock Press, 1988) pp. 46-48 (with regard to the metaphor of the money changer
applied to the examination of thoughts).

30. "He undertook to write only on the instigation of Castor, bishop of Apt and founder of a community. The institutions that he proposed to set down in two works were those he had studied and practiced in Egypt" (M. Olphe-Galliard, "Cassien," col. 217). The title of "most blessed Pope" ("*beatissimus papa*") (*Institutions*, Preface, p. 23; *Institutes*, Preface, p. 199), which Cassian accords Castor, is purely honorific.

31. *De institutis coenobiorum et de octo principalium vitiorum remediis*, or, according to the title used most often by Cassian himself, *The Institutes*, written around 420-424; Fr., Jean Cassien *Institutions cénobitiques*, ed. J.-C. Guy; Eng., John Cassian, *The Institutes* (see above, note 29, and p. 109, note 7).

32. *Conlations* (title of the translation manuscript) or, according to later custom, *Collationes patrum in Scithico eremo commorantium*; *Conférences*, ed. E. Pichery; *The Conferences*, (see above, note 29, and p. 109, note 7).

33. See *Regula Benedict* (*La Règle de saint Benoît* [sixth century]), Introduction, trans., and notes by A. de Vogüé (Paris: Cerf, CS, no. 181-182, 1972); English translation by Carolinne White, *The Rule of Benedict* (London: Penguin Books, 2008). "Saint Benedict owes a great deal to the lessons of the Eastern masters, if not directly, for he did not know Greek, at least indirectly through translations (*Rules* of Saint Basil, *Vitae Patrum*) and especially through Cassian whom he quotes all the time and earnestly recommends be read" (G. Bardy, "Direction spirituelle. III. En Occident: A Jusqu'au 11ᵉ siècle," *DS*, III, 1957, col. 1074). On these sources, see in particular Rule 73.

34. *Apophtegmata Patrum*, PG, 65, 71-440 (i.e., the alphabetical collection rather than the systematic collection, *Vitae Patrum*, PL 73, col. 851-1062, a Latin version made by Pelagius and John in the sixth century, not yet published in Greek); translation of the first collection by L. Regnault, *Les Sentences des Pères du Désert. Collection alphabétique* (Solesmes, 1981), and of the second by L. Regnault, J. Dion, and G. Oury, *Les Sentences des Pères du Désert. Recueil de Pélage et Jean* (Éd. de Solesmes, 1966). See also ed. and trans. J.-C. Guy, *Les Apophtegmes des Pères*, systematic collection, ch. I-XXXI, (Paris: Cerf, 3 vols., 1993-2005); *The Sayings of the Desert Fathers: The Alphabetical Collection*, trans. Benedicta Ward (Cistercian Publications: 2005), and *The Desert Fathers: Sayings of the Early Christian Monks*, trans. Benedicta Ward (London: Penguin, 2003). See J.-C. Guy, *Recherches sur la tradition grecque des Apophthegmata Patrum* (Brussels: coll. "Subsidia Hagiographica," XXXVI, 1962.

35. Palladius, *Histoire lausiaque (Vies d'ascètes et de Pères du désert)*, Greek text, Introduction and trans. A. Lucot (Paris: A. Picard et Fils, coll. "Textes et documents pour l'histoire du christianisme," 1912), based on the critical edition of Dom Butler, *The Lausiac History of Palladius* (Cambridge: Cambridge University Press, "Texts and Studies," 6, 2 vols., 1898 and 1904). After a stay of a dozen years with the hermits of Egypt, Palladius was ordained bishop of Helenopolis, in Bithynia, in 400, then of Aspuna in Galatia: he wrote his work around 420. See O. Chadwick, *John Cassian*, p. 32, who notes the "curious parallels" in the respective careers of Palladius and Cassian (departure from Egypt at the same time, as a result of the Origenist crisis, link with John Chrysostom, works illustrating the period of the first Egyptian monasticism); R. Draguet, "L'*Histoire lausiaque*, une œuvre écrite dans l'esprit d'Évagre," *Revue d'histoire ecclésiastique*, t 41, 1946, pp. 321-364, and 42, 1947, pp. 5-49. See also *Sécurité, territoire, population*, lecture of 22 February 1978, p. 191 note 30; *Security, Territory, Population*, p. 188 note 30. To the works referred to, the *Historia Monachorum* should be added, cited by historians of early monasticism as an important source of information on the subject. This text from the end of the fourth century was translated into Latin by Rufinus, and was for a long time attributed to him. Greek text established by A.-J. Festugière, *Historia Monachorum in Aegypto* (Brussels, coll. "Subsidia Hagiographica" XXXIV, 1961; translated by same author as *Les Moines d'Orient* (Paris: Cerf, t. 4, 1964); English translation by Benedicta Ward, *The Lives of the Desert Fathers: Historia Monacharum in Aegypto* (Kalamazoo: Cistercian Publications, Cistercian Studies, No. 34, 2006).

36. See the critical edition of the Pachomian Rule by A. Boon, *Pachomiana latina, Règle et épîtres de S. Pakhôme, épître de S. Théodore et 'liber' de S. Orsiesius, texte latin de S. Jérôme* (Louvain: Bibliothèque de la Revue d'histoire ecclésiastique, "Monastica" 7, 1932, pp. 13-74; French translation in P. Deseille, *L'Esprit du monachisme pakhômien* (Begrolles-en-Mauges: Abbaye de Bellefontaine, coll. "Spiritualité orientale" 21, 1968, 2nd ed. 1980); English translation by Armand Veilleux in *The Lives, Rules, and Other Writings of Saint Pachomius. Volume 2: Pachomian*

Chronicles and Rules (Kalamazoo: Cistercian Publications, 2006). The Greek text used by Saint Jerome is lost. Only fragments of the original survive, written in Coptic.

37. The Latin translation of the Rule of Pachomius by Jerome, in 404 (*Regula patris nostri Pachomii hominis Dei*, PL 73, col 67d-86d) is one of the important sources for Cassian's *Institutes* (see the reference to this translation in his preface, § 5, Fr., p. 27; Eng., p. 13).

38. Cassien, *Institutions*, préface, § 3, p. 25; Cassian, *Institutes*, Preface, 3, p. 12: "the simple life of holy men."

39. "... which" Cassian notes ibid., "the ancients fixed as eight" ; Eng., ibid., 7, p. 13: "to explain, as well as I can with the Lord's help, just the institutes of these men and the rules of their monasteries and, in particular, the origins and causes and remedies of the principal vices, which they number as eight, according to their traditions." See Books V-XII concerning the spirit of gluttony, fornication, avarice, anger, sadness, acedia, vainglory, and pride. See also the fifth *Conference*: "Of the eight principal vices." This list is taken from Evagrius of Ponticus: see below, lecture of 26 March 1980, p. 317, note 32. See O. Chadwick, *John Cassian*, p. 89, and pp. 94-95; C. Stewart, "John Cassian's Schema of Eight Principal Faults and his Debt to Origen and Evagrius," in C. Badilita and A. Jakab, eds., *Jean Cassien entre l'Orient et l'Occident* (Paris: Beauchesne, 2003), pp. 205-220.

40. Cassien, *Institutions*, préface, § 7, p. 29; Cassian, *Institutes*, Preface, 7, p. 13.

41. Ibid., § 8, p. 31; Eng., ibid., 8, p. 13: "my plan is to say a few things not about the marvelous works of God but about the improvement of our behavior and the attainment of the perfect life."

42. See A. Lucot, Introduction to *Histoire lausiaque*, p. xxxviii: "One competed in austerities, collected ascetic virtues in succession, strove to hold the record for a particular mortification, and readily boasted of it. Hence, the multiplicity and novelty in the practices, but soon the strangeness, then a hyper-asceticism, a doctrinal encratism that Saint Paul was aiming at from the First Epistle to the Corinthians, chapter 7, that the Church had to repress [note: DTC, fasc. 34, pp. 4-14: 'Encratites'], and which was justified by the apocryphal Gospels, the Acts of Peter, the Ascensions of James, and the Acts of Paul and Thomas."

43. See *Sécurité, territoire, population*, lecture of 1 March 1978, pp. 208-211 and p. 228 notes 44 and 45; *Security, Territory, Population*, pp. 204-208 and pp. 222-223 notes 44 and 45.

44. Palladius, *Histoire lausiaque*, XXVII, p. 201 (regarding the monk Ptolemy): "he became a stranger to the teaching, intercourse, and benefits of holy men, and to a constant communion of the mysteries, he departed so much from the straight (path), that he said these things were nothing; but it is reported that he became haughty, wandering about in Egypt to the present day, devoting himself to gluttony and drunkenness without restraint, and not communicating anything to anyone. And this misfortune happened to Ptolemy as a result of his unreasonable presumptuousness, according to what is written: 'Those without direction fall like leaves' (Proverbs, 11, 14)"; English translation by W. K. Lowther, *The Lausiac History of Palladius* (London: Macmillan Company, 1918), p. 108: "And he became a stranger to the teaching of holy men and intercourse with them, and the benefit derived therefrom, and the constant communion of the mysteries, and diverged so greatly from the straight way that he declared these things were nothing; but they say he is wandering about in Egypt up to the present day all puffed up with pride, and has given himself over to gluttony and drunkenness, speaking no (edifying) word to anyone. And this disaster fell on Ptolemy from his irrational conceit, as it is written: 'They who have no directing influence fall like leaves.'" Cited by I. Huasherr, *Direction spirituelle*, p. 156 in reference to Dorotheus of Gaza, *Doctrina* V, PG 88, according to the "very literal" translation of B. Cordier (Anvers, 1646): "It is said in the Proverbs: those who are not governed fall like leaves; salvation lies in much counsel." See also Cassien, *Conférences*, 2, 4, p. 116: "It [*discretio*] is also that of which it is written that it is the rudder (*gouvernail*) of our life (*vitae nostrae dicitur gubernatio*): 'Those who are not directed fall like leaves (*quibus non est gubernatio cadunt un folia*).'"; Cassian, *Conferences*, Second Conference, IV, p.86: "It is also said to be the guidance of our life, as it is written: 'Those who have no guidance, fall like leaves.'" The quotation cannot be found in this form in the Vulgate, it is taken from the Septuagint, English translation by Johann Cook, in *A New English Translation of the Septuagint* (London: Oxford University Press, 2009), Proverbs, 11, 14, p. 631: "They who have no direction [*kubernēsis*] fall like leaves."

45. See Saint Jérome, *Lettres*, trans. J. Labourt, t. 7, 1961, letter 125, 15 ("Ad Rusticum monachum") p. 127: "All of this has but one aim: to teach you not to rely on your own will alone, but

that you should live in a monastery under the authority of a single abbot and in a large community. There you will learn humility from one, patience from another; this one will teach you
silence, and that one mildness"; English translation as "To Rusticus" in St. Jerome, *The Letters*
in *NPNF2*, Vol. VI, p. 249: "... my drift is simply this. Do not rely on your own discretion, but
live in a monastery. For there, while you will be under the control of one father, you will have
many companions; and these will teach you, one humility, another patience, a third silence, and
a fourth meekness." Reference to this letter is given by J.-C. Guy in Cassien, *Institutions*, p. 195,
note 1.

46. Cassien, *Institutions*, 5, 4, p. 195; Cassian, *Institutes*, 5, IV, 2, p. 118: "... the monk who, like a
most prudent bee, is desirous of storing up spiritual honey must suck the flower of a particular
virtue from those who possess it more intimately." This sentence, attributed to Saint Anthony,
as J.-C. Guy emphasizes, is addressed "to the monk already perfectly tested in the cenobitic
life." For the beginner, Pinufius advised rather that "the model for the perfect life should not
be taken from many, but from a small number of monks and even just one or two" (*Institutions*,
4, 40, pp. 181-183); "you should seek out, while you live in the community, examples of a perfect life that are worthy of imitation; they will come from a few, and indeed from one or two,
but not from the many" (*Institutes*, 4, XL, p. 100).

47. Ibid., Fr.: "One ... is adorned with the flowers of science, the other is better equipped with the
technique of discrimination, another has as foundation the weight of patience, another excels
in the virtue of humility, another in continence ... [etcetera]"; Eng., ibid., 5, IV, 1, p. 118: "For
there is one who is adorned with the flowers of knowledge, another who is more strongly forti-
fied by the practice of discretion, another who is solidly founded in patience, one who excels
in the virtue of humility and another in that of abstinence, while still another is decked with
the grace of simplicity, this one surpasses the others by his zeal for magnanimity, that one by
mercy, another one by vigils, yet another by silence, and still another by toil."

48. Ibid., 5, 36, 1, Fr., pp. 247-249: "[The anchorites] first of all stay for a long time in the monasteries (*in cenobiis*) where they are taught the rules of patience and discernment. When they have
acquired the virtues of both humility and nakedness and are completely purged of their vices,
they penetrate the deepest recesses of the desert to engage the devil in fearful combat"; Eng.,
5, XXXVI, 1., p. 138: "the anchorites...dwelling first for a long time in cenobia, having been
carefully and thoroughly instructed in the rule of patience and discretion, having mastered the
virtues of both humility and poverty and having totally destroyed every vice, penetrate the deep
recesses of the desert in order to engage in terrible combat with the demons."

49. As the title of the Fourth Book indicates: "*De institutis renuntiantium*" (On the training of those
of renounce [the world]), ibid., p. 119; Eng., ibid., p. 75: "The Institutes of the Renunciants."

50. Ibid., 4, 3, p. 125; Eng., ibid., 4, III, 1, p. 79: "purposely rebuked and disdained by everyone, as
if he wished to enter the monastery not out of devotion but out of necessity, and ... visited with
numerous insults and taunts." The reason for this testing is set out later by Abba Pinufius, in
his famous "discourse on taking the habit", often reproduced on its own in medieval manuscripts (see J.-C. Guy, p. 171 note 2); Fr., ibid., 4, 33, p. 173: "... we fear that by receiving
you without hesitation we might make ourselves guilty before God of thoughtlessness, and of
drawing upon you greater torment if, being admitted too easily, and without having properly
understood the importance of the life you desire to embrace, you were to abandon this life later,
or if you were to fall into half-heartedness"; Eng., ibid., 4, XXXIII, p. 97: "You were put off
by us for a very long while...so that we may not receive [those who wish to turn to Christ]
heedlessly, and, before God, make ourselves guilty of light-mindedness and you of a harsher
punishment if, having been accepted easily now without appreciating the gravity of this profession, you were afterwards to show yourself lukewarm and a backslider."

51. Ibid., 4, 2, 2-4, pp. 125-127; Eng., ibid., 4, III-V, pp. 79-81.

52. Ibid., 4, 7, p. 131; Eng., ibid., 4, VII, p. 81. This period of one year outside the monastery is
a requirement peculiar to Cassian. It does not correspond to the practice of the Pachomian
monasteries and will not be taken up by Benedict in his *Rule* (see rule 58). See O. Chadwick,
John Cassian, p. 57.

53. Ibid.: "he is entrusted to another elder who is charged by the Abbot with their instruction (*alii
traditur seniori, qui decem iunioribus praeest, quos sibi creditos ab abate instituit partier et gubernat ...*)";
Eng., ibid., p. 82: "he is given over to another elder who is responsible for ten younger men,
who have been entrusted to him by the abba and whom he both teaches and rules."

54. Ibid., 4, 3, p. 124; "*Cum ... experimentum dederit constantiae suae ...*"; "when he has given proof of his constancy"; ibid., 4, III, 1, p. 79 : "when he... has given proof of his constancy."
55. Ibid., Eng.: patience, obedience, humility.
56. Ibid., 4, 5, p. 127. More exactly, Cassian writes that the postulant must "be so stripped of all his previous wealth that he is not even permitted to keep the clothes he is wearing"; ibid., Eng., 4, V, p. 80: "all his former possessions are removed from him, such that he is not even permitted to have the clothing that he wore." But the brothers cannot accept any money from him, from fear that, if he turns out to be unable to "persevere under the rule of the monastery, he seeks, on leaving ... to have it returned to him in a sacrilegious spirit ..." (4, 4); ibid., 4, IV: "Therefore they do not even agree to accept money from him... The reason for this is that ... he might ... when he was unable to remain under the discipline of the cenobium he would leave and would with sacrilegious spirit endeavour ... to take back and claim what he had brought in ...."
57. In reality Cassian writes, ibid., 4, 6, p. 129: "The clothes that the postulant has set aside are kept by the bursar until such a time as, by various temptations and trials, the value of his progress, the seriousness of his way of living, and his steadfastness have been recognized." If he is allowed to remain in the monastery, these clothes will be given to the poor. In the opposite case, "he is stripped of the monastery clothes with which he has been covered and driven out, wearing the old clothes which had been put aside"; Eng., ibid., 4, VI, p. 220: "The clothing that he has taken off is deposited with the bursar and kept until, thanks to various trials and tests, he has made progress and they clearly recognize the virtue of his way of life. And when they see ... that he can stay in that place ... they give it to the poor. But if they notice that he has committed the sin of complaining or is guilty of an act of disobedience ... they strip him of the garb of the monastery ... and dressed once more in what he used to wear ... they drive him out."
58. Ibid. (a rather free quotation): "... *copia nulli penitus palam discedendi conceditur, nisi aut in morem servi fugacis captans densissimas tenebras nocte effugiat ...*"; "... no one has the right to leave the monastery freely: unless like a fugitive slave, he will leave by night, seeking the darkest shadows ..." and "or, judged unworthy of the order and the monastic profession, he will be driven out, marked with shame, after being stripped of his monastery garments before all the brothers"; Eng., ibid.: "... the possibility of leaving openly is never granted to anyone, unless either he escapes by night like a runaway slave on the watch for the thickest darkness or, having been judged unworthy of his state and profession, the garb of the monastery is removed from him and he is driven out with shame and notoriety in the presence of all the brothers."
59. Ibid., 4, 7, p. 131: "giving proof of his service towards strangers without complaint" ("*Cum ... absque ulla querella suum circa peregrinos exhibuerit famulatum*"); Eng., ibid., 4, VII, p. 81: "And when he has served for a full year there and has without any complaining waited upon travelers ..."
60. Ibid., 4, 8, p. 131: "The concern and principal object of his teaching (*sollicitudo et eruditio principalis*), which will make the young man capable of raising himself to the peaks of perfection, will be to teach him to vanquish his wishes"; ibid., 4, VIII, p. 82: "The chief concern and instruction of this man, whereby the young man who was brought to him may be able to ascend even to the loftiest heights of perfection, will be, first of all, to teach him to conquer his desires."
61. Ibid.: "... [The elder] will always make sure expressly to order him to do what he has observed to be contrary to his temperament"; ibid.: "he will purposely see to it that he always demands of him things that he would consider repulsive."
62. Ibid., 4, 9, p. 133; Ibid., 4, IX, p. 82: "... they are then taught never, through a hurtful shame, to hide any of the wanton thoughts in their hearts but to reveal them to their elder as soon as they surface."
63. See *Sécurité, territoire, population*, lecture of 22 February 1978, pp. 184-186; *Security, Territory, Population*, pp. 180-183. Foucault returns at length to this comparison in *Mal faire, dire vrai*, pp. 128-139.
64. See above, lecture of 12 March 1980, pp. 233-234.
65. See L. Bieler, ΘΕΙΟΣ ΑΝΗΡ. *Das Bild des 'göttlichen Menschen' in Spätantike und Früfchristentum* (Vienna: O. Höfels, 2 vols., 1935-1936; republished Darmstadt: Wissenschaftliche Buchgesellschaft, 1967); J.-P. Vernant, *L'Individu, la Mort, l'Amour. Soi-même et l'autre en Grèce*

ancienne (Paris: Gallimard, 1989) p. 218, with regard to the *"theoiándres*, who from their living rise from the mortal condition to the status of imperishable beings ... [and] in periods of crisis in the seventh and sixth centuries will play a role comparable to that of the lawgivers, of legislators like Solon, in order to purify communities of their defilement, pacify seditions, arbitrate conflicts, promulgate institutional and religious regulations." Foucault had already referred to this figure of the *theios anēr* in *Leçons sur la volonté de savoir*, lecture of 6 January 1971, p. 36; *Lectures on the Will to Know*, p. 36: "Certainly, the philosopher is no longer the *theios anēr* Hesiod spoke about, and who rightfully said what is necessary ...."

66. See above, lecture of 12 March, pp. 241-242.

67. On this quality of the elder, or of the old man, linked to the gift of *diakrisis* and not to age, see I. Hausherr, *Spiritual Direction*, p. 91.

68. Cassien, *Institutions*, 2, 3, p. 63: "To direct others and be directed well is, they declare in fact, the distinctive character of the wise man (*Bene enim regere vel regi sapientis esse*); and they affirm that it is the highest gift and a grace of the Holy Spirit"; Cassian, *Institutes*, 2, III, 4, p. 38 : "For they declare that to rule well and to be ruled well is typical of the wise person, and they insist that this is a most lofty gift and a grace of the Holy Spirit." The translation used by Foucault here is taken from J. Brémond, *Les Pères du désert* [see above, p. 68, note 9], t. II, p. 298: "For these admirable men recognize that it is the height of wisdom to conduct others well and let oneself be conducted well. They say openly that in this single point consist the greatest gift of God and the effect of the greatest grace of the Holy Spirit." However, in the following sentence Cassian establishes a relation of anteriority between the moment of obedience and that of command. It is necessary to have learnt to obey before commanding, to have been novice before being abbot: "For no one can establish salutary precepts for his subordinates unless that person will first have been instructed in all the disciplines of virtue (*nisi eum qui prius universis virtutum disciplinis fuerit instructus*)," p. 63; Eng., p. 38: "a person cannot enjoin beneficial precepts on his subjects unless he has first been instructed in every virtuous discipline."

69. See *Sécurité, territoire, population*, lecture of 22 February 1978, p. 180; *Security, Territory, Population*, p. 177: "Now in Christian obedience, there is no end, for what does Christian obedience lead to? It leads quite simply to obedience. One obeys in order to be obedient, in order to arrive at a state of obedience."

70. See Cassien, *Institutions*, 4, 30-31, pp. 165-171; Cassian, *Institutes*, 4, XXX-XXXI, pp. 94-96; *Conférences*, 20, 1, pp. 57-59; *Conferences*, 20, I, pp. 496-497. The Twentieth Conference, "On the end of penance (*pénitence*) and the sign of satisfaction" [Eng.: "On the End of Repentance and the Mark of Reparation"] is entirely devoted to this Egyptian father, "that excellent and remarkable man" (20, 1), whom Cassian had met during his stay at the Bethlehem monastery, ibid., pp. 58-59: "[After having again fled his monastery (at Panephysis in Lower Egypt)] he embarked secretly for Palestine, a province of Syria. He was received as a beginner and novice in the monastery where we were staying. But not even there could his virtues and merits remain hidden for long. Discovered in the same way as the first time, he was taken back to his monastery with the greatest marks of honor, amidst a concert of praise, and finally forced to be what he had been"; Eng., ibid., 20, I, 5, p. 694 : "stealthily taking passage on a boat, he went off to the province of Palestine in Syria. There he was accepted as a beginner and a novice in a house of the monastery where we were staying, and he was ordered by the abba to live in our cell. But his virtue and his worth could not remain hidden there for long, to be sure, for by a similar betrayal he was discovered and brought back to his own monastery with considerable honor and praise." When, "urged by the desire to be instructed in the science of the saints," Cassian and Germain reach Egypt in turn, "they sought after him with great feelings of affection and an immense desire to see him" (ibid., 20, 2, p.59); Eng.: "When, therefore, after a short while a desire for holy instruction had compelled us to come to Egypt ourselves ... we ... sought out this man with great longing and desire" (ibid., 20, II, 1, p. 694). An almost identical account appears in *Institutions*, 4, 31-32, p. 171; *Institutes*, 4, XXXI-XXXII, pp. 135-136. See O. Chadwick, *John Cassian*, p. 12.

71. See *Institutions*, 4, 30, p. 169; *Institutes*, 4, XXX, p. 135; *Conférences*, 20, 1, p. 58: "Almost three years passed in this labor and humiliating subjection (*desideratis tam iniuriosae subjectionis*) for which he had longed"; *Conferences*, 20, I, 3, p. 694: "he ... spent nearly three years there, rejoicing in the longed-for labors of his burdensome submission."

72. *Conférences*, 1, 2, p. 80 (Abbot Moses): "It is this same goal [the kingdom of heaven] ... that made you despise your parents' love, the soil of your fatherland, the delights of the world, and cross so many countries, in order to seek out the company of people like ourselves, uncouth and ignorant (*ad nos homines rusticos et idiotas*), lost in the desolate horizons of this desert"; *Conferences*, 1, II, 3, p. 42: "Without doubt it is for its sake that you yourselves have spurned the affection of relatives, despised your homeland and the delights of the world and have journeyed through so many foreign parts in order to come to us, men rude and unlearned, living harshly in the desert."

73. *Institutions*, 4, 24, pp. 155-157; *Institutes*, 4, XXIV, pp. 90-91. See *Sécurité, territoire, population*, lecture of 22 February 1978, pp. 179-180 and p. 191, note 32; *Security, Territory, Population*, pp, 175-176 and pp. 188-189 note 32, with regard to the "test of absurdity." On the different versions of this episode, see note 1 of J.-C. Guy, pp. 156-157: it is in the *Apophtegmata Patrum* (PG 65, col. 204C) that "the miracle of the stick taking root and bearing fruit is added"; see also O. Chadwick, *John Cassian*, p. 21. On the character of John de Lyco (or Lycopolis), see below, lecture of 26 March 1980, p. 315, note 20.

74. *Institutions*, 4, 27, p. 161; *Institutes*, 4, XXVII, pp. 92-93.

75. Ibid., 4, 28, p. 163: "The elder [who had ordered Patermucius to throw his son in the river] had the revelation that, by this obedience, he had fulfilled the work of the patriarch Abraham"; ibid., 4, XXVIII, p. 93: "For it was straightaway revealed to the elder that by this obedience he had performed the deed of the patriarch Abraham."

76. Ibid., 4, 27, p. 163; ibid., 4, XXVII, p. 93. See *Sécurité, territoire, population*, lecture of 22 February 1978, p. 180 and pp. 191-192, note 33; *Security, Territory, Population*, pp. 176-177 and p. 189 note 33, with regard to the "test of breaking the law."

77. The distinction does not appear in this form in Plato's text, which is organized nevertheless around the opposition teaching/being useful. See *Apologie de Socrate*, trans. M. Croiset (Paris: Les Belles Lettres, CUF, 1959). *Didaskein* and its derivatives are recurrent. See notably the indictment, 19b, p. 142 and, among Socrates' responses, 33a, p. 161: "*ego de didaskalos men oudenos pôpot egenomēn* (literally: "I have never been any man's teacher"). *Ophelos* is used more rarely here. See 28b, p. 155 where he opposes the fear of death to the sense of his usefulness, of his ability to be helpful (*ôphelos estin*), and 36c, p. 166, where he justifies his choice by his concern to be useful (*ôphelos einai*), to turn away from public affairs. Foucault's probable source here is I. Hausherr, *Spiritual Direction*, p. 5: "We know that Socrates refused the title[of *didaskalos*]: 'I was never anyone's teacher' [*Apology*, 33a]. What he wanted to do was not to teach, but to be useful (*ophelein*), to perform the good."

78. Here, and in the following sentence, Foucault uses this word, which cannot be found in Cassian, instead of *subjectio*. He takes up the same term in his fourth Louvain lecture (*Mal faire, dire vrai*, lecture of 6 May 1981, pp. 136-137). The word *subditio* seems to be a fairly late usage. Dictionaries of classical Latin are unaware of it; Du Cange, *Glossarium Mediae et Infimae Latinitatis*, expanded edition (Niort: Le Favre, 1883-1887), t. 7, col 627c, who gives "Subjectio, servitus" as equivalents, cites only one occurrence (Gregory the Great, *Regesta Pontificum Romanorum*, 12, 23), and Maign d'Armis translates it as "Vassalage, condition of vassal" in *Lexicon manual ad scriptores mediae et infimae latinitatis* (Paris: Migne, 1858), col. 2123. It is attested, for example, in the Carolingian capitularies relative to the *potestas* of bishops over their subjects. See S. Patzold, *Episcopus. Wissen über Bischöfe im Frankenreich des späten 8. Bis frühen 10. Jahrhunderts* (Ostfildern: Jan Thorbeke, Verlag, "Mittelalter-Forschungen" 25, 2008). *Subditus*, on the other hand, appears several times in Cassian's text (see *Collationes*, 7, 5 and 22, 11; *Institutiones*, 4, 1 and 12, 28). Of these usages, only *Institutiones*, 4, 1 refers to the monks' relationship with their superior, p. 123: "[In the Pachomian community of Tabenna] more than five thousand brethren are directed by a single Abbot, and ... yet this great number of monks live constantly subject (*subditus*) to the elder in such obedience that not one of would be able to obey another nor command him for a short time"; Eng., *Institutes*, 4, I, p. 79: "[In the cenobium of the Tabennisiots there are] more than five thousand brothers ... ruled by a single abba, and this huge number of monks is subject at every moment to their elder with an obedience such as, among us, one could neither render to another nor demand of another even for a short while." But Cassian, immediately after, qualifies this attitude as, 4, 2, p. 125: "persevering and humble submission (*subjectio*)"; Eng., 4, II, p. 79: "great perseverance and

humility and subjection." Citing the word *subditus*, Foucault refers to this passage in *Sécurité, territoire, population*, lecture of 22 February 1978, p. 180; *Security, Territory, Population*, p. 177.

79. Cassien, *Institutions*, 4, 10, pp. 133-135; *Institutes*, 4, X, p. 83: "… the young men do not even presume to attend to their common and natural necessities on their own authority."

80. Dositheus (sixth century): young novice of the monastery of Abbot Peridos in southern Palestine, disciple of Dorotheus of Gaza, who wrote his *Life*, in *Œuvres spirituelles*, trans. Dom L. Regnault and Dom J. de Préville (Paris: Cerf, SC no. 92, 2001 [1963]), pp. 122-145.

81. Ibid., p. 139: "He was suffering greatly and called to the Great Elder [Barsanuphius]: 'Let me go, I can bear no more!' The Elder replied: 'Patience, my child, God's mercy is at hand.' … Again, after a few days, Dositheus said to the Elder: 'Master, I am at the end of my strength!' Then the Elder replied: 'Go in peace! Sit by the Holy Trinity and intercede for us.'" In this *Life*, Dositheus appears as a model of perfection "for being attached to obedience and for having broken his own will" (p. 145).

82. Saint Basil (Basil of Caesarea), *Exhortatio de renunciation saeculi*, 4, PG 31, col. 633B: "*Quidquid enim sine ipso … efficitur furtum est et sacrilegium, quod mortem infert, non utilitatem, tametsi tibi videtur esse bonum*." The sentence is quoted by I. Hausherr, *Direction spirituelle*, pp. 190-191: "Any action not ordered or permitted by the superior is a theft and a sacrilege which leads to death and not to advantage, even if it seems good to you." See too the *Rule of Benedict*, 49, p. 74 ("Observance of Lent"): "whatever is done without the father's permission might be attributed to unwarranted pride and a desire for self-glorification rather than to any reward."

83. Saint Jérome, *Lettres*, 22, 35, t. 1, p. 150: "Their primordial pact is to obey the Elders and to carry out all their orders"; Saint Jerome, *Letters*, XXII, 35, NPNF2, Vol. VI, p. 37: "Among these the first principle of union is to obey superiors and to do whatever they command." Jerome is speaking here about Egyptian cenobites.

84. On this notion, see Cassien, *Conférences*, 18, 13-16, t. 3, pp. 24-26; Cassian, *Conferences*, 18, XIII-XVI, pp. 644-654.

85. "Like a corpse" is Ignatius Loyola's formula in the sixth chapter of his *Constitutions*: "Every order must be acceptable to us. We shall renounce for our part any other way of seeing and any other opinion in a sort of blind obedience and this in everything that is not sin. Each must be convinced that whoever lives in obedience must let themselves be guided and directed by Divine Providence, with the intermediary of his superiors, as if he were a corpse (*perinde ac cadaver*) that can be transported anywhere and treated in any way, like again the old man's cane, which serves everywhere and for anything" (quoted by J. Lacouture, *Jésuites. Une multibiographie* (Paris: Seuil, 1991), t. 1, p. 112). On this doctrine of obedience of Ignatius, see too his *Lettre aux Jésuites portugais* of 23 March 1553: "We may suffer that we are outdone in fasting, vigils, and other austerities by other religious orders … But I earnestly desire, dear brethren, that those in this Company who follow God are distinguished by the purity and perfection of obedience … and the abnegation of judgment" (ibid., p. 111).

86. Nilus of Ancyra [Saint Nilus], *Logos askētikos/De monastica exercitatione*, 41, PG 79, col. 769D-772 A. See I. Hausherr, *Spiritual Direction*, p. 197, where the quotation from Saint Nilus used by Foucault continues as follows: "Just as the soul functions in the body at will and the body offers no resistance, and just as the artist shows his art in the material and the material does not resist him, so does the teacher apply his knowledge of virtue upon obedient disciples who do not contradict him in anything."

87. The word is not found in the text of *Institutions*, 4, 27; *Institutes*, 4, XXVII. The idea, however, is expressed by the verb "*tolerari*": Fr., p. 162: "He was not concerned about the present injustices, rejoicing rather because he saw that they were never endured without profit"; Eng., p. 93: "nor did he worry about his present sufferings; instead he rejoiced because he saw that they were not being borne fruitlessly." For the multiple occurrences of the word in the *Institutions*, see the index, p. 524.

88. On this notion, see *Institutions*, 4, 39, 2, p. 181: "the signs by which humility is recognized," among which are the mortification of all his will, hiding nothing from his elder, not relying on his own judgment, constantly practicing patience, declaring himself the last of all, "not only in words … but in an inner feeling of his heart"; *Institutes*, 4, XXXIX p. 232: "Humility … is verified by the following indications: … if a person has put to death in himself all his desires; … if he conceals from his elder not only none of his deeds but also none of his thoughts; … if he commits nothing to his own discretion but everything to his [elder's] judgment …; … if in

every respect he maintains a gracious obedience and a steadfast patience; ... if he neither brings injury on anyone else nor is saddened or sorrowful if anyone else inflicts it on him; ... if he does nothing and presumes nothing that neither the general rule nor the example of our forebears encourages; ... if he is satisfied with utter simplicity and ... considers himself unworthy of everything that is offered him; ... if he does not declare with his lips alone that he is inferior to everyone else but believes it in the depths of his heart ..."; *Conférences*, 2, 10, p. 120: "True discretion is acquired only at the cost of a true humility. The first proof of this will be leaving all one's actions and even one's thoughts to the judgment of the elders, such that one will place no trust at all in one's own judgment, but will acquiesce in their decisions in all things and wish to know what should be considered good and what bad only from their mouths"; *Conferences*, 2, X, pp. 90-91: "True discretion not obtained except by true humility. The first proof of this humility will be if not only everything that is to be done but also everything that is thought of is offered to the inspection of the elders, so that, not trusting in one's own judgment, one may submit in every respect to their understanding and may know how to judge what is good and bad according to what they have handed down." See also 9, 3, p. 42; Eng., 9, III, p. 330; 15, 7, p. 217: "It is ... humility which is the mistress of all the virtues (*omnium magistra virtutum*), the unshakeable foundation of the heavenly building, the Savior's special and magnificent gift"; Eng., 15, VII, p. 542: "Humility, then, is the teacher of all the virtues; it is the most firm foundation of the heavenly edifice; it is the Savior's own magnificent gift"; 24, 16, t. 3, pp. 187-188; Eng., 24, XVI, p. 838.

89. See *Sécurité, territoire, population*, lecture of 22 February 1978, pp. 181-182 and p. 192 notes 36 and 37; *Security, Territory, Population*, pp. 178-179 and p. 189 note 36. But Foucault does not raise here the question of the relations between ancient *apatheia* and Christian *apatheia*. On this notion, see especially M. Spanneut, "*Apatheia* ancienne, *apatheia* chrétienne. Ier partie: L'*apatheia* ancienne," in *Aufstieg und Niedergang der römischen Welt*, Teil II, Heft 36/7, 1994 (Berlin and New York: Walter de Gruyter), pp. 4641-4717. Central in the thought of Evagrius, (see A. Guillaumont, Introduction to the *Traité pratique*, pp. 98-112): "Impassivity is 'the flower of *practikē*' (ch. 81); it is towards it that the latter leads, as to safety the person who practices it. It is also, like *practikē* itself, the subject of the *Traité pratique* ..." (p. 98), this concept corresponds, in Cassian, to those of *puritas cordis, puritas mentis, quies* (see the index of *Institutions*, pp. 525-526; O. Chadwick, *John Cassian*, p. 102).

90. In *Mal faire, dire vrai*, lecture of 6 May 1981, pp. 130-131, Foucault illustrates this analysis of the principal characteristics of ancient direction with a passage from Athenaeus, a first century doctor, passed on by Oribasius in *Œuvres d'Oribase*, t. 3, trans. C.-V. Daremberg (Paris: Chez J.-B. Baillière, Imprimerie imperial, "Collection des médecins grecs et latins," 1885).

Christian direction according to Cassian (continued). Correlation of the three principles of obedience without an end, incessant self-examination, and exhaustive confession. ⌒ *The practice of* discretio, *between laxity and excess. Anti-ascetic meaning of this notion. Historical context: monastic organization against individual asceticism without rule. Difference from ancient conception of* discretio: *the Christian no longer finds his measure in himself.* ⌒ *Two questions: 1. Why does man lack* discretio? *The presence of the devil, source of illusion, within the subject. The need to decipher the secrets of one's conscience. 2. How to make up for this lack of* discretio? *The examination-confession apparatus (*dispositif*). (a) Object of the monk's examination: his thoughts (*cogitationes*). The activity of sorting (the metaphor of the moneychanger). Descartes' malicious demon, a constant theme of Christian spirituality. (b) Function of confession in the exercise of* discretio. *An indispensable mechanism; its never-ending and permanent character.* Exagoreusis. *Paradox of an alethurgy of oneself linked to renunciation of self.* ⌒ *Three concluding remarks: 1. Christian critique of the gnosis: dissociation of salvation and perfection, knowledge of God and knowledge of self; 2. The obligation to tell the truth about oneself in Western societies; 3. The form of power this presupposes.*

[LAST WEEK] I READ to you the passage from Book IV of Cassian's *Institutes* in which he set out the method for training novices [when] they arrive at the convent and in their first years there. You remember that in this text the first imperative was to teach the novices to conquer their will by imposing on them a complete, exhaustive, and permanent regime of obedience. This involved them having constantly to obey the orders they might be given, and those giving the orders being advised to ensure that they were as contrary as possible to the inclinations of the novices. Thanks to this the novices had to arrive at that renunciation of self that is called humility. Now I also read to you the passage immediately following this in which it was said that, in order to arrive at this perfect and complete form of obedience,* beginners must be taught "not to hide with false shame any of the thoughts that gnaw at their heart," but rather, as soon such thoughts arise, to "reveal them to the elder."[1] Last week, then, I tried to explain the passage concerning obedience. Now I would like to try to explain the passage concerning examination and confession.

The second passage I have just read reveals, I think, two important elements. The first is the link between obedience to the other and examination of oneself. If one really wants to teach the novice to obey the other completely and exhaustively, it is also necessary, and as a condition of this, to teach him to examine himself. To be able to listen to the other, I must look at myself. The second important element is that within this examination, in this obligation to examine oneself, you see a very strange coupling between the obligation to keep watch on oneself, to open one's eyes to what is happening in oneself—so the obligation to look—and correlatively, immediately linked to this duty to look, the obligation to speak. I must see everything in me, but I must tell all of what I see and I must tell it as I am seeing it. So, in Christian direction we have an apparatus (*dispositif*) with three fundamentally linked and interdependent elements: the principle of obedience without an end, the principle of incessant examination, and the principle of exhaustive confession. A triangle: listening to the other, looking at oneself, speaking to the other about oneself. It is the organization, the articulation of this triangle that I would like to study a bit today.

To justify the necessity of the link between obedience and examination, or rather, if you like, the necessity of a link between obedience and

---

* M.F. adds: in order to arrive at this stage of humility in which the monk ... [two or three inaudible words: crackling on the tape].

this packet formed by examination and confession, the examination-confession, Cassian gives a series of reasons which, truth to tell, contain nothing unexpected. For Cassian, the point, in fact, is to make sure that the monk avoids two dangers at the same time. First, the danger of a laxity that insinuates its way into the soul on the basis of all the monk's minor self-indulgences. The monk has to keep watch on himself for all that could be the first signs of a laxity that would lead progressively to the greatest weaknesses. Thus Cassian makes very interesting analyses of, for example, the genesis of avarice from a single small feeling of ownership that the monk might still have towards objects available to him.[2] So, on the one hand laxity is to be avoided, and, on the other, excess must also be avoided. Excessive rigor is to be avoided, excessive ascesis in which, of course, self-confidence, pride, vanity, the desire to dazzle others could be mixed.

That both laxity and excessive rigor are to be avoided, you will say—and I entirely agree—is an absolutely banal theme, and ancient philosophy continually inflected this theme of "not too much and not too little," neither excess in one direction nor excess in the other, neither too much weakness nor too much rigor. This is a very old theme of ancient wisdom. To this necessity or form of the happy medium, Cassian, and in truth all the Christian authors, gave a word that is important, and you will see that if we try to follow it a little and force out its meanings, it reveals a number of important things. Cassian, like other Christian authors, gives the name *discretio*[3] to the principle that one must fall into neither one excess nor the other, neither laxity nor excessive ascesis.

Discretio, discretion: the word is the approximate Latin translation of the Greek term *diakrisis*. What do these two words, *diakrisis* and then *discretio*, or rather *discrimen* in classical Latin—well, no matter—designate? In the first place they designate the ability to separate what is mixed: that is to say, actually, between right and left, excess on one side and excess on the other, finding the dividing line that will enable a straight line to be drawn between two dangers. Second, *discretio*, or *diakrisis*, or *discrimen* is at the same time the activity that allows one to judge: placing oneself in the middle, seeing what is too much or not enough. So, an activity of separation and an activity of judgment. Here again, Cassian basically only reproduces and extends the notions and analyses produced by ancient wisdom on the need to separate things, to stick to the happy medium and the straight road, to draw the straight line between one thing and another. Cassian defines *discretio* in this way: "Keeping away from the two opposite extremes, [*discretio*] teaches always to walk along a royal road. It does not permit straying either to the right, towards a foolishly presumptuous virtue and an exagerrated fervor that exceeds the limits of just temperance, or to the left, towards laxity and vice."[4] As commonplace as it is, this notion of *discretio* actually becomes one of the key notions of the Christian technique of direction. How and why?

I think we should first of all note that in Christian authors and, any-way, very clearly in Cassian, the notion of *discretio* takes on a particular accentuation. It takes on a particular accentuation in the sense that, if it is true that *discretio* is required in order to struggle against laxity, the examples actually given by Cassian, the most developed examples, those on which he works, those regarding which he shows the need for an effective *discretio*, [are] practically always examples of an excess of ascesis, of the excessive rigor of this or that practice of the monastic life or of asceticism. There is a whole series of examples showing the consequences of the absence of *discretio* in precisely those who are most advanced on the road to holiness. There is the example of Abbot John of Lycon, to which we will return, who undertook exaggerated fasts but finally realized that they were inspired by the devil.[5] There is the story of the monk Heron, who, after living fifty years of the most perfect absti-nence in the desert—taken to the point of not even eating any vegetables on Easter day—thought that he could throw himself in a well and God or his angels would get him out safely, but who, of course, remained at the bottom.[6] There is the story of the two monks, whose names Cassian dares not give out of human respect, who thought they could cross the entire desert without food.[7] There is also the monk, whose name he does not give, who thought he could sacrifice his son like Abraham (but this is not the monk I spoke about last week, Patermucius, who agreed to sacrifice his son because he was ordered to do so[8]). It was not a good sacrifice because it was not carrying out an order but was purely and simply presumptuous. There is the story of the monk Benjamin, who instead of eating a little bread every day, ate two portions every two days.[9] There is above all the dire story of the abbot Paul, who had a holy and justified horror of women, but who took this horror to the point that one day, while on his way to visit another ascetic who had need of him, he met some women and took to his heels,[10] giving up his visit, thus showing that he would rather give up his charitable work than see a woman. Well, he should not have behaved in this way and was punished: four days later he was paralyzed and for four years was looked after in a women's convent.[11] The examples Cassian gives of *discretio*, or rather of the absence of *discretio* and the harmful effects of this absence, all—well, the great majority—have a very pronounced anti-ascetic point. *Discretio* must be much more a curb, moderator, and measure of ascesis than a mainspring and principle of an amplification or intensification of the ascetic life.[12] Cassian quotes a text of Saint Antony, true or false it doesn't matter, which says: "How many have we seen give themselves up to the most vigorous fasts and vigils, eliciting admiration for their love of solitude, throwing themselves into utter deprivation, keeping not a single day's provisions ... And then fall into illusion; unable to complete satisfactorily the work they have undertaken; bringing ... a life worthy of praise to an abominable end."[13]

This point, this sharp manifestly anti-ascetic edge in Cassian's analysis of *discretio* arises, of course, from a precise and particular historical context. I refer to it in a few words. Obviously, there is a whole series of very interesting problems. We should not forget that monasticism, as it was developed, institutionalized, and regularized in the fourth century, and especially, of course, in the regulated and communal forms of the cenoby, was not in fact developed as an intensification, but against a certain, let's say untrammelled intensification of ascetic practices current at the end of the third and the start of the fourth century.[14] A wild intensification taking the form of an individual asceticism with no rule, of a geographical vagrancy, but also an uncontrolled speculative vagrancy and wandering accompanied by a blossoming of exploits, visions, extraordinary ascesis, miracles, and rivalries and jousts in ascetic rigor as well as in thaumaturgic marvels. All this had to be taken in hand, regularized, and brought back into the ecclesiastical institution in general and the dogmatic system that was being constructed at this time through successive expurgations of heresies. In short, ascesis and the rules of ascesis had to be brought back into the system of the Church itself. It was basically a matter of warding off that old figure known by the Greeks under the term *theios anēr*, the divine man,[15] the perfect man, the man endowed with so many powers beyond those given to other men that he is able to

produce a number of effects on himself and others due to a divine presence in him. You can see that it is always this problem of perfection and
of the necessity or, at any rate, of the objective that the Christian church
set for itself against certain internal or neighboring tendencies, the effort
it made to distinguish the system of salvation and the requirement of
perfection. There is no need to be perfect to earn one's salvation. The
task of salvation does entail a work of striving for perfection; it does not
postulate the existence of perfection.

The monastic organization, the regularization of monastic practice
and the requirement of *discretio* therefore have mainly, and for historical
reasons, an anti-ascetic point. Given this, it is understandable that there
is a crucial difference between *discretio* as it developed in the theorists
of monastic life and what we find in the philosophers and moralists of
Antiquity. And the difference is this. In Book Two, chapter five of the
Institutes, Cassian gives the example of the very foundation of the first
great practice of *discretio*, of moderation. He reports what is, of course,
the somewhat legendary apostolic origin of the cenoby[16]: that is to say,
for him, the Apostles founded and lived in a sort of convent that was
the model of future convents ... Well, no matter. In this first convent
of the Apostles themselves, each one was, of course, driven by great
zeal, by a great individual and particular zeal, and they each chanted
a number of quite remarkable psalms. Each was free to do what he
wished and to chant as many psalms as he liked or could. But these first
monks became aware that this contained the danger of "internal strife."
"Dissonance and even variety," they thought, might engender "the germ
of future error, rivalry and schism."[17] So, faced with this danger, they
decide to meet one evening to discuss and fix the number of psalms to
be imposed as a general measure, *modus*, on their successors. They meet,
and a brother they do not know is in their midst. The brother rises,
sings one psalm, two, ten, eleven psalms, and then at the twelfth psalm
he stops while singing the hallelujah, and he has not finished the hallelujah when, of course, he disappears. You've guessed: he was an angel.[18]
Obviously, there is nothing extraordinary in this anecdote of the divine
establishment of an institution, the divine establishment of this measure imposed on the zeal of private asceticism. But despite its quite banal
character, I think this story has a particular meaning: although the participants in this meeting were the Apostles themselves,[19] that is to say

people of the highest holiness, their holiness was not sufficient by itself for them to be able to define, by themselves, the principle of moderation that was nevertheless necessary for them to achieve their goal. The Apostles themselves were not the measure of themselves. They needed this divine intervention for moderation, the principle of moderation, that is to say for the principle of discretion, of the just measure between one thing and another to be imposed on them and for them to be able to accept it. In other words, we arrive at the idea that even in these most holy figures, even in those closest to the truth there was a blind spot, a point that eluded them; they could not be their own measure for themselves. They are unable to know exactly what they must do, for they do not really know what they can do and they do not know what they can do because basically they do not know what they are. There is no natural *discretio* immanent to man. And this is where, as I was saying to you, the different accentuation of *discretio* in Cassian indicates a radical difference from the *discretio* of ancient wisdom. To what is the *discretio* of ancient wisdom due, to what does the ancient sage owe the possibility of making the division between too much and too little? He owes it to his *logos*, to that *logos*, that reason that he has in himself and that is perfectly clear to his own eyes on the sole condition, of course, that he is not temporarily confused by the passions: it is, in any case, from himself and from himself alone that the ancient sage will ask for his measure. The holy Christian, the ascetic Christian, cannot find his measure in anything in himself. He cannot ask himself for the principle of his own measure. In short, *discretio* is indispensable. There is only one problem: [this is that]* man lacks it.

First question: why does man lack *discretio* or, if you like, what is the mode of absence of *discretio*? And second, how to make up for the absence of *discretio*?

First question: why, how, and in what way is man lacking *discretio*? Example: this is [the one] of the abbot John of Lycon. At the end of his Twenty-Fourth Conference, Cassian refers to this abbot John of Lycon who had reached such a great point of holiness, who was so close to perfection, and who, as a result, was so full of light that all the sovereigns of the world came to consult him and ask him what it was necessary to

---

* Audition uncertain: crackling on the tape.

do.[20] Now this abbot John of Lycon, so full of light that all the sovereigns of the world came to consult him, is the same as the John we saw in the First Conference falling into excessive fasting. He fasted too much, and at the end of his fast, when he thought he had thereby attained greater perfecton, cuckoo, the devil appears to him and tells him: "It was I who who told you to fast, and I told you to fast excessively so that you would be weakened and resist temptation less easily."[21] He advised sovereigns; he could not measure his own fasting. This story, of course, speaks very clearly. On the one hand, it indicates a fundamental difference between this holy personage and the ancient sage. The ancient sage was precisely someone who renounced wanting to master the order of the world and rule over it, but who had at least a little empire over which he could cast his gaze and exercise his power, and this was himself. He could not be dispossessed of this empire and thus was happy to give up advising sovereigns when he was certain of exercising his sovereignty over himself. This was the ancient sage. Here, on the other hand, we see the holy man who is capable of advising the princes of the world. It is easier to tell those who command the whole world what they must do than to tell myself what I must do.[*] What I must do eludes me if I do not refer to someone else. Second element of the story, its second aspect: what is the the explanation of this obscurity, to what is this uncertainty regarding himself due? The story tells us: it is due to the devil. The devil who is present in an ascetic; the devil does not let go even at the highest [degree][†] of holiness. The devil, secondly, as you see in the story, who is so hidden that the ascetic could think that the idea of fasting for longer came either from himself or from God, whereas it came from the devil. The devil, finally, who has deceived and deluded, presenting as a good what turns out in fact to be an evil.

In Cassian, as in the authors of this whole period of course, there is a theology of the presence of the devil in man, a whole series of explanations of how and in what way the evil spirit may be both constantly present and constantly active in man. I will not go back over this. I would just like to hold on to three elements that seem essential to me. First: the devil's presence is never warded off. No degree of holiness

---

* The manuscript adds in quotation marks: "Not having an idea of one's own soul."
† M.F.: point.

can absolutely and definitively ensure that the devil will not be present in me. Second: this presence is brought about within the subject himself and in a kind of intrication with [his] subjectivity.* How does this come about? Cassian explains, in a spirit entirely in line with what most of the authors of the time said, [that] this penetration of the devil does not take place in the soul exactly. In other words, man's soul is not directly taken, possessed, overrun, or impregnated by the evil spirit or spirits. There is no penetration. This is physically and theologically impossible for reasons that Cassian gives.[22] On the other hand, if the human soul is not penetrated directly by the evil spirit, even so the latter greatly resembles it. The evil spirit and the soul both have the same nature.[23] They are related and it is this resemblance, this analogy, this close kinship that allows the evil spirit to come alongside the human soul impregnating the body, commanding it, giving it orders, troubling it, shaking it. And to that extent there is not possession of the soul by the evil spirit, but co-possession, co-penetration, co-existence of the evil spirit and the soul in the body. The body is the seat of both of them. From the body the evil spirit sends the soul representations, suggestions, and ideas[24] whose distinctive characteristic is that, first, they disguise the evil under kinds of good so that it is very difficult for the soul to recognize whether the suggestion it receives is good or bad, but above all the soul is unable to distinguish whether the suggestion comes from the individual himself, or from Satan, or from God.[25] That is to say the point of origin, the identity, the original stamp of the suggestion is completely scrambled. In sum, through its co-presence in the body, through its analogy and resemblance with the soul itself, the evil spirit's mode of action is such that it produces in the soul the illusion or, at any rate, the non-distinction of good and evil, of Satan and God, of Satan and the subject himself.

Under these conditions you can see that the devil's mode of action in the soul is not passion, *pathos*; it is illusion, deception, error. So that, quite naturally, whereas for the ancient sage or Stoic sage the problem, the enemy, the danger, the serious thing with which one had to cope through *discretio* was the uncontrollable impulses of passion, of *pathos*, the mechanics of the body reverberating in the soul and provoking

---

* M.F.: the subjectivity of the subject himself.

uncontrollable impulses, for Christian direction the problem, question, and danger was, on the contrary, illusion, the lack of discrimination between the representation of good and the representation of evil, between the representation or suggestion coming from God, that coming from Satan, and that coming from oneself. In other words, we can say that whereas the *discretio* of ancient wisdom had to focus primarily on things, on the value of things, the problem of *discretio* in Christian holiness or in Christian work of striving for perfection will focus on oneself, what happens in oneself, and on the ideas that come to me, of which I become conscious. It is not the value of things that one must recognize, it is the secrets of conscience that must be deciphered. *Arcana conscientiae, exploratio conscientiae*:[26] this will be the task of Christian discretion—very different, you can see, from taking the measure of the value of things and of the relation of things to oneself that was asked of the [ancient]* sage. The *diakrisis* of ancient wisdom was a judgment that the individual's sovereign conscience brought to bear itself, by distinguishing between good and evil in the confusion of the passions. It involved determining the value of things in relation to the subject. This was *diakrisis*, the *discretio* of the, let's say, Stoic sage. In Christian spirituality, *discretio* no longer focuses on the value of things, it focuses on the subject himself, on the subject insofar as he is inhabited by another principle, by a foreign principle that is at the same time a source of illusion. So it involves *discretio* being exercised on the subject himself insofar as he is obscure to himself. It is no longer a question of the value of things in relation to the subject, it is the internal illusion of the self about itself. This then is the reason for the subject himself not having *discretio*.

[Second question:] how to make up for this lack of autonomous *discretio*? *Discretio* is lacking, then, for the reasons I have just given (the presence of the devil as a principle of illusion and uncertainty in relation to oneself), so what will replace it? Precisely the structure, the examination-confession apparatus (*dispositif*) I talked about at the beginning. What is this examination-confession, the reason for whose indispensability I have tried to explain? The first thing to note is, as will be clear to you, that it cannot have either the same form or the same objects as ancient examination. Ancient examination—you recall Seneca, for

---

* M.F.: Christian.

example, [reviewing]* his day to see what he had done and whether
he had done it well—focused primarily on actions performed. Christian
examination will not get rid of this practice. In fact it is mentioned by
a number of Christian spirituals. You find it in Saint John Chrysostom
saying, in a very Seneca-like style: "Let us call on our conscience, let us get
it to give an account of actions, words, and thoughts. Let us examine what
profits us or harms us."[27] This practice exists, but it is no longer the most
important practice, far from it, and at best, and not without some signs
of mistrust moreover, to which I will come back shortly, it is only a secondary structure in relation to what is basically a very different practice.
In fact, Christian examination, first, focuses on a raw material that is not
at all the same as that of ancient examination. You remember from the
passage I began with, Book Four, chapter nine of the *Institutes*: "Do not
hide with false shame any of the thoughts, *nullas cogitationes [celare]*,"[†28]
an expression found again throughout Cassian's texts.[29] It is always the
problem of *cogitatio*, of *cogitationes*, thoughts. Examination focuses on
thoughts and not on acts. It goes without saying that *cogitatio*, thought,
is a fundamental element in the monastic institution. When the monk's
goal is contemplation, and he must advance towards contemplation by
prayer, orison, meditation, and reverence, then *cogitatio* is obviously the
central problem of the monk's life. Consequently, the danger that arises
for the monk is the flux of his thoughts, the course, the agitation of ideas
that come to his mind. In his *Practical Treatise*, which was an important
source of inspiration for Cassian, Evagrius Ponticus said: "With seculars"
(with people living in the world) "the demons prefer to struggle by
using objects," *pragmata* he says. "But with monks, it is usually by using
thoughts," and he employs the fundamental word, *logismoi*.[30]

The history of this word is very interesting, because what did *logismos* designate in classical Greek? It designated reasoning, that is to say
the way *logos* is employed in order to arrive at the truth.[31] Now in the
vocabulary of Christian spirituality—and here Evagrius Ponticus is
fundamental in the inversion, or inflection of the word's meaning[32]—
logismos is not the positive use of a positive *logos* enabling one to arrive
at truth. *Logismos* is thought that comes to the mind along with all the

---

* M.F.: going back over.
† The word "*celare*," omitted by M.F., is added in the manuscript.

uncertainties of its origin, nature, and content, and consequently of what one can extract from it. *Logismos* is something dubious and, if it comes to it, even something negative inasmuch as if the goal of monastic life is contemplation, and contemplation of a single thing, namely God, then the mere fact of thinking about something, about anything whatsoever, the mere fact that a *logismos* appears in the striving of the conscience directed by God is already negative and the *logismos*, as emergence of any idea whatsoever in the mind aiming at God, is something bad. The connotation of the word *logismos* is inflected, and in Cassian (and in Latin generally) it is the same with the word *cogitatio*, which takes on a rather negative sense in the vocabulary of Christian spirituality: in Cassian we find a whole series of statements of the negative roles of *cogitatio*, that is to say of the mere fact of beginning to think of something when one should think of nothing or, rather, when one should think only of God himself.

So, there is a whole series of references that I could multiply. For example, in the third chapter of the Seventh Conference: "Sometimes, we feel that our heart's gaze is directed on its object"—namely God—but immediately, "our mind slips insensibly from these heights to rush with a more fiery spirit towards its previous divagations."[33] *Cogitatio, [e]vagatio:** the simple fact of having *cogitationes* is already a divagation. In the First Conference, someone questions the abbot Moses and says to him: "Even despite ourselves, and what is more, without our knowledge, *nolentibus...nescientibus*, unwanted thoughts steal into us so subtly and secretly that it is difficult not only to drive them away, but to be aware of them and recognize them" (to make the division, exercise *discretio* therefore).[34] Abbot Moses replies to his disciple's question: "It is [in fact] impossible for the mind not to be crossed by multiple thoughts."[35] In the Seventh Conference, entirely devoted to precisely the mind's mobility, we read the following: The human mind is defined as—and here Cassian uses Greek words—"*aeikinētos kai polukinētos*," something always mobile that shifts in every sense and direction, shaken by a whole multiplicity of impulses. "It is prey to perpetual and extreme mobility...Its nature is so formed that it cannot remain idle,...its natural fickleness necessarily leads it to wander, flitting about [here and there]

---

* M.F.: *divagatio.*

over everything it comes across."[36] In sum, the great peril, the permanent danger for the monk and consequently the major problem that
will be encountered in the exercise of *discretio*, of examination, of obedience, etcetera, is not so much the agitation of the passions therefore, as
the agitations of thoughts. A mulitiplicity of thoughts which appear,
an onrush which means it is difficult to distinguish between them, to
master the movement, to recognize them for what they are, that is to say
to recognize their origin and direction.

Such, then, is the raw material of Christian examination: *cogitatio*. To
catch hold of the flow of thought and then try to sort through the ceaseless flow of the multiplicity in this *nous*, this perpetually mobile mind,
to sort through that flow is the role of examination. How is examination
to be carried out? On this point Cassian employs a series of metaphors.
The metaphor of the mill [first of all]. He says: So the mind is always
agitated. It is agitated like the water of an ever flowing stream or river
and which, while flowing, turns the millwheel, and the miller can do
nothing about it. He can do nothing. The water is agitated, it runs and
this is very good or very bad, no matter, that's how it is, and it is what
turns the millwheel. But the mill[37] can grind good or bad grain. One
can put darnel in, or one can put wheat. Consequently, the role of the
monk, or the role of examination, of the person who examines himself
is to carry out a sorting in this flow of thought so that thought mills
good and not bad grain.[38] The second metaphor is that of the centurion,
of the officer who, when presented with soldiers or candidate soldiers,
inspects them, looks at them, measures their qualities, sees who is strong
and who is weak, suspects if one is courageous, if the other is cowardly,
and thus sorts out those he will accept and those he will reject, those to
whom he will give responsibility for one thing and who for another.[39]
Finally, the third metaphor is that of the money-changer. He is given
some coins. Before accepting them and giving other coins in exchange,
he will quite certainly [examine]* them, gauge them.[40]

These three metaphors enable us to see clearly the role of examination. It is not, as in Seneca, that of an inspection afterwards: one has
managed one's day as one has been able to and then, at the end of the
day, one inspects what one has done and sees whether one has acted as

---

* M.F.: accept.

one [ought].* What is involved here is an activity exercised on the flow of thought and thoughts at the same time as these thoughts pour out. Examination must focus on the present reality of thought and not retrospectively on what has been done. It involves catching hold of thought at the moment it begins to think, catching hold of it at root, when one is in the process of thinking about whatever one is thinking of. Strictly speaking, examination is a final exam, a final exam in present reality, the function of which is, what? To exercise a sorting, to exercise [what was called, precisely] *discriminatio.*† So it is not a matter of re-evaluating actions afterwards in order to find out whether or not they are good, but of grasping thoughts at the very moment of their appearance and then trying, as quickly as possible, immediately, to separate those that one must be able to accept into one's consciousness and those that must be rejected, expelled from one's consciousness.

How is this operation carried out? The metaphor of the money-changer, which occurs several times in Cassian, is undoubtedly the best for enabling us to work out how Cassian thinks this examination of conscience must be carried out in the actuality of the flow of ideas that come to mind. What in fact does the moneychanger do? Cassian says the moneychanger is someone who checks the metal of the coin, who checks its nature, its purity, and also the image stamped on it, someone who questions the coin's origin. It is the same for thought, he says, and for the examination one must continuously make of one's thought. [First possibility: an idea comes to mind with all the brilliance of philosophical language],‡ one thinks it pure gold—and God knows how philosophers can gild their ideas—but they are only the ideas of philosophers and not truly Christian. So they must be rejected.[41] False metal. Second possibility: an idea may be of good metal, but has a false image stamped on it, and this is very interesting. He says, for example: A text of Scripture comes to mind, which is of good metal, pure gold, of course, but I may, or rather the evil spirit in me may suggest a bad interpretation of this text and give it a meaning that is not its own, as if this pure metal had been stamped with a false image. The interpretation is, as it

---

* M.F.: has.

† M.F.: what they call, precisely, a *discriminatio.*

‡ Phrase from the manuscript; incomplete passage of the recording, due to tape being turned over. All that can be heard is "flashy."

were, the image of the idea, of Scripture itself, and may be inspired by the usurper, by the deceiver.[42] Third possibility: the thought appears in a valid form, made of good metal, and with an apparently correct image, but it comes from a bad workshop and is, in [reality], made for shameful ends. For example, I have the idea that it is good to fast, I have the idea that it would be good to become a cleric, or to perform some charitable works. All this is good. But, in fact, it may come from a bad workshop, it may come from the devil.[43] This is what happened to the abbot John of Lycon, for example, who, basically put in circulation this coin (one must fast) for ends that were harmful, namely to weaken the monk.[44] Finally, fourth possibility: everything is good, the image is correct, the metal is good, and it's been issued by a good workshop. Only there is some rust, it has been worn away, it is weakened and cannot completely make the weight and is as it were eaten away by a sort of rust. So it may be that an imperative one follows—the obligation to fast, for example—is eaten away by the desire to be appreciated by others, a desire of vanity, by the concern to show others how far one can go in asceticism.

Through these four possibilities,[45] it is clear that the examination to be carried out at the very moment that the idea begins does not focus on what the idea is an idea of, that is to say on what will later be called its objective content. It is not that. What is important, what the examination, the sorting activity focuses on is as it were the grain, the substance, the origin, the very hallmark of the idea. What is involved is the material examination of the thought and not an examination of the objective content of the idea. Moreover, Cassian says so, "one must observe the *qualitas cogitationum*, the quality of the thoughts."[46] So, observation of thought, of the flow of thought in its quality, its grain, its origin: searching deep in oneself for how and with what it was fabricated, leaving somewhat to one side the problem of what it is the idea of. So, there is the problem of the origin, fabrication, and material reality of the idea, and also the problem not so much of whether I am mistaken in what I think—for, after all, I am not mistaken when I tell myself that it is necessary to fast—[but] whether I am deceived by someone, by someone other, by an other within me. Grain of thought, quality of thought, and the problem of being subject to deceit.

I think we are at a very important point here, because in the Stoic type of examination, acts were examined, but a problem of truth was also posed. In fact the question was: when acting as I did, was I the victim of a common or ready-made opinion, had a truth eluded me? For example, I tried to convince someone that they were wrong to do this or that, but I was too angry and did not reflect on the truth that one must take into account the ability of the person one reprimands to understand and grasp the truth. Therefore, I committed an error. So in the Stoics there was analysis of the act and identification of the error. But you can see that, for them, the question bore on the truth of what I think, that is to say on the objective content of my ideas or opinions, and I examined this objective content afterwards, in the evening, in the dark, when my wife was silent, that is to say when I could exercise my conscience as subject in a sovereign manner. In Christian examination, on the other hand, you can see that the question does not bear on the objective content of the idea, but on the material reality of the idea in the uncertainty of what I am, the uncertainly of what is taking place deep within myself, and while searching—for what? Whether my idea is true? Not at all. Whether I am right to hold this or that opinion? Not at all. What is in question is not the truth of my idea; it is the truth of myself who has an idea. It is not the question of the truth of what I think, but the question of the truth of I who thinks.

I think we have here a very significant inflection in the history of the relations between truth and subjectivity. A history so significant that we can take it up again by its other end, its extremity, I was going to say by its outcome: we should never forget that Descartes' malicious demon is not at all the bizarre and extreme invention of a radical attempt by philosophy to retake possession of itself. The malicious demon, the idea that there is something in me that can always deceive me and that has such power that I can never be completely sure that it will not deceive me is the absolutely constant theme of Christian spirituality. From Evagrius Ponticus or Cassian to the seventeenth century, it is absolutely fundamental that there is something in me that can deceive me and that nothing assures me that I will not be deceived, even though I am sure of not being mistaken. And the Cartesian reversal, which precisely will again tip the truth-subjectivity relationship in a different direction, takes place when Descartes says: "Let me be deceived, or not deceived, let whoever wants to deceive me, there is in any case something that is indubitable and in which I am not deceived, which is that for me to be deceived, I must exist."[47] At that point, he will have made the "I am not mistaken" emerge from the fundamental danger of being subject to deceit, and from the indefinite spiritual doubt that the Christian practice of direction and examination introduced into the relationship between subjectivity and truth. Descartes, finally, will have made the first philosophical affirmation.

So that is examination. But precisely, if what I tell you is true, that is to say there is always something in me that can deceive me, and if I must constantly be on guard, the centuriun of my conscience, the ferryman of my ideas, if I must be like* a vigilant customs officer who, at the threshold of my consciousness, keeps watch over what enters and what must not enter, then how is it I can make this discrimination myself, if I do not have *discretio*, that is to say if I cannot be my own judge and measure? How can I be the good centurion, the good [night] watchman, the good miller when I lack in myself any instrument of measure, when there may always be in me this source of illusion and this great deceiver? How can I carry out this sorting when I do not myself possess the yardstick with which I could measure my thoughts.[48] This is where avowal comes in. To this possibility of being deceived, Descartes will oppose the fact that there is at least one certainty, which is that I must exist in order to be deceived. Christian spirituality will say: Since you may always be deceived about yourself, since there is always something in you that may deceive you, you must speak, you must confess.

Why does confession enable me to escape the paradox or uncertainty of an examination that is called for by the deception in me, but which at the same time is rendered impossible by the fact that this deception is inescapable? Why does confession enable me to escape this paradox of the possibly deceived examination? For a number of reasons. Confession puts one right, of course, because in confiding in the other what I know of myself, he will be able to give me advice, indicate what I must do, what prayers I must make, what reading is recommended, what conduct I must follow. But, actually, this is not what is fundamental for Cassian, and it is not the advice given by the other that makes confession effective with regard to the truth of the examination, the production of the truth of oneself. One can trust confession as an operator of discrimination, not

---

* Foucault adds: a stockbroker or.

so much because the person to whom I speak is trustworthy, but simply due to the fact of speaking to another person. The form itself of confession is a principle of discrimination, even more than the wisdom of the person to whom I speak, and there are three reasons for this.

First, because if the quality of the thoughts is good, Cassian says, if their origin is pure, if they have been issued in me with only good intentions, then they will have no difficulty in being confessed. If, on the other hand, they come from evil, are of evil intent, then precisely they will have difficulty in being expressed. They will refuse to be expressed, they will tend to conceal themselves. Refusal to be expressed, shame at being formulated, is the indubitable criterion of good and evil regarding the thought's quality. Shame at confessing is a sign of the nature of what one confesses. "However subtle the devil," says Cassian, "he will not be able to bring about the young man's fall unless he entices him, out of pride or human respect, to conceal his thoughts. The elders affirm, in fact, that it is a universal and diabolic sign when we blush to reveal it to the elder."[49] So, mechanism of shame, of the impossibility of speaking. If I cannot say what I think, it is because what I am thinking is not of good quality. The *qualitas* of the *cogitatio* is bad. Criterion of shame.

The second mechanism of sorting is the following: basically, bad thoughts prefer to loosen their grip and withdraw from the soul, to flee swiftly rather than have to pass through confession. And there is a theological or, if you like, cosmo-theological reason for this, which is that Satan was the angel of light who was condemned for his fault. To what was he condemned? To darkness. That is to say he was forbidden daylight. He can therefore live only in darkness, he can live only in the mysteries of the heart, in the recesses of the soul where the light does not penetrate. And the light, simply by virtue of the fact that it is light and there is henceforth a fundamental incompatibility between the devil, Satan, and the light, by virtue of the fact that there was light and the word brings light to the soul, makes Satan loosen his grip. "A bad thought," Cassian says in the tenth chapter of the Second Conference, "immediately loses its venom when it is brought into the light. Even before discretion has passed judgmnent, the hideous serpent that this confession has dragged out, so to speak, from his dark underground lair in order to shed light on him and display his shame, hastens to beat a retreat."[50]

The third mechanism is that the simple fact of speaking, of making the words come out of one's mouth, constitutes an act of expulsion, of material expulsion. What is now on the tongue is already no longer in the heart. This analogy of confession with exorcism appears very clearly in a number of texts and in particular in a story of the Abbot Serapion given by Cassian in the eleventh chapter of the Second Conference. When he was a child, the Abbot Serapion used to steal bread rolls and, of course, carefully hid the fact that he stole them. He did not want to admit that it was him. Finally, one day, he agrees to confess and at the very moment of doing so sees a sulphurous lamp come out from his chest and fill the room with an unbearable odor. It is his gluttony flee-ing. He is freed from it simply by the confession.[51] You can see that the quality of the person to whom one speaks, the advice he might be able to give, and his experience play no role in any of these mechanisms. It really is the sole fact of speaking that constitutes the principle of dis-crimination, of sorting out, of expulsion of the bad and acceptance of the good. What is interesting in this analogy of confession with exorcism is that the main component is not the pedagogical or medical role of the master, [but] the fact that one utters it to someone who is basically an x. It is the form of verbalization.[52]

And here we come to what will be the final point of this analysis, which is that if it is true that this expulsion in itself, the externalization in discourse that is the factor of sorting or choice, of discrimination, in other words, if the indispensable mechanism of *discretio* that human nature lacks can be re-established by the fact of confession, or rather by the very form of confession that is the principle of *discretio*, this entails that confession be perpetual and continuous. One must supervise the flow of thoughts that ceaselessly agitate the monk's soul and prevent him from advancing towards the point of contemplation. If one wishes to exercise *discretio* on this flow of thoughts it will have to be constantly examined, one will have to try to sort through it. How will this sorting be carried out? By a confession that will perpetually double the flow of the soul. One must verbalize completely what is unfolding in the soul. *Cogitatio* must become speech, it must become discourse. One must constantly hold a discours about oneself, of oneself, telling all that one thinks, telling all as one thinks it, telling all of the most subtle and imperceptible forms of thought, always looking into oneself so as to [catch hold straightaway of] the thought as soon as it forms, there, on the threshold of its emergence into consciousness, to turn it into discourse, to utter it, to utter it in the direction of someone, of someone = *x*. That is where the re-establishment of that *discretio*, that measure takes place, that measure of oneself that man cannot possess once he is perpetually inhabited by the devil. The need, the obligation to tell all of the depths of one's thought as soon as one has scarcely begun to think it is what Greek spirituality called *exagoreusis*, a practically untranslatable word,[53] which is putting oneself into discourse, the perpetual putting oneself into discourse.[54]

I don't have the time now to contrast *exagoreusis* and a different form I have talked about.[55] You remember *exomologesis*. In penance, the penitent was not so much asked to say what had happened, what he had done. He was not required to make a detailed confession of the fault he had committed. This was not what was in play. By his attitude, gestures, dress, grief, fasting, prayers, supplications, and genuflections he had to display in a dramatic form the fact of being a sinner. The nature of the act committed, the nature of the sin and the details of its cirumstances were not important. *Exomologesis* was this manifestation in truth of being a sinner. It was the alethurgy of the sinner as sinner. *Exagoreusis*, on the other hand, putting oneself into discourse, is a completely different type of alethurgy. Here there is no longer any dramatic and spectacular element of bearing, gesture, and dress. It is a relationship of oneself to oneself that is as fine, permanent, analytical, and detailed as possible, a relationship that can be established and is effective only insofar as it is sustained from end to end by an activity of discourse, by a discursive activity such that it is I myself who puts myself in discourse as I am, as I think, as the flow of thoughts appears to me and as I must sort through them in order to know ultimately from whence comes what I think, in order, in short, to decipher the power of illusion and deception that inhabits me constantly throughout my existence.

In brief, let's say that with its practices of provisional obedience, regular examination, and indispensable confiding in the master, ancient wisdom aimed to enable the subject to exercise constant jurisdiction over his actions. For the ancient sage, for Seneca, it involved reflecting on oneself in the evening, being one's own instance of jurisdiction, becoming the law to oneself. The objective of Christian direction, on the other hand, is not at all to establish a jurisdiction or codification.

It involves establishing a relationship of obedience to the other's will and at the same time establishing, in correlation with, as condition of this obedience, what I would call not a jurisdiction, but a veridiction: the obligation constantly to tell the truth about oneself, with regard to oneself, and in the form of confession. The aim of ancient direction is a jurisdiction of actions with a view to the subject's autonomisation; the formula for [Christian] direction is, I think, obedience to the other with veridiction of oneself for its instrument.[*]

You can see that this mechanism of perpetual confession connected to permanent obedience complies with a number of laws that seem to me to be very important for the history of the relationships between truth and subjectivity in the Christian West. Law of ever deeper probing: nothing is ever too small in the depths of myself for me not to pay attention to it.[†] Law of externalization, insofar as it is not a matter of defining a zone of interiority inaccessible to assaults from outside, but rather of the need to drag interiority from itself, to bring it out in order to display it in a relationship of exteriority and obedience. Law of tropism, of inclination towards the secret, in the sense that the principle is that of always going towards the most hidden in myself, the most fleeting, scarcely perceptible thoughts. It is not just a matter of detecting what is hidden, but of detecting what is hidden in the hidden, of unmasking the evil in every kind of good, of unmasking Satan in every kind of piety, of unmasking the other deep within myself. Finally,[‡] it involves a law of production of truth, insofar as it is not just a matter of registering what is taking place in myself, as the *suneidēsis* of ancient wisdom demanded.[56] It involves revealing something in me that I could not know and that becomes known through this work of self-exploration. It involves actually producing a truth, a truth that was unknown. Now, here is the paradox, this alethurgy of myself, this need to produce

---

[*] M.F. leaves out here the following remarks of the manuscript (two unnumbered sheets): "Concl[usion]. In ancient direction obedience and confession had an instrumental value, a provisional role, and a function relative to the aim of autonomy and self-control. In Christian monasticism they have an absolute value; they constitute an indefinite obligation. They owe their importance to their form, to a pure relationship of dependence on the other. These two obligations, to obey and to confess, refer back to each other."

[†] The manuscript adds: nothing indifferent.

[‡] In the manuscript, this fourth law is followed by a fifth: the "law of self renunciation" (see the next footnote).

the truth that I am, this need of alethurgy is fundamentally linked, you recall, to the renunciation of oneself. It is insofar as I must renuounce entirely my own wishes by substituting another's will for my own, it is because I must renounce myself that I must produce the truth of myself, and I produce the truth of myself only because I am working at this renunciation of myself. The production of the truth of self is in no way polarized, indexed to the will finally to establish in being what I am, but rather if I want to know what I am, if I must produce in truth what I am, it is because I must renounce what I am.[*] And this linkage between production of truth and renunciation of self seems to me to be what could be called the schema of Christian subjectivity, let's say more exactly the schema of Christian subjectivation, a procedure of subjectivation historically formed and developed in Christianity and characterized paradoxically by the obligatory link between self-mortification and production of the truth of oneself.[†]

Three remarks and I will have finished. First, you see that all this elaboration of Christian subjectivation, veridiction of self for renunciation of self, is developed in comparison and contrast with the theme of perfection. It was set not so much against ancient wisdom and innocence as against the presumption of perfection. It was in order to establish a religion of salvation uncoupled from the presumption of perfection. Now where above all do we find this linkage between salvation and perfection in a way that is threatening for Christianity, or at any rate in a form from which Christianity wanted to detach itself? It is, of course, in the Gnostic movements where we [encounter][‡] the idea that the *pneuma*, spirit, is a spark, a fragment, an emanation of the divinity and that salvation is its deliverance, that consequently the problem for the Gnostic is to rediscover, buried in this body and imprisoned in this matter, that

---

* At this point there is a rather different text in the manuscript: "Law of renunciation of self. Insofar as this obedience-confession apparatus (*dispositif*) involves replacing one's own will with the will of another, of discovering in the depths of oneself this "other" power that inhabits it (Satan), of dragging this other out from oneself, not however so as to re-discover oneself, but in order to contemplate God without darkness and to do his will without hindrance."

† The manuscript adds: "How is this link established? In the form of a structural subjection (*assujettissement*) to the will of the other (understood as whoever is able to function as master) and in the form of the verbal and exhaustive externalization of interiority—of the indefinite interiority peopled by the thoughts, illusions, and tricks of the Other (the other [illegible word], the Other par excellence, namely the Enemy)."

‡ M.F.: find.

element of perfection, that divine element that is within him.[57] So that, for the Gnostic, knowing God and recognizing oneself is the same thing. What one is seeking deep within oneself is God, and if one knows God it is because and insofar as one has become transparent to oneself, insofar as one has rediscovered God in oneself. The gnosis is necessarily linked to a structure of memorization. Knowledge of self in the gnosis appears only in the form of memory of the divine.* Knowledge of self and knowledge of God cannot be separated in this memory of the divine. [Now], Christianity precisely broke away from all these Gnostic movements by separating salvation and perfection. It promised the imperfect the possibility of salvation. It marked with permanent imperfection all those who might think they are saved. But, thereby, Christianity separated knowledge of God and knowledge of self, knowledge of God and transparency to oneself. Christianity autonomized knowledge of self as an endless task, an always unfinished labor of perfection. Christianity detached itself from the promises of Platonic memory: Remember God who is in you and seek out deep within yourself the God therein you have forgotten. Against these promises of Platonic memory, Christianity disconnected a knowledge of God, on the one hand, and a knowledge of self [on the other]; knowledge of self which is, of course, indispensable for advancing towards one's perfection, but which is sufficiently autonomous in relation to knowledge of [God]† for it to have its own form and for the one not to lead to the other. I will not find God deep within myself since, as you have seen, what I find is Satan, evil. Consequently, Christianity replaced the Platonic structure of memory of the divine lying deep within oneself with the indefinite task of penetrating the uncertain secrets of conscience, and it imposed on Christians the task, the obligation—I was going to say: of a gnosis of self different from the gnosis of God ... in truth, [the] word gnosis is not appropriate here—it articulated, but as two different forms, the obligation to believe in God, of course, and the indefinite task of knowing oneself.

Second remark. You have seen that the subjectivity and truth relationship takes different forms in the different institutional fields of

---

* The manuscript notes: "[and not] in the form of a permanent investigation of the most dubious impulses of conscience."
† M.F.: self.

Christianity: probation of the soul in baptism, public presentation of self in penance and exomologesis, and finally exploration of conscience, of its secrets and mysteries in direction and *exagoreusis*. You can see how quite specific techniques for establishing a relationship between subjectivity and truth, for linking the obligation of truth and subjectivity, are organized differently and in increasingly complex ways from baptism to direction. [And you can see] in each of these three forms, be it probation of the soul in baptism, public presentation of self in penance, or exploration of conscience in spiritual direction, relations between the same three elements, namely: death as mortification of self, the other as either the other = x to whom one speaks [or] the Other that one must recognize, Satan, and finally the truth. It is indeed a question of death, the other, and the truth in the three forms. But direction—and this is no doubt why it has a much greater historical importance from the point of view I am adopting, namely the history of subjectivity and truth and their relationships—is more important than baptism, or even penance, because in direction these relations between death, the other, and truth are established only by way of the obligation to speak, the obligation to tell, the obligation to tell the truth, to produce a true discourse on oneself, and to do so indefinitely. Whatever form this linkage between death, other, and truth through truth-telling, through veridiction, might have taken in the fourth century in Cassian, this obligation to tell the truth about oneself has never ceased in Christian culture, and probably in Western societies. We are obliged to speak of ourselves in order to tell the truth of ourselves. In this obligation to speak about oneself you can see the eminent place taken by discourse. Putting oneself in discourse is in actual fact one of the major driving forces in the organization of subjectivity and truth relationships in the Christian West. Subjectivity and truth will no longer connect so much, primordially, or anyway not only in the subject's access to the truth. There will always have to be this inflection of the subject towards its own truth through the intermediary of perpetually putting oneself into discourse.

In short, one no longer needs to be king, to have killed one's father, married one's mother, and ruled over the plague to be forced to discover the truth of oneself. It is enough to be anyone. One does not have to be Oedipus to be obliged to seek one's truth. No people in the grip of the plague asks it of you, but merely the whole, institutional, cultural, and religious system, and soon the whole social system to which we belong. The only difference, supplementary benefit or misfortune in comparison with Oedipus: [Oedipus] could grasp this truth about himself only by forcing the truth from the mouth of the slave he summoned from the elevated position of his power, whereas for us to be obliged, for us to tell the truth about ourselves, there is no need to be king and interrogate a slave, we just have to interrogate ourselves and to do so within a structure of obedience to another, to any other. So one does not have to be Oedipus to be obliged to discover the truth of oneself. You don't have to be Oedipus, unless, of course, an amusing mind tells you: but yes, yes you do! If you are obliged to tell the truth it is because, without knowing it, despite everything, there's a bit of Oedipus in you too.*58 But you see that the person who tells you this in the end does no more than turn the glove inside out, the glove of the Church.

Third and final point: this institutionalization of truth/subjectivity relationships through the obligation to tell the truth about oneself, the organization of this linkage cannot be conceived without the existence and functioning of a form of power, which, of course, I have not wanted to undertake [to study] this year. You recall Septimius Severus, the Roman Emperor who had the truth of the world displayed above his head in the picture representing the order of the stars, with the exception of the part concerning his life and death—someone highly qualified has told me that this was not possible, that one could not represent the astral sky while leaving out the part that concerned the life of the individual, but this is what the Roman historians tell us, so I take it to be true. So Septimius Severus had the truth of the world displayed above his head, except the part concerning him, and it was from this truth of the world from which he had subtracted his own truth, it was from this manifestation of the truth of the world that he asked for the sign and promise of the durability of his own power. The Christian does not have the truth of the world above his head, with the exception of his own truth, the truth concerning himself. The Christian has the truth deep within himself and he is yoked to this deep secret, indefinitely bent over

* This last sentence—after "but yes, yes you do!"—is written as follows in the manuscript: "It is because you are all Oedipus that you all need to set off in search of what Cassian called *arcana secretorum*."

it and indefinitely constrained to show to the other the treasure that his work, thought, attention, conscience, and discourse ceaselessly draw out from it. And by this he shows that putting his own truth into discourse is not just an essential obligation; it is one of the basic forms of our obedience. Well, thank you.

1. Cassien, *Institutions*, 4, 9, p. 133; Cassian, *Institutes*, 4, IX, p. 82. On the need for "openness of conscience," a "practice essential to early monasticism," J.-C. Guy, p. 132 note 1, refers to I. Hausherr, *Spiritual Direction in the Early Christian East*, pp. 155-184.
2. See *Institutions*, 4, 13, pp. 137-139 and especially 7, 7-15, pp. 299-313; *Institutes*, 4, XIII, p. 84, 7, VII-XV, pp. 171-176.
3. On the history of this word in Christian thought, see F. Dingjan, *Discretio. Les origins patristiques et monastiques de la doctrine sur la prudence chez Saint Thomas d'Aquin* (Assen: Van Gorcum N.V., 1967), pp. 14-88 (on Cassian); I. Hausherr, *Spiritual Direction*, pp. 77-98; I. Hausherr, "Direction spirituelle. II. Chez les chrétiens orientaux," *DS*, III, 1957, col. 1024-1028, and A. Cabassut, "Discrétion," ibid., cols. 1311-1330; Dom P. Miquel, *Mystique et Discernement* (Paris: Beauchesne, 1997), Part III, chapter 1: "Le discernement," pp. 105-117. In Cassian, see *Conferences*, especially First Conference, chapters XVI-XXIII, and the whole of the Second Conference.
4. Cassian, *Conférences*, 2, 2, p. 113 (translation slightly modified by Foucault); *Conferences*, 2, II.4, p. 85: "discretion...avoids excess of any kind and teaches the monk always to proceed along the royal road and does not let him be inflated by virtues on the right hand—that is, in an excess of fervor to exceed the measure of a justifiable moderation by a foolish presumption—nor let him wander off to the vices on the left hand because of a weakness for pleasure." On this image of the "royal road" (*via regia*) taught by *discretio*, see also ibid., Fr., 4, 12, p. 178 (*itinere regio*); Eng., 4, XII.5, p. 163; Fr., 6, 9, p. 228; Eng., 6, IX.3, p. 223; Fr., 24, 24, p. 197; Eng., 24, XXIV.5, p. 845; *Institutions*, 11, 4, p. 431 (*via regia*); *Institutes*, 11, IV, p. 241. See F. Dingjan, *Discretio*, p. 37; A. Cabassut, "Discrétion," col. 1313; see also col. 1312: "Cassian appears to have been the first to express the idea of moderation by *discretio* by using it to designate the virtue that keeps the zeal for perfection from any excess and maintains it in the happy medium."
5. *Conférences*, 1, 21, p. 105; *Conferences*, 1, XXI, pp. 61-62.
6. Ibid., 2, 5, p. 117: "the brethren had great difficulty in pulling him out more than half-dead. He expired two days later"; Eng., ibid., 2, V.4, p. 88: "When, after a great deal of effort on the part of the brothers, he was pulled out of it nearly dead, he expired three days later."
7. Ibid., 2, 6, pp. 117-118; Eng., ibid., 2, VI, pp. 88-89.
8. Ibid., 2, 7, pp. 118-119; Eng., ibid., 2, VII, p. 89. On Patermucius, see above, lecture of 19 March, p. 270 and p. 273.
9. Ibid., 2, 24, p. 135; Eng., ibid., 2, XXIV, pp. 102-103.
10. Ibid., 7, 26, p. 268. The text says that "by chance there was a woman on the road," and the abbot Paul "fled back to his monastery, faster than would someone who had seen a lion or a monstrous dragon"; Eng., ibid., 7, XXVI.3, p. 265: "For when a woman from nearby chanced to meet him on his way ... he ... ran back to his own monastery in greater haste than a person would use to flee from a lion or an immense dragon."
11. Ibid., p. 269; Eng., ibid., XXVI.4, p. 266
12. On *discretio* as "mother of all moderation (*moderationis generatrix*)," see ibid., 1, 23, p. 108; Eng., 1, XXIII.3, p. 64: "begetter of moderation"; see also, 2, 16, p. 131: "the good of discretion ... will be to keep us unharmed by two opposed excesses"; Eng., 2, XVI.1, p. 99: "the good of discretion ... which can keep both extremes from hurting us." The lack of moderation in abstinence is even worse, in its consequences, than gluttony (ibid., 2, 17, p. 132; Eng., 2, XVII, p. 100).
13. Ibid., 2, 2, p. 113 (sentence slightly modified by Foucault); Eng., ibid., 2, II.3, p. 85: "For we often see that those who keep fasts and vigils most rigorously and who live far off in the solitude in wondrous fashion, who also deprive themselves of any belongings to such an extent that they do not so much as allow a single day's food or one denarius ... are so suddenly deceived that they are unable to bring to a satisfactory conclusion the work that they have begun, and they cap off the highest fervor and a praiseworthy way of life with a disreputable end."
14. On this point see *Sécurité, territoire, population*, lecture of 1 March 1978, pp. 208-209; *Security, Territory, Population*, pp. 204-208.
15. See above, lecture of 19 March, p. 267 and note 65.
16. It is a matter, as J.-C. Guy explains in Cassien, *Institutions*, p. 65, note 2, of "the 'Alexandrian version' of the myth of the apostolic origin of monasticism ... Cassian was inspired by Philo, known through Eusebius of Ceasarea, *Church History*, II, 17." The first monks, Cassian writes, *Institutes*, 2, V, p. 39, received that "form of life from the evangelist Mark ... the first to rule

as bishop over the town of Alexandria"; Philo "says that they were called Therapeutes, and Therapeutrides the women who lived with them … either because they treated and cured the souls of those who came to them, delivering them, like doctors, from the sufferings of vice, or because of the chaste and pure care and worship they rendered the Deity," Eusèbe, *Histoire ecclésiastique*, II, 17, trans. E. Grapin (Paris: A. Picard, "Textes and documents pour l'étude historique du christianisme," 1911), pp. 170-171; English translation by Arthur C. McGiffert and Ernest C. Richardson as, Eusebius Pamphilus, *Church History*, Book II, chapter 17, in *NPNF2*, Vol. I, eds. Philip Schaff and Henry Wace (Grand Rapids, Michigan: W.B. Eerdmans Publishing, 1994), p. 117: Philo "says that these men were called Therapeutae and the women that were with them Therapeutrides … from the fact that they applied remedies and healed the souls of those who came to them, by relieving them like physicians, of evil passions, or from the fact that they served and worshipped the Deity in purity and sincerity." On the bibliography relative to this myth, see *Histoire ecclésiastique*, p. 31 note 3. See also *Conférences*, 18, 5, t.3, pp. 14-15 where the "Hierosolymitana version" is set out: "The cenobite life arose at the time of the apostolic preaching. This is, in fact, what we see appearing in Jerusalem in that all that multitude of believers whose picture is drawn in the *Acts*: 'The multitude of believers have but one heart and one soul …'"; *Conferences*, 18, V, p. 637: "The discipline of the cenobites took its rise at the time of the apostolic preaching. For such was the whole multitude of believers in Jerusalem, which is described thus in the Acts of the Apostles: 'The multitude of believers had but one heart and one soul.'" In the first version, the first monastic community is not confused with that of the Apostles themselves.

17. Cassien, *Institutions*, 2, 5, p. 67; Cassian, *Institutes*, 2, V.3, p. 40: "for they feared that … some discord or difference might arise and that sometime thereafter it would burst forth into error or rivalry or hurtful schism."

18. Ibid., p. 69; Eng., ibid., 2, V.5, pp. 40-41. See already, 2, 4, p. 65: "[The number of twelve psalms] was sent from heaven to our fathers by the ministry of an angel"; Eng., 2, IV, p. 206: "This number (twelve) … was not established by human whim but was given to the fathers from heaven by the teaching of an angel."

19. Ibid., p. 67: "*venerabiles patres*" (see above, note 16). See 2, 6, p. 69: "the venerable assembly of the Fathers (*patrum senatus*)"; Eng., 2, VI, p. 41: "the venerable gathering of fathers."

20. Cassien, *Conférences*, 24, 26, t. 3, p. 205; Cassian, *Conferences*, 24, XXVI.17, pp. 851-852. This reputation was due to the gift of prophecy (*karisma prorrēseōn*) that he would have obtained after thirty years of reclusion. See *Histoire lausiaque*, 35, pp. 235-237: "Having spent thirty years completely shut away, and receiving the necessaries from an attendant through a window, he was judged worthy of the gift of predictions. Among others he sent different predictions to the blessed Emperor Theodosius, and, with regard to the tyrant Maximus, after having conquered him, he would return from the Gauls. And likewise, he gave him good news regarding the tyrant Eugenius. The considerable fame of his virtue was widespread"; *The Lausiac History of Palladius*, trans. W. K. Lowther Clarke (London/New York: The Macmillan Company, 1918), pp. 120-121: "Having completed thirty years thus immured, and receiving the necessaries of life through a window from one who ministered to him, he was counted worthy of the gift of predictions. Among other instances he sent various predictions to the blessed Emperor Theodosius, one concerning Maximus the tyrant, that he would conquer him and return from the Gauls; similarly also he gave him good news about the tyrant Eugenius. His reputation as a virtuous man was widespread." According to Cassien, *Institutions*, 4, 23, p. 155, it was "because of his obedience" that he "was raised to the grace of prophecy (*propter obedientiae virtutem usque ad prophetiae gratiam sublimatus*)"; Cassian, *Institutes*, 4, XXIII, p. 90: "on account of the virtue of obedience he was raised to the grace of prophecy itself."

21. See above p. 291 and p. 314, note 5. *Conferences*, 1, XXI.1, p. 61: "'Pardon me, for it was I who inflicted this labor on you.'"

22. See *Conférences*, 7, 12, t. 1, pp. 256-257: "It is not at all by a diminution of the soul, but by a weakening of the body that these things happen …"; *Conferences*, 7, XII.1, p. 256: "It is very clearly understood that this takes place not through some kind of diminution of the soul but through a weakening of the body."

23. Ibid., 7, 10, p. 255: "Between them, as between men, there is a similarity of nature and kinship. The proof of this is that the definition we give of the essence of the soul likewise applies to their essence. But it is absolutely impossible for them to penetrate or mutually unite with

each other to the point that one contains the other. This prerogative is justly attributed only to the Divinity, because it alone is an incorporeal and simple nature"; Eng., ibid., 7, X, p. 255: "For among them, as among human beings, there is a certain substantial similarity and relationship, since the understanding of the nature of the soul may likewise be applied to their substance. But, on the other hand, it is completely impossible for them to enter into and be united with one another in such a way that one can contain the other. This is rightly attributed only to the Godhead, which alone is an incorporeal and simple nature." See also 7, 13, p. 257; 7, XIII, pp. 256-257.

24. Ibid., 7, 15, p. 258: "Whether the same thoughts that they [= the spirits of evil] suggest are welcomed and how, it is not at all by the very essence of the soul that they know them, that is to say by the inner movement, hidden, so to speak, in its very marrow, but through the movements of the external man and the signs he reveals"; Eng., ibid., 7, XV.2, p. 257: "Likewise, they come up with the thoughts that they insinuate, whether they are accepted and however they are accepted, not from the nature of the soul itself—that is, from its inner workings, which are, as I would say, concealed deep within us—but from movements and indications of the outer man."

25. Ibid., 7, 9, p. 255: "... such is the union existing between them and our soul that it is almost impossible, without God's grace, to distinguish what results from their excitations and what from our will"; Eng., ibid., 7, IX, p. 255: "... so that there is so close a union between them and the mind that, apart from the grace of God, one can hardly determines what comes from their instigation and what from our own will."

26. See Cassien, Institutions, 6, 9, p. 123: "... what others desire to arrive at in purity of the body, we must possess in the secret of our conscience (in arcanis conscientiae)"; Cassian, Institutes, 6, IX, p. 157 : "For what those others wish to acquire in terms of purity of body, we must ourselves possess in the depths of our conscience." "See also ibid., 12, VI.2, p. 459: "That is why, although [the blessed David] guarded his heart (cordis sui arcana) with such vigilance that he dared declare to The One for whom the secrets of his conscience (secreta suae conscientiae) were not unknown ..."; Eng., ibid., 12, VI, p. 257: "Hence, although blessed David guarded the recesses of his heart with great care (so that he boldly declared to him from whom the secrets of his conscience were not hidden ..."; Conférences, 19, 12, t. 3, p. 50: "[The solitary must not] display his purity, but [strive] to offer it inviolate to the sight of The One from whom the most intimate secrets of the heart (cordis arcana) cannot hide"; Conferences, 19, XII.4, p. 678: "Thus even the solitary, who strives not to show his purity to human beings but to manifest it inviolate before him from whom no secrets of the heart can be hidden, perceives from telltale indications whether the roots of each vice are implanted in him." The expression exploratio conscientiae refers, no doubt, to this passage of Conférences, 19, 11, t. 3, p. 48 (where conscientiae, however, is the subject and not the object of exloratio): "How can the gaze of our conscience, which explores the inner movements of the soul (exploratrix internorum motuum conscientiae), discern in us the presence or absence of these virtues?"; Conferences, 19, XI.2, p. 677: " Or how will our conscience, which searches into interior movements, understand the virtues that it has and those that are lacking to it?"

27. See above, lecture of 19 March, p. 258 and p. 278, note 22.

28. See above, p. 289 and p. 314, note 1.

29. In the manuscript, Foucault refers to Conférences, 2, 10: "Nullas cogitationes obtegere." See the translation, SC, p. 120: "... no cleverness of the devil will take advantage of the ignorance of a man who is unable to hide from false shame any of the thoughts which arise in his heart (qui universas cogitationes in corde nascentes perniciosa verecundia nescit obtegere), but leaves it to the mature appreciation of the elders whether he should accept or reject them"; Conferences, 2, X.2, p. 91: "... nor shall the crafty foe be able to take advantage of the ignorance of a person who does not know how to hide all the thoughts coming to birth in his heart because of a dangerous embarassment but either rejects them or accepts them according to the considered opinion of the elders."

30. Évrage le Pontique [Evagrius Ponticus], Logos praktikos / Traité pratique ou le Moine, trans. A. and C. Guillaumont (Paris: Cerf, 1971, SC, 170-171) t. 2, p. 609. See below, note 32.

31. See for example Platon, Ménon, 97e, trans. M. Canto-Sperber (Paris: Flammarion, GF, 1991) p. 198: "True opinions ... are not worth much unless they are bound by a reasoning that gives their explanation (aitias logismos)." As the translator clarifies, p. 311, note 310, "the most common meaning of the term logismos is 'reasoning,' 'calculation.'" Plato, The Meno, trans. W.

K. C. Guthrie, in *Protagoras and Meno* (Harmondsorth: Penguin Books, 1956) p. 154: "True opinions...are not worth much until you tether them by working out the reason." See also 100b; *La République*, IV, 440b, trans. E. Chambry (Paris: Les Belles Lettres, CUF, 8th printing, 1975), p. 38: "... when a man is driven by his passions despite reason (*para ton logismon*), he rebukes himself"; Plato, *The Republic*, Book IV, 440b, trans. Desmond Lee (London and Harmondsworth: Penguin Books, 2nd revised ed., 1987), p. 216: "And don't we often see other instances of a man whose desires are trying to force him to do something his reason disapproves of, cursing himself ... ?" (*logismos* here is a synonym of *logos*, employed twice a few lines further on). Aristotle links *logismos* more specifically to the domain of action: See *On the Soul*, Book III, 10, 433a and 11, 434a; *Eudemian Ethics*, Book II, 10, 1226b. This is why H. Lorenz, *The Brute Within. Appetitive Desire in Plato and Aristotle* (Oxford: Clarendon Press, 2006), who cites these references, translates it as "deliberative reasoning" (p. 178).

32. Evagrius Ponticus (?345-399). On his life as an ascetic in Egypt and his relations with the Egyptian anchorites (Antony, Macarius, John of Lycon), see *The Lausiac History of Palladius*, chapter XXXVIII; on his relations with Cassian (who would have met him during his stay in the Kellia desert, although he does not cite him, "but by the time that Cassian wrote, the name of Evagrius was suspect of heresy"), see O. Chadwick, *John Cassian*, p. 26. See A. and C. Guillaumont, "Évagre le Pontique," *DS*, IV, 1961, cols. 1731-1744. Dividing spiritual life into two phases, the *praktikē* ("practical" life) and the *gnostikē* ("gnostic" life), he defines the first as "the spiritual method that purifies the impassioned part of the soul" (*Traité pratique*, t. II, chapter 78, p. 667; the distinction is taken up by Cassian in *Conferences*, 14, II. The goal to be reached is *apatheia*, impassivity, the condition of access to the *gnosis*. It is the demons who move the passions, by making use either of objects themselves, *pragmata*, with seculars or cenobites, or of thoughts, *logismoi*, against anchorites. "Evagrius played a decisive role in perfecting the later classical theory of the 'eight thoughts' (later reduced to seven, hence the seven capital sins) [gluttony, fornication, avarice, sadness, anger, despondency or accidie, vanity, and pride: see *Traité pratique*, chapter 6, 14: 'On the eight thoughts']." (A. and C. Guillaumont, col. 1738). These eight *logismoi*, as has already been noted (see above, lecture of 19 March, p. 281, note 39), are the object of Books 5-8 of Cassian's *Institutes*, and the Fifth of his *Conferences*. On the process which led, with Gregory the Great, from the eight thoughts to the seven capital sins, see O. Chadwick, *John Cassian*, p. 95. According to A. Guillaumont, in his Introduction to the *Traité pratique*, the designation of the vices by the word *logismoi* is probably linked, through Origen (pp. 58-60) to the Jewish notion of *yêsèr*, "thought" or "thinking," which is found in Ecclesiastes and the Testaments of the Patriarchs (pp. 60-62).

33. Cassien, *Conférences*, 7, 3, p. 247: "*insensibiliter mens inde revoluta ad priores evagationes inpetu vehementiore prolabitur*"; Cassian, *Conferences*, 7.3, III, pp. 248-249: "For when we think that our heart is stretching out toward its goal, our mind, insensibly turned away from that to its former wanderings by a powerful impetus ..." Lower down Cassian employs the word *pervagatio* (ibid., "we come to see in these divagations (*has animae pervagationem*) less a personal fault than a vice inherent in human nature"; Eng., ibid., we are drawn to the opinion: "We believe that these wanderings of the soul which exist in the human race are not our own fault but nature's"). See also 7, 4, p. 248: "this dissipation of the mind (*hanc evagationem cordis nostri*)"; Eng., 7, IV.3, p. 250: "this wandering of our heart"; 7, 6, p. 253: "the divagations of the soul (*evagationibus animae*)"; Eng., 7, VI.2, p. 253: "these wanderings of the soul"; 10, 10, p. 88; Eng., 10, X.10, p. 381: "my wandering thoughts"; 14, 11, t. 2, p. 198: "the divagation of the mind (*cogitationum pervagatione*)"; Eng., 14, XI.5, p. 516: "wandering thoughts"; 22, 3, t. 3, p. 117: "the vagabond multitude of thoughts (*multimoda cogitationum pervagatio*)"; Eng., 22, III.4, p. 764, "numerous roving thoughts"; 23, 5, p. 147; Eng., 23, V.8, p. 796, "wandering," etcetera.

34. Ibid., 1, 16, p. 98; Eng., ibid., 1, XVI, p. 56: "Why is it, then, that superfluous thoughts insinuate themselves into us so subtly and hiddenly when we do not even want them, and indeed do not even know of them, that it is not only very difficult to cast them out but even to understand them and to catch hold of them?"

35. Ibid., 1, 17; Eng., ibid., 1, XVII.1: "It is, indeed, impossible for the mind not to be troubled by thoughts."

36. Ibid., 7, 4, p. 248; Pichery translation: "*de çà de là*"; Eng., ibid., 7, IV.2, p. 249: "The *nous*, therefore, which is the mind, is understood as *aekinētos kai polukinētos*—that is, as always

changeable and manifoldly changeable … Because of its nature, then, it can never stand idle but … will inevitably run about and fly everywhere due to its own changeableness."

37. Cassian writes, ibid., 1, 18, p. 99: "it is in the power of the master of the mill (*in eius qui praeest situm est in potestate*)"; Eng., ibid., 1, XVIII.1, p. 57: "it is in the power of the one who supervizes [the millwheel]."

38. Ibid.; Eng., ibid.

39. Ibid., 7, 5, pp. 249-251; Eng., ibid., VII, V, pp. 363-364. See Matthew 8, 9.

40. Ibid., 1, 20, pp. 101-103; 1, 21-22, pp. 105-107; 2, 9, p. 120; Eng., ibid., 1, XX, pp. 59-60; 1, XXI-XXII, pp. 61-63; 2, IX, p. 90. See above, lecture of 19 March, p. 279, note 29, on other references, in later works by Foucault, to the analysis of this metaphor. To the three metaphors cited by Foucault (and which he refers to again in "Le combat de la chasteté"; "The Battle for Chastity," with regard to "'discrimination' that lies at the heart of the technology of oneself as developed in the spirituality inspired by Evagrius," pp. 305-306; Eng., p. 194) is added that of the fisherman, in *Conférences*, 24, 3, t. 3, p. 174 (the abbot Abraham): "I suppose some spiritual fisherman seeking his food by the method learned from the apostles. He observes the shoal of thoughts swimming in the calm depths of his heart. As from an overhanging shelf, he casts an avid gaze into the depths, and discerns with a sagacious eye (*sagaci discretione*) those he must pull in to himself with his line and those he must leave and reject as bad and dangerous fish"; *Conferences*, 24, III.2, pp. 827-828: " like a clever fisherman looking out for his food with apostolic skill, he may catch the swarms of thoughts swimming about in the calmest depths of his heart and, like someone gazing intently into the depths from a jutting promontory, may with wise discretion judge which fish he should draw to himself with his saving hook and which ones he should let go and reject because they are wicked and harmful."

41. Ibid., 1, 20, p. 101 and p. 102; Eng., ibid., 1, XX, pp. 59-60.

42. Ibid., pp. 101-102, p. 103; Eng., ibid., p. 60.

43. Ibid., pp. 103-104; Eng., ibid., p. 61.

44. Ibid., p. 105: "He was deceived by a false coin, and bowed before the image he saw of the legitimate king without sufficiently examining if its stamp was genuine"; Eng., 1, XXI.1, p.62: "He was deceived by a counterfeit coin, and while he was venerating the image of the true king on it he was too little aware of whether it was lawfully minted." See above, pp. 294-295.

45. Ibid., 1, 22, p. 106; Eng., ibid., 1, XXII.1 pp. 62-63. In the first paragraph Cassian recapitulates all the foregoing.

46. Ibid., 7, 4, p. 248: "the quality of our thoughts depends on us (*a nobis [cogitationum] qualitas pendet*)"; Eng., ibid., 7, IV.3, p. 250; "Their quality, therefore, depends on us." See also 1, 17, p. 98: "it depends on us, to a great extent, to raise the tone of our thoughts (*ut cogitationum qualitas emendetur*)"; Eng., 1, XVII.2, p. 56: "it is, I say, largely up to us whether the character of our thoughts improves." See *Institutions*, 6, 11, p. 275 (regarding the spirit of fornication): "… the quality of thoughts (*qualitas cogitationum*), watched over more negligently during the day because of distractions, is put to the test by the calm and quiet of night"; *Institutes*, 6, XI, p. 157 : "For the character of our thoughts, which is rather negligently paid heed to in the midst of the day's distractions, is made trial of in the calm of night."

47. Descartes, *Méditations métaphysiques*, II, p. 418 (AT, IX, 20); *Meditations on First Philosophy*, Second Meditation, in *The Philosophical Writings of Descartes*, Vol. II, p. 17: "I too undoubtedly exist, if he is deceiving me; and let him deceive me as much as he can, he will never bring it about that I am nothing so long as I think that I am something."

48. See Cassien, *Conférences*, 2, 10, p. 120, the question put to the abbot Moses: "What use will it be to us to know the excellence of the virtues of discretion and the value of its grace if we do not know how to seek it and acquire it?"; Cassian, *Conferences*, 2, IX.2, p. 90: "For what profit will it be to have known the dignity of its [discretion's] virtue and grace if we do no know how it is to be sought for and acquired?"

49. Cassien, *Institutions*, 4, 9, p. 133 (sentence slightly modified); Cassian, *Institutes*, 4, IX, pp. 82-83 : "Indeed, the devil in all his slyness will not be able to deceive or cast down a young man unless he inveigles him, either by haughtiness or by embarrassment, into covering up his thoughts. For they [the elders] declare that it is an invariable and clear sign that a thought is from the devil if we are ashamed to disclose it to an elder."

50. Cassien, *Conférences*, 2, 10, pp. 120-121; the text adds: "and his pernicious suggestions hold sway over us only so long as they remain hidden in the depths of the heart"; Cassian, *Conferences*,

2, X.3, p. 91: "For as soon as a wicked thought has been revealed it looses its power, and even before the judgment of discretion is exercised the loathsome serpent—drawn out as it were into the light from its dark and subterranean cave by the power of the confession—departs as a kind of laughing stock and object of dishonor. For his harmful counsels hold sway in us as long as they lie concealed in our heart."

51. Ibid., 2, 11, pp. 121-122; Eng., ibid., 2, XI, pp. 91-92.

52. Ibid., p. 122 (Abbot Theonas to Abbot Serapion): "Your deliverance is acccomplished; without me saying a single word, the confession (*aveu*) you have just made sufficed (*absoliut te ab hac captivitate etiam me tacente confessio tua*). Your adversary was victorious; you triumphed over him today; and your confession (*aveu*) brings him down more completely than he himself beat you through your silence ... This horrible serpent will no longer be able wrongfully to make is lair in you after your salutary confession (*confession*) has dragged him from the darkness of your heart into the light"; Eng., ibid., 2, XI.4, p. 92: "'Take heart, my boy. Your confession freed you from this captivity even before I spoke. Today you have triumphed over your conqueror and adversary, defeating him by your confession more decisively than you yourself had been overthrown by him because of your silence... nor shall the filthy serpent ever again seize a place to make his lair in you, now that by a salutary confession he has been drawn out from the darkness of your heart into the light.'"

53. See I. Hausherr, *Direction spirituelle*, p. 337: "*Exagoreusis*, a word derived from the verb *exagureuo*, to speak out, to make known, 'to confess'. The 'revelation [*manifestation*] of thoughts' ... to an elder; later, sacramental confession." In the chapter he devotes to this practice (see the following note), the expression *exagoreusis tōn logismōn* is translated as "revelation [*manifestation*] of thoughts" (p. 157). The word *exagoreusis* itself, however, is frequently employed. Bailly, *Dictionnaire grec-français* (Paris: Hachette, 1929), p. 692, which translates the word by "Enunciation, revelation," refers, for the ecclesiastical usage ("confession"), to Basil, 3, 1016, 1236, Gregory of Nyssa, 2, 229, 233, and John Chrysostom, 12, 766 in Migne, *Patrologia Graeca*. *Exagoreuein* is used in the Septuagint to translate the Hebrew word *hitwaddâ* ("confession") in Numbers, 5, 7: "*exagoreusei tēn amartian ēn epoiēsen*"; Vulgate translation: "*confitebuntur peccatum suum*"; English translation by Peter W. Flint in *A New English Translation of the Septuagint* (Oxford: Oxford University Press, 2009), p. 114: "he shall confess the sin he has committed"; and Leviticus, 5, 5: "*exagoreusei tēn amartian*"; 16, 21; 26, 40: "*exagoreusousin tas amartias autōn kai tas amartias tōn paterōn autōn*"; English translation by Dirk L. Büchner as *Leuitikon* in *A New English Translation of the Septuagin*, p. 105: "And they shall confess their sins and the sins of their fathers." See T.R. Ashley, *The Book of Numbers* (Grand Rapids, Michigan: W.B. Eerdmans, 1993), p. 114 note 12, who comments; "This verb means 'to divulge.' The reason why this Greek word is chosen rather than the far more common *exomologein* ... may be to emphasize the verbal nature of this confession."

54. For a different analysis see, for example, O. Chadwick, *John Cassian*, pp. 103-104, who clearly separates, in the "perfect" (those who, according to Cassian have attained the state of *puritas cordis*), the continuous analysis of thoughts from the obligation of confession (*aveu*) to another: "The 'perfect' man, unlike a junior monk, need[s] no longer confess his sin to another—though he might. The eight capital sins must be confessed to another. But, once the stage is passed, the pure in heart confess only before God. Though to him sin is a heavy burden, he is to remember how free and merciful is the forgiveness of God ....."

55. The absence of pagination of the manuscript means that we do not know whether Foucault envisioned here a particular exposition on the subject that he would have used later for a lecture or a seminar. See "About the Beginning of the Hermeneutics of the Self: Two Lectures at Dartmouth" (1980), *Political Theory*, 21, 2, May 1993, 2nd lecture, pp. 220-221, where, returning briefly to the relations between *exomologesis* and *exagoreusis*, he emphasizes this common element: "... the rule of confession in *exagoreusis*, this rule of permanent verbalization, finds its parallel in the model of martyrdom which haunts *exomologesis*. The ascetic maceration exercised on the body and the rule of permanent verbalization applied to the thoughts, the obligation to macerate the body and the obligation of verbalizing the thoughts—those things are deeply and closely related. They are supposed to have the same goals and the same effect." On *exagoreusis* itself, see I. Hausherr, "Direction spirituelle. II," cols. 1037-1039, and in particular *Spiritual Direction in the Early Christian Easty*, the whole of chapters V ("The Need for Openess of Heart") and VII ("The Revelation [*manifestation*] of Thoughts in Practice"), pp. 152-177 and pp. 212-229.

56. See H. Osborne, "ΣΥΝΕΣΙΣ and ΣΥΝΕΙΔΗΣΙΣ," *The Classical Review*, 45 (1) February 1931, pp. 8-9: "*suneidēsis* occurs twice only in classical Greek [Democritus, fragment 297; Chrysippus, in Diogenes Laertius, VII, 35] and in both cases it means not Conscience but Consciousness in the broadest sense ... It does not reappear in literature until the Book of Wisdom (XVII, 10), Dionysius of Halicarnassus and Diodorus Siculus. From this time onwards it is not infrequent ... Its primary meaning remains Self-consciousness, not as an abstract faculty, but as introspective awareness of particular states or chracteristics of the Self, or of past behaviour regarded as a manifestation of character"; Ibid., "ΣΥΝΕΙΔΗΣΙΣ," *Journal of Theological Studies*, XXXII, January 1931, pp. 167-179. In the first translations of *suneidēsis* by *conscientia*, see G. Molenaar, "Seneca's Use of the Term 'Conscientia,'" *Mnemosyne*, 4th Series, 22(2), 1969, pp. 170-180. See also the old work, which has a wealth of references, of M. Kähler, *Das Gewissen Die Entwickelung seiner Namen und seines Begriffes* (Halle: J. Fricke, 1867), pp. 23-54, on *suneidēsis*, and pp. 55-73, on *conscientia* in Cicero and Seneca. See above, lecture of 23 January, p. 54 and p. 69, note 20 ("*suneidōs*").

57. On the gnosis and its criticism by Christianity, see above the lectures of 20 and 27 February, p. 118 and pp. 182-183.

58. See Cassien, *Institutions*, 5, 2, p. 193: quotation of Isaiah 45, 2-3: "... I will open up for you sacred treasures and secret mysteries (*arcana secretorum*)"; and a bit further on: "[The word of God] will make [the evil passions] succomb to our inquiry and exposition, and 'breaking thus the doors' of ignorance and 'breaking the locks' of the vices which exclude us from the true science, it will lead us to our 'secret mysteries' (*secretorum nostrum arcana*) and, according to the Apostle, will reveal to us, once illuminated, 'the secrets of the darkness' (*abscondita tenebrorum*) and show to us the thoughts of the hearts (1, Corinthians, 4, 5)"; Cassian, *Institutes*, 5, II.2, pp. 117-118: "'... And I will open to you hidden treasures and concealed secrets.' Then the word of God ... will make [these same harmful passions] submit to our investigation and our exposure. And, breaking open the gates of ignorance and smashing the bolts of the vices that shut us out from true knowledge, it will lead us to our concealed secrets and, according to the Apostle, it will, once we have been enlightened, reveal to us 'the hidden things of darkness and make manifest the counsels of hearts.'"

Course Summary[*]

THE COURSE THIS YEAR took off from the analyses carried out in the preceding years concerning the notion of "government," this being understood in the broad sense of techniques and procedures for directing men's conduct. Government of children, government of souls or consciences, government of a household, of a State, or of oneself. Within this very general framework we studied the problem of the examination of conscience and of confession (*aveu*).

With reference to the sacrament of penance, Tommaso de Vio called the confession (*confession*) of sins an "act of truth." Let us keep this phrase with the meaning Cajetan gave to it. The question posed then is this: how is it that in Western Christian culture, the government of men requires of those who are directed, in addition to acts of obedience and submission, "truth acts" that have the distinctive characteristic of requiring not only that the subject tell the truth, but that he tell truth about himself, about his faults, desires, the state of his soul, etcetera? How was a type of government of men formed that does not just require one to obey, but to manifest what one is by stating it?

After a theoretical introduction on the notion of "regime of truth," the longest part of the course was devoted to the procedures of the examination of souls and of confession (*aveu*) in early Christianity.

* Published in the *Annuaire du Collège de France, 80ᵉ année, Histoire des systèmes de pensée, année 1979-1980*, 1980, pp. 449-452, and in *Dits et Écrits, 1954-1988*, ed. D. Defert and F. Ewald, with the collaboration of J. Lagrange (Paris: Gallimard, 1994), Vol. 4, pp. 125-129; "Quarto" ed., Vol. 2, pp. 944-948. An earlier translation of this summary by Robert Hurley appears with the title "On the Government of the Living" in M. Foucault, *The Essential Works of Michel Foucault, 1954-1984, Vol. 1: Ethics: subjectivity and truth*, ed. Paul Rabinow, trans. Robert Hurley and others (New York: The New Press, 1997), pp. 81-85.

Two concepts must be distinguished, each corresponding to a particular practice: *exomologēsis* and *exagoreusis*. Study of exomologesis shows that the term is often employed with a very wide meaning: it designates an act that is intended to manifest both a truth and the subject's adherence to that truth; to make the exomologesis of one's belief is not just to assert what it is one believes, but to assert the fact of believing; it is to make the act of assertion an object of assertion, and so to authenticate it either for oneself or before others. Exomologesis is an emphatic assertion in which the emphasis falls above all on the fact that the subject binds himself to this assertion and accepts its consequences.

Exomologesis as an "act of faith" is indispensable to the Christian for whom revealed and taught truths are not just a matter of beliefs that he accepts, but obligations by which he commits himself—the obligation to maintain his beliefs, to accept the authority that authenticates them, possibly to profess them publicly, to live by them, etcetera. But we quickly encounter another type of exomologesis: this is the exomolegesis of sins. Here again distinctions have to be made: the obligation to acknowledge that one has sinned is imposed on both catechumens who apply for baptism and on Christians guilty of a few weaknesses: for the latter, the *Didascalia* prescribes that they make the exomologesis of their faults to the assembly. Now, at that time, this "confession (*aveu*)" does not seem to have taken the form of a detailed public statement of the sins committed, but was rather a collective rite during which each individual acknowledged to himself, before God, that he was a sinner. It is with regard to serious sins, those of idolatry, adultery, and homicide, and with the occurrence of persecutions and apostasy that the exomolegesis of sins acquires its specificity: it becomes a condition for reintegration and is linked to a complex public rite.

The history of penitential practices from the second to the fifth century shows that exomologesis in this period did not take the form of an analytical verbal confession of different faults together with their circumstances; and it did not obtain remission by virtue of it being performed in the canonical form [by] someone who had received the power to remit them. Penance was a status into which one entered after a ritual and which came to an end (sometimes on the deathbed) after a second ceremony. Between these two moments, the penitent made the exomologesis of his sins through his mortifications, austerities, mode of life, clothes, and the manifest attitude of repentance—in short by a whole dramatics the main part of which was not verbal expression and [from which] the analytical statement of specific sins seems to have been absent. It may well be that a special rite took place before reconciliation and that the term "exomologesis" was more specifically applied to this. But even here, it was still a matter of a dramatic and synthetic expression by which the sinner acknowledged before everyone the fact of having sinned; he attested this acknowledgment in a manifestation that visibly bound him to a sinner's state and at the same time prepared his deliverance. Verbalization of the confession of sins in canonical penance will take place systematically only later, first with the practice of tariffed penance, then from the twelfth and thirteenth centuries with the organization of the sacrament of penance.

In monastic institutions, the practice of confession (*aveu*) took very different forms (which, when a monk committed certain important offences, did not exclude forms of exomologesis before the assembled community). To study these practices of confession in monastic life, we resorted to the more detailed study of Cassian's *Institutes* and *Conferences* from the perspective of techniques of spiritual direction. Three aspects in particular were analysed: the mode of dependence on the elder or teacher, the way of conducting the examination of one's own conscience, and the duty to tell all regarding the impulses of thought in a formulation that was meant to be exhaustive: the *exagoreusis*. On these three points, considerable differences emerge in comparison with the processes of spiritual direction to be found in ancient philosophy. Schematically, we can say that the relationship to the teacher in the monastic institution takes the form of unconditional and continuous obedience concerning every aspect of life that in principle leaves the novice no margin of initiative; if the value of this relationship depends on the teacher's qualification, it is true nevertheless that the form of obedience, regardless of its object, has a value in itself; finally, if obedience is indispensable in novices and the teachers are in principle elders, difference in age is not sufficient by itself to justify the relationship—both because the ability to direct is a charisma and obedience, in the form of humility, must constitute a continuous relationship to oneself and to others.

The examination of conscience is also very different from that recommended by the philosophical schools of Antiquity. Certainly, like the latter, it included two great forms: evening recollection of the day gone by and continuous vigilance over oneself. The second form is most important in the monasticism Cassian describes. Its procedures show clearly that it is not a matter of determining what one must do so as not to commit a sin or even of recognizing whether one has committed a sin in what one has done. It is a matter of catching hold of the movement of thought (*cogitation* = *logismos*), of examining it thoroughly in order to grasp its origin and decipher where it is from (God, oneself, or the devil), and to carry out a sorting (which Cassian describes with several metaphors, the most important of which is probably that of the money-changer who checks the coins). Reporting the views of Serenus, Cassian devotes one of the most interesting *Conferences* to the "mobility of the soul," which constitutes the domain of an examination of conscience that can clearly be seen to have the role of making the unity and conti-nuity of contemplation possible.

As for the confession (*aveu*) Cassian prescribes, this is not the simple statement of faults committed or a presentation of the overall state of the soul; it must strive for the continuous verbalization of all the move-ments of thought. This confession enables the director to give advice and provide a diagnosis: Cassian thus recounts examples of consultation; sometimes several elders take part and give their views. But verbaliza-tion also entails intrinsic effects due solely to the fact that it transforms the impulses of the soul into statements addressed to another person. In particular, the "sorting," which is one of the objectives of the examina-tion, is carried out through verbalization thanks to the triple mecha-nism of shame that makes one blush at formulating any bad thoughts, of the material realization by the words uttered of what is taking place in the soul, and of incompatibility between the demon (who seduces and deceives while hiding in the inner recesses of consciousness) and the light that reveals them. What then is involved in confession thus understood is a continuous externalization of the "arcana" of conscious-ness through words.

Unconditional obedience, uninterrupted examination, and exhaus-tive confession thus form a whole in which each element implies the other two; the verbal manifestation of the truth hidden in the depths of oneself appears as an indispensable component in the government of men by each other as this was put to work in monastic, and especially cenobitic institutions from the fourth century. But it needs to be stressed that the aim of this manifestation was not to establish one's sovereign mastery over oneself; rather, what was expected from it was humility and mortification, detachment with regard to oneself and the constitution of a relation to self that strives for the destruction of the form of the self.

*   *   *

The seminar this year was devoted to certain aspects of nineteenth century liberal thought. Presentations were given by N. Coppinger on economic development at the end of the nineteenth century, by D. Deleule on the Scottish historical school, P. Rosanvallon on Guizot, F. Ewald on Saint-Simon and the Saint-Simonians, P. Pasquino on Menger's place in the history of liberalism, A. Schutz on Menger's epistemology, and C. Mevel on the notions of the general will and the general interest.

COURSE CONTEXT

Michel Senellart*

IN 1978-1979, MICHEL FOUCAULT delivered a course of lectures on biopolitics,[1] a concept introduced in 1976[2] and the analysis of which he began the previous year through several examples of techniques for regulating populations,[3] before reorienting his inquiry towards the study of modern "governmentality," its genesis (from the Christian pastorate), forms of exercise (*raison d'État*, police), and its transformations.[4] However, far from returning to an empirical analysis of the mechanisms of bio-power,[5] Foucault endeavors to clarify the latter's conditions of intelligibility by reconstructing the "framework of political rationality"[6] within which it functions, "liberalism" understood as governmental technique modeled on the rationality of the governed:

> "... only when we know what this governmental regime called liberalism was, will we be able to grasp what biopolitics is."[7]

This approach led him, first of all, to describe the specific features of the liberal art of government as it appeared in the eighteenth century, and then to a closer examination of the two major, German and American versions of contemporary neoliberalism. Taking stock of his progress on

---

* Michel Senellart is Professor of Political Philosophy at the École Normale Supérieure, Lyon. He edited Michel Foucault's lectures at the Collège de France: *Sécurité, Territoire, Population* (1978) and *Naissance de la biopolitique* (1979), Paris, Gallimard-Seuil ("Hautes Études"), 2004; English translations by Graham Burchell, *Security, Territory, Population* and *The Birth of Biopolitics* (London: Palgrave Macmillan, 2007 and 2008).

7 March he acknowledged that he had left out biopolitics[8] and, after the course had ended, he observed that the lectures had "ended up being devoted entirely to what should have been only its introduction."[9]

Hence the title, registered in Spring 1979, of what should have been the following year's lectures: "On the Government of the Living." Clearly, the intention was to extend the reflection opened up in 1976 and enriched with new concepts, but the further study of which was constantly deferred, by refocusing it on the way in which, for three centuries, power related to men not only as subjects of right, but as living beings. The title given signified the resumption, within the framework of the problematic of "government," of the study of the means by which power takes charge of the life of men and women as population. In sum, how "the biological is reflected in politics" in our societies as the result of a decisive transformation of the traditional relations of power.[10]

But in the end the lectures delivered in 1980 deal with something else entirely: not the government of the living, but the "government of men by the truth";[11] not the species-body[12] in its relation to techniques of the control of populations, but the subject in is relation to the manifestation of truth; not modalities of taking charge of life in a society of normalization,[13] but Oedipus and the truth acts peculiar to Christianity in the first centuries.

STRUCTURE OF THE COURSE

The Summary gives a very partial idea of the content of the course, describing in fact, after some theoretical reminders and clarifications, only the last five lectures.[14] So before anything else we should provide a basic account of its general structure. The course is divided into two quite distinct parts: the first (the second and third lectures, of 16 and 23 January, and the beginning of the fourth lecture, 30 January), is devoted to the analysis of Sophocles' *Oedipus the King*, and the second, and longer (from the fifth to the twelfth lecture, 6 February to 26 March), is devoted to the study of the three major practices around which the obligation of men to express in truth what they are, with a view to the remission of their sins, is structured in Christianity: baptism (the fifth, sixth, and seventh lectures, 6, 13, and 20 February), canonical or ecclesial penance (*pénitence*) (eighth and ninth lectures, 27 February and

5 March), and spiritual direction (from tenth to twelfth lecture, 12, 19, and 26 March).

How are such apparently heterogeneous sets connected to each other? Their unity is assured by the problematic of the government of men by the truth set out in the first and reformulated in the fourth lecture.

(I) To start with, Foucault distinguishes his analysis from the conception of a purely instrumental relation between power and truth. If the exercise of power entails some specific knowledge, it is accompanied by a manifestation of truth that is irreducible to these. Foucault then coins the word "alethurgy" to designate,

> the set of possible verbal or non-verbal procedures by which one brings to light what is laid down as true as opposed to false, hidden, inexpressible, unforeseeable, or forgotten,[15]

and he gives as one example among others, the struggle, correlative of *raison d'État*, against the type of production of truth (or "alethurgy") represented by the knowledge (*savoir*) of witches, seers, and astrologers in the entourage of princes.[16] The notion serves as a basis for freeing himself from the theme of knowledge-power around which his research was organized from the start of the 1970s.[17] After a first shift in 1978-1979 from the concept of power to that of government, the objective of the course is now to "develop the notion of knowledge in the direction of the problem of the truth."[18] This is the object of the analysis of Sophocles' *Oedipus the King* developed in the following lectures, of which Foucault, returning once again to this text,[19] here puts forward an "alethurgic" re-reading, with a view to showing

> how you cannot direct men without carrying out operations in the domain of truth, and operations that are always in excess of what is useful and necessary to govern in an effective way.[20]

Two complementary types of alethurgy frame the character Oedipus: on one side that of the gods, corresponding to the old forms of oracular consultation, and on the other that of the slaves, corresponding to the new rules of judicial procedure, entailing the summoning of witnesses.[21]

Faced with these, what is Oedipus's knowledge (*savoir*), and how does it function? It is an art (*tekhnē*) directed towards discovery by means of clues. It is an alethurgy of discovery, therefore, that he puts to work to defend his own power.[22] Oedipus is the man in whom the unity of knowledge and power is realized: knowledge of government since, by means of inquiry, it involves avoiding the reefs—the gods' decrees that weigh on the city—and directing the ship to safe harbor,[23] but also organized by reference to the preservation of his sovereignty (his "tyranny"). Now what the drama condemns, in the person of Oedipus himself, is not this alethurgy, since it leads to disclosure of the truth, but the claim to make oneself master of it for one's own advantage: not the procedure itself, but the use Oedipus makes of it. The latter, through the alignment of the two, divine and judicial alethurgies, which takes place without him knowing, thus becomes the "surplus character": "a supernumerary of knowledge," in short, "and not an unconscious."[24]

The drama thus stages the need for the manifestation of truth for the exercise of power, a manifestation, however, that exceeds the purely utilitarian objective of knowledge and escapes control by the tyrant. This is a reading that, in many respects, is close to that set out in 1972 in terms, not of alethurgy, but of rituals or procedures of knowledge.[25] But whereas in *Oedipal Knowledge* the axis of the analysis was the confrontation of forms of power-knowledge,[26] in 1980 analysis is re-focused on a new object: "the element of ... the "I," of the "*autos*," of the "myself""[27]—what Foucault calls the "point of subjectivation"[28]—in the cycle of alethurgy. The slave-witness is no longer the only seeing subject, the possessor of a knowledge founded on sight;[29] he is the one who, knowing the truth because he saw it, states it in his own name. Identification of having-seen with truth-telling[30]: it is this first person assertion as instance of veridiction that enables Foucault, at the end of the third lecture, to introduce the specific question of the course: "What is this game of the myself or this game of the oneself within procedures of truth?"[31] What is involved in the "relation between *autos* and alethurgy,"[32] and how is this problem linked up with that of the government of men? These three elements—subject, manifestation of truth, government—mark out the field of study of Christianity that Foucault undertakes from the fourth lecture.

(II) This transition leads him, first of all, to a clarification of his theoretical approach, which he describes with humor as "anarcheology."[33]
Rather than a philosophical thesis, this is an attitude that is distinguished
from skepticism by the fact that it does not consist in suspending all
certainties, but of positing "the non-necessity of all power of whatever
kind."[34] The question then becomes "what of the subject and relations
of knowledge do we dispense with when we consider no power to be
founded either by right or necessity."[35] Using the example of his works
on madness or criminality, Foucault thus contrasts an analysis based on
the notion of ideology, which postulates the existence of a non-alienated
human essence, with an approach founded on the refusal of universals[36]:
starting from the contingency of practices (confinement, imprisonment)
and showing the knowledge relations and mode of constitution of the
subject to which they have given rise.

He then establishes new concepts needed for his analysis of
Christianity. The reading of *Oedipus the King* had brought out, with the
slave-witness, a form of insertion of the subject in a procedure of truth.
Now it is a matter of passing to another level: no longer that of simply
picking out a singular historical figure, but that of the genealogy of the
bonds that in our culture unite relation of power and manifestation of
truth in the double sense of the word "subject."

The first concept is that of "truth act (*acte de vérité*),"[37] by which
Foucault designates "the part that falls to a subject in the procedures of
alethurgy."[38] The subject may play the role of operator (that, for example, of the priest in a sacrifice), spectator (that of the witness), or the
object itself of the alethurgy, when it is a question of oneself in the truth
act. It is with this reflexive form, of which confession (*aveu*) represents
the "purest and also historically most important form,"[39] that Foucault
choses to concern himself in the rest of the course, based on the study
of early Christianity.

The second, no doubt more decisive,[40] but also more problematic
concept is that of "regime of truth," introduced in the fourth lecture
and to which Foucault devotes a lengthy justification at the beginning
of the fifth lecture (later on,[41] we shall see what turning point in his
journey is marked by taking up this concept that he had already used
previously).[42] How does he define it here?

A regime of truth is then, that which constrains individuals to these truth acts, that which defines, determines the form of these acts and establishes their conditions of effectuation and specific effects.[43]

Such a "regime"—the word is explicitly taken up with its political and juridical connotations[44]—is not exercised only when the truth is powerless to "make its own law." In other words, it does not apply solely to the domain of non-scientific knowledge, but goes beyond the science/non-science (or science/ideology) opposition, science functioning as one possible regime of truth among others (although the constraint being assured by truth itself in science, the regime seems to lose all exteriority in relation to the subject of enunciation).

Foucault then comes to the central object of the course: Christianity viewed from the point of view of the truth acts that characterize it—more precisely the acts of confession, and not the acts of faith to which more attention is generally accorded; both, in fact, fall under two distinct regimes of truth, which, although strictly interdependent, nonetheless have very different morphologies.[45] To the *continuum* of taught truth-extracted truth, by which in 1978 Foucault described the "system of truth" peculiar to the Christian pastorate,[46] thus succeeds a relationship of tension —the emergence of which he locates in Tertullian[47]—between the poles of faith (acts of adherence to a revealed truth) and confession (acts of manifestation of a hidden truth).

Foucault had already studied the progressive formation and ritualization of the pole of confession through the history of Christian penance from the end of the Middle Ages to the Counter Reformation.[48] The obligation of confession (*aveu*) was gradually imposed in penitential practice in the form, codified in 1215, of regular, continuous, and exhaustive confession (*confession*).[49] In that way, confession (*aveu*) seemed to merge with [sacramental] confession (*confession*).[50] Now in reality the latter is only

the result, and the as it were most visible and superficial result, of much more complex, numerous, and rich processes by which Christianity bound individuals to the obligation to manifest their truth…[51]

In 1980 the objective is therefore to bring to light the regime of truth that the ritual practice of the verbalization of sins, inscribed in the foundation of the sacrament of penance, had ended up hiding. It is a matter, in short, no longer of the history, but of the archeology of confession (*confession*). Hence the need to go back to early Christianity.

The regime of confession in the first centuries is organized around three major practices: baptism, ecclesial penance (*pénitence*), and on a different plane, spiritual direction. Foucault devotes the end of the fifth lecture and the two following lectures to the first; the eighth and ninth lectures to the second; and the three last lectures to the third. In the Course Summary this analysis is focused on two essential concepts: exomologesis, a sort of dramatic manifestation of oneself by which the sinner, in the rite of second repentance (*pénitence*), or canonical penance (*pénitence*), asks to be reintegrated into the Church, and *exagoreusis*, or manifestation of thoughts, corresponding to the practice of examination of conscience in the framework of monastic direction. Since the Summary does not say anything about the lectures dealing with baptismal theology, it seems necessary to clarify briefly their content. In fact, Foucault explains here how, with Tertullian, the question of access to baptism lead to the profound renewal of the Christian conception of the relations between subjectivity and truth.

The Tertullian moment

Baptism, the believer's act of entering into a new life, is strictly linked to the idea of purification. Until the second century, it is connected to a procedure of truth that takes the form of a pedagogical type of initiation. At the end of catachesis, the postulant gains access to divine illumination through the sacrament of water. The soul is thus inscribed in a process that gradually qualifies it as a subject of knowledge. According to Foucault, Tertullian represents a decisive turning point of Christian thought in relation to this structure of teaching.[52] His conception of original sin (the doctrine of which, Foucault recalls several times, Tertullian invented)[53] leads him in fact to a radical redefinition, not of baptism itself, the purifying effectiveness of which he defends against the Gnostics, but of the time preparing for it. The fact of the state of corruption in which men are born means that purification cannot be simply the effect of the light. It entails a complete transformation of our nature before the baptismal act: "We are not bathed in the water in order to be purified, but because we are purified."[54] That our nature has become other is not the only consequence of sin, however, but also that the other—Satan—henceforth lives in us. Preparation for baptism, consequently, appears as a time of struggle and confrontation, dominated by the fear of ceding to the demon's assaults. Fear from which the remission of sins could not deliver the faithful, but to which he must remain subject throughout his life,[55] in a perpetual anxious relationship to himself:

> fear about oneself, of what one is ... this fear is ... will obviously be of absolutely decisive importance in the whole history of what we may call subjectivity, that is to say the relationship of self to self, the exercise of self on self, and the truth that the individual may discover deep within himself.[56]

From this new conception of the time before and after baptism flows the need for a "discipline of repentance (*pénitence*)"[57] extending to the entire life. It is around the problem of conversion (*metanoia*), reinterpreted as repentance (*pénitence*)[58] and mortification, that the question of the relations between subjectivity and truth in Christianity are reorganized and, consequently—as a decisive passage from the manuscript clarifies— that of the government of men:

> The paradox of a form of power with the intended purpose of being exercised universally over all men insofar as they have to convert, i.e., gain access to the truth by a radical ... change that must be authenticated by manifesting the truth of the soul. Governing the being-other through the manifestation of the truth of the soul, so that each can earn his salvation.
>
> ...
>
> Christianity assures the salvation of each by authenticating that they have in fact become completely other. The relation government of men/manifestation of the truth is entirely recast. Government by the manifestation of the Completely Other (*Tout Autre*) in each.[59]

COURSE CONTEXT

There are, to tell the truth, few external elements of contextualization related to this course, which is as "untimely (*inactuel*)" as the previous year's course on neoliberalism was directly at grips with current reality (*actualité*). If the analysis of this theme is pursued in the framework of the seminar,[60] we find no trace of it, as we have already stressed, in the general problematic of *On the Government of the Living*. The first months of 1980 were marked, moreover, by several deaths: that of Roland Barthes on 16 March—the day of the last session of the course—taken by "the stupid violence of things"[61] and whose funeral eulogy was given by Foucault at the Collège de France,[62] then that of Sartre, in April, whose funeral he attended. But these deaths occurred after the course. However, another, earlier death perhaps finds its echo in some of the questions broached by Foucault: the sudden death of Maurice Clavel on 22 April 1979, with whom he had spoken the day before

> of a book that he had enjoyed regarding Freud; and then of different things; and then of Christian penance: why, he said, does the obligation to tell the truth bring with it the ashes, dust, and the death of the old man, but also rebirth and the new day? Why is the moment of truth at this threshold?[63]

Likewise, of the two major events with religious resonance in which Foucault found himself involved—the Iranian uprising at the end of 1978 and the beginning of 1979,[64] and the Solidarnosc resistance to the state of siege declared in Poland at the end of 1981—the first came to an end some months earlier with a wave of executions of opponents, in the name of purification of the country,[65] and the establishment of a theocratic dictatorship, and the premises of the second are not yet discernible (the major strike that will give rise to the Solidarnosc union took place in August 1980).

It is therefore withdrawn from all immediate intellectual or political actuality that Foucault, faced with a rather disconcerted audience, set out his research on early Christianity. This attitude may be explained in part by his desire to stand back from a media scene with a tendency he deplored to create ephemeral events around authors placed under the spotlight, rather than practice genuine critical thought. It is significant that he chose to make this observation in an interview in *Le Monde*, in April, published under the anonymity of the "masked philosopher."[66] The mask expresses his need to escape the game of effects of opinion linked to fame. But it also serves to put philosophy back on the terrain of a fundamental questioning, beyond the division established between scholarly research and channels of information:

> I was saying...that philosophy was a way of reflecting on our relationship to the truth. It should also be added that it is a way of interrogating ourselves: If this is the relationship that we have with the truth, how must we conduct ourselves? I believe that a considerable and varied amount of work has been done and is still being done that alters both our relationship to the truth and our way of conducting ourselves. And this has taken place in a complex conjunction between a whole series of investigations and a whole set of social movements. It's the very life of philosophy.[67]

The true actuality from which the course arises is here, in that "complex conjunction," linked to the stakes of the present by an unexpected detour.

No doubt Foucault's readers were hoping, for years, finally to see the new volume of the *History of Sexuality* that was announced in the *The Will to Know** with the title *The Flesh and the Body*.[68] They were unaware that in 1975, following a disagreement with Gallimard, Foucault had decided to publish nothing further for five years after this book.[69] But there would have been nothing surprising in him returning, following in the tracks of the latter, to the study of the post-Tridentine Christian pastorate. However, Foucault chose to devote his analyses to a completely different epoch of Christianity without any explicit link with the problematic of the flesh. There was, then, a double surprise in the face of the object of the course and the apparent decoupling from the program of *The Will to Know*.[70]

We know that Foucault finally abandoned this program after beginning "to write two books in accordance with my original plan,"[71]

---

* Published in English as *The History of Sexuality, Vol. I: An Introduction.*

choosing, at the end of a long development,[72] to refocus his work on the genealogy of "desiring man"[73]: how was "a certain relation to the self" formed "in the experience of the flesh"[74] in the first centuries C.E.? A thematic and chronological shift the result of which was the still unpublished volume *Aveux de la chair (Confessions of the Flesh)*.

As we will see shortly,[75] the 1980 course is closely linked to the writing of that book. *On the Government of the Living* thus appears as the first course for a long time in which the material is inscribed within the perspective of a future book (the same is true for the following year, with the course "Subjectivity and Truth"[76]). However, nothing in the general organization of the course gave the least indication to his audience of this connection between the oral teaching and the resumption of the project of the History of Sexuality.

The reorientation of his project was also accompanied by a change in Foucault's usual ways of working. Weary with the slow service at the Bibliothêque nationale, from the summer of 1979[77] he decided to frequent henceforth the Dominican library of Le Saulchoir, rue de la Glacière, in the 13th arrondissement. Here, in the small reading room[78] giving on to a pleasant internal garden, there was free access to the major collections of classical and patristic texts he needed to write his book. He spent entire days there, seated at the same table near the window.[79]

Foucault was not satisfied with reading the Church Fathers. He also sought to compare his views with those of specialists of history and religious philosophy. In April he met a young Jesuit, James Bernauer, then a doctoral student in Paris (he was preparing a thesis on "The Thinking of History in the Archeology of Michel Foucault"), who had followed the course and wanted to question him about his work. At the end of this interview, Foucault asked him if he could organize a meeting with some theologians, in order to discuss his study of Christianity. This took place on 6 May 1980, at the Jesuit home, 42 rue de Grenelle. Those who took part were the fathers Alfonso Alfaro, Mario Calderon, Charles Kannengiesser (who then taught patristics at the Catholic Institute of Paris), Gustave Martelet, and William Richardson, all Jesuits apart from the first.[80] Some days earlier, J. Bernauer had given them an introductory text in which he presented briefly the authors and themes dealt with in the course.[81] Foucault showed that he wanted clarifications about certain Christian categories and inquired about critical editions of authors on whom he was working. His very first question, notably, bore on the origins of the notion of *debitum* in Christian marriage (the obligation, for both spouses, to accept the sexual act). Contrary to the view of one of those present, Foucault was doubtful that it stemmed from canon law. He also spoke about Tertullian, Cassian, and other authors studied in the course.[82] If the exchange was open and warm, to the young Jesuit it seemed nevertheless that "however well-intentioned the theologians, they did not really understand Foucault's point of view on these subjects."[83]

STAKES OF THE COURSE

This course connects together several levels of problematization in a complex way. In the first place, it is in continuity with the general project of a "morphology" of the "will to know"[84] set out by Foucault in 1970. No doubt the same goes for several of the previous courses, the program for which was sketched out, in its major lines, in the opening lecture,[85] although their content is not reducible to the unfolding of a pre-established schema of analysis. But in 1980 Foucault quite explicitly links his course to his inaugural problematic:

> Basically, what I would like to do and know that I will not be able to do is write a history of the force of truth, a history of the power of the truth, a history, therefore, to take the same idea from a different angle, of the will to know.[86]

It is quite significant that, in this respect, this course begins, in the mode of a fully acknowledged repetition,[87] with a lengthy analysis of *Oedipus the King*, to which Foucault had already devoted the final lecture of the 1970-1971 course.[88] We cannot speak of a simple return to the initial project however. Behind the appearance of its resumption, Foucault resolutely endeavors to open up new perspectives on the basis of the theoretical and conceptual displacements carried out in the previous years.

Freeing himself of power-knowledge

The first displacement is marked by the transition, in 1978 and 1979, from the concept of power to that of government. Initially introduced in a series of lectures on the theme of bio-power, with reference to the management of populations as opposed to the power of sovereignty,[89] the concept of "government," defined as the way of conducting men's conduct, very quickly came to occupy the center of Foucault's analysis[90] and gradually replaced that of "power."[91] It is in this way that Foucault, from the start of the 1980 course, bids farewell to the latter, henceforth deemed "less operational" than that of "government"

> in the broad sense, and old sense moreover, of mechanisms and procedures intended to conduct men, to direct their conduct, to conduct their conduct,[92]

and inscribes his new research in continuity with his previous works on raison d'État and contemporary liberalism.[93]

Now a correlate of the analysis of power developed from the beginning of the 1970s in the framework of the problematic of the "will to know" was the establishment of a circular relation between truth and power:

> 'Truth' is linked in a circular relation with systems of power which produce and sustain it, and to effects of power which it induces and which extend it.[94]

The notion of "power-knowledge,"[95] coined in 1972 to designate that level of reality, distinct from the plane of the history of the sciences,[96] where knowledge and power reciprocally reinforce each other, answered to the problem posed the previous year, on the basis of Nietzsche,[97] of the "origin" of knowledge (*connaissance*), or rather of the site from which the question of origin, peculiar to classical metaphysics, is invalidated: not the subject of knowledge, driven by the desire for truth, but that "other side of knowledge" that cannot be reached—and all the difficulty is here—except by placing oneself outside of it.[98] The "other side" described then in terms of struggle and violence.[99] Going back over this analysis, Foucault writes, in the manuscript for the course "Penal Theories and Institutions":

> The Nietzschean analysis ... seeks [behind knowledge (*connaissance*)] something altogether different from knowledge. Something altogether different in relation to which the knowing subject and knowledge itself are effects. It is this altogether different something that was to be inventoried.
>
> What is behind the "form" of knowledge, the secret of knowledge, the open field of what is to be known, the corpus of knowledge, what is behind all this are relations of power: it is the bringing into play of forms of power that creates knowledge (*savoir*), which in turn enhances power: an indefinite interplay of formation, displacement, circulation, and concentration in which supplements, excesses, and reinforcements of power are produced incessantly, and the increase of knowledge, the most knowledge, the *sur*-knowledge. This is the level of "power-knowledge."[100]

This critique of the metaphysical foundation of knowledge is extended, in the following course, "The Punitive Society," by the (until then merely subjacent) critique of the Marxist concept of ideology. As he explains in one of the lectures—a transcription of which was circulated, at the time, in the form of a small typed pamphlet ("Power and the norm")[101]—it is important to "differentiate oneself" from the analysis according to which power "can only ever produce ideological effects in the domain of knowledge."[102] Far from power being "held in the alternative: violence or ideology,"

> every point of exercise of power is at the same time a site of the formation of knowledge. And, on the other hand, all established knowledge enables and assures the exercise of a power. In other words, there is no opposition between what is done and what is said.[103]

The analysis of power in terms of ideology rests, in fact, on the idea that knowledge and power are antinomic. For knowledge to be developed, relations of power must be suspended. And where power is exercised, only the interplay of interests reigns.[104] This conception leans on the representation of a knowledge naturally oriented towards the truth that only the economic and political conditions in which men live disturb or obscure.

> Ideology is the mark, the stigma of these political or economic conditions of existence on a subject of knowledge who rightfully should be open to the truth.[105]

On one side, then, a discourse organized by reference to truth, and on the other, the veil or obstacle for the act of knowledge constituted by socio-economic determinations: the science/ideology couple thus leads back to the metaphysical postulate of a pure knowing subject, ideally free in relation to power, but that power tends to subject and instrumentalize, to which Foucault, in his first course, had opposed the Nietzschean model of the "will to know." It is in fact from the latter, through the concept of power-knowledge, that the critique of the notion of ideology draws its theoretical premises.[106] Conversely, the whole program of research developed since 1970 could be read as a series of more or less discontinuous inquiries on different apparatuses (*dispositifs*) of power-knowledge—forms of analysis of measure, the inquiry, and the examination,[107] the emergence of the judicial apparatus, carceral penality, penal psychiatry, the model of war as "analyzer of power relations," and the economic government of populations—from Ancient Greece to the nineteenth century.[108]

From this it is easy to imagine the surprise of Foucault's audience when, in the first lecture of the course, distancing himself from "the now worn and hackneyed theme of knowledge-power," he declare he wants to "get rid of" it.[109] Just as that concept had enabled him to put the notion of dominant ideology out of play, so henceforth it must give way to the new concept that Foucault propose to develop of "government by the truth."

What is a regime of truth?

Certainly this is a new concept, even if it was already sketched out in previous years' courses. In *The Birth of Biopolitics*, Foucault analyzed how, in the eighteenth century, political economy marked the appearance of a new "regime of truth" founded on the principle of self-limitation.[110]

And, through a typical retrospective modification of perspective, he presented his earlier research in the light of the following problem: how a series of practices, linked to a certain regime of truth, inscribes in reality something that in itself does not exist[111]—madness, disease, delinquency, sexuality, the economy—in order to submit it to the division between true and false. This practices-regime of truth coupling, defined, however, in terms of "knowledge-power,"[112] was not yet a reformulation of the approach adopted since 1971. "Regime of truth" certainly signified more than the simple domain of knowledge and techniques coextensive with a certain practice of power.[113] It was to be understood as "the set of rules enabling one to establish which statements in a given discourse can be described as true or false," which is why from the following lecture Foucault chose to speak of "regime of veridiction."[114] A regime, therefore, that determines the conditions of truth-telling and which, through the interplay of a variety of factors, connects up with governmental practice. If there could have been a question, in this sense, of government by the truth with regard to liberalism, it is to the extent, nevertheless, that this "regime" was still analyzed from the point of view of discursive rules alone, in their relation to a practice of power.

In 1980, on the other hand, Foucault entirely reconstructs his analytical schema. The question is no longer how discourse is connected to practice, but by what procedures, according to what mode, in view of what ends is a subject bound to the manifestation of truth. It is this relationship between procedures of manifestation of the true (or alethurgy) and forms of the subject's implication (operator, witness, or object) that defines the word "regime."[115] The latter does not designate a system of constraints exerted from outside on the individual (subject in the passive sense); but no more does it designate the activity by which this individual, in his relation to a given truth, is constituted as a subject (in the active sense). It designates the specific type of obligations an individual submits to in the act by which he becomes the agent of a manifestation of truth. Thus, in Christianity, the truth act par excellence is "confession (*confession*)" (in its double signification of profession of faith and act of confession of self (*aveu*)[116]), but we will not say that this constitutes the Christian regime of truth. The regime consists in a certain correlation between two major obligations: to believe, on the one hand, and for each to explore the secrets of their heart on the other.[117] And confession (*confession*) is situated here, at the hinge of these two obligations of truth.[118]

We can see, from this, how this concept enables the idea of a "government by the truth" to replace the schema of power-knowledge, in which the subject, far from playing an active role, was simply objectivized.

The flesh and confession

The second shift with regard to the initial program of the "will to know" is related to the study of sexuality. Whereas in his inaugural lecture of 1970 the problem of the putting of sexuality into discourse was still posed in terms of prohibition,[119] in 1976 this approach is, if not impugned, at least relegated to second rank,[120] to the advantage of a new interpretive hypothesis founded on the foregrounding of mechanisms of incitement to discourse and the production of confession (*aveu*). We saw above how, after conceiving the plan of a History of Sexuality in six volumes, Foucault finally reoriented his project in an entirely different direction.[121] From this turning point came the first version of *Confessions* (aveux) *of the Flesh*. It remains to clarify the relations between that book and this course.

According to Daniel Defert's "Chronologie," Foucault began to write on the Church Fathers[122]—principally Cassian, Augustine, and Tertullian[123]—in August 1977, his interest arising from the study of the history of confession (*confession*). Until 1976, in fact, these names do not appear anywhere in his work. The first reference to Tertullian appears the following year (in the form of a joke, "as a joke, to make a fable") in a casual interview with psychoanalysts around the introductory volume of *The History of Sexuality* (*La Volonté de savoir*):

> We have had sexuality since the eighteenth century, and sex since the nineteenth. What we had before was no doubt the flesh. The basic originator of it all was Tertullian.[124]

The 1978 course, *Security, Territory, Population*, calls in, alongside Cassian, a number of Christian authors of the first centuries, from Cyprian to Jerome and Gregory the Great. This corpus, recently brought together no doubt for the analysis of the pastorate,[125] is considerably enriched over the following months, thus forming the material of the second volume of the History of Sexuality: *The Confessions of the Flesh*, instead of the volume *The Flesh and the Body* initially announced,[126] the manuscript of which was partially destroyed.[127] Work on this book, begun at the beginning of 1979,[128] therefore precedes the course *On the Government of the Living*, and it is likely that its writing accompanied its development. In October and November 1980, in fact, Foucault presents the results of his research in the United States. At Berkeley first of all, within the framework of a seminar on "The Sexual Ethics of Late Antiquity and nascent Christianity,"[129] then at New York (a seminar partially published with the title "Sexuality and Solitude"[130]) and, finally, at Dartmouth College (lectures: "Subjectivity and Truth" and "Christianity and Confession"[131]). If the latter, in particular, summarizes the 1980 course fairly faithfully,[132] "Sexuality and Solitude," on the other hand, which starts from the same premises—the truth obligation to which every Christian is subject in his relationship to himself, and the technique of self that derives from it—deals with a completely different subject: the turning point of Christian sexual ethics represented by the Augustinian conception of *libido*, the "principle of autonomous movements of sexual organs."[133] This question is completely absent from the course (Saint Augustine himself is cited only rarely), but here Foucault relates it directly to the practice of the examination of conscience according to Cassian.[134] It is on the basis of this "libidinization of sex"[135] by Augustine that the monastic activity of the control of thoughts, analyzed at length some months earlier,[136] acquires it full meaning. Thus we see, with this precise example, how the two axes of analysis of the course and the book on which he was working intertwine.

So the question arises of what links them and to what extent the themes developed orally in the first months of 1980 reflect a specific moment of the construction of *The Confessions of the Flesh*.[137] The only extract we have from this volume is the chapter published by Foucault in 1982 with the title "The Battle for Chastity,"[138] in number 35 of *Communications* devoted to "Western sexualities."[139] Its object—the struggle against the spirit of fornication—appears to be fairly distant from that of the eleventh and twelfth lectures of the course based on Cassian: the function of confession, correlated with the principle of direction and the rule of obedience, in the monastic practice of the examination of conscience. However, they are rigorously connected to each other. In the article in *Communications*, after making clear that the target of the ascetic battle is not so much fornication strictly speaking, as impure thoughts, Foucault stresses in fact the "state of perpetual vigilance" demanded of the monk in his relation to the impulses of his soul.[140] A vigilance that is nothing other, he notes, than the exercise of the virtue of *discretio*, or "discrimination," around which "the technology of oneself" is organized "in the spirituality inspired by Evagrius Ponticus."[141] And to illustrate this, Foucault takes up again the metaphors of the miller, the centurion, and the moneychanger analyzed in the last lecture of the course,[142] but the sexual background of which is brought out here.

Such, no doubt, is the schema according to which the course is, as it were, fit into the general structure of the book. Just as the problem of concupiscence in Augustine is indissociable from the elaboration of a "constant hermeneutic of oneself,"[143] so the latter, in Cassian, is anchored in the attention focused on the problem of "voluntary/involuntary pollution"[144] and the psychical acts that give rise to it. By what ways, as a result of what developments, in terms of what strategic choices was that "technique of self"[145] formed that requires each to decipher the truth of his soul? It is indeed this interrogation, in the light of the problem of the "flesh," that underpins the whole approach of the course. The analysis developed by Foucault of the progressive emergence of the "pole of confession" distinct from the "pole of faith" thus acquires its full significance in relation to the book, the aim of which, as its title indicates, is to study

the experience of the flesh in the first centuries of Christianity, and [the] role in this of the purifying hermeneutics and decipherment of desire.[146]

So it seems that, from the fifth lecture, the course sets out the elements of a part of the book, whatever the state of its writing was at this time. Although the vocabulary of sexuality—desire, *libido*, flesh, concupiscence, etcetera—does not appear at any point in the course, it is quite clearly inscribed in the framework of the general problematic of the *Confessions of the Flesh*.

However, the hermeneutic of the Christian flesh is not Foucault's final development of the theme of confession. He returns to it the following year, in a series of lectures delivered at the Catholic University of Louvain, in the framework of the Chaire Francqui, with the title "Wrongdoing, Truth-telling. Functions of Avowal (*Mal faire, dire vrai. Fonctions de l'aveu*)."[147] Invited by the Faculty of Law, on the initiative of the School of Criminology, he undertook the study of penal confession (*aveu*) by situating it "in the more general history [of] "technologies of the subject,"" that is to say of the "techniques by which the individual is led, either by himself, or with the help or under the direction of another, to transform himself and modify his relation to himself."[148] The lectures form a course-balance sheet, a masterly synthesis of research conducted over ten years (on Greek pre-law, on the Christian pastorate, on criminal justice from the Middle Ages to the eighteenth century, on psychiatric expertise), but hitherto set out in separate parts and on distinct planes, the assemblage of which on a single axis—that of a "political history of veridictions"[149]— manifests remarkable coherence. But a course, equally, that, through the driving force of the questions dealt with, leads Foucault to expound at greater length than he had foreseen on the specifically Christian history of confession from the second to the thirteenth century.[150] Far from solely redeploying, with new inflections, the material already presented at the Collège de France (although in many passages he gives the impression of having the same manuscript in front of him), he makes it more complex and enriches it on several points, invoking different references, bringing certain connections into greater and sharper relief (as with regard to the "fundamental bond in Christianity between reading the text and verbalization of oneself"[151]) or expanding the field of analysis (see, especially, the exposition on the Pacomian monasteries in Egypt[152]). The additions clearly show that the "Christian dossier"—as the last lecture of the 1984 course, *The Courage of Truth* will confirm[153]—was by no means closed with the completion of *Confessions of the Flesh.*

SOURCES

The corpus of texts used by Foucault in the fifth to the twelfth lecture of this course is easily identifiable: it is that of the patristic writings of the first centuries, as established by Church tradition. The apostolic fathers, from the *Didache* (end of the first, beginning of the second century) to the *Pastor* of Hermas (middle of the second century),[154] and, to a lesser extent, the apologists,[155] Greek fathers of the Alexandrian school (Clement and Origen), and the first Latin fathers (Tertullian—we have seen the place Foucault attributes to him in the evolution of baptismal penance—and Cyprian), and Cassian, finally, for the genesis of Western monasticism. Foucault gives lengthy quotations from the texts—indicating a new style of work that he will pursue in his courses in the following years—whose internal references he often clarifies, without indicating, with some exceptions, the edition used. The difficulty therefore was discovering this, taking account of the fact that Foucault sometimes retranslates himself the passage on which he comments or adapts the translation chosen, sometimes resorts to different translations of the same text, some of which—like that of the Abbé De Genoude—go back to the nineteenth century. For the critical apparatus we are indebted to the fine work of Philippe Chevalier who, in his doctoral thesis, carried out a meticulous survey of these editions.[156]

As for the secondary literature consulted by Foucault—theses, scholarly works and articles, introductions to critical editions—the reader will find the extent of these through our notes. His use of this literature in the course is mainly for purposes of information and identification. It provides Foucault with examples, factual elements, and sometimes the quotations he needs or that enables him to orient himself in the field of this or that exegetical controversy (see, for example, his reference to the great book by Poschmann, *Paenitentia secunda* (1940), regarding the interpretation of the text of Hermas). But the substance of his analyses is drawn mainly from the direct reading of the texts.

*　*　*

The text of the course was transcribed on the basis of the recording made by J. Lagrange. With the exception of the inevitable breaks, linked to the cassette being turned over, this sound archive of excellent quality did not raise any particular problem. The manuscript, on the other hand, which includes numerous gaps—it is incomplete for the first four and the ninth lecture—has only been able to be used for a part of the course.

Written in a fairly discontinuous fashion (fully formed passages, read by Foucault as they are, alternate with schematic indications or isolated quotations) it presents scarcely any differences, generally speaking, from the text delivered. We have cited them in the notes when it seemed that they complete the latter usefully.

1. *Naissance de la biopolitique. Cours au Collège de France, 1978-1979*, ed. M. Senellart (Paris: Gallimard-Seuil, "Hautes Études," 2004); English translation by Graham Burchell, *The Birth of Biopolitics. Lectures at the Collège de France, 1978-1979*, English series editor, Arnold I. Davidson (Basingstoke: Palgrave Macmillan, 2008).

2. See *"Il faut défendre la société." Cours au Collège de France, 1975-1976*, ed. M. Bertani and A. Fontana (Paris: Gallimard-Seuil, "Hautes Études," 1997), lecture of 17 March 1976, p. 216; English translation by David Macey, *"Society Must Be Defended." Lectures at the Collège de France. 1975-1976*, English series editor Arnold I. Davidson (New York: Picador, 2003) p. 243; *La Volonté de Savoir* (Paris: Gallimard, "Bibliothèque des Histoires," 1976, p. 184; English translation by Robert Hurley, *The History of Sexuality. Volume 1: An Introduction* (London: Allen Lane, 1979) p. 139. See *Sécurité, Territoire, Population. Cours au Collège de France, 1977-1978*, ed. M. Senellart (Paris: Gallimard-Seuil, "Hautes Études," 2004), "Situation du cours," pp. 393-394; English translation by Graham Burchell, *Security, Territory, Population. Lectures at the Collège de France, 1977-1978*, English series editor Arnold I. Davidson (Basingstoke: Palgrave Macmillan, 2007), "Course context," pp. 377-378.

3. See the three major "apparatuses (*dispositifs*) of security" in the seventeenth and eighteenth century analyzed in the first lectures of *Security, Territory, Population* on the basis of problems of the town, scarcity, the circulation of grain, and smallpox and inoculation.

4. On this theoretical turning point, see ibid., "Situation du cours," pp. 396-400; Eng., "Course Context," pp. 379-382.

5. Foucault, then, employed the two concepts, "biopolitics" and "bio-power," without distinguishing them. See, for example, ibid., lecture of 11 January 1978, p. 23; Eng., p. 22, with regard to Moheau, "who was no doubt the first great theorist of what we could call biopolitics, bio-power."

6. *Naissance de la biopolitique*, "Résumé du cours," p. 323; *The Birth of Biopolitics*, "Course Summary," p. 317.

7. Ibid., lecture of 10 January, 1979, p. 24; Eng., p. 22. See too the passage from the manuscript for this lecture quoted on pp. 23-24 footnote *; Eng, pp. 20-22, footnote *, which ends with these words: "Studying liberalism as the general framework of biopolitics."

8. Ibid., lecture of 7 March 1979, p. 191; Eng., p. 185: "… I really did intend to talk about biopolitics and…I have ended up talking at length, and maybe for too long, about neoliberalism."

9. Ibid., "Résumé du cours," p. 323; Eng., "Course Summary," p. 317.

10. *La Volonté de savoir*, p. 187; *The History of Sexuality. 1: An Introduction*, p. 142 (translation modified).

11. Above, this volume (hereafter *GL*), lecture of 9 January 1980, p. 11.

12. See *La Volonté de savoir*, p. 183; *The History of Sexuality 1*, p. 139, where Foucault distinguishes the "body as machine," the object of disciplinary power, from the "species body, the body imbued with the mechanics of life and serving as the medium for biological processes," the object of a "bio-politics of population" (translation slightly modified).

13. On this concept see *"Il faut défendre la société,"* lecture of 17 March 1976, p. 225; *"Society Must be Defended,"* p. 253.

14. See above, p. 321 et seq.

15. *GL*, lecture of 9 January 1980, p. 7.

16. Ibid., pp. 10-11.

17. See below, pp. 338-340 for further clarification.

18. *GL*, lecture of 9 January 1980, p. 12.

19. On his previous readings of Sophocles' tragedy, see *GL*, lecture of 16 January 1980, p. 43, note 2.

20. *GL*, lecture of 9 January 1980, p. 17.

21. *GL*, lecture of 16 January 1980, pp. 34-42.

22. *GL*, lecture of 23 January 1980, pp. 58-65.

23. Ibid., p. 59.

24. Ibid., p. 67.

25. See M. Foucault, *Le Savoir d'Œdipe*, appendix to *Leçons sur la volonté de savoir. Cours au Collège de France, 1970-1971*, ed. Daniel Defert (Paris: Gallimard-Seuil, "Hautes Études," 2011), p. 233 and p. 241; English translation by Graham Burchell, *Oedipal Knowledge* in *Lectures on the Will*

to Know. Lectures at the Collège de France, 1970-1971, and Oedipal Knowledge, English series ed. Arnold I. Davidson (Basingstoke: Palgrave Macmillan, 2013), p. 238 and p. 246.

26. Ibid., p. 256.
27. *GL,* lecture of 23 January 1980, p. 48.
28. *GL,* lecture of 30 January 1980, p. 84.
29. See *Le Savoir d'Œdipe,* pp. 232-233; *Leçons sur la volonté de savoir,* lecture of 17 March 1971, p. 179; *Oedipal Knowledge,* pp. 237-238; *Lectures on the Will to Know,* p. 186.
30. *GL,* lecture of 23 January 1980, pp. 49-50.
31. Ibid., p. 67.
32. Ibid., and see already p. 49.
33. *GL,* lecture of 30 January 1980, p. 79.
34. Ibid., p. 78.
35. Ibid.
36. Ibid., p. 80.
37. On this concept, attributed to Cajetan in the Course Summary (above, p. 321), see p. 90, our note 8.
38. *GL,* lecture of 30 January 1980, p. 81.
39. Ibid., p. 82.
40. Insofar as the procedure of truth focuses on the subject himself, the formally distinct concepts of "alethurgy" and "truth act" tend to merge (see, for example, ibid., p. 88; lecture of 5 March 1980, p. 214, etcetera). This identification is confirmed in the 1984 course: M. Foucault, *Le Courage de la vérité. Cours au Collège de France, 1983-1984,* ed. F. Gros, (Paris: Gallimard-Seuil, "Hautes Études," 2009), lecture of 1 February 1984, First hour, p. 5; English translation by Graham Burchell, *The Courage of Truth. Lectures at the Collège de France 1983-1984,* English series ed. Arnold I. Davidson (Basingstoke: Palgrave Macmillan, 2011), p. 3: "Etymologically, alethurgy would be the production of truth, the act by which the truth is manifested."
41. See below, "Stakes of the course," pp. 340-342.
42. This is the moment of the "theoretical introduction" Foucault refers to in the Course Summary (above, p. 321), as if, in fact, the course really began at this point.
43. *GL,* lecture of 6 February 1980, p. 93.
44. Ibid., p. 94.
45. On this distinction see *GL,* lecture of 30 January 1980, pp. 83-84, and lecture of 6 February 1980, pp. 102-103.
46. *Sécurité, territoire, population,* lecture of 1 March 1978, p. 216; *Security, Territory, Population,* p. 212: "pastoral power developed a system of truth that ... went from teaching to examination of the individual; a truth conveyed as dogma to all the faithful, and a truth extracted from each of them as a secret discovered in the depths of the soul." See also ibid., French: p. 208, lecture of 8 March 1978, p. 241, and lecture of 15 March, p. 279; English: p. 205, pp. 235-236, p. 273 (in which he speaks of "cycle of truths").
47. See *GL,* lecture of 13 February 1980, pp. 134-135.
48. M. Foucault, *Les Anormaux. Cours au Collège de France, 1974-1975,* ed. V. Marchetti and A. Salomoni (Paris: Gallimard-Seuil, "Hautes Études," 1999) lecture of 19 February 1975, pp. 158-180; English translation by Graham Burchell, *Abnormal. Lectures at the Collège de France, 1974-1975,* English series ed. Arnold I. Davidson (New York: Picador, 2003), pp. 170-193.
49. Ibid., p. 162; English, p. 174.
50. See *La volonté de savoir,* p. 78; *The History of Sexuality, 1,* p. 58: "Since the Middle Ages at least, Western societies have established the confession [*l'aveu*] as one of the main rituals we rely on for the production of truth: the codification of the sacrament of penance by the Lateran Council in 1215, with the resulting development of confessional techniques [*techniques de confession*] ...."
51. *GL,* lecture of 6 February 1980, p. 103. This decentering of the history of confession (*aveu*) in relation to [the modern sense of] confession (*confession*) alone already appeared in *Sécurité, territoire, population,* lecture of 22 February 1978, p. 186; *Security, Territory, Population,* pp. 182-183 (with regard to examination of conscience).
52. As he stresses in various places, in fact, Tertullian is in no way an isolated figure but translates a more general movement of thought. See in particular *GL,* lecture of 20 February 1980, p. 146: "[His analyses] appear simply as a more particularly elaborated form of what is happening, evidence for which can be found not only in contemporary texts, but also and especially in

institutions of Christianity." In particular, Foucault relates Tertullian's principles to the cat-echumenate, to which he devotes a large part of the lecture of 20 February.

53. On Tertullian's "invention" of original sin, see *GL*, lecture of 13 February 1980, p. 138, note 23.

54. Quotation from *De paenitentia*, VI, 17, fairly freely translated by Foucault (see ibid., p. 136, note 4).

55. As testifies the problem of relapse (*rechute*) studied by Foucault on the basis of the major question of the relapsed in the lecture of 27 February 1980, p. 181 and pp. 199-200.

56. *GL*, lecture of 13 February 1980, p. 127.

57. Ibid., p. 128.

58. As Foucault explains, *paenitentia* is the Latin word by which *metanoia* was translated in the first Christian centuries. See ibid., and lecture of 20 February 1980, p. 153.

59. See the end of the lecture of 20 February, p. 160, footnote *.

60. See above, Course Summary, p. 325. In a manuscript of thirteen pages, inserted in the file of documents relative to the 1979 course and with the title: "Liberalism as art of government," Foucault refers to the seminar in these terms: "In a liberal government society constitutes the site of precipitation of intervention that has to be suspended in the specific domain of the economy. It is the surface of transfer of governmental activity. What we saw last year with regard to theory: Scottish, Guizot, Saint-Simon, Menger, the general will. The other of liberal government. Society was practiced by government before becoming an object of scientific knowledge. Practiced through reflections and forms of knowledge (*savoirs*)" (folio 12).

61. M. Foucault, "Roland Barthes (12 novembre 1915-26 March 1980)" in *Dits et Écrits, 1954-1988* [hereafter *DÉ*], ed. D. Defert and F. Ewald, collab. J. Lagrange (Paris: Gallimard, 1994), 4 vols.: No. 288, Vol. IV, p. 125/Quarto edition, 2001, 2 vols.: Vol. II, p. 945.

62. See the previous note.

63. M. Foucault, "Le moment de vérité," *Le Matin*, No. 673, 25 April 1979; *DÉ*, Vol. III, No. 267, p. 788/Quarto, Vol. II, p. 788. See also, in homage to Clavel, "Vivre autrement le temps," *Le Nouvel Observateur*, 30 April-6 May 1979; *DÉ*, Vol. III, No. 268, pp. 788-790/ Quarto, Vol. II, pp. 788-790. The link will be noted between this text—"What escapes history [according to Clavel] is the moment, the fracture, the tear, the interruption. To grace corresponds (and maybe responds), on the human side, the *uprising* [Foucault's emphasis]"—and the famous article published shortly after in *Le Monde*, 11 May 1979, "Inutile de se soulever?"; English translation "Useless to Revolt?" in Michel Foucault, *Essential Works of Foucault 1954-1984, Vol. Three. Power*, ed. James D. Faubion, trans. Robert Hurley and others (New York: The New Press, 2000).

64. See our "Situation du cours" in *Sécurité, territoire, population*, pp. 389-392; "Course Context," *Security, Territory, Population*, pp. 375-377.

65. See the article by C. Brière and P. Blanchet, "Corrupteur de la terre," which was alongside Foucault's "Inutile de se soulever?" *Le Monde*, 11 May 1979, p. 2. On Foucault's relationship with these two journalists of *Libération*, see our "Situation du cours" in *Sécurité, territoire, population*, p. 389 note 39; ; "Course Context," *Security, Territory, Population*, p. 394 note 39.

66. "Le philosophe masqué," *DÉ*, Vol. IV, No. 285, pp. 104-110/Quarto, Vol. II, pp. 923-929; English translation by Alan Sheridan (amended by the editors) as "The Masked Philosopher" in Michel Foucault, *The Essential Works of Foucault 1954-1984. Volume One: Ethics, Subjectivity and Truth* [hereafter, *Ethics, Subjectivity and Truth*], ed. Paul Rabinow, trans. Robert Hurley and others (New York: The New Press, 1997). This interview with C. Delacampagne took place in February 1980. On the circumstances of the interview, see the presentation by the editors, *DÉ*, IV, p. 104/Quarto, II, p. 79. D. Defert, in his "Chronologie," *DÉ*, Vol. I, p. 57/Quarto, Vol. I, p. 79, also links this "desire for discretion" with Foucault's refusal to play "the role of major intellectual" that increasingly suited the media with the approaching disappearance of Sartre. From this point of view, the latter is not entirely unrelated, if not to the course itself, at least to the state of mind in which Foucault undertook it.

67. "Le philosophe masqué," p. 110/p. 929; "The Masked Philosopher," p. 327.

68. See below, p. 354, notes 126 and 127.

69. On the reasons for this decision, see D. Defert, "Chronologie," *DÉ*, Vol. I, p. 50/Quarto, I, p. 68, which notes that many interpreted this silence "as a crisis in his reflection."

70. We recall the series of five volumes announced on the back cover of the book: *The Flesh and The Body; The Children's Crusade; The Woman, The Mother, and The Hysteric; The Perverts; Populations and Races.*

71. "Le souci de la vérité" (1984), *DÉ*, Vol. IV, No. 340, p. 668/Quarto, Vol. II, p. 1487; English translation by Alan Sheridan, "The Concern for Truth," in Michel Foucault, *Politics, Philosophy, Culture. Interviews and Other Writings 1977-1984*, ed. Lawrence D. Kritzman (New York and London: Routledge, 1988), p. 255.

72. On the reasons that led Foucault to reorganize his initial project, see "Préface à l'"Histoire de la sexualité"," *DÉ*, Vol. IV, No. 340, pp. 583-584/Quarto, Vol. II, pp. 1402-1403; English translation by William Stock, amended by the editors, "Preface to *The History of Sexuality*, Volume Two," in *Ethics, Subjectivity and Truth*, pp. 204-205; *Histoire de la sexualité, Vol. II: L'Usage des plaisirs* (Paris: Gallimard, "Bibliothèque des Histoires," 1984), Introduction, pp. 11-15; English translation by Robert Hurley, "Introduction" to *The Use of Pleasure. The History of Sexuality Volume Two* (New York: Pantheon Books, 1985), pp. 5-9.

73. *L'Usage des plaisirs*, p. 12; *The Use of Pleasure*, p. 6.

74. "Préface à l'"Histoire de la sexualité'," p. 584/p. 1403; "Preface to *The History of Sexuality* Volume Two," p. 205.

75. See below, pp. 342-345.

76. See the summary of this course in *DÉ*, Vol. IV, No. 304, p. 213/Quarto, Vol. II, p. 1032; English translation by Robert Hurley, "Subjectivity and Truth" in *The Essential Works of Foucault, I. Ethics, Subjectivity and Truth*, p. 87: "This year's course is to be the object of a forthcoming publication."

77. At the invitation of the brother Michel Albaric, director of the library, whom Foucault had met the previous Spring. See D. Eribon, *Michel Foucault* (Paris: Flammarion, 1989) p. 310; D. Macey, *The Lives of Michel Foucault* (New York: Vintage, 1995). In 1983, Foucault expressed his gratitude to him in this way: "I thank the library of Le Saulchoir and its director; they have helped me, especially since, recently, working conditions at the Bibliothèque nationale have deteriorated considerably" ("Usage des plaisirs et techniques de soi" in *DÉ*, Vol. IV, No. 338, p. 549 note 1/Quarto, Vol. I, p. 1368, note 2; see also *L'Usage des plaisirs*, p. 279 note 1 (not included in the English translation).

78. Opened to the public in 1974.

79. See the photograph in [collective] *Michel Foucault. Une histoire de la vérité* (Paris: Syros, 1985), p. 25.

80. See J.R. Carrette, ed., *Religion and Culture / Michel Foucault* (New York: Routledge, 1999) p. 2, note 7. As the author comments, "this meeting is unfortunately not discussed in any of the biographies."

81. "For many in his audience, the lectures Foucault presented this year, from January through March, must have seemed as though they were written by someone else. Certainly the cast was new: Philo of Alexandria, Hermes, Justin, Tertullian, Hippolytus, Cyprian, Origen, Jerome, Cassian. These were not figures with whom Foucault has been identified ... thought and praxis were continually introduced into his course and his interrogation of them reflects his current concern with theology in general and pastoral theology in particular" (J. Bernauer, quoted by J.R. Carrette, ibid., p. 2).

82. I thank J. Bernauer for providing me with this information.

83. Letter from J. Bernauer, February 2012. Foucault also visited with J. Bernauer the Jesuit Library of Centre Sèvres. See the latter's account in J.R. Charrette, ibid., p. xiii: "At one point ... he did take a look at the Jesuit Library of Centre Sèvres, to which I escorted him one afternoon. I remember that when we came to the first section of books, which a sign announced as 'dogmatic theology,' he joked that this was not his place and rushed towards the section farther down the long room as his goal: moral theology."

84. See *Leçons sur la volonté de savoir*, lecture of 9 December 1970, p. 4; *Lectures on the Will to Know*, p. 1: "all these analyses—past or still to come—could be seen as something like so many 'fragments for a morphology of the will to know'."

85. See M. Foucault, *L'Ordre du discours* (Paris: Gallimard, 1971), pp. 62-65. Foucault grouped the analyses he proposed to undertake into two sets, one "critical" and the other "genealogical." The first, notably, was to include a series of works on the system of exclusion that constitutes the "will to truth," through, on the one hand, the study of the three major scansions of the

"morphology of our will to know" (Ancient Greece, the sixteenth and seventeenth century, the beginning of the nineteenth century), and on the other, that of psychiatric expertise and its role in the practice of the penal system. It is easy to recognize in this program the object of the first four courses: "The Will to Know," "Penal Theories and Institutions," "The Punitive Society," and "Psychiatric Power."

86. *GL*, lecture of 6 February 1980, p. 101.

87. See ibid., lecture of 16 January 1980, p. 23.

88. *Leçons sur la volonté de savoir*, lecture of 17 March 1971, pp. 177-186; *Lectures on the Will to Know*, pp. 183-193.

89. See *Sécurité, territoire, population*, lecture of 25 January 1978, p. 77; *Security, Territory, Population*, p. 76: "While I have been speaking about population a word has constantly recurred … and this is the word 'government.' The more I have spoken about population, the more I have stopped saying 'sovereign'"; and Fr., p. 68/Eng., p. 66: "The government of populations is, I think, completely different from the exercise of sovereignty over the fine grain of individual behaviors. It seems to me that we have two completely different systems of power."

90. See ibid., lecture of 1 February 1978 on "governmentality."

91. See *Naissance de la biopolitique*, lecture of 7 March 1979, pp. 191-192; *The Birth of Biopolitics*, p. 186: "The term itself, power, does no more than designate a domain of relations which are entirely still to be analyzed, and what I have proposed to call governmentality, that is to say, the way in which one conducts the conduct of men, is no more than a proposed analytical grid for these relations of power."

92. *GL*, lecture of 9 January 1980, p. 12.

93. Ibid., p. 12. See also the Course Summary, p. 321.

94. M. Foucault, "La fonction politique de l'intellectuel" (1976), *DÉ*, Vol. III, No. 184, p. 114/Quarto, Vol. II, p. 114 (see the complete version of this text, "Entretien avec Michel Foucault," ibid., No. 192, p. 160/Quarto, Vol. II, p. 160); English translation by Colin Gordon as "Truth and Power" in *Essential Works of Foucault. Volume 3: Power*, ed. James D. Faubion (New York: The New Press, 2000), p. 133. See also the interview, "Pouvoir et savoir" (1977), *DÉ*, Vol. III, No. 216, p. 404/Quarto, Vol. II, p. 404. On the circular relation between knowledge and power see M. Foucault, "Résume du cours," *Le Pouvoir psychiatrique. Cours au Collège de France, 1973-1974*, ed., J. Lagrange (Paris: Gallimard-Seuil, "Hautes Études," 2003), p. 351; English translation by Graham Burchell, "Course Summary," *Psychiatric Power. Lectures at the Collège de France 1973-1974*, English series ed. Arnold I. Davidson (Basingstoke: Palgrave Macmillan, 2006), p. 346; *Surveiller et Punir* (Paris: Gallimard, "Bibliothèque des Histoires," 1975), p. 225; English translation by Alan Sheridan, *Discipline and Punish. The Birth of the Prison* (London: Allen Lane, 1977).

95. It is in this form that Foucault at first uses it most often. See, for example, "Théories et institutions penales," (course summary), *DÉ*, Vol. II, No. 115, p. 390/Quarto, Vol. I, p. 1258; English translation by Robert Hurley, "Penal Theories and Institutions," in *Ethics, Subjectivity and Truth*, p. 17; Résumé du cours, *Le Pouvoir psychiatrique*, p. 341; Course Summary, *Psychiatric Power*, p. 346; *Surveiller et Punir*, p. 32; *Discipline and Punish*, p. 27; *La Volonté de savoir*, p. 130 and p. 131; *The History of Sexuality. Volume 1*, p. 98 and p. 99. The form "knowledge-power," employed at the beginning of the 1980 course, follows it from 1976. See *"Il faut défendre la société,"* lecture of 11 February, p. 113; *"Society Must Be Defended,"* p. 129 [the English here has "power-knowledge"; G.B.]; *Sécurité, territoire, population*, lecture of 18 January 1978, p. 44; *Security, Territory, Population*, p. 42; *La naissance de la biopolitique*, lecture of 10 January 1979, p. 22; *The Birth of Biopolitics*, p. 19.

96. This distinction is clearly established in the last lecture of the (unpublished) 1971-1972 course, "Penal Theories and Institutions" in which Foucault explains how, by a double "decoupling (*décrochage*)," one passes from the history of the sciences to archeology (through the intermediary of "epistemological matrices") and from that to power-knowledge ("through the intermediary of those "juridical-political" matrices of knowledge, which are measure, the test, and the inquiry") (manuscript, folios 18 and 19).

97. On the Nietzschean sources of the concept of "will to know" in the 1970-1971 course, see D. Defert, "Situation du cours" in *Leçons sur la volonté de savoir*, p. 264; Course Context, *Lectures on the Will to Know*, p. 268 (the concepts *Wissensgier, Wissenstrieb, Erkenntnistrieb*).

98. Ibid., lecture of 16 December 1970, p. 26; Eng., p. 26.

99. Ibid. See also the lecture of 17 March 1971, p. 198 and the "Lecture on Nietzsche" (April 19) published in the same volume, p. 209, on the "'altogether different' of violence, which acts as framework to knowing and presents itself in knowledge." This links up with "La vérité et les formes juridiques" (1974), *DÉ*, Vol. I, No. 139, pp. 544-545/Quarto, Vol. I, pp. 1414-1415; English translation by Robert Hurley, "Truth and Juridical Forms" in *Essential Works, 3: Power*, pp. 9-10.

100. "Théories et institutions penales," last lecture, manuscript, folios 16-17.

101. Listed in the catalogue of the Fonds Michel Foucault of the Bibliothêque du Salchoir, now at the IMEC, under the classification mark D67r. Joined with "Faces et surfaces" (dialogue between Gilles Deleuze and Stefan Czerkinsky) in G. Deleuze and Michel Foucault, *Mélanges: pouvoir et surface*, [no publication details; Paris, 1973?] (two notebooks stapled together back to back, 22 pages); English translation of "Faces and Surfaces" by Michael Taormina in Gilles Deleuze, *Desert Islands and Other Texts 1953-1974*, ed. David Lapoujade (Los Angeles and New York: Semiotext(e), 2004).

102. "La société punitive," lecture of 28 March 1973. Three other parallel themes are put in question: those of power-property ("the theoretical schema of the appropriation of power"), the "localization of power," and of "subordination." Deleuze had this course in mind (or, more likely, the text in front of him) when, in December 1975, he commented on pages 31-33 of *Surveiller et punir*; *Discipline and Punish*, pp. 26-29 ("Ecrivain non: un nouveau cartographie," *Critique*, No. 343, December 1975, pp. 1208-1210). Listing the postulates that Foucault in these pages would "suggest abandoning" (postulates of property, localization, and subordination) he clarified in a note (p. 1208) that "in a lecture at the Collège de France in 1973, Foucault himself listed these postulates." This comment disappears from the version of the article republished in G. Deleuze, *Foucault* (Paris: Minuit, "Critique," 1986), p. 32; English translation by Seán Hand, *Foucault* (Minneapolis: Minnesota Press, 1988).

103. "La société punitive," lecture of 28 March 1973.

104. See *Surveiller et Punir*, p. 32; *Discipline and Punish*, p. 27.

105. "La vérité et les formes juridiques," p. 552/p. 1420; "Truth and Juridical Forms," p. 15.

106. On this point, see D. Defert, "Le "dispositif de guerre" comme analyseur des rapports de pouvoir," in J.-C. Zancarini, ed., *Lectures de Michel Foucault*, Vol. I (Paris: ENS Éditions, "Theoria," 2000), pp. 60-61. Foucault briefly recapitulates his arguments against the notion of ideology in the lecture of 9 January 1980, *GL*, pp. 11-12.

107. On their presentation in terms of power-knowledge, see the course summary for 1971-1972, "Théories et institutions penales," *DÉ*, Vol. II, No. 115, p. 390/Quarto, Vol. I, p. 1258; English translation by Robert Hurley, "Penal Theories and Institutions," *Essential Works, I: Ethics, Subjectivity and Truth*, pp. 17-18.

108. See D. Defert, "Le "dispositif de guerre" comme analyseur des rapports de pouvoir," pp. 61-62.

109. *GL*, lecture of 9 January 1980, p. 12.

110. *Naissance de la biopolitique*, lecture of 10 January 1979, p. 21; *The Birth of Biopolitics*, p. 19. See Fr., p. 20; Eng., p. 17: "self-limitation by the principle of truth."

111. This formulation is to be compared with that of P. Veyne, "Foucault révolutionne l'histoire," in his *Comment on écrit l'histoire* (Paris: Seuil, "Points Histoire," 1978), p. 226; English translation by Catherine Porter, "Foucault Revolutionizes History," in Arnold I. Davidson, ed., *Foucault and His Interlocutors* (Chicago and London: University of Chicago Press, 1997), p. 167: "... there are no things: there are only practices ... Madness exists as an object only in and through a practice, but the practice in question is not itself madness." The nominalist theses developed by Paul Veyne in this text was the object of a discussion in a working group that Foucault brought together in his office at the Collège de France, "during the two years he was dealing with governmentality" (D. Defert, "Chronologie," p. 53/p. 73). On the methodological nominalism adopted by Foucault, see the same lecture of 10 January 1979, Fr., p. 5/Eng., p. 3—"Let's suppose that madness does not exist. If we suppose that it does not exist, then what can history make of these different events and practices which are apparently organized around something that is supposed to be madness?"—and Fr., p. 26 note 4/Eng., p. 23 note 4. In *GL*, lecture of 30 January 1980, p. 80, Foucault objects to the concept of nominalism with regard to his own approach, preferring to speak of "refusal of universals."

112. *Naissance de la biopolitique*, p. 22; *The Birth of Biopolitics*, p. 19.

113. See *Surveiller et Punir*, p. 27/*Discipline and Punish*, p. 23, where the phrase "regime of truth" appears for the first time. [The English translation has "system of truth"; G.B.]

114. On "regimes of veridiction": *Naissance de la biopolitique*, lecture of 17 January 1979, p. 37; *The Birth of Biopolitics*, p. 35. This concept, to which maybe not enough attention has been given, testifies to a new relation, on Foucault's part, to the language of law, his project being "a history of truth that is coupled, from the start, with a history of law."

115. See *GL*, lecture of 6 February, 1980, p. 100: "... regimes of truth, that is to say, the types of relations that link together manifestations of truth with their procedures and the subjects who are their operators, witnesses, or possibly objects."

116. On this double signification, see *GL*, lecture of 30 January 1980, pp. 84-85.

117. In 1980, Foucault relates these obligations to two interconnected, but distinct regimes of truth (one revolving around acts of faith and the other around acts of confession) at the heart of Christianity. See above, note 45. In *Mal faire, dire vrai*, the following year, he gives greater emphasis to their strict interdependence. See below, note 151.

118. This is why truth-telling about oneself in the framework of the psychoanalytic relationship cannot be reduced to the Christian practice of confession, as if the former derived directly from the second. They are truth acts that no doubt present structural analogies and of which the genealogy of their filiation it is important to establish, but which nonetheless fall under very different regimes of truth.

119. See *L'Ordre du discours*, p. 63: "... one could try to analyze a system of prohibition of language: the one concerning sexuality from the sixteenth to the nineteenth century"; p. 69: "... a possible study: that of the prohibitions affecting discourse about sexuality."

120. See *La Volonté de savoir*, p. 18; *The History of Sexuality*, 1, p. 10: "Are prohibition, censorship, and denial truly the forms through which power is exercised in a general way, if not in every society, most certainly in our own?"; and p. 20/p. 12: "I do not maintain that the prohibition of sex is a ruse; but it is a ruse to make prohibition into the basic and constitutive element from which one would be able to write the history of what has been said concerning sex starting from the modern epoch."

121. See above pp. 335-336

122. D. Defert, "Chronologie," p. 51/p. 71.

123. Ibid., p. 56/p. 77.

124. "Le jeu de Michel Foucault" (1977), *DÉ*, Vol. III, No. 206, p. 313/Quarto, Vol. II, p. 313; English translation by Colin Gordon as "The Confession of the Flesh" in *Power/Knowledge*, p. 211. In response to a comment by J.-A. Miller criticizing his designation of Tertullian as a point of origin of the Christian discourse of the flesh, Foucault clarifies that he said that "in a fictive manner, as a joke" (ibid., Fr., p. 316/p. 316; Eng., p. 214).

125. The latter, in the 1978 course, is not directly connected to the problem of sexuality, but is nonetheless inscribed within its horizon, as is shown by the lecture "Sexualité et pouvoir" (*DÉ*, Vol. III, No. 233), delivered at the University of Tokyo in April 1978. Recapitulating his analysis of the pastorate (p. 560 et seq./p. 560 et seq.), Foucault applies himself to showing the importance this mechanism of power had for the history of sexuality in the West, according to the hypothesis that "what Christianity has contributed to this history ..." is not new moral ideas or new prohibitions (as P. Veyne has shown: pp. 558-559/pp. 558-559 [see "La famille et l'amour sous le Haut-Empire romain," *Annales ESC*, 1978/1, pp. 35-63]) but "new techniques" (p. 560/p. 560), and discusses, in fairly general terms, the role of "very difficult and obscure conception of the flesh" (p. 565/p. 565) in Christian discourse of the second and third century.

126. See *La Volonté de savoir*, p. 30 note 1; *History of Sexuality*, 1, p. 21 note 4. It was a matter "of a genealogy of concupiscence through the practice of confession in Western Christianity and of spiritual direction as it developed after the Council of Trent" (D. Defert, "Chronologie," p. 53/p. 73).

127. And not "entirely," as D. Defert thought in 1994 (ibid.). For a precise description of the manuscript of 40 pages entitled "The flesh and the body," recently found in his archives, see P. Chevallier, *Michel Foucault et le Christianisme*, pp. 149-150 and his doctoral thesis, presented with the same title (Université de Paris, XII-Val de Marne, 2009), vol. I, p. 236. Written at the beginning of 1978, the manuscript "focuses on the way in which the problem of diurnal pollution was dealt with by confessors in the sixteenth and seventeenth century. Its condition

[is] that of a text written out in full, in a clear and well spaced out presentation, divided into numbered sections, with notes at the bottom of the page. The division into sections open with "2. Diurnal pollution" and is continued by "II—Delectation," indicating that the forty pages formed part of a larger set." The period covered, the sixteenth and seventeenth century, corresponds to the general problematic recalled by D. Defert (see the previous note). Is this the work that Foucault alludes to in 1983, in his interview: "À propos de la généalogie de l'éthique: un aperçu du travail en cours," *DÉ*, Vol. V, No. 344, p. 611/Quarto, Vol. II, p. 1430, Foucault's modified French version of the original English, "On the Genealogy of Ethics: An Overview of Work in Progress," in *Essential Works, 1: Ethics, Truth, and Subjectivity*, p. 255: "I have more than a draft of a book about sexual ethics in the sixteenth century, in which also the problem of the techniques of the self, self-examination, the cure of souls, is very important, both in Protestant and Catholic churches"?

128. D. Defert puts the genesis of the work at January 1979 ("Chronologie," p. 56/p. 77).

129. Ibid., p. 58/p. 80.

130. "Sexuality and Solitude" in *Essential Works, 1: Ethics, Subjectivity and Truth*. In this talk Foucault refers for the first time to Peter Brown, author of *Augustine of Hippo. A biography* (London: Faber and Faber, 1967), according to whom "what we have to understand is why it is that sexuality became, in Christian cultures, the seismograph of our subjectivity" (p. 179). On this exchange see Peter Brown, "A Life of Learning," Charles Homer Haskins Lecture, American Council of Learned Societies, Occasional Papers No. 55 (9 May 2003): "... a lively two-hour argument on the relation between Augustine's notion of concupiscence and John Cassian's notion of the spiritual struggle in the Bear's Lair at Berkeley, in late 1980, formed the basis of an intellectual friendship ...."

131. "About the Beginning of the Hermeneutics of the Self: Two Lectures at Dartmouth" (1980), *Political Theory* 21/2, May 1993, pp. 188-227.

132. More precisely, after a general introduction on the two forms "truth obligation" peculiar to Christianity (pp. 211-212), it summarizes the last four lectures on exomologesis and *exagoreusis*. The first lecture dealt mainly with ancient spiritual direction based upon the example of Seneca.

133. "Sexuality and Solitude," p. 182.

134. Ibid., p. 183.

135. Ibid., p. 182.

136. See *GL*, lecture of 26 March 1980, p. 289 et seq.

137. On the state of the manuscript left by Foucault, see D. Defert, "Je crois au temps ...," *Recto/Verso*, No. 1, June 2007, pp. 4-5.

138. "Le combat de la chasteté," *DÉ*, Vol. IV, No. 312, pp. 295-308/Quarto, Vol. II, pp. 1114-1127; English translation by Anthony Forster, "The Battle for Chastity," in Philippe Ariès and André Béjin, *Western Sexuality. Practice and Precept in Past and Present Times* (Oxford: Blackwell, 1985); republished, translation amended, in *Essential Works, 1: Ethics, Subjectivity and Truth*.

139. This issue, edited by Philippe Ariès and André Béjin (republished, Paris: Seuil, "Points Essais," 1984; *Western Sexuality*, see previous note), is essentially the result of Philippe Ariès 1979-1980 seminar at the *École des Hautes Études en sciences sociales* in which Western sexuality was studied "in its different aspects—the indissolubility of marriage, homosexuality, passivity, autoerotism, etc." (Preface, p. xi). As well as several contributions from Ariès and Béjin themselves, it included notably articles by P. Veyne ("Homosexuality in ancient Rome") and J.-L. Flandrin ("Sex in married life in the early Middle Ages: the Church's teaching and behavioural reality").

140. "Le combat de la chasteté," p. 305/p. 1124; "The Battle for Chastity," *Essential Works, 1: Ethics, Subjectivity and Truth*, p. 193.

141. Ibid.; Eng., p. 194 (translation modified).

142. *GL*, lecture of 26 March 1980, pp. 300-301; see note 40.

143. "Sexuality and Solitude," p. 182.

144. "Le combat de la chasteté," p. 304/p. 1123; "The Battle for Chastity," p. 192.

145. The expression, absent from the course, is used by Foucault shortly afterwards in his American lectures.

146. Text of the insert written by Foucault, for the first edition of *L'Usage des plaisirs* and *Souci de soi*.

147. *Mal fire, dire vrai. Fonction de l'aveu* (April-May 1981), edition established by F. Brion and B. Hacourt (Louvain and Chicago: Presses universitaires de Louvaine/University of Chicago Press, 2012). (I thank the editors for having provided me with the proofs of this work). On these lectures, see J. François, "Aveu, vérité, justice et subjectivité. Autour d'un enseignement de Michel Foucault," *Revue interdisciplinaire d'études juridiques*, No. 7, 1981, pp. 163-182.
148. *Mal faire, dire vrai*, end of the inaugural lecture, p. 13.
149. Ibid., p. 9.
150. Ibid., lectures of 29 April and 6 and 13 May 1981 (or one half of the series of lectures).
151. Ibid., lecture of 13 May, p. 164.
152. Ibid., p. 171.
153. *Le Courage de la vérité; The Courage of Truth*, lecture of 28 March 1984. The whole of the second part of this lecture is devoted to the analysis of Christian *parrhēsia*. In the first hour, Foucault declared: "Maybe I will try to pursue this history of the arts of living, of philosophy as form of life, of asceticism in its relation to the truth...after ancient philosophy, in Christianity" (Fr., p. 290; Eng., p. 316).
154. Texts brought together in the collection used by Foucault, *Les Écrits des Pères apostoliques*, published by Cerf in 1962.
155. See *GL*, lecture of 6 February 1980, p, 110, note 15.
156. P. Chevallier, see above, p. 354, note 127, Vol. I, pp. 214-246. This inventory appears in a condensed form in the book that came from the thesis, *Michel Foucault et le christianisme*, pp. 188-194 (see especially the summary table pp. 193-194), and in the article "Foucault et la patristique," *[Cahier de] L'Herne: Michel Foucault*, 2011, pp. 136-141 (on the "green notebook," notably, bibliographical index written by Foucault betrween 1975-1976 and 1978, in which appear references of several historical studies—Dölger, Dondeyne, Grotz, Holstein—used by Foucault in preparing the course).

INDEX OF NOTIONS
Compiled by Sue Carlton

Page numbers followed by n refer to endnotes

subjectivity 75-7, 80-2, 115, 128, 143, 145-6, 159, 225, 333
sumbolon 32-3, 45n
supplication 174-5, 203, 206-7, 213, 214, 227

Tauftheorie 169, 170, 171
tekhnē (technical knowledge) 51, 52, 53-5, 329
tekhnē tekhnēs (supreme art) 51-2, 67
  see also spiritual direction
tekmēria (clues, signs) 57-8, 59, 67
terror, principle of 15-16
test(s) 265
  of exorcism 150, 151-2
  and preparation for baptism 148, 152-3, 224
  of the soul (*probatio animae*) 143-4, 201, 211, 223-5, 227, 228, 311
  structure of 13
  of truth 148, 151-2, 155, 157
Thebes, salvation of 3, 26, 28, 64-5, 66, 67, 74
theios anēr (divine man) 267, 292-3
tragedy, and alethurgy 23-5, 29, 66
truth
  access to 143-5
  discovery of 25, 27, 29-39, 54-61, 65-7, 145
  and knowledge 5-6, 7, 12-13, 33-4
  and liberation of the city (Thebes) 74
  and logic 97-8
  manifestation of *see* alethurgy

regimes of 93-103, 321, 330-1
  self-indexation of 96, 98, 100
truth acts 81-4, 198-215, 321, 327, 331, 341
  objective acts 198-201
  and purification 104-5
  reflexive acts (manifesting own truth) 88-9, 198, 201-15, 330
  see also confession; *exomologēsis*
truth-telling 23-4, 38, 42, 47, 48-9, 54, 329
  see also veridiction
turannis (tyrannical power) 53
turannos (absolute ruler) 25, 62
tyrants/tyranny 62-7, 329

verbalization 102, 224-9, 305-7, 319n, 323, 324, 332
  coupled with self-exploration 225-9, 233, 235, 236-7
veridiction 25, 40, 47-8, 308, 309, 311, 329, 341, 345
  see also truth-telling

water 104, 117-20, 142, 156, 168, 332, 333
witch hunt 10-11
witnesses 29-30, 58, 66
  and alethurgy 39, 49-50, 81-2, 85, 88, 100, 330
  servants/slaves 36-7, 328, 329, 330
  testifying for postulants 149, 150, 153

INDEX OF NAMES
Compiled by Sue Carlton

Printed by Books on Demand, Germany